Robustness a1

This volume focuses on the assessments political actors make of the relative fragility and robustness of political orders. The core argument developed and explored throughout its different chapters is that such assessments are subjective and informed by contextually specific historical experiences that have important implications for how leaders respond. Their responses, in turn, feed into processes by which political orders change. The volume's contributions span analyses of political orders at the state, regional, and global levels. They demonstrate that assessments of fragility and robustness have important policy implications but that the accuracy of assessments can only be known with certainty ex post facto. The volume will appeal to scholars and advanced students of international relations and comparative politics working on national and international orders.

Richard Ned Lebow is the author of 50 books on international relations, comparative politics, political theory, history, classics, and philosophy of science. He has also recently published his first novel and a book of short stories. Lebow is a fellow of the British Academy and the recipient of many book awards and honorary degrees.

Ludvig Norman studies European politics, democratic theory, and social science methodology. He is the author of the book *The Mechanisms of Institutional Conflict in the European Union* (2016) and recent articles in *Journal of Common Market Studies, Political Studies, European Journal of International Relations, European Journal of Social Theory,* and *Cooperation and Conflict.*

Robustness and Fragility of Political Orders

Leader Assessments, Responses, and Consequences

Edited by

Richard Ned Lebow
King's College London

Ludvig Norman
Stockholm University

CAMBRIDGE
UNIVERSITY PRESS

CAMBRIDGE
UNIVERSITY PRESS

Shaftesbury Road, Cambridge CB2 8EA, United Kingdom

One Liberty Plaza, 20th Floor, New York, NY 10006, USA

477 Williamstown Road, Port Melbourne, VIC 3207, Australia

314–321, 3rd Floor, Plot 3, Splendor Forum, Jasola District Centre, New Delhi – 110025, India

103 Penang Road, #05–06/07, Visioncrest Commercial, Singapore 238467

Cambridge University Press is part of Cambridge University Press & Assessment, a department of the University of Cambridge.

We share the University's mission to contribute to society through the pursuit of education, learning and research at the highest international levels of excellence.

www.cambridge.org
Information on this title: www.cambridge.org/9781009265072

DOI: 10.1017/9781009265058

© Cambridge University Press & Assessment 2023

This publication is in copyright. Subject to statutory exception and to the provisions of relevant collective licensing agreements, no reproduction of any part may take place without the written permission of Cambridge University Press & Assessment.

First published 2023
First paperback edition 2023

A catalogue record for this publication is available from the British Library

Library of Congress Cataloging-in-Publication data
Names: Lebow, Richard Ned, editor. | Norman, Ludvig, 1976- editor.
Title: Robustness and fragility of political orders : leader assessments, responses, and consequences / Edited by Richard Ned Lebow, King's College London, Ludvig Norman, Stockholm University
Description: New York : Cambridge University Press, 2022.
Identifiers: LCCN 2022023481 (print) | LCCN 2022023482 (ebook) | ISBN 9781009265027 (hardback) | ISBN 9781009265072 (paperback) | ISBN 9781009265058 (epub)
Subjects: LCSH: State, The. | Order–History. | Comparative government. | Failed states–History. | Communication in politics. | Political stability.
Classification: LCC JC11 .R482 2023 (print) | LCC JC11 (ebook) | DDC 320.01–dc23/eng/20220705
LC record available at https://lccn.loc.gov/2022023481
LC ebook record available at https://lccn.loc.gov/2022023482

ISBN 978-1-009-26502-7 Hardback
ISBN 978-1-009-26507-2 Paperback

Cambridge University Press & Assessment has no responsibility for the persistence or accuracy of URLs for external or third-party internet websites referred to in this publication and does not guarantee that any content on such websites is, or will remain, accurate or appropriate.

Contents

	List of Figures	*page* vii
	List of Contributors	viii
1	Introduction RICHARD NED LEBOW AND LUDVIG NORMAN	1
2	Robustness and Fragility of Political Orders RICHARD NED LEBOW	25
3	End of Democracy or Recurrent Conflict: Minimalist Democracy, Legitimacy Crisis, and Political Equality PETER BREINER	54
4	Politics and the Administrative State: Perceptions of Stability and Fragility in Weimar Germany PAUL PETZSCHMANN	92
5	Roots in Common: The Fragility–Robustness of Democratic and Ecological Regimes ANDREW LAWRENCE	115
6	The End of Communist Rule in Europe: A Comparative Perspective on the Fragility and Robustness of Regimes ARCHIE BROWN	141
7	Democracy's Fragility and the European Political Order: Functionalism, Militant Democracy, and Crisis LUDVIG NORMAN	176
8	The American Fragility–Robustness Nexus ARIANE CHEBEL D'APPOLLONIA	202

9 The Perils of Choice: Structure and Agency in EU
  Crisis Management   229
  DOUGLAS WEBBER

10 Conclusions   270
   RICHARD NED LEBOW AND LUDVIG NORMAN

   Index   313

Figures

2.1 Leader Questions and Responses *page* 38
10.1 Feasibility Flowchart 274

Contributors

Peter Breiner is Associate Professor of Political Science at the University at Albany, State University of New York. He is the author of *Max Weber and Democratic Politics* (1996), Cornell University Press and numerous articles on Weber, Mannheim, and German political theory, along with articles on Machiavelli, Rousseau, and Tocqueville. He is working on a book entitled *Political Equality: Movement and Countermovement*, in which he argues that the tension between liberal rights and Schumpeterian democracy leads to a constant and unending struggle over political equality much like the Polanyi's recurrent movement and countermovement between the market and democracy.

Archie Brown is Professor Emeritus of Politics at the University of Oxford and an Emeritus Fellow of St Antony's College, Oxford. His most recent books are *The Human Factor: Gorbachev, Reagan, and Thatcher, and the End of the Cold War* (2020), *The Myth of the Strong Leader: Political Leadership in the Modern Age* (2014) and *The Rise and Fall of Communism* (2009). He has been Visiting Professor of Political Science at Yale, the University of Connecticut, Columbia University, and the University of Texas at Austin. Brown is a Fellow of the British Academy (elected 1991) and an International Honorary Member of the American Academy of Arts and Sciences since 2003.

Ariane Chebel d'Appollonia is Professor at Rutgers University – State University of New Jersey (School of Public Affairs, and Division of Global Affairs). She also teaches at Sciences Po Paris. She has been Visiting Chaired Professor at Northwestern University and the University of Central European University, EU-US Fulbright Transatlantic Researcher at the University of Pittsburgh, and Visiting Professor at New York University (NYU) and at the Universidad Complutense of Madrid. Her main recent publications include *Frontiers of Fears: Immigration and Insecurity in the United States and Europe* (Cornell University Press, 2012); *How Does It Feel to Be a*

Threat? Migrant Mobilization and Securitization in the US and Europe (Palgrave Macmillan, NYU Series, 2015); and *Violent America: The Dynamics of Identity Politics in a Multiracial Society* (Cornell University Press, 2022).

Andrew Lawrence (Wits School of Governance, Wits University) has written extensively on energy and climate politics, comparative and global political economy, and worker and employer collective action, with recent articles in *Competition and Change, Renewable and Sustainable Energy Reviews*, and *Review of International Political Economy*. His most recent books are *South Africa's Energy Transition* (Palgrave, 2020) and *Employer and Worker Collective Action* (Cambridge University Press, 2014). His current book project is on reworking global governance under conditions of climate crisis.

Richard Ned Lebow is Professor of International Political Theory at King's College London and Bye-Fellow of Pembroke College, University of Cambridge. He is the author of almost fifty books on international relations, comparative politics, political theory, history, classics, and philosophy of science. He has recently published his first novel and a book of short stories. Lebow is a fellow of the British Academy and the recipient of many book awards and honorary degrees.

Ludvig Norman is Associate Professor at Stockholm University, Department of Political Science and Senior Fellow at the Institute of European Studies at UC Berkeley. His research focuses on the institutions of the European Union, democratic theory, and social science methodology. He is the author of the book *The Mechanisms of Institutional Conflict in the European Union*. His recent works have appeared in *Political Studies, European Journal of International Relations, European Journal of Social Theory, Journal of Common Market Studies* and *Cooperation and Conflict*.

Paul Petzschmann is Senior Lecturer and Director of European Studies at Carleton College, Minnesota. He has been a research fellow at the University of Cape Town and the Norwegian Institute of International Affairs. His interests are in modern American and European political and administrative thought, especially in the politics of economic emergency. He has published in Public Administration, contributed to multiple edited volumes, and is working on a book on the American Public Administration Clearinghouse (PACH) as a transatlantic network of administrative knowledge.

Douglas Webber is Professor Emeritus of Political Science at the international business school, INSEAD. He has been a guest professor at the University of California Berkeley, a visiting fellow at Monash University (Melbourne) and the Australian National University (Canberra), and a Jean Monnet Fellow and Robert Schuman Fellow at the European University Institute (Florence). He has published extensively on issues of German politics and foreign policy, Franco-German relations, EU politics, and European and Asian regional political integration. His most recent book is *European Disintegration? The Politics of Crisis in the European Union* (Red Globe Press/Macmillan).

1 Introduction

Richard Ned Lebow and Ludvig Norman

The relative robustness and fragility of political orders is a central concern of scholars and political elites alike. What factors account for broad political shifts, sudden ruptures, and gradual processes, through which orders decline, break down, and are replaced by new ones? How do fledgling political orders, especially democratic ones, consolidate themselves and become more robust over time? Our volume focuses on an underexplored aspect of these questions by studying assessments of robustness and fragility made by both scholars and political actors. The core argument we develop and explore throughout the different chapters in this volume is that such assessments have important implications for how leaders behave and that their behavior feeds into processes by which political orders change. Assessments of fragility and robustness of political orders, we argue, is intimately associated with ideas of what is politically prudent and feasible, and equally important, which actions are not. This also prompts us to ask questions regarding how these understandings among political elites develop, how they influence each other, and how scholarly ideas shape the outlooks of political actors.

Our contributors explore these questions in the context of national, regional, and global political orders, collectively developing a multifaceted perspective on political orders at these respective levels. Our focus on leaders' assessments relies on a common perspective that underlines the highly context-dependent nature of scholarly and leader understandings of robustness and fragility. Here we provide an alternative view to prevalent perspectives in political science and international relations research that aim to develop objectivist measures of fragility and robustness. Our interpretive perspective instead relies on the fundamental assumption that assessments are shaped by recognized role models, historical lessons, political commitments, and the broader Zeitgeist in which leaders and analysts are embedded. We do not argue that external factors, be they slow-moving shifts in broad material conditions, sudden technological leaps or crises, are inconsequential. We do argue, however, that leaders' assessments of such factors and their potential impact on political orders will be highly uncertain and that such processes need to be studied from the horizon of the actors that engage in them. Contextual factors shape assessments of fragility and robustness as well as responses to these assessments. The contributors to this volume will help identify patterns of assessments and responses in an effort to balance the general against the particular, allowing us to establish analytically general insights regarding these dynamics.

Political Orders and Leaders' Assessments

Our authors, while offering a broad set of perspectives on robustness and fragility share a set of assumptions that are foundational to our arguments and important to foreground in this introduction. First and foremost, we accept political orders as the units of our analysis. Political orders can be seen as assemblages of formal as well as informal institutions and procedures that work to regulate collective life and understood as serving the purpose of governing the social orders on which they ultimately depend. Political orders also exist at the regional and international levels. They are admittedly thinner, but increasingly important to regional and international relations. Our contributors address all three levels of order.

Regimes and political orders are increasingly synonymous in common parlance. Regime is a term usually applied to a type of government. In democratic states we can effectively distinguish between governments and regimes.[1] The former can come and go while the latter may endure. Our focus in this volume is on how leaders assess the fragility or robustness of their political orders. These are units, like the Soviet Union, the Ottoman Empire, Great Britain, the European Union (EU), or the United States, that are imbued by particular ways of organizing political life. They appear, change, and break down much less frequently than governments change. But when they do, it is often associated with momentous consequences. A case in point is Hungary's termination of its union with Austria and the declaration of independence by Czechs in October 1918, followed quickly by that of South Slavs, Slovaks, Ukrainians, and Poles that led to loss of control of peripheral territories to new breakaway states. Emperor Karl was encouraged to abdicate in November, the monarchy collapsed, and a new Austrian Republic emerged, effectively redrawing the political map in Europe.[2]

In some circumstances, the collapse of a regime leads to the collapse of a political order. This happened to the ex-communist-run countries of Eastern Europe, Libya after Gadaffi's overthrow, and Iraq after the defeat of Saddam Hussein. Much less commonly, the end of a regime and order can result in the collapse of a country as well, as it did for the Soviet

Introduction 3

Union and Yugoslavia in the aftermath of the Cold War. The weakening of communist regimes in both countries encouraged component provinces or republics to declare and ultimately make good on their independence.[3] How do leader's assessments of the order's fragility and robustness feed into such processes of change?

We start off from the observation that assessments of robustness and fragility wax and wane in often unpredictable ways. If there seems to be widespread agreement on the general robustness of political orders, fears of their fragility can emerge abruptly and unexpectedly. Such shifts are evident irrespective of whether political orders are organized according to autocratic principles or democratic ones.

Shifting perceptions of democracy's robustness or fragility in the period after World War II offer an example. From about 1950 on, the robustness of democracies was all but taken for granted. Democracy seemed to be developing roots in Germany, Japan, and Italy, only a few years after being ruled by fascist regimes. In the course of the next couple of decades in Europe there was some threat of backsliding that quickly passed, as in the attempted General's Putsch in France in 1961, a failed left-wing coup in Portugal in 1975, and an unsuccessful military putsch in Spain in 1981.[4] Portugal and Spain had only recently put authoritarian regimes behind them so their ability to withstand these shocks was regarded as that much more impressive.[5]

These successes helped to spawn a large and optimistic literature that linked democratization to economic development, the growth of a middle class, and desire to emulate Western Europe and the North America.[6] This literature spoke of waves of democratization and reached its high point in the aftermath of the collapse of communism and the Soviet Union.[7] Some Americans celebrated what they described as unipolarity and the end of history.[8] Thomas Friedman, among others, insisted that globalization would usher in a world of peaceful, liberal trading states.[9] Relatively few voices warned that it was the harbinger of vast disparities in wealth with far-reaching social and political consequences.[10]

In the last decade, the pendulum has swung in the other direction. Optimism has given way to pessimism as democracy appears threatened, even in its core regions of Western Europe and North America. The collapse of so many democracies in Europe in the interwar period generated a considerable literature on democracy's fragility.[11] These discussions were largely shelved with the apparent spread and consolidation of democracy across the globe.[12] At the present juncture, the literature on fragility is undergoing a revival and receiving considerable attention in the media. Popular and academic debates are replete with warnings related to the possible collapse of democracy.[13] It is far from obvious that these assessments rely on any unambiguous evidence that would prompt such an analysis, but they have quite suddenly emerged as the dominating perspective on contemporary democracies.

In the United States, specifically, there is growing concern for the survival of democracy for the first time since the Great Depression. To some it seems that a political order that appeared for a long time unshakeable is threatened with collapse. Some 70 million people voted for Donald Trump in 2020 and there was a widespread belief among liberals that democracy in America would not have survived his second term.[14] Propaganda, fake news, and nationalist voices find growing audiences, and hate crimes and paramilitaries are more frequent. Trust in government and politicians is in decline, and political systems are routinely depicted as secretive, uncaring, and inefficient, if not downright evil, even by politicians themselves.[15] This kind of rhetoric generates fears among those that perceive it as a threat to democratic institutions. It may also prompt a greater willingness to violate norms among those that see such rhetoric as cues to restore the perceived former glory of the country. In the run up to the 2020 American presidential election, the liberal media carried almost daily stories about President Trump refusing to accept defeat if he lost the election.[16] One of his former aides, the convicted and pardoned Roger Stone, publicly urged Trump to declare martial law and arrest the Clintons among others, if Biden were to win.[17] Trump was impeached a second time after leaving office for inciting a mob assault on the capitol building that led to the deaths of five people and the hospitalization of many others.[18]

In September 2020, when we wrote the first draft of this introduction, the American presidential election was six weeks away. The media was full of speculation about what would happen if Trump was defeated. Would he leave office gracefully, as all his predecessors had, or dismiss the election as a fraudulent attempt to stay in power? If the latter, how would others respond? Would the Secret Service or the military physically remove him from the White House, or stand aside? What would Biden and his supporters do, and how would those actions be perceived by those who supported Trump? Would there be violence in the streets?[19] In this instance, fears, or even expectations of preemption, had important consequences for voter turnout and plans for possible counter-preemption. We know now that Trump did his best to delegitimate the election, compelled many Republican representatives and senators to pretend that he had only lost because of alleged voter fraud, and encouraged a mob to storm the capitol.[20] His behavior also appears to have prompted the massive turnout of voters that led to his defeat, and

Introduction 5

his postelection behavior to the victory of two Democratic senatorial candidates in Georgia. The Democrats have the presidency and control of both houses of congress, but democracy does not look more robust to many.[21] In the immediate aftermath of the occupation of the capitol building, American faith in democracy dropped, although it recovered after Biden's inauguration.[22] No doubt, it will continue to rise and fall in response to on-going events now that survival of democracy has become a question in the eyes of many.

Faced with these developments, political leaders and analysts today, as in the past, are assessing the strength of democratic political orders, not on the basis of any objective, or even consensual metrics of robustness or fragility but in relation to evolving and uncertain understandings of what is at stake and how their political order might be saved or strengthened. Among democratically minded actors, there is something of a consensus that the principal threat is from right-wing, nationalist opinion and would-be authoritarian leaders. Their opponents, by contrast, see the threat to democracy as coming from the woke, socialist, left.

There is no agreement about what actions to take, or even what the developments before and after the US election tells us about the robustness or fragility of the political order. Some observers contend that the Trump presidency constituted a stress test of democratic institutions and that their survival demonstrates the fundamental robustness of the political order. Others are less optimistic and see Trump as a manifestation of slow but steady, and still ongoing, erosion of democratic institutions. These competing assessments imply different perspectives on fragility and robustness and also imply different avenues of political action that leaders may embark upon. Some propose reforms that would make politics more open and inclusive. Others demand structural changes in the economy and tax structure. Still others fear that either of these responses will strengthen the right, promote a violent reaction, and put democracy at greater risk. These assessments as well as the likely consequences of the responses that they prompt are uncertain.

The historical record suggests that such consequences can be far-reaching. In the 1920s, there was misplaced confidence in democratic robustness combined with exaggerated fears of left-wing revolution.[23] Many fragile democracies in southern and eastern Europe were considered more robust than they turned out to be. In Britain and the United States, a desire to outflank and defuse the left strengthened workers' rights and prompted other social reforms and programs. At the same time, the focus on threats from the left led many in Western political elites to discount the gravity of the rise of fascist and authoritarian regimes on the continent. Even many sensible Germans erred at the outset of the Nazi regime by dismissing Hitler as an *Irrtum* [error] of history that would soon pass.[24]

The post hoc assessments of democracy's collapse in the interwar years led after the war to a reevaluation of the conditions required for ensuring the robustness of democratic political orders. For many, the so-called Weimar lesson encouraged fear of mass involvement in politics and highlighted the fragility of democracy.[25] Karl Löwenstein described Hitler's appointment to *Reichskanzler* and the subsequent destruction of democracy as in no little part facilitated by "the generous and lenient Weimar republic." The problem he identified and that came to shape the perspective of many analysts was a constitution that allowed for the dismantling of democracy through legal means.[26] This specification of democracy's inherent fragility led to a reconceptualization that focused more on ensuring stability than on deepening public participation. As Norman's chapter argues, these understandings also shaped how political elites throughout Western Europe, organized international cooperation after the war.

By the 1970s, faith in democracy's stability was restored. So much so, we noted, that estimates of its worldwide robustness were increasingly rooted in a liberal teleology that made analysts less sensitive to possibilities of democratic breakdown. In the current decade, democracy is again perceived under threat and upbeat teleological thinking rarely rears its head. This concern may be realistic; large right-wing, antidemocratic parties are evident almost everywhere in Europe and have come to power in Hungary and Poland. It is possible that analysts are exaggerating the threat, just as they did with prior expectations of democracy's universal triumph. Either way, the beliefs of political actors – and sometimes, even of analysts – matter as they may have far-reaching consequences.

The misreading of tea leaves is not a peculiarly democratic phenomenon. Stalin imagined nonexistent wreckers and anticommunist conspiracies within the Soviet Union, leading to the enactment of repressive measures on a colossal scale. Khrushchev was unreasonably optimistic about the Soviet Union's future, which encouraged his reforms, including his exposure of Stalin and his crimes. Arguably, the Soviet Union never recovered from Khrushchev's de-Stalinization; Brezhnev and his circle were probably right in worrying about the survival of their political system and country.[27] Gorbachev exaggerated the robustness of the Soviet Union, and initially his ability to democratize while preserving the leading role of the communist party. His views evolved and he came to recognize that he would have to jettison the communist party. In the months before the attempted coup he moved toward the concept of a voluntary union with a different name and minus the Baltic republics and possibly several other components of the USSR. In practice, he and his opponents set in motion the events that led to the collapse of communism and the breakup of the Soviet Union.[28] KGB Chairman Vladimir Kryuchkov and his coconspirators worried that *glasnost*, *perestroika*, and the new Union Treaty that decentralized power would promote the disintegration of the Soviet Union. The assessment of the conspirators was undoubtedly accurate but their poorly conceived and failed coup proved to be the catalyst for the country's rapid unraveling.[29]

The Soviet case reveals how policies that may have appeared reasonable in the short term had longer-term consequences that could not easily have been imagined at the time. It further indicates how leaders can delude themselves about the prospects of policies they are committed to pursuing and motivated to make quite unreasonable judgments about the relative fragility of their political order and what might best strengthen it. Different political actors would almost certainly have behaved differently.[30]

In Eastern Europe, some leaders made different assessments, more attuned it seems to the fragility of their regimes and well aware that radical reformist change in Moscow would destabilize them. None, however, recognized until early 1989 that they and their political orders were about to go under.[31] In some instances, assessments can exacerbate fears and even encourage preemptive action. Had their assessments of the relative fragility of their orders been different, we would expect their responses to have differed as well. Whether they could have saved their regimes is another matter. In his chapter, Archie Brown is inclined to think not.

A characteristic where authoritarian political orders differ from democratic ones concerns their response to dissent. While the use of repression against perceived anti-systemic threats is not foreign to democracies it dominates the authoritarian playbook. Their greater reliance on repression implies that authoritarian leaders may be more concerned with their orders' fragility. In China, for instance, leaders seem to share an enduring sense of their fragility. The post-Maoist leadership has been extremely sensitive to challenges and willing to use brute force against dissidents, as they did in the 1989 Tiananmen Square massacre or against independent social movements not initially antagonistic to the regime, as in their continuing vendetta against Falun Gong.[32] Under President Xi Jinping, crackdowns against political dissidents and Muslims in Xinjiang and elsewhere have increased, as have efforts to suppress political liberties and expression in Hong Kong.[33] The Chinese leadership appears convinced that such actions will make their political order more robust and not provoke costly international opposition.

What are the long-term consequences of these policies? Are China's leaders acting wisely in terms of making their political order more robust? History offers no clear guidance. Sometimes suppression has succeeded, or has at least bought time for regimes. It has also been a contributing cause of their collapse. In some countries, it has done both, as was arguably true for the Russian and Austro-Hungarian empires; it bought time but made their downfall more likely in the longer term.[34] The Western literature on China is divided on the question of repression, although the majority of commentators, rooted in the Western liberal tradition, are disinclined to believe that a repressive regime can survive in the long term.[35] Leninist-Stalinist regimes depend on bureaucracies that enforce conformity. Once self-doubt takes root within these institutions, their confusion, disillusionment, and uncertainty ultimately undermine the system. The intelligentsia that populate the higher levels of the bureaucracy gave rise to the most effective critics of the Soviet Union and Eastern European communist regimes because they were better educated, better able to turn the official ideology and sanctioned texts against the political order, and the general public was used to the idea of them taking the lead.[36] Only time will tell if this – or something else as yet unforeseen – happens in China.

We also encounter concerns about survival in regional and international organizations.[37] Here too we need to be aware of how the specifics of such political orders inform assessments of fragility and robustness and how diverse the consequences of particular responses might prove to be. Assessments will invariably be influenced by different perspectives on the more general conditions for cooperation between states. They are likely to differ considerably among actors who subscribe to *Realpolitik* versus those who stress the binding features of shared norms, values, and identities.[38]

It is important to recognize that actors populating international political orders will also be influenced, like domestic actors, by lessons derived from previous successes and failures. The United Nations long lived in the shadow of the League of Nations and its failure in the 1930s. European postwar cooperation and its institutional design were heavily influenced by the perceived weaknesses of prewar arrangements and the perceived fragility of democracy. Leaders and supporters of the European project have from this perspective worried about its fragility from the outset.[39] Douglas Webber tells us in his chapter that one of the striking features of today's European Union is how repeated successes and survival have not reduced widespread fears of its vulnerability among political actors. Scholars, by contrast, have, until recently, tended to take its survival for granted.

There is understandably great interest in regime survival among political actors and scholars. Both appear to hold strong opinions about the relative robustness or fragility of their own and other political orders. For different types of orders, democratic and authoritarian, national and international, assessments are often influenced by what has recently occurred elsewhere in the world and is refracted through underlying assumptions about the nature of political order. These assessments help shape how leaders behave. Success and failure of efforts to shore up political orders in turn influences assessments others make of their orders and possible responses to challenges.

These fluctuations and overall uncertainty about robustness do not stop leaders and analysts from making judgments, nor should they. But it ought to make them cautious, more willing to hedge their bets, and on the lookout for information at odds with their expectations. More often than not, we believe, the opposite occurs: leaders and analysts stick with their judgments and dismiss or explain away information that appears to contradict them. Misjudgments of both kinds – the over- and undervaluation of the robustness of regimes demonstrate just how difficult it is to make such assessments and frame appropriate responses.

Robustness and Fragility

We assume that actor assessments of robustness and fragility bear only a passing relationship to the actual state of affairs. In the next chapter, Ned Lebow will elaborate this argument and offer evidence in support of our claim that robustness and fragility really only become fully apparent in retrospect. What we offer here are provisional starting points for thinking about leaders' understandings of robustness and fragility, their assessments of the robustness and fragility of their own and other orders, and the implications of those assessments for their behavior.

It is tempting to frame robustness and fragility as polar opposites of a continuum. This only makes sense if we conceive of these poles as ideal types. No political order is ever fully robust, and fragile orders invariably collapse before they lose all their support. All orders are arrayed somewhere along this continuum, but we suspect, closer to the fragility than the robustness end as entropy, decline, and collapse are default states. All political orders have ultimately collapsed and a handful at best has endured more than a couple of 100 years.

Fragility, in contrast to robustness, has an endpoint: the collapse of a regime, order, or political unit. This does not make assessments of fragility any more straightforward. Fragility is a condition whose existence and degree may only become known when a catalyst comes along that brings about an actual collapse – or might be expected to and does not. Their condition is known with certainty only ex post facto. The same is true of many other phenomena that rely on a concatenation of underlying causes and immediate causes or triggers. Ned Lebow has argued that this is true of war; even when underlying conditions make it likely it will not occur in the absence of an appropriate catalyst. Studies of war – especially those that focus on underlying conditions – unreasonably assume that catalysts are like streetcars and that one will come along if you wait long enough. However, catalysts are often independent of underlying causes.[40]

Robustness and fragility are similar in the sense that movement in the direction of either is more often than not gradual, and almost always so in the case of robustness. Political orders can become more fragile as a result of shocks of various kinds. Political orders can also undergo phase transitions from robust to fragile and from fragile to collapse. The latter kind of transition happened in the Soviet Union, Romania, and East Germany. Moving in the other direction, political orders take time to consolidate. The construction of legitimacy, and with it regime robustness, is a gradual process. There are no instances in which robustness can be described as an overnight phenomenon.

We want to emphasize that fragility and robustness are difficult to theorize and even more difficult to assess. Because they are reifications, they can be defined in different ways and different markers for them devised. Assessments of them by analysts and political actors depend very much on the markers used. Their choice of markers may influence, if not determine, their assessments of robustness and fragility but also the responses they think appropriate.

Consider contemporary debates about the fragility of Western democracy. Some attribute it to increasing economic disparities and diminishing prospects for social mobility.[41] Others focus on how political parties have evolved from mass movements into something similar to political cartels, producing governments that are unable to respond effectively to popular discontent in a productive way and thereby generating support for anti-system parties.[42] These diagnoses, as Peter Briener demonstrates in his chapter, lead to different assessment and policy prescriptions.

Another crucial aspect of actor assessments is priming. Political leaders are arguably aware of how they and their states are evaluated, ranked, and perceived by scholars and the myriad of other analysts in the business of providing measures on the performance of states.[43] International rankings of health, education, crime, corruption, and democracy are often highly publicized and can encourage or further undermine trust in a particular set of institutions. So too can dramatic events, which focus attention on certain problems as did COVID and the January 2021 assault on the US capitol, and perhaps the extreme Chinese lockups in the unrealistic hope of eradicating COVID.

Actor estimates are never uniform, as these events illustrate. Being perceived as performing well or badly during the pandemic presumably enhanced or reduced the robustness of political orders, not just their leaders of the moment. In New Zealand, democracy was a big winner, at least for the first year of the pandemic, and the United Kingdom a big loser. The joint report by the House of Commons health and science committees was brutal in its criticism.[44] Public opinion polls indicate that the COVID disaster led to greater disenchantment with democracy within England and increased support for Scottish independence and Northern Irish unification with the Republic of Ireland.[45] In the United States, it aggravated the already acute polarization of the country, which bodes ill for democracy's survival in the long term. In the short term it was a gift to democracy as Trump's egregious handling of the epidemic helped to elect Joseph Biden.[46]

Trump's claim to have lost the election due to alleged ballot cheating by Democrats culminated in an attack on the United States Capitol by his supporters. For many, the refusal of Trump to accept the outcome of a fair election and the violence he encouraged in its aftermath were serious signs, not only of disorder but of a fragile democracy at great risk. For others, the Senate's affirmation of Biden's victory, his peaceful inauguration, and the prosecution of many of those who assaulted the capitol is evidence of democratic robustness. It remains to be seen who is right.

These events drive home the difficulty of trying to make any objective assessments of robustness or fragility. Open-minded and thoughtful analysts can credibly come down on opposite sides. Any adjudication of these opposing assessments must await further events. For this reason, as noted, we eschew any attempt to study robustness and fragility directly but rather focus on the understandings of political actors, why and how they form, and the consequences they have. Needless to say, those consequences can only be determined in retrospect. That is why we have sought a balance in this book between historical and contemporary political orders. Although we do not offer measures of robustness and fragility, our book still speaks to analysts and political actors. It can make them more aware of the consequences of their beliefs for the assessments and encourage rethinking, or at least open questioning of these beliefs. It also has the potential to promote caution, rather than confident assertions, of any estimates they make.

Structure of the Book

Our common assumptions about robustness and fragility generate a large research agenda. They also point to what might be the most feasible set of questions to ask and how they might be addressed. The chapters that follow pick up on these questions and address them in widely varying circumstances. Our contributors explore robustness and fragility, although most focus more on the latter. They do so in the context of states, regional, and international organizations. Given our common set of assumptions the chapters speak to one another even though they address different questions in different settings.

Chapter 2, by Ned Lebow, more fully elaborates two of the assumptions broached in this introduction: that assessments of stability made by political actors and analysts are largely hit-or-miss, and that leader responses to fragility or robustness are unpredictable in their consequences. He suggests that leader assessments are often made with reference to historical lessons derived from dramatic past events that appear relevant to the present. These lessons may or may not be based on good history and may or may not be relevant to the situation at hand. Assessments are also influenced by cognitive biases and are often highly motivated. They rely on selective use of information and can be confirmed tautologically. On occasion, they promote a much needed but largely unsupported belief in robustness. But they are just as likely to encourage exaggerated estimates of fragility and responses.

Lebow suggests that scholars do not do demonstrably better than political actors in their estimates. This is attributable to the impossibility of making any kind of objective assessment of the relative robustness or fragility of political orders. There are few agreed upon markers, and most of them applicable only to regimes situated toward both ends of the robustness continuum. These indicators, moreover, are of limited help because underlying conditions are only part of the story. There are multiple pathways to robustness, and even more to collapse, and most, if not all, of them require catalysts. As in the case of wars, these catalysts may be independent of underlying conditions, and may or may not appear. Efforts to predict the success or failure of political systems based on underlying conditions will accordingly be hit-or-miss.

This two-step process consists of conditions and pathways, and good prediction requires not only correct assessment of relevant conditions but identification of multiple pathways to robustness or fragility and the catalysts that might set them in motion. Even then, predictions or forecasts can be wrong because pathways are rarely determinant. What happens will depend on context, a catchall term for situation-specific

Introduction 13

conditions that includes agency, confluence, path dependence, and accident. At best, the monitoring of appropriate underlying conditions, identifications of possible pathways to great robustness or fragility, and speculation about appropriate catalysts to these pathways constitute the basis for forecasts. Given the complexity of the problem it is hardly surprising that leaders and analysts are often taken by surprise. In effect, the relative robustness or fragility of political orders is only really apparent in retrospect.

Lebow draws on Janis and Mann's theory of conflict decision-making and Brian Rathbun's typology of personalities to offer some propositions about leader beliefs and some of the circumstances influencing them. One of the most important are historical lessons that sensitize them to particular pathways of regime success and failure and offer positive and negative role models. These role models legitimate and delegitimize certain kinds of policy responses and influence leader estimates of their freedom of action. He concludes with some general observations about the differences and similarities between leader and scholarly assessments of robustness and fragility.

Chapter 3 by Peter Breiner addresses the shift from the 1990s wave of optimism about the spread and consolidation of democracy and markets to the present counter-wave that worries about the danger to "democracy" from authoritarian leaders, populism, or simple complacency. He argues that new wave of "end of democracy" commentary – in particular, the writings of Steven Levitzky and Daniel Ziblatt, David Runciman, and Yascha Mounk – suffer from a series of problems. Most stem from their identification of "democracy" with liberal democracy, and liberal democracy with the minimalist Schumpeterian model of democracy.

What these "end of democracy" commentators view as new phase in liberal democracy is in fact an artifact of the internal logic of the minimalist model. The moment of harmony and consensus in the competitive party model that the "end of democracy" theorists claim has been lost, encourages political arrangements that provide space for right-wing authoritarian movements and left democratic populism to claim that the political system has betrayed its democratic credentials, in particular its claim to realize political equality with regard to governance. Movements and parties will attempt to fill this political space if social democracy leaves it unfilled.

This problem, he maintains, does not arise from some abandonment of the norms of liberal democracy, inadequate barriers to authoritarians, complacency in democracy's survival, or patching up the severe political and economic inequalities of liberal democracy. Rather, it is a product of a chronic failure of the minimalist model to deliver on its claim to political legitimacy: namely, it fails to produce political equality in its full sense of civil and political rights, inclusion and membership, and influence and power. It accordingly provides a space for political actors – whether right-wing authoritarian movements, left populist movements and parties, or insurgent members of established political parties, and even social democratic parties willing to give up their participation in political cartel arrangements – to make a claim to fulfill the unfilled promise of political legitimacy based on equality with regard to popular sovereignty. This is precisely the promise of legitimacy that liberal democracy in its minimalist variant cannot fulfill.

Chapter 4, by Paul Petzschmann, speaks to two questions at the heart of this volume. It examines beliefs about the Weimar Republic's robustness by its contemporaries. Administrative elites and academic observers regarded the Republic as much more stable than we might expect. Their judgments were rooted in a particular view of politics as driven by administration and administrators. They regarded bureaucracy and the courts as providing long-term continuity regardless of who or what type of political regime was in power.

Participants in the early debates about the causes of Weimar's collapse of the Republic were divided in their opinion about whether 1919 and 1933 – or either – constituted decisive historical breaks that marked the end of one kind of political order and the beginning of another. Today, we routinely differentiate among "monarchist," "republican," and "totalitarian" periods of German history in the first half of the twentieth century. At the time, the distinction between democracy and non-democracy was not regarded as relevant to the questions of political stability. Critiques of mass democracy associated parliamentary representation with fragility and regarded the central state and its administrative machine as an anchor of robustness. From this point of view, 1919 and 1933 were by no means decisive turning points.

Confidence in administrative stability was accompanied by a belief in elite administrators as agents capable of steering the fledgling Republic into calmer waters. This confidence was borne out of their experience of the civil service in Prussia with its highly efficient bureaucratic apparatus and stable coalition of pro-democratic parties. Many of the reform-minded civil servants placed their hopes of saving the Republic – paradoxically – in the Prussian state apparatus and the "Prussian spirit" that later observers would condemn as one of the most important nails in the coffin of Weimar.

Chapter 5 by Andrew Lawrence investigates proximate and underlying reasons why democratic liberal regimes failed to identify and confront the climate crisis in a timely fashion, or to adequately protect and empower their populations in light of it. He argues that states' legitimation and democratic crises are fundamentally intertwined with the more basic ecological crisis, in ways that implicate assessments of relative fragility or robustness in one sphere with those in the others.

In order to understand why most elite as well as non-elite actors do not adequately perceive the extent to which their political orders are ecologically embedded – and thus do not perceive the fragility of these political orders – the chapter first explores how perceptions and preferences came to be structured in everyday institutions, discursive tropes, and ways of seeing that collectively have come to constitute a hegemonic common sense he terms, following Brand and Wissen, "the imperial mode of living." He then argues that in order to become counter-hegemonic, critiques of the status quo need to identify collective actors as well as oppositional policies that can effectively counter this common sense. After tracing its structuring logic at the level of ideology via a brief genealogy of ideas in Descartes, Locke, Hegel, and Marx, the chapter explores some of its current institutional and practical manifestations. The conclusion reflects upon how elite and popular forms of climate leadership differ in their epistemologies and ontologies of nature. The core logic of commodification for profit, Lawrence argues, cannot be channeled or reformed in ways that strengthen the ecological, and thus also the liberal-democratic order. This necessarily implies that liberal-democratic actors need to recognize that the adequate defense of their order requires the subordination of commodification processes to the necessary goals of ecological and social well-being.

In Chapter 6, Archie Brown argues that fundamental change in the Soviet political system and of Soviet foreign policy was of decisive importance for the de-Communization of Eastern and Central Europe, as the peoples of those countries would have dispensed with the services of their Communist rulers years earlier but for the realistic expectation that this would lead to Soviet intervention, making a bad situation worse.

This had little or nothing to do with the "Third Wave" of democracy of the 1970s in Southern Europe and Latin America, but was a discrete Fourth Wave in which transnational influences were crucial – in the first instance, the new tolerance, liberalization, and ideological change (the

New Thinking) emanating from Moscow. Once pluralizing change got underway in both the Soviet Union and Eastern Europe, there was democratic "contagion" from one country to another and a circular flow of influence.

The facilitating conditions for East European democratization and independence were created by change in Moscow, but when Poles, Hungarians, and Czechs speedily asserted their independence without any coercive response by the Soviet leadership, the most disaffected nations within the USSR – the three Baltic states, in the first instance – acquired the confidence to move beyond pressing for greater national autonomy within the USSR to demanding the same kind of independent statehood that had been obtained by the Central and East European states.

Within the Soviet Union itself, Brown emphasizes the distinction between the system and the state. He argues that it is *wrong* to think that the end of the former was an unintended consequence of Mikhail Gorbachev's reforms, although the end of the Soviet state *was*, inasmuch as the new tolerance had allowed national movements to develop and the democratization process – in particular, contested elections – had provided institutional mechanisms for nationalists to advance the cause of separate statehood. Whereas Gorbachev devoted much time and energy to preserving some kind of Union, but without resorting to repression, he was from mid-1988 onward engaged in dismantling the political system he had inherited. All generalizations about Gorbachev's aims, Brown argues, should have a time dimension, for this was a leader whose views greatly evolved, even during the period of less than seven years in which he led the Soviet Union. He came to power as a Communist reformer in 1985 but turned into a systemic transformer in 1988, and he was prepared to go still further in democratization by 1990.

The agency of leaders mattered greatly – above all, Gorbachev's, in association with the institutional power of the General Secretaryship. This enabled him, for example, to replace the entire top foreign-policymaking team within his first year as Soviet leader. The transformation of Soviet foreign policy went alongside the dismantling of the Communist political system, and both of those fundamental changes were primarily Gorbachev's doing.

For the breakup of the USSR the agency of Boris Yeltsin was also of decisive consequence. A Union – which Gorbachev accepted need no longer be called the *Soviet* Union – could have survived without Estonia, Latvia, and Lithuania, which were not part of the USSR until they were forcibly incorporated in 1940. But clearly, such a Union could not exist without Russia. It was unusual, to say the least, for a Russian leader to think that the disintegration of the Soviet Union was in Russia's national interest, and Yeltsin himself was ambivalent about it. However, by presenting his struggle for supremacy with Gorbachev in terms of Russia versus the federal authorities, and ultimately supporting separate Russian statehood, Yeltsin made the preservation of a Union unattainable.

Chapter 9 by Ludvig Norman focuses on order at the regional level. It does so by looking at the origins of the institutions that would eventually evolve into the European Union. It argues that a focus on perceptions of fragility provides a fruitful but underexplored perspective on these institutions. It applies this perspective to discussions surrounding the creation of the early institutions of European postwar political cooperation. It demonstrates that discussions about the creation of these institutions were informed by perceptions of fragility associated with democratic governance. The functionalist story of the EU, where cooperative institutions were set up to prevent the formerly warring countries from entering into new conflicts, has long had a dominant position in the understanding of these origins. While not inaccurate, this narrative often obscures how the reconstruction of the European political order was also an answer to the breakdown of European democracy before the war. Notions of democracy's fragility informed the functionalist perspective on politics as well as the perceived need for a 'militant' protection of democratic institutions, most clearly articulated by constitutional scholar Karl Löwenstein. Apart from shaping the origins of the European political order, Norman argues that perceptions of fragility have continued to inform the institutional development of the EU and even ongoing efforts to strengthen its democratic aspects.

Chapter 8 by Ariane Chebel d'Appollonia investigates American understandings of the fragility and robustness of their democracy. Chebel d'Appollonia emphasizes three main points. First, Americans perceived the meaning of democracy in a multidimensional way (as a unique set of values and principles, a political regime, a form of government, an ideology, a sense of destiny, and an expression of national character, if not a model for humanity). This explains why political leaders' estimates of the state of democracy have never been just context-dependent; they have also been ideologically contingent, framed by beliefs in US exceptionalism that are often disconnected from reality.

Second, US democracy has been and still is more fragile and more resilient than commonly perceived (by analysts, political elites, and the mass public) – which suggests we need to put into perspective both an overconfidence in robustness and pessimistic accounts of fragility. Chebel d'Appollonia, therefore, examines the relationship between "the weakness of robustness" and "the strength of fragility" in order to demonstrate how robustness and fragility are organically related, for better or worse, in terms of perceptions and practices.

Third, assessments of US democracy oscillate between overconfidence and declinism, with no stable equilibrium between these two poles. Political elites, scholars, and public opinion historically shared the positive view of US democracy – at least until the late 1990s. In the opening decade of the 2000s, Americans started to express distrust in US institutions (but still valued US democracy). Political elites, however, continued to praise the US model (both domestically and internationally). Today, the assumption that US democracy is in crisis is shared by political and intellectual elites, and by most Americans. The three are in sync again, but at the opposite side of the optimism–pessimism spectrum. While it is premature to evaluate what the state of US democracy will be in the coming years, Chebel d'Appollonia identifies major threats that can seriously damage US democracy – such as the denial of actual problems by leaders, or conversely, the use of declinist arguments to legitimize undemocratic practices allegedly designed to protect democracy. Any exaggeration of a vulnerability to threats, as well as overconfidence in US exceptionalism, will have dire consequences.

Chapter 9 by Douglas Webber is the second chapter that focuses on the EU. In the decade from 2010 to 2020 the EU endured several major crises that its political leaders feared could lead to its collapse. He explores how leaders managed these crises, the extent to which EU became more fragile because of them, and how far EU crisis management was structurally determined or shaped by agency. The crises resulted in divergent outcomes. The EU emerged politically more closely integrated from the Eurozone crisis and slightly less so from the refugee crisis. In the third, the Brexit crisis, it lost one of its three most important member states. The more "disintegrative" outcomes can be attributed to a large extent to decisions that were made relatively autonomously. Thus, agency is not necessarily a recipe for the rescue of crisis-afflicted political orders. Nor does the existence of structural constraints that limit the range of politically feasible responses to respond to crises condemn regional orders to collapse.

In Chapter 10, as editors, we try to pull together the findings of our contributors. We include a flowchart that attempts to capture leader responses to fragility by asking how they perceive their orders, whether they see an effective response if they judge their orders fragile, and their freedom to act. Answers to each of these questions create branching points, which we subsequently illustrate with examples from our chapters. We also consider factors outside of our scheme that influence leader decisions. They include role models, historical lessons, path dependency, and the kind of expectations that are dominant in the era. We then consider the consequences of leader initiatives or lack of them. In this connection, we consider key features of context. We offer some generalizations about contingency and agency, and the differences and similarities in fragility and robustness at different levels of analysis: state, regional, and international. We also consider how the lessons learned from the collapse of prior orders influences present-day responses to nationality and regional fragility.

Threats and tensions offer an incentive to address problems, inequalities, dissatisfaction, alienation, and opposition that might otherwise become more pronounced and threatening to existing orders. It may well be that in some others there is a point of no return – as scientists warn may be the case with climate change – where a process becomes irreversible and intervention in the hope of reversing the process will be fruitless. It is difficult to know about such turning points in advance, but it is still useful to theorize them and make them the subject of study. Knowledge about them might generate more support for intervening at an earlier stage when it is still possible to reduce fragility.

Notes

1 Regime changes may occur in democratic states, sometimes peacefully, as in the transition from the Fourth to the Fifth Republic in France, see Jean-Jacques Chevallier, Guy Carcassonne, and Olivier Duhamel, *Histoire de la Ve République: 1958–2017*, 16th ed. (Paris: Dalloz, 2917).
2 Mark Cornwall, ed, *The Last Years of Austria-Hungary* (Exeter: University of Exeter Press, 2002).
3 Susan L. Woodward, *Balkan Tragedy: Chaos and Dissolution after the Cold War* (Washington, DC: Brookings, 1995); Misha Glenny, *The Fall of Yugoslavia*, 3rd ed. (London: Penguin, 1996); Ronald Suny, *Revenge of the Past: Nationalism, Revolution, and the Collapse of the Soviet Union* (Stanford: Stanford University Press, 1993); Archie Brown, *The Human Factor: Gorbachev, Reagan, and Thatcher and the End of the Cold War* (Oxford: Oxford University Press, 2020), ch. 15–16.
4 Pierre Abramovici, ed., *Le Putsch des Généraux* (Paris: Fayard, 2011); Catarina Falcão, "25 de Novembro. O fim da revolução, mas só para alguns," *Observador*, 24 November 2015, https://observador.pt/2015/11/24/25-de-novembro-o-fim-da-revolucao-mas-so-para-alguns/ (accessed September 11, 2020); Amadeo Martinez Ingles, *23-F: El Golpe que nunca existio* (Madrid: Foca, 2001).
5 The only successful coup was staged by colonels in Greece. They were in power from 1967 to 1974, when democracy was restored. See C. M. Woodhouse, *The Rise and Fall of the Greek Colonels* (London: Olympic, 1985).
6 For example, W. W. Rostow, *The Stages of Economic Growth: A Non-Communist Manifesto* (Cambridge, MA: Cambridge University Press, 1960);

Seymour M. Lipset, "Some Social Requisites of Democracy: Economic Development and Political Legitimacy," *American Political Science Review* 53, no. 1 (1959), pp. 69–105; Dankwart Rustow, "Transitions to Democracy: Toward a Dynamic Model," *Comparative Politics* 2, no. 3 (1970), pp. 337–63. Barrington Moore, Jr., *Social Origins of Dictatorship and Democracy* (Boston, MA: Beacon Press, 1966); Guillermo O'Donnell and Philippe Schmitter, *Transitions From Authoritarian Rule: Tentative Conclusions about Uncertain Democracies* (Baltimore, MD: The Johns Hopkins University Press, 1986); Guillermo O'Donnell, Philippe Schmitter, and Laurence Whitehead, eds., *Transitions from Authoritarian Rule: Prospects for Democracy* (Baltimore, MD: The Johns Hopkins University Press, 1986); Larry Diamond, Juan J. Linz, and Seymour Martin Lipset, eds., *Democracy in Developing Countries: Africa* (Boulder, CO: Lynne Rienner, 1989); Dietrich Rueschemeyer, Evelyne Huber Stephens, and John D. Stephens, *Capitalist Development and Democracy* (Chicago, IL: University of Chicago Press, 1992).

7 Juan J. Linz and Alfred Stepan, *Problems of Democratic Transition and Consolidation: Southern Europe, South America and Post-Communist Europe* (Baltimore, MD: The Johns Hopkins University Press, 1986); Richard Gunther, P. Nikiforos Diamandouros, and Hans-Jürgen Puhle, eds., *The Politics of Democratic Consolidation: Southern Europe in Comparative Perspective* (Baltimore, MD: Johns Hopkins University Press, 1995); Adam Przeworski, *Democracy and the Market. Political and Economic Reforms in Eastern Europe and Latin America* (New York: Cambridge University Press, 1991); Adam Przeworski, Michael E. Alvarez, José Antonio Cheibub, and Fernando Limongi, *Democracy and Development: Political Institutions and Well-Being in the World, 1950-1990* (New York: Cambridge University Press, 2001); Geoffrey Pridham, ed., *Transitions to Democracy: Comparative Perspectives from Southern Europe, Latin America and Eastern Europe* (Brookfield, VT: Dartmouth Publishing, 1995); Laurence Whitehead, ed., *The International Dimensions of Democratization: Europe and the Americas* (New York: Oxford University Press, 1996); Samuel P. Huntington, "Democracy's Third Wave," *Journal of Democracy* 2, no. 2 (1991), pp. 12–34, and "After Twenty Years: The Future of the Third Wave," *Journal of Democracy* 8, no. 4 (1997), pp. 3–12; Scott Mainwaring, and Fernando Bizzarro, "The Fates of Third-Wave Democracies," *Journal of Democracy* 30, no. 1 (2019), pp. 99–113; Luke Martell, "The Third Wave in Globalization Theory," *International Studies Review* 9, no. 2 (2007), pp. 173–96.

8 Francis Fukuyama, *The End of History and the Last Man* (New York: Free Press, 1992). An earlier claim was made by Daniel Bell, *The End of Ideology: On the Exhaustion of Political Ideas in the 1950s* (Glencoe, IL: Free Press, 1960).

9 Thomas Friedman, *The Lexus and the Olive Tree* (New York: Farrar, Strauss & Giroux, 1999); Richard Rosecrance, *Rise of the Trading State: Commerce and Conquest in the Modern World* (New York: Basic Books, 1987).

10 David Harvey, *A Brief History of Neoliberalism* (Oxford: Oxford University Press, 2007); Michel Foucault, *The Birth of Biopolitics: Lectures at the Collège de France, 1978—1979*, trans. Graham Burchell (London: Palgrave-Macmillan, 2008); Stefan Hedlund, *Russia's "Market" Economy: A Bad Case of Predatory Capitalism* (London: University College London Press, 1999).

11 See Paul Petzschmann's chapter in this volume on the Weimar Republic and the literature that developed about its collapse. At least since Tocqueville, there has been a literature on the breakdown of democratic orders. Alexis de Tocqueville, *Democracy in America*, trans. and ed. Harvey C. Mansfield and Debra Winthrop (Chicago, IL: University of Chicago Press, 2000).

12 There was however a small literature about postwar democratic failures, or the threat of them. See Juan J. Linz, *The Breakdown of Democratic Regimes. Crisis, Breakdown, and Reequilibration* (Baltimore, MD: Johns Hopkins University Press, 1978); Juan J. Linz and Alfred Stepan, eds., *The Breakdown of Democratic Regimes* (Baltimore, MD: Johns Hopkins University Press, 1978); Howard Handelman and Mark A. Tessler, eds., *Democracy and Its Limits: Lessons from Asia, Latin America and the Middle East* (Notre Dame, ID: University of Notre Dame Press, 2007).

13 For example, David Runciman, *How Democracy Ends* (London: Profile, 2018); Steven Levitsky, *How Democracies Die* (New York: Penguin, 2018); Timothy Snyder, *The Road to Unfreedom: Russia, Europe, America* (New York: Random House, 2018); Anne Applebaum, *Twilight of Democracy: The Seductive Lure of Authoritarianism* (New York: Doubleday, 2020). Peter Breiner's chapter in this volume discusses some recent and prominent.

14 "What If Trump Wins? The Washington Monthly explores the policy consequences of a second Trump term," *Washington Monthly*, May-June 2020, https://washingtonmonthly.com/magazine/april-may-june-2020/what-if-trump-wins/; Symposium, "A Trump second term: How President Trump could change America with four more years in office," *Vox*, August 27, 2020, www.vox.com/21514447/trump-2020-second-term-policy-agenda; Thomas Wright, "Order from Chaos: What a Second Trump Term Would Mean for the World," *Brookings*, October 1, 2020, www.brookings.edu/blog/order-from-chaos/2020/10/01/what-a-second-trump-term-would-mean-for-the-world/ (all accessed February 3, 2021).

15 Wolfgang Streeck, *How Will Capitalism End?* (London: Verso, 2016); John Foster Bellamy and Fred Magdoff, *The Great Financial Crisis: Causes and Consequences* (New York: Monthly Press, 2009); George A. Akerloff and Robert J. Shiller, *Phishing for Phools* (Princeton, NJ: Princeton University Press, 2015).

16 For studies on polarization and fears of violence across the political spectrum, Thomas B. Edsall, "Will Trump Ever Leave the White House?" *New York Times*, October 2, 2019, www.nytimes.com/2019/10/02/opinion/trump-leave-white-house.html. Masha Gessen, "What Could Happen If Donald Trump Rejects Electoral Defeat?" *New Yorker*, July 21, 2020, https://www.newyorker.com/news/our-columnists/what-could-happen-if-donald-trump-rejects-electoral-defeat (both accessed September 13, 2020).

17 Martin Pengelly, *"Roger Stone to Donald Trump: Bring in Martial Law If You Lose Election," Guardian*, September 13, 2020, www.theguardian.com/us-news/2020/sep/13/roger-stone-to-donald-trump-bring-in-martial-law-if-you-lose-election (accessed September 13, 2020).

18 For constantly updated coverage, Wikipedia, *2021 Storming of the United States Capitol*, February 3, 2021, https://en.wikipedia.org/wiki/2021_storming_of_the_United_States_Capitol (accessed February 3, 2021).

19 Thomas B. Edsall, "Whose America Is It?," *New York Times*, September 16, 2010, www.nytimes.com/2020/09/16/opinion/biden-trump-2020-violence.html?action=click&module=Opinion&pgtype=Homepage (accessed September 16, 2020).
20 Luke Broadwater and Alan Feuer, "Jan. 6 Panel Tracks How Trump Created and Spread Election Lies," *New York Times*, 13 June 2022, www.nytimes.com/2022/06/13/us/politics/trump-january-6-hearings-day-2.html (accessed 13 June 2022).
21 Although less so, to Europeans. Christine Huang and Richard Wike, "Even before Capitol riot, most people in Germany, France and the UK had concerns about U.S. political system," *Pew Research Center*, January 19, 2021, www.pewresearch.org/fact-tank/2021/01/19/even-before-capitol-riot-most-people-in-germany-france-and-the-uk-had-concerns-about-u-s-political-system/ (accessed February 3, 2012).
22 Hannah Hartig, "In their own words: How Americans reacted to the rioting at the U.S. Capitol," *Pew Research Center*, January 15, 2021, www.pewresearch.org/fact-tank/2021/01/15/in-their-own-words-how-americans-reacted-to-the-rioting-at-the-u-s-capitol/ (accessed February 3, 2021).
23 Robert K. Murray, *Red Scare: A Study in National Hysteria, 1919-1920* (Minneapolis, MN: University of Minnesota Press, 1955).
24 Henry Pachter, "On Being an Exile," *Salamagundi*, nos. 10-111 (Fall, Winter 1969-70), pp. 12–51.
25 Karl Popper, *The Open Society and Its Enemies* (Princeton: Princeton University Press, 1945); Karl Löwenstein, "Autocracy versus Democracy in Contemporary Europe," *American Political Science Review* 29, no. 4 (1935), pp. 571–93; William Kornhauser, *The Politics of Mass Society* (Glencoe, IL: Free Press, 1959).
26 Karl Löwenstein, "Autocracy versus Democracy in Contemporary Europe," *American Political Science Review* 29, no. 4 (1935), pp. 571–93. There is a comprehensive and more contemporary literature on legal and political thought in Weimar and its influence on postwar thought, in particular in the field of constitutional law. See for instance David Dyzenhaus *Legality and Legitimacy: Carl Schmitt, Hans Kelsen, and Hermann Heller in Weimar* (Oxford: Oxford University Press, 1997); Jan-Werner Müller, *A Dangerous Mind: Carl Schmitt in Post-War European Thought* (New Haven, CT: Yale University Press, 2003); Cindy Skach, *Borrowing Constitutional Designs: Constitutional Law in Weimar Germany and the Fifth Republic* (Princeton, NJ: Princeton University Press, 2005); William E. Scheuerman, *The End of Law: Carl Schmitt in the Twenty-First Century* (Boulder, Co: Rowman and Littlefield, 2020).
27 Edwin Bacon and Mark Sandle, eds., *Brezhnev Reconsidered* (London: Palgrave-Macmillan, 2002), esp. chs. 2, 7, and 10; Thomas Crump, *Brezhnev and the Decline of the Soviet Union* (London: Routledge, 2016), esp. chs. 6 and 13.
28 Archie Brown, *The Gorbachev Factor* (Oxford: Oxford University Press, 1996), and his chapter in this volume; Serhii Polkhy, *The Last Empire: The Final Days of the Soviet Union* (New York: Basic Books, 2014), pp. 29–30, 395–97.

29 Archie Brown, *The Human Factor: Gorbachev, Reagan, and Thatcher and the End of the Cold War* (Oxford: Oxford University Press, 2020), chs. 15 and 16; Polkhy, *The Last Empire*, ch. 5. Among other failings, they left Yeltsin and his supporters unmolested and in constant contact with foreign media and leaders.
30 Breslauer and Lebow, "Leadership and the End of the Cold War" offer counterfactual experiments about the end of the Cold War using different combinations of possible Soviet and American leaders. They reveal wide variation in their consequences.
31 Jacques Lévesque, *The Enigma of 1989: The USSR and the Liberation of Eastern Europe*, trans. K. Martin (Berkeley, CA: University of California Press, 1997), pp. 149–64; Mary Elise Sarotte, *The Collapse: The Accidental Opening of the Berlin Wall* (New York: Basic Books, 2014), chs. 6–7; Archie Brown, *The Rise and Fall of Communism* (London: Bodley Head, 2009), ch. 6, 25–26.
32 Michael Dillon, *Religious Minorities and China* (London: Minority Rights Group International, 2001); Amnesty International, "China: The crackdown on Falun Gong and other so-called 'heretical organizations,'" March 23, 2000, www.refworld.org/docid/3b83b6e00.html (retrieved September 14, 2020).
33 Human Rights Watch, "China: Events of 2018," www.hrw.org/world-report/2019/country-chapters/china-and-tibet and "China: Events of 2018," www.hrw.org/world-report/2020/country-chapters/china-and-tibet (both accessed September 14, 2020).
34 See the next chapter for elaboration.
35 Martin Dimitrov and Richard Ned Lebow, "China," in Richard Ned Lebow, *The Rise and Fall of Political Orders* (Cambridge, MA: Cambridge University Press, 2018), pp. 274–303.
36 Leszek Kołakowski, *Main Currents of Marxism*, trans. P. S. Falla (New York: Barnes & Norton, 1978), pp. 1049–50.
37 Maria Josepha Debre and Hylke Dijkstra, "Institutional Design for a Post-Liberal Order: Why Some International Organizations Live Longer than Others," *European Journal of International Relations* 20 no. 4 (2021), pp. 311–39; Mette Eilstrup-Sagiovanni "Death of International Organizations: The Organizational Ecology of Intergovernmental Organization, 1815-2015," *The Review of International Organizations* 15 (2020), pp. 339–70.
38 John Mearsheimer "The False Promise of International Institutions," *International Security* 19 no. 3 (1994/95) pp. 5–49; James G. March and Johan P. Olsen "The Institutional Dynamics of International Political Orders," *International Organization* 52 no. 4 (1998), pp. 943–69.
39 Ludvig Norman, "Defending the European Political Order," *European Journal of Social Theory* 20 no. 4 (2017), 531–49.
40 For a debate on this subject, Richard Ned Lebow, "Contingency, Catalysts, and International System Change," *Political Science Quarterly* 115, no. 4 (2000–2001), pp. 591–616; William R. Thompson, "A Streetcar Named Sarajevo: Catalysts, Multiple Causation Chains, and Rivalry Structures," *International Studies Quarterly* 47, no. 3 (2003), pp. 453–74; Richard Ned

Lebow, "A Data Set Named Desire: A Reply to William P. Thompson," *International Studies Quarterly* 47, no. 3 (2003), pp. 475–58

41 Robert Putnam, *Our Kids: The American Dream in Crisis* (New York: Simon & Schuster).
42 Peter Mair, *Ruling the Void: The Hollowing of Western Democracy* (London: Verso, 2013).
43 Judith G. Kelley and Beth A. Simmons, *The Power of Global Performance Indicators* (Cambridge, MA: Cambridge University Press, 2020).
44 Peter Walker, "'Extraordinary omission': key findings in scathing UK Covid report," *Guardian*, October 2012, 12, www.theguardian.com/world/2021/oct/12/extraordinary-omission-key-findings-in-scathing-uk-covid-report (accessed October 13, 2021).
45 Gerry Moriarty, "Poll finds majority favours holding a Border poll in next five years," *Irish Times*, January 2021, 24, www.irishtimes.com/news/ireland/irish-news/poll-finds-majority-favours-holding-a-border-poll-in-next-five-years-1.4466826 (accessed February 5, 2021).
46 Diedre Shesgreen, "How COVID-19 shaped the 2020 election, swinging some voters to Biden but bolstering Trump with his base," *USA Today*, November 9, 2020, www.usatoday.com/story/news/politics/elections/2020/11/09/covid-19-shaped-2020-election-amid-split-biden-trump-response/3729201001/; Ashley Parker, Josh Dawsey, Matt Viser, and Michael Scherer, "How Trump's erratic behavior and failure on coronavirus doomed his reelection," *Washington Post*, November 7, 2020, www.washingtonpost.com/elections/interactive/2020/trump-pandemic-coronavirus-election/; Christina Wilkie, "Coronavirus changed the 2020 money race — and helped Biden erase Trump's massive cash advantage," *CNBC*, September 29, 2020, (all accessed February 4, 2021).

2   Robustness and Fragility of Political Orders

Richard Ned Lebow

I begin with a paradox: Knowledge about the relative robustness or stability of a political order is more important than ever before in today's world but also more difficult to determine for reasons that I will elaborate.[1] This does not deter leaders, elites, other political actors, talking heads, and scholars from making and publicizing assessments of the stability and fragility of their political systems and those of other states. These judgments matter and can determine how and if leaders respond to warnings of fragility or positive assessments of robustness of their regimes. There may be underlying conditions associated with regime robustness or fragility, but they are only one piece of a much larger puzzle. What matters more is what leaders think about the problem, what kinds of responses they deem appropriate, and the degree to which they think them feasible to implement.

I make two related claims: (1) that assessments of stability made by political actors and analysts are largely hit-or-miss; and (2) that leader responses to fear of fragility or confidence in robustness are unpredictable in their consequences. Leader assessments are often made with respect to historical lessons derived from dramatic past events that appear relevant to the present. These lessons may or may not be based on good history and may or may not be relevant to the case at hand. Leaders and elites who believe their orders to be robust can help make their beliefs self-fulfilling. However, overconfidence can help make these orders fragile. I argue that leader and elite assessments of robustness and fragility are influenced by cognitive biases and also often highly motivated. Leaders and their advisors use information selectively and can confirm tautologically the lessons they apply.

I do not believe that scholars do demonstrably better than political actors. This is not so much their fault as it is the impossibility of making any kind of objective assessment of the relative robustness or fragility of political orders. There are few agreed-upon benchmarks, and these indicators may be misleading because underlying conditions are only part of the story. There are multiple pathways to robustness, and even more to fragility and collapse, and most, if not all, of them are context-dependent. They also require catalysts and they may be independent of underlying conditions.[2] Efforts to predict the success or failure of political system based on underlying conditions must accordingly be hit-or-miss.

This two-step process consists of conditions and pathways, and good prediction requires not only correct assessment of relevant conditions but identification of multiple pathways to robustness or fragility and the catalysts that might set them in motion. Even then, predictions or forecasts can be wrong because pathways are rarely determinant. What happens will depend on situation-specific conditions that include agency, confluence, path dependence, and accident. At best, the monitoring of appropriate underlying conditions, identifications of possible pathways to great robustness or fragility, and speculation about appropriate catalysts to these pathways constitute the basis for forecasts. Given the complexity of the problem it is hardly surprising that leaders and analysts are often taken by surprise.

Accurate assessments of fragility and robustness are only really possible after the fact, when it is too late to benefit politically from them. It is certainly possible to identify a set of conditions that have the potential to contribute to the survival of orders – or their downfall – and I try to identify some of them. They are, however, indeterminate for the reasons noted. This situation gives rise to several distinct but related analytical questions: Why is it so difficult to assess the robustness and fragility of regimes; and why do leaders make the assessments that they do? And why are many leaders confident about their judgments? I have offered a partial answer to the first question and will explore it further in the opening section of the chapter.

The following section focuses on the beliefs and behavior of leaders. Drawing on Janis and Mann's theory of conflict decision-making and Brian Rathbun's typology of personalities, I offer propositions about the importance of leader beliefs, how these beliefs form, and the circumstances that influence different responses to perceptions of fragility. These beliefs have multiple sources. One of the most important is historical lessons that sensitize them to particular pathways of regime success and failure and offer positive and negative role models. These role models legitimate and delegitimize certain kinds of policy responses. They may also influence leaders' estimates of their freedom of action.

The choice of lessons and role models is not always obvious and worth investigation. Various features of context affect their availability and appeal. Timing is particularly important in this regard. It is critical for other reasons as well. Some political strategies intended to reduce fragility hold promise but may be counterproductive if introduced at the wrong moment. I conclude with some general observations about the differences and similarities between leader and scholarly assessments of robustness and fragility.

Problems of Assessment

Assessments of robustness are deeply influenced, if not determined, by the political assumptions people bring to the task. In the decade before the French Revolution, the otherwise astute David Hume worried about the prospect of political upheaval in Britain because of its chaotic party structure and diffusion of power. He thought France remarkably stable because of its more rigid hierarchy and centralized government.[3] In the aftermath of the Bolshevik coup, Lenin and his fellow revolutionaries felt terribly insecure but also expected revolution in the West because they believed in the inevitability of socialism. Their insecurity justified their turn to large-scale terror. For Lenin and Stalin, terror then became a principal means of retaining power. In the words of Stalin's most recent biographer, "the threat of a counterrevolution was a gift that kept giving."[4]

Throughout the Cold War, Western analysts thought the Soviet Union robust and most worried more about their own internal weaknesses. They were as surprised by its rapid collapse as eighteenth-century observers had been of the French Revolution. Today, there is something of a consensus among Western scholars that China's communist political order is fragile and must ultimately liberalize or go under.[5] This judgment too may also be based on an inappropriate assumption: that corrupt, single-party regimes cannot survive in the long term. Chinese leaders appear to regard their political system as fragile, although for entirely different reasons. Only time will tell which set of expectations – if either – was on target.

These and other examples make clear that policymakers and respected analysts routinely describe as stable orders on the verge of collapse, and as fragile those that have endured without serious challenge. There are, I believe, multiple generic reasons why assessment is so difficult. The first, noted in the introductory chapter is that change – and especially the breakdown of orders – is a two-step process that requires appropriate underlying conditions and catalysts that set change in motion. I suspect that leaders focus more on the latter and academic analysts on the former. This is a question worthy of serious examination.

Orders most often change gradually over time. Not all change is gradual. The collapse of communism in Europe was rapid and dramatic, as were the events of the so-called Arab Spring. Both upheavals began with internal changes in one country that affected others in a ripple effect. We can borrow the concept of phase transition from physics and chemistry and use it metaphorically to describe these kinds of transformations in domestic politics and international relations. In the case of the DDR, groups of East Germans on holiday in Hungary in July and August of 1989 were the precipitants. Thousands of them wanted to flee to the West, and the Hungarian government considered letting them pass through its border with Austria. On 6 October, Gorbachev came to Berlin to attend the fortieth-anniversary celebrations of the East German regime and was welcomed as a liberator by huge crowds in East Berlin. Shortly afterward, the DDR Politburo forced Erich Honecker to step down as general secretary and replaced him with Egon Krenz. Demonstrations spread and more East Germans fled to the West via Czechoslovakia, which opened its borders. East Germans gathered at the Berlin Wall and demanded the right to leave without prior permission. Events escalated with new demonstrations in Leipzig and elsewhere, the Wall was breached, and the rest is history.[6]

As these examples indicate, political orders sometimes transition rapidly from order to chaos. The most fragile orders tend to be rigid and resistant to change and ignore or suppress demands for change, and the people who make them. This can create a false appearance of tranquility, but the order can unravel quickly in response to unanticipated internal or external shocks. Had public opinion polls been available, been politically acceptable, and asked the right questions, they would have been unlikely to have revealed that these political systems – and their countries – were at the edge of the precipice. In East Germany, public protest against the regime did not occur – and probably could not have – until citizens became aware of just how widespread opposition to the regime was. The divided and weak response of the government to protest then proved to be its undoing.

Agency can be considered another monkey wrench. The relative robustness of orders is very much influenced by the assessments of key actors and public opinion. Belief in robustness can help make it self-fulfilling – or blind leaders to the need for reforms and make their political system more fragile. Belief in fragility can prompt reforms that shore up a regime and build legitimacy.[7] It can also set leaders against meaningful reform, as happened in Brezhnev's Soviet Union. When leaders fear for the survival of their regimes, they may be tempted to engage in a combination of denial and political repression. The Russian,

Austro-Hungarian, and Ottoman Empires, and more recently the Soviet Union, are cases in point. I will return to this seeming paradox.

Context is critical to outcomes. The same policies in different contexts can have divergent consequences.[8] This renders historical lessons of dubious value, even when – which is not often the case – they are carefully constructed and based on good historical evidence. Two telling examples of leaders drawing the opposite conclusions from roughly comparable events offer graphic evidence of the importance of context. Early nineteenth-century British leaders saw the opposition of the French monarchy to reform as the fundamental reason for its collapse and accordingly become more predisposed to manage change.[9] The Chinese leadership concluded that Gorbachev's political reforms were responsible for the collapse of the Soviet Union and shared a commitment to avoid them and repress those who campaigned for them.[10]

Context also determines how long fragile orders can endure. The Roman, Russian, Austro-Hungarian, and Ottoman Empires endured well past what some considered their "use by" date. Their collapse depended upon an appropriate catalyst, which was World War I for the three modern empires. The Weimar Republic may well have survived in the absence of the Great Depression. North Korea is currently hanging on longer than most analysts expected. Other features of context may be just as important. Mette Eilstrup-Sangiovanni shows that the death or survival of international nongovernmental organizations is often a function of the timing and sequencing of institution-building efforts. This in turn can influence their scope, membership, degree of support, and others' perceptions of their utility.[11]

It is often difficult to identify the relevant features of context. They too may only become evident ex post facto. Donald Trump's political career offers a telling example. He ran for the Republican nomination in 2012 and found no traction whatsoever with voters.[12] In 2016, to the amazement of pols and pollsters, he won primary after primary, and then the presidential election. Donald Trump had not changed, but the context had; there were many more voters angry and disillusioned with "the system" and willing to vote for someone perceived as an outsider who appeared to sympathize with their plight.[13]

Beliefs and Consequences

Political actors sometimes exaggerate the robustness of their political orders. Less often they worry without good reason that they are at risk. They can also pretend that that their orders are fragile. Donald Trump is only the most recent example of a would-be dictator propagating a false estimate of fragility to justify the illegal use of force to advance his political ends. Ironically, by doing so, he arguably helped to make that order more fragile.

Leader beliefs and behavior obviously have important implications for their policies and for the survival of their political orders. Beliefs about robustness and fragility are nevertheless indeterminate in their policy implications. How leaders respond will depend on key features of context. The two most important determinants in this regard may be their perceived freedom of action and the positive or negative role models they find compelling.

Freedom to act is largely a function of domestic institutional and political constraints. Leaders routinely misjudge their freedom of action, although estimates about what they might have done are counterfactual and difficult to establish. Leaders can fail to introduce or push for reforms they think advisable, even necessary, because they do not believe they have the power to carry them through. They may also fear that arousing hopes that might then be dashed is worse than doing nothing. Leaders who feel compelled to act to preserve their order may be motivated to exaggerate their ability to do what is necessary, as was Mikhail Gorbachev.[14] Conversely, those who believe they lack the freedom to carry out reforms may downgrade the fragility of their orders in their minds. Context and agency are all-important and interactive.

Leader assessments of their freedom to act are highly subjective. For this reason there may be sharp differences of opinion within a government about what is feasible. President Kennedy put civil rights legislation on the back burner, thinking it might only be possible in his second term. Following Kennedy's assassination, President Johnson pushed forward with both tax reform and civil rights. He insisted, moreover, on a civil rights bill with teeth, not one that would be watered down in the Senate by opposition and filibuster from segregationists.[15] Johnson's advisors thought he was foolhardy. One of them recalled that in a strategy session "'one of the wise, practical people around the table' told him to his face that a President shouldn't spend his time and power on lost causes, no matter how worthy those causes might be. 'What the hell is the Presidency for?' Johnson responded."[16] To their surprise – and of many of his Senate colleagues – the President achieved his goals through astute manipulation of Senate rules, exquisite timing, and a combination of carefully calibrated bribes and threats based on intimate knowledge of what really mattered to friends and foes alike in the Congress.[17]

Leader goals are difficult to separate from their estimates of authority. Goals can expand and contract in response to what is considered feasible. These changing estimates are hard to document and we must avoid the circularity of inferring them from observable behavior. When possible we must do this so on the basis of internal conversations or documents. A case in point is the program Archduke Franz Ferdinand had drawn up for the restructuring of the Austro-Hungarian Empire once he came to power. He envisaged a tripartite monarchy, with southern Slavs constituting the third major political grouping. This would have required extension of the franchise, which he favored. It was strongly opposed by the Hungarians, who controlled Slavic lands by keeping the population disenfranchised. Nevertheless, nobody really knows what the new emperor would have done once he was wearing the crown.[18]

Role models greatly influence the beliefs of leaders and elites. They learn lessons from their personal experience and recent history. The obvious lessons will be one's own country if it has experienced a political upheaval or revolution in the recent past. For postwar Germans, the collapse of the Weimar Republic and the rise of Hitler were the relevant past and the Federal Republic was designed to avoid its predecessor's constitutional weaknesses. In its first few decades, the success of the Federal Republic was measured by politicians and analysts alike against that of its ill-fated predecessor.[19] Weimer, as Paul Petschmann elaborates in his chapter, provided a lesson for democracies more generally, and one whose substance evolved over time.

For many countries, the success and failure of other political systems is critical. Their experience provides lessons thought relevant to one's own country. They can be positive in character, in the sense of suggesting pathways to follow, or negative by indicating those to avoid. Work in cognitive psychology suggests that so-called lessons of history are often based on superficial comparisons between situations.[20] Such analogies can nevertheless generate strong imperatives in the minds of leaders and elites, especially when it concerns pathways to avoid. These understandings may be shared or contested within an elite.

For Britain, Prussia, and Austria-Hungary in the late eighteenth and early nineteenth centuries, France provided a very strong negative role model. Leaders in these countries were desperate to avoid the kind of revolution that had engulfed the continent's leading powers. They did not see the same imperatives arising from recent events. At different times the British and Prussians drew opposing lessons. The Prussians liberalized after their invasion in 1805–6 by France in the hope of mobilizing popular support against Napoleon. They turned to extensive repression once the French were expelled.[21] The British initially became repressive but then liberalized at home and in Ireland when Napoleon was safely exiled on St. Helena. The British elite convinced itself that they were preserving the old order in substance, not changing it.[22]

Chinese leaders have made the Soviet Union their negative model. They rightly understand Gorbachev's reforms as setting in motion a political process that led to the demise of communism in the Soviet Union and Eastern Europe and the breakup of the Soviet state. The Chinese elite have accordingly become extremely sensitive to the risks of democratic political change. They carried out the Tiananmen massacre while Gorbachev was at the height of his authority, and in retrospect, have come to regard it as the proper and necessary response to organized opposition.[23] Even today, Gorbachev is reviled for advocating what he called "humane, democratic socialism," which China understands as a threat to the political system because of its promotion of human rights and competitive multiparty elections.[24]

The origins of World War I became an important negative role model in the 1930s and had the effect of making appeasement more attractive than confrontation for many in Britain and France almost across the political spectrum.[25] World War II had both effects for Soviet and American leaders; it made them more fearful of war but also less willing to give in to intimidation.[26] Neither the choice of role models nor their associated lessons are obvious. They are social constructions, generally advanced by people in support of political projects, and for this reason frequently contested. A good example is the 1989–90 debate in Germany over intervention as part of NATO in the former Yugoslavia. Arguments for and against turned on two different readings of German identity and of Nazi Germany as a negative role model. They led to two different policy lessons – no more war and no more Auschwitz – that were mobilized to support or oppose intervention.[27]

The importance of positive and negative role models provides more evidence of the centrality of context and the subjective nature of assessment. The so-called lessons to which these events give rise are the outcome of a highly political process. They reflect that ability of politicians, the media, and intellectuals to impose readings consistent with their political ideology or objectives. Historical interpretations change, and often cycle between traditional and revisionist, making some readings more accessible or attractive to political actors.

There is considerable evidence that political actors and publics exaggerate threats to their political and social orders. Conservatives in 1950s postwar America worried that rock 'n' roll was corrupting the young and threatening the social and political order.[28] The oil shock of 1973 convinced the Trilateral Commission, a group of American, European, and Japanese officials and policy intellectuals, that thirty years of unprecedented growth was coming to an end due to stagflation: a combination of high unemployment and inflation. They feared – quite incorrectly as it turned out – that the international order was on the verge of collapse.[29] The rock 'n' roll example suggests that threats to social values from people you can no longer control – teenagers in this instance – are likely to be regarded as severe. To some degree these concerns were warranted; rock 'n' roll was the harbinger of dramatic social change, but American culture and society, although evolving rapidly, remained robust. The Trilateral Commission's fears are amusing in retrospect and attributable to faulty conceptions. The leaders and analysts involved deserve the Cassandra prize. If we take a broader sweep of history, intellectuals on the right and the left have been consistently predicting the imminent collapse of the Western order or civilization since the Renaissance.[30]

Leaders focused on averting threats to regime survival can blind themselves to other equally grave threats. They can unwittingly intensify these threats by forceful responses to the ones they perceive. British leaders in the 1760s and 1770s worried about the collapse of the East India Company and the survival of their domestic political system if they had to raise domestic taxes to pay for the maintenance of the empire in India and North America. Unwilling to tax the landed gentry, and already having placed a high tax burden on trades people and ordinary folk, they imposed consistently higher taxes instead on North American colonists. Vigorous opposition to the Sugar Act, Currency Act, Stamp Act, Townsend Acts, Tea Act, and Coercive Acts from Massachusetts to South Carolina prompted some amelioration. Colonial opposition did not deflect the British government from its policies of higher taxation and greater political control of the colonies through administrators and armed forces stationed in the colonies and paid for by local taxes. Improving living standards and political freedoms, subsequently reversed by British policies provoked widespread anger and made local elites more sympathetic to radical calls for independence.[31] In retrospect, it is apparent that British leaders exaggerated their domestic threat and greatly minimized the American one.

Even in regimes widely recognized by their ruling elites to be in decline we find that elites often downplay the precariousness of their situation. This was true of the Ottoman, Austro-Hungarian, and Russian empires in the nineteenth and early twentieth centuries. Austria-Hungary was living on borrowed time but that was not the feeling at all in the decade before World War I. Complacency was the order of the day and is captured effectively and vividly in after-the-fact in novels like Joseph Roth's *Radetzky March* and Robert Musil's *The Man Without Qualities*.[32] In 1914 in Austria-Hungary, Archduke Franz Ferdinand was about the only major figure who believed that a war with Russia was likely to destroy both empires.[33] As in Germany, most officials thought that war would strengthen their empires and the positions of their leading classes. Failure to recognize that their regimes were at the edge of chaos was equally evident among the leaderships of Soviet Union and the communist regimes of Eastern Europe.[34]

Despite ex post facto claims that World War I and the collapse of the old European order were inevitable, most political authorities and commentators at the time thought that European society was robust and that great power war was becoming less rather than more likely[35] Few political upheavals have been expected beforehand by leaders and elites, or by outside analysts. The French and American revolutions, the European revolutions of 1848, the 1908 Turkish Revolution, World War I, Franco's coup in Spain in 1936, the 1974 Portuguese coup, the collapse of communism in the Soviet Union and Eastern Europe, and more recently, the so-called Arab Spring caught political leaders and observers by surprise. The so-called failure to predict either the Soviet collapse or the Arab Spring generated a large literature. Much of it is based on the assumption – erroneous in my view – that such events could have been foreseen, even predicted.

Under- and overestimates of stability have important consequences. The latter can occasionally be made self-fulfilling, but only in orders that are reasonably robust. When not, false beliefs in robustness can make leaders or entire political elites unreasonably confident and less willing to endorse meaningful and risky initiatives. At best, it postpones the inevitable. Exaggerations of vulnerability can have equally divergent consequences. In England in the decades after the Glorious Revolution fears of disorder were greatly exaggerated. They prompted repression but made the regime more pliant in other respects and keener to build support among wider constituencies. These fears became acute again after the French Revolution and led to a new series of repressive measures. They were never serious enough to stimulate the kind of popular backlash that might have raised the prospect of revolution.[36] The British were clever and lucky. The French Revolution's failure to find wide support among the masses in Britain – most rallied in support of king and country – convinced many to support Catholic Emancipation and extension of the electoral franchise. These reforms proved central to Victorian stability and the country's evolution into a stable democracy.[37]

This is an irony in the British case. Leaders were convinced that they were preserving the existing order by introducing reforms. Instead, they set in motion a chain of events that undermined the old order and set the stage for modern, mass politics and democracy.[38] Those espousing, voting for, and implementing reforms, thought they were making concessions that would co-opt opposition groups, or would-be opponents, and by doing so preserve the existing order, not change it. Support for the status quo was unwittingly the vehicle for its transformation. In retrospect, the strategy of unconflicted change was unwarranted, but reforms succeeded in enhancing robustness, if in a way never envisaged or desired by their strongest governmental supporters.[39]

When regime failure is anticipated it is often only close to the event. The Russian Revolution of 1917 and the collapse a year later of the German, Austro-Hungarian, and Ottoman empires are cases in point. By the early twentieth century, the Ottoman and Austro-Hungarian empires were perceived to be on the decline by foreign observers, although much less so by their leaders and populations. Prior to 1914, almost everyone in Austria-Hungary assumed the Empire would last, including its opponents. The only exceptions were some right wing nationalists who feared that any sign of weakness would be exploited by internal and external enemies. These were the same people who succeeded in using Sarajevo as pretext for war against Serbia in 1914 and set in motion the chain of events that led to the Empire's demise. In November 1918, Emperor Karl renounced the throne and soon took up residence in Switzerland. In Vienna, a small monarchist faction kept talking about his imminent return but an overwhelming majority of Austrians supported the Republic. Before 1914, the nationalist right failed to see their regime's fragility. After 1918, they greatly exaggerated it.

Some foreign observers, notably in Germany, regarded Russia as a stable, rising power. These perceptions did not change until well into World War I when foreign observers began to expect and even plan for the collapse of the Ottoman and Russian Empires. Most Russians and foreigners on the eve of the 1917 revolution and the 1918 Bolshevik coup anticipated neither event. "It's staggering and so unexpected" exclaimed one exiled revolutionary upon hearing that the monarchy had been overthrown.[40] Germany's political system was transformed during the war from a quasi-constitutional monarchy to a quasi-military dictatorship. The collapse of this dictatorship, the flight of Kaiser Wilhelm, and the proclamation of a republic at the end of the War were equally unanticipated by Germans of every political persuasion.

These cases suggest a nearly universal propensity to regard the status quo as stable and to express surprise when it undergoes dramatic change. This phenomenon might have a cognitive explanation: The present is vivid because it is experienced. To the extent that people are cognitively open to change, it is of the gradual and even marginal kind. Here too, such change is easier to imagine than more dramatic and far-reaching transformations. They require the construction of different worlds, and to be credible, pathways that lead to them. This is a difficult task for most people. It is more difficult still because it requires escaping from a world that is so well-known. Laboratory experiments repeatedly find support for the prediction – derived from Tversky and Kahneman's classic work on the availability and simulation heuristics – that merely imagining multievent scenarios increases the perceived likelihood of the component events.[41]

Cognitive processes may also account in part for exaggerated fears of fragility. This phenomenon appears to be associated with two situations: new and radical regimes attempting to establish themselves, and status quo regimes confronted with revolutionary neighbors. It is reasonable for revolutionary regimes to worry about their survival. Lenin and Trotsky made direct comparisons to the French Revolution and breathed a sigh of relief when the Soviet regime was still in power on the ninth of Thermidor.[42] The Chinese communists maintained their sense of insecurity long after their regime was well-entrenched. This concern is more difficult to explain cognitively. Anxiety in the face of revolutionary regimes was acute in Europe in the aftermath of the French Revolution, and globally, following the Soviet and Chinese revolutions. Left-wing regimes in the Caribbean, Central and South America have triggered similar, exaggerated fears. The revolutions were perceived as grave threats to the social order and their spread became easy to imagine. There were also actors with strong political interests in fanning and exploiting these fears. I experienced this phenomenon first-hand during the McCarthy era in the United States.

Vigilance vs. Avoidance

In this section, I emphasize motivated reasons for assessments. My argument can be formulated as a sequence of three questions that leaders and other political actors might reasonably be expected to ask themselves about their political orders: Is our order fragile? If so, how should we respond? Do we have the freedom to respond as we should?

Answers to these questions are rarely a simple "yes" or "no." They are almost always matters of degree. Orders are perceived as more or less stable, and leaders believe that their freedom to act depends on what they attempt to do. Even then it may be uncertain. Perceptions of both relative robustness and freedom to act change over time. Assessments, moreover, are rarely uniform across a political elite. The best strategy for studying perceptions of robustness and their possible policy consequences are case studies that track changes in leader and elite estimates of robustness, their freedom of action, and goals, the ways in which they are related in their minds, and the catalysts for change.

To guide such research, I offer a set of propositions about the relationships among what I consider to be the most important considerations: perceptions of fragility-robustness, leader freedom of political action, relevant role models, and their policy lessons. I start from the assumption that acceptance of fragility is anxiety-provoking and that leaders – really, people in general – seek to reduce or avoid anxiety as it makes them uncomfortable. Extreme anxiety, it has been shown, can be incapacitating. Uncertainty is a primary cause of anxiety, but only when a problem or decision matters. For political leaders, few things matter as much as the survival of their leadership and the political system in which they govern.

The best conceptualization of anxiety and its consequences for political behavior is that of Irving Janis and Leon Mann. I rely on their theory of decision-making and also Brian Rathbun's typology of leaders.[43] I attempt to combine the two because Janis and Mann focus on situational triggers of stress and treat people as if they all respond the same way. Rathbun focuses on leaders and thus allows me to work in agency, and on dimensions I think appropriate to my questions.

Janis and Mann describe people more as emotional beings than rational decision-makers. They are beset by doubts and uncertainties, struggle with incongruous longings, antipathies, loyalties, and are generally reluctant to make irrevocable choices. Important decisions accordingly generate conflict, defined as opposing tendencies to accept or reject a course of action. This conflict and the stress it generates become acute when decision-makers recognize risk of serious loss associated with any available choice. More often than not they respond to such situations by procrastinating, rationalizing, or denying their responsibility for a decision.[44]

Janis and Mann present their "conflict model" of decision-making in terms of a series of questions that decision-makers must ask themselves when they are in the receipt of new information. Their answers determine which of five possible coping patterns they will adopt (see Figure 2.1).[45]

Leaders ask themselves: What is the risk of the current course of action? If it is assessed as low there is no stress and policymakers are likely to remain committed to their current courses of action. This pattern of coping is "unconflicted inertia."[47]

If information conveys serious risks, decision-makers must identify alternative courses of action. If good and feasible alternatives are found, they can adopt them without internal conflict. This coping strategy is "unconflicted change."[48]

If the information conveys risks considered to be serious, but upon first assessment no acceptable alternatives can be identified, decision-makers experience stress. They become committed to finding feasible alternatives but will terminate their search if none is found. This results in a pattern of "defensive avoidance," characterized by efforts to avoid fear- and anxiety-arousing warnings. There are three forms of defensive avoidance: procrastination, shifting responsibility for the decision, and bolstering. The first two are self-evident. With bolstering, decision-

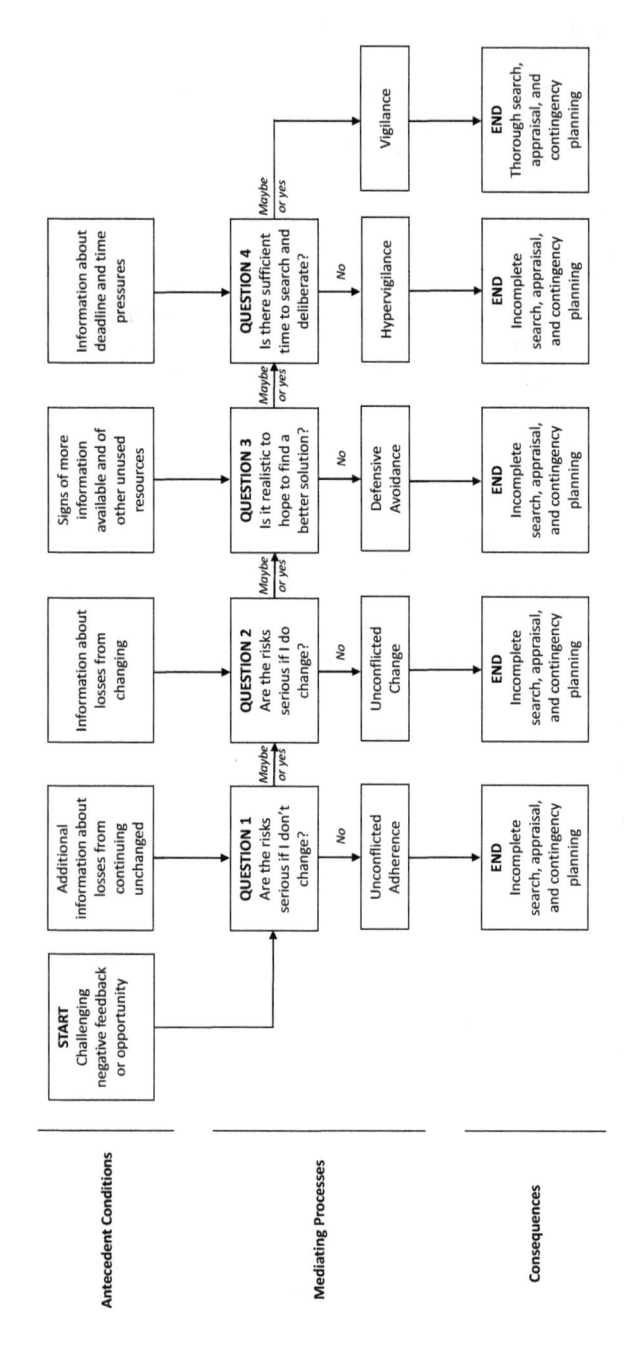

Figure 2.1 Leader Questions and Responses[46]

makers commit to the least objectionable course of action and proceed to exaggerate its benefits and downgrade its likely risks and costs. They may deny aversive feelings, emphasize the remoteness of the consequences, and minimize their responsibility for any related decisions and their consequences. Decision-makers will cope with threatening information by ignoring it, denying its import, or explaining it away.[49]

If decision-makers find an alternative that holds out the prospect of avoiding serious loss they must have sufficient time to implement it. If not, the likely response will be "hypervigilance." It is characterized by indiscriminate openness to information and suggestions of all kinds with a corresponding failure to make any effort to determine if that information is relevant, accurate, or useful. Hypervigilant people will be unduly influenced by the opinions and behavior of others. In its most extreme form it leads to panic.[50]

Unconflicted inertia, unconflicted change, defensive avoidance, and hypervigilance are different means of coping with psychological stress. The last two are unlikely to result in good policies. Good decision-making, Janis and Mann insist, requires vigilance and it is promoted by four conditions: recognition that the current policy is problematic, belief that a good alternative can be found, and that there is adequate time – and I would add, freedom – to implement it.[51]

Janis and Mann focus on external conditions and how they are understood by actors. Not everyone responds the same way to the same stimuli. We must account for personality differences, and I attempt to do so in, admittedly, a crude manner, by drawing on Brian Rathbun's distinction between realists and romantics.[52] Realists, whom he thinks are uncommon, have clearly thought-out, feasible goals. They are rational in their assessment of information and risk. Romantics are in many ways the opposite. They believe in the power of their agency. They pursue idealistic goals and are convinced that they are capable of overcoming what others might see as daunting odds by virtue of their resolve, charisma, and commitment. Romantics have goals but do not pursue them in a measured, deliberate way. Rathbun offers Winston Churchill and Ronald Reagan as examples. Many rational models distinguish between leaders who are risk-averse and risk-prone. I do not make use of this binary because it is captured, at least in part, by Rathbun's distinction between realists and romantics.

Let us return to Janis and Mann's category and factor in, where relevant, Rathbun's distinction between realist and romantic leaders. Janis and Mann intend their typology and theory to apply to singular decisions. Here I extend it to a general problem: determination of the relative fragility of a political order and how to maintain or shore it up.

Unconflicted inertia: This coping strategy can be effective if decision-makers are correct in their belief that their current policy is succeeding. If they do not perceive an existential threat there is no need for policy change, or of denial if change is politically impossible. The *ancien régime* in France was supremely confident of its stability. The French king, his advisors, and many other nobles were convinced that the existing order was sanctioned by god. Nor could they imagine an alternative, which made it that more difficult for them to take any opposition seriously.[53] In the decades before 1789, their failure to see what was coming was due to lack of imagination; they could not conceive of an organized uprising of the lower orders in contrast to a mere Jacquerie – a disorganized peasant mob motivated by local grievances. Their smugness promoted unconflicted inertia.

One of the few people to understand the need for meaningful reform was the French statesman and writer Anne Robert Jacques Turgot. He was minister of the navy and then controller of finances in the 1770s.[54] He did not have the authority to implement the far-reaching program he envisaged, beginning with a free market for grain. As this example indicates, unconflicted inertia is not always justified. It can represent a gross failure to see what might lie ahead. This is most likely to happen to political elites whose focus of attention and circle of acquaintances is narrow and restricted, as it was in *ancien régime* France. Here, the cognitive explanation is compelling.

Unconflicted change: We have many examples of reforms, prompted by the belief that they would make political orders less fragile or more robust. Far-reaching reforms, however, are rarely, if ever, unconflicted. There are almost always members of the elite who worry that change will lead to more demands and weaken the existing order, as Leonid Brezhnev and his colleagues did in the Soviet Union and China's leaders do today. Leaders implementing major reforms are likely to have qualms, anxieties, and doubts about how they will work out, and with good reason because the future is unknowable.

Those who espouse far-reaching reforms are always attempting something difficult because they envisage a major departure from the status quo. The likelihood of success is not high, which is one reason why such reform programs are only infrequently attempted. Given their low odds of success, they often require the kind of leaders who Rathbun characterizes as romantic. They believe in both the justness and necessity of their cause and convince themselves that their charisma and commitment will overcome any obstacles.[55] Examples of Romantic leaders include Anwar el-Sadat and Mikhail Gorbachev, and arguably Turgot, the Young Turks, and Mustafa Kemal Atatürk.[56] Gorbachev convinced himself that *glasnost* and *perestroika* would succeed, just as he persuaded himself that he could end the Cold War and make the West his willing partner. He succeeded in overcoming Western suspicions and hostility by committing himself and his country to multiple acts of reassurance: withdrawal from Afghanistan, arms control, allowing Eastern Europe to choose its own political systems, and finally, the unification of Germany. The latter was the final step in ending the Cold War and a powerful symbol of East-West collaboration.[57]

Gorbachev was clever and very lucky – up to a point. He exploited a series of unexpected events early in his secretary generalship – including the 1986 nuclear power plant disaster at Chernobyl and the 1987 surprise landing in Red Square of Matthias Rust's Cessna – to purge the military and civilian *nomenklatura* of hundreds of hardline officials who opposed his reforms.[58] Gorbachev deluded himself into believing that he could use reforms to generate pressure from below on recalcitrant bureaucrats and party officials. He also thought he could turn the tap of reform off when it threatened to carry the country in directions he did not wish to go.[59] Instead, he provoked a coup against him that failed but quickly led to the unraveling of the Soviet Union. One of the ironies of the Soviet system is that centralization gave the general secretary power to initiate the kind of sweeping changes that could not be made by a democratic leader. However, efforts to decentralize authority and increase political participation undermined the authority not only of the leader but of the political system.[60]

Less lucky was Anwar el-Sadat. He was equally committed to transforming his country by ending its decades-long conflict with Israel and shifting Egypt's political and economic ties from the Soviet Union to the United States. He hoped this would bring peace, American aid and investments, and create the conditions for economic growth and political stability. Sadat's reforms were cut short by his assassination.[61] In the Soviet and Egyptian cases, it seems evident that motivated bias played in important role in leader assessments. It encouraged overconfidence, which paid off in the ending the Cold War, but was an impediment to reforming either political system.

Defensive avoidance: If leaders recognize they have no freedom of action, or not enough to implement what they consider to be necessary reforms, they have strong psychological incentives to deny the need for reforms. They may convince themselves that their order is not as fragile as some suppose and certainly not on the verge of collapse. Janis and Mann describe denial as a uniformly bad response. Their logic is impeccable. Refusal to recognize that a course of action is failing and take appropriate action will guarantee failure, providing the initial assessment is accurate.

In practice, the political record of defensive avoidance is mixed. Pre-revolutionary France, Austria-Hungary, and Russia engaged in varying degrees of repression and denial. Repression is often preferred over reform because it does not require shifts in the distribution of power. Leaders convince themselves – rightly or wrongly – that they can control effectively the organs of repression. Many political systems and their leaders also find it organizationally and psychologically easier to rely on coercion than reform. This strategy is particularly attractive when combined with denial. It has the double benefit of suppressing warnings and the people voicing them. Denial and repression can buy time but arguably make regime collapse more likely in the longer term. The opening acts of the French revolution caught the king and his advisors by surprise, and their response, a mix of repression and concession, was the worst possible strategy. Concessions led to the demand for additional and more dramatic reforms and repression turned the people against the king. Alexis de Tocqueville later observed that "a grievance comes to appear intolerable once the possibility of removing it crosses men's minds.[62]

After 1789, other European states had their eyes opened to the possibility of revolution, and for many leaders, the almost equal danger of concessions. This fear was especially pronounced in Austria, where censorship was intensified and relatively harmless groups were proscribed, like the Free Masons to which Emperor Joseph II had formerly belonged.[63] Defensive avoidance can sometimes prolong the life of a political order by buying time to consolidate. It arguably did this for Prussia and Austria; these regimes survived the French Revolutionary and Napoleonic eras and the Revolutions of 1848. In Prussia, a policy of repression and concessions and victorious foreign wars – skillfully implemented by Bismarck – succeeded in building a robust political order.[64]

By contrast, Austria – Austria-Hungary after 1867 – became increasingly fragile. By the early twentieth century, the Empire was widely regarded as a declining power but its leaders did little to placate or otherwise address centrifugal nationalist forces. They attempted to repress southern Slav nationalism. They largely ignored or denied pan-German nationalism because as they felt powerless to overcome it. They also bowed to the refusal of Hungarians to accede to universal male suffrage, which all but ruled out any reforms that might have placated southern Slavs. Northern Slavs, notably the Czechs, were demanding cultural autonomy, which the government refused to grant. The German-speaking population, the dominant political force in the

Empire, was increasingly drawn to German nationalism and away from membership in the Austro-Hungarian multiethnic state. This domestic deadlock made Austrian leaders, Franz Ferdinand aside, all the more concerned with defending their honor and prestige in foreign affairs, lest any restraint signal weakness to their domestic as well as foreign opponents.[65] Austria-Hungary pursued a largely incoherent mix of repression, concession, and denial. It was ultimately responsible for the Empire's collapse.

In Russia, Pyotr Durnovo, Pyotr Stolypin, and Nicholas II did not take revolution or protests seriously. They relied on crackdowns, executions, and exile to suppress dissidents. They were not prepared to make any concessions. Theirs was not so much a thought-out strategy as it was an unqualified commitment to authoritarianism.[66]

In its final days, the German Democratic Republic switched from its strategy of extreme surveillance and repression of dissent to some degree of toleration and finally, offered concessions. Rather than placating its citizens, it inspired them to further challenges, led to a breach in the Wall, and a quick end to the German Democratic Republic.[67] The East German narrative very much resembles that of *ancien régime* France.

If leaders believe they have the authority and charisma to carry out meaningful reforms, they will be more willing to credit opinion and information indicating they are necessary. Defensive avoidance can nevertheless work in both directions when it comes to reform and fragility. Leaders can convince themselves that major reforms are feasible to the degree they regard them as necessary. It is also possible for leaders committed to reforms for other reasons to exaggerate regime fragility as a conscious tactic to sell their proposed reforms.

Hypervigilance: Leaders resort to this coping strategy when they believe there may be a better policy available to them but lack the time to find and implement it. It is only relevant in crisis situations in which there is great time pressure. In September 1989 Hungary opened its borders, allowing thousands of East Germans to flee to the West. In November, other East Germans who had found refuge in West German embassies were allowed to transit East Germany by train to West Germany. Their passage provoked huge public demonstrations in East German cities. The East German police chief prepared for a Tiananmen Square style showdown but the leadership lost its nerve. Events followed in quick succession: Hardliner Erich Honecker was replaced by more reform-inclined Egon Krenz; schools closed; services began to fail as so many people were protesting; a Politburo member made a public announcement that people would be free to leave the country; thousands gathered at the Berlin Wall; guards at the Wall, unable to contact their superiors, opened the gates. In a crucial seventy-two hours, the communist party flitted from one course of action to another and quickly lost control of the situation and of the country.[68]

Context

Context is all-important in shaping the relationship between perceptions of robustness and freedom of action. It determines the extent to which one helps to shape the other. It determines which, if any, role models are thought relevant. It helps determine the success or failure of attempts at repression or reform. One of the key features of context is timing. It is all-important with respect to role models and their lessons and can be to the success of policy initiatives.

Gorbachev's reforms and the collapse of the Soviet Union did not have to happen when they did. Had someone else been chosen as general secretary it is highly unlikely that he would have gone down the same radical pathways as Gorbachev. George Breslauer and I maintain that communism and the Soviet Union were probably doomed in the long term. However, they might have endured for decades longer and their ultimate demise might have come about in different ways and as the result of different catalysts.[69] If so, Gorbachev's reforms and the collapse of the Soviet Union would not have been a negative role model for Chinese leaders. In their absence, Chinese leaders may have been less averse to political change.

Consider too the implications of the end of the Cold War for the acute conflicts associated with divided nations and partitioned countries. South Korea and India were long committed to the weakening and isolation of North Korea and Pakistan in the hope of reunification on their own terms. Leaders in both countries rethought their goals in the aftermath of German reunification. Germany was richer and more developed and struggled, with only partial success, to make the old east resemble the west. They realized how much more problematic this challenge would be for their countries. If the Soviet Union and the Cold War had endured for some decades longer Germany would have remained divided and South Korea and India would still be seeking the destruction of their adversaries.

Timing was critical in a different way for Britain's relations with Ireland. In England, Wales, and Scotland parliamentary reforms might be said to have been ahead of the political curve. Electoral and other reforms were introduced in a timely way, alleviating more pressures from below than they invited. These reforms also made it possible to address subsequent pressures by legislative means; they helped to reconcile the rising middle class, and later, the working class, to the political system. In Ireland, the reverse was the case because Catholic Emancipation, disestablishment of the Protestant Church, and Home Rule in 1914 were all late in coming. Each was regarded in Ireland as a concession extracted only because British leaders feared the likely violent consequences of denying them. Rather than reconciling Irish Catholics to union with Britain they increased the appeal of nationalism and support for independence.[70]

If we step back from individual cases and adopt a longer historical perspective on events we can see the ways in which so-called historical lessons are connected across problems and eras. Consider the pathway created by Khrushchev's reforms. Khrushchev sought to distance himself from Stalin and reinvigorate the communist party. His reforms arguably failed as much because of the manner of their implementation as their substance.[71] Leonid Brezhnev nevertheless drew the lesson that any easing of political restraints or decentralization of the economy would set in motion a process that could unravel the communist system. Under his long leadership the Soviet Union stagnated, creating the political conditions for another round of reforms.[72]

Gorbachev was a young man in the Khrushchev era and greatly admired his predecessor's courage in attacking the cult of Stalin and beginning the process of de-Stalinization. Gorbachev and his advisors thought they had learned important lessons and that their reform program would succeed.[73] The Post-Stalin Soviet Union was something of a pendulum, swinging back and forth between reform and repression. Neither succeeded, and each arguably made what followed it more likely to fail. Brezhnev's crackdown was motivated by his belief, widely shared in the Politburo, that any loosening of cultural controls would inescapably lead to more vocal political dissent, and even rebellion. Gorbachev's policies of glasnost and perestroika had just this effect, confirming Brezhnev's fears in the eyes of conservatives. However, the Soviet Union of 1964 was not the Soviet Union of 1985. Meaningful reform and easing of cultural and intellectual restraints in 1964 might have prolonged the life of the country and its regime.[74]

Twentieth-century international relations also reveal a seesaw pattern. Lessons learned from the last conflict were applied to the next one, where they were largely inappropriate. Revisionists concluded that military buildups and alliances – what today we would call deterrence – were responsible for World War I. This lesson was one of the justifications for appeasing Hitler. In the aftermath of World War II, scholars and policymakers made the counterfactual case that early and credible efforts to deter Mussolini and Hitler could have prevented World War II.

Deterrence was re-legitimized and applied with a vengeance to the Soviet Union and China. Arguably, it intensified conflict with these countries. Deterrence, as practiced by both superpowers, was unquestionably responsible for the Cuban missile crisis, the most serious crisis of the Cold War.[75]

Conclusion

My arguments and examples foreground agency. The ways in which political actors understand the problems they face, their freedom to address them, and any role models and historical lessons they identify, are all-important in shaping perceptions of robustness and fragility and responses to them. Actor judgments are neither arbitrary nor fully rational. Leaders may lack the imagination to grasp problems or their gravity. Or, they may be motivated to deny problems or the difficulties that stand in the way of properly responding to them. I have offered examples of both types of motivated error.

Theories and models that all but exclude agency by purporting to explain and predict behavior as rational responses to environmental constraints and opportunities are of questionable value.[76] They assume that the constraints and opportunities of the environment that they identify are "objective" and accordingly understood the same way – or should be – by political actors. So-called system pressures are invariably the products of theories and more in the imagination of scholars than they are features of the world.[77] Political elites rarely share similar understandings of the constraints and opportunities they face, the policies they adopt often have little to do with the constraints and opportunities they do perceive, and may have entirely unintended consequences. Change, like order, is more often an emergent, even accidental, property than the product of design. Beyond their often-crude determinism, theories of this kind invoke multiple mechanisms (i.e., evolution, adaptation, imitation) and often fail to identify them properly or distinguish among them.[78]

Leaders make decisions in context so we must consider their local and broader settings – but *their* understandings of them. This is particularly true of leadership assessments of fragility. We need to construct or reconstruct them on the basis of empirical evidence, not inference from some theoretical formulation.

We must also approach leader and elite beliefs through the broader cultural and political zeitgeist. Seventeenth-century political leaders and intellectuals considered their culture in decline, in part a response to the religious wars, but also due to confusion and uncertainty about the nature of truth and where to find it. This pessimism undoubtedly influenced judgments of individual leaders about the relative fragility of their respective political units.[79] The late Victorian era offers a sharp contrast. Political, business, and banking leaders were upbeat and optimistic about the future. Most believed that war was increasingly unlikely.[80] Leaders were accordingly less concerned with deviance and the perceived need to maintain order.

We should be sensitive too to perceptions of external threat. When they are high, as they were in early Georgian Britain and the first decades of the existence of the People's Republic of China, so too were perceptions of regime fragility. Concern for regime survival can encourage reform, but not in these circumstances. Reforms are only likely to occur once these threats are seen to have receded. The external environment, I have argued, is also likely to influence, if not shape in some circumstances, assessments of regime robustness or fragility. However, the degree to which this occurs and what consequences it has depend almost entirely on domestic conditions, traditions, and politics and how both external and internal conditions are understood by relevant political actors.

Let me conclude by revisiting the distinction I introduced between leader assessments of the relative robustness or fragility of their political orders and those made by scholars. The principal difference, I believe, is that leader assessments are always case-specific. They are only comparative or general in nature to the extent that they rely on role models and lessons generated by the experience of other states. Scholarly assessments are most often rooted in more general theories of regime stability, democracy, or authoritarianism. As we will discover in the subsequent chapters, these theories often grow out of historical lessons. If so, the principal difference between leader and scholarly assessments may be the extent to which the former are ad hoc and often strongly felt but largely unconceptualized and the latter formally expressed and developed in some detail.

The greatest similarity between leader and scholarly assessment may be the failure of many leaders and scholars to take context into account. At best, any kind of theory of robustness or fragility, democracy, authoritarianism – or theory of anything else – is at best a starting point for explanatory narratives or forecasts that fold in agency and other features of context. They will determine whether and how more general factors featured in these theories play out. We must tack back and forth between these narratives and our theories but in the recognition that they will never be more than frames of reference for the analysis of single cases.

Notes

1 There is an interesting parallel here to a central claim I make in *Reason and Cause: Social Science in a Social World* (Cambridge: Cambridge University Press, 2020), that cause is more important in the modern age but correspondingly more difficult to establish.
2 Richard Ned Lebow, *Forbidden Fruit: Counterfactuals and International Relations* (Princeton, NJ: Princeton University Press, 2010), ch. 3.
3 David Hume, "Of the Liberty of the Press," in Knud Haakonssen, ed., *Hume, Political Essays* (Cambridge: Cambridge University Press, 1994), pp. 1–3.
4 Stephen Kotkin, *Stalin, vol. I: Paradoxes of Power, 1879–1928* (New York: Penguin, 2014), p. 291.
5 See David Shambaugh, "Contemplating China's Future," *Washington Quarterly* 39 no. 3 (2016), pp. 121–30 and *China's Future* (Cambridge: Cambridge University Press, 2016); Christopher Adolph Victor and Mingxing Liu, "Getting Ahead in the Communist Party: Explaining the Advancement of Central Committee Members in China," *American Political Science Review* 106 no. 1 (2012), pp. 166–87; Yasheng Huang, "Democratize or Die: Why China's Communists Face Reform or Revolution," *Foreign Affairs* 92 no. 1 (2013), pp. 47–54; Minxin Pei, "The Beginning of the End," *Washington Quarterly* 39 no. 3 (2016), pp. 131–42 and *China's Crony Capitalism: The Dynamics of Regime Decay* (Cambridge, MA: Harvard University Press, 2016); Richard Ned Lebow, *Rise and Fall of Political Orders*, (Cambridge: Cambridge University Press, 2018); ch. 4 and Martin Dimtrov and Richard Ned Lebow, "China," in Lebow, *Rise and Fall of Political Orders*, pp. 274–303, for a discussion of appropriate ways of thinking about fragility and their application to China.
6 Jacques Lévesque, *The Enigma of 1989: The USSR and the Liberation of Eastern Europe*, trans. K. Martin (Berkeley, CA: University of California Press, 1997), pp. 149–64; Mary Elise Sarotte, *The Collapse: The Accidental Opening of the Berlin Wall* (New York: Basic Books, 2014), chs. 6–7.
7 Legitimacy is a troubled concept and a term I avoid. Max Weber, who made it central to his analysis in *Economy and Society*, used it as a way of saying that people accept the claims of authority made by their rulers. Peter M. Blau, "Critical Remarks on Weber's Theory of Authority," *American Political Science Review* 57 no. 2 (1963), pp. 305–16; David Beetham, *The Legitimation of Power* (London: Macmillan, 1991). For a critique of more recent literature on legitimacy, see Rodney Barker, *Legitimating Identities: The Self-Presentations of Rulers and Subjects* (Cambridge: Cambridge University Press, 2001).
8 David Bohmer Lebow, "Leviathans Unbound: Irrationalist Political Thought in Interwar United States and Germany," *Journal of Political Ideologies* 24 no. 1 (2019), pp. 32–53.
9 Lebow, *Rise and Fall of Political Orders*, ch. 7.
10 Hua Yang, *Dong'ou jubian jishi* [Record of the Eastern European Collapse] (Beijing: Shijie shishi chubanshe, 1990); Ma Zhou Xincheng, "Sulian yanbian guocheng zhong de yishi xingtai yu zhishifenzi" [Ideology and Intellectuals

during the Evolution of the Soviet Union], in Li Shenming, ed., *Shijie shehui zhuyi genzong yanjiu baogao* [Follow-Up Report on World Socialism] (Beijing: Shehui kexue wenxian chubanshe, 2012), pp. 740–48; Mary Elise Sarotte, "China's Fear of Contagion: Tiananmen Square and the Power of the European Example," *International Security* 37 no. 2 (2012), pp. 156–82.
11 Mette Eilstrup-Sangiovanni, "What Kills International Organisations? When and Why International Organisations Terminate," *European Journal of International Relations* 21 no. 1 (2020), pp. 215–39.
12 Ewen MacAskill, "Donald Trump Bows out of 2012 US Presidential Election Race," *Guardian*, 16 May 2011, www.theguardian.com/world/2011/may/16/donald-trump-us-presidential-race (accessed 23 July 2019).
13 Emily Ekins, "Five Kinds of Trump Voters: Who Are They and What They Believe," Voter Study Group, June 2017, www.voterstudygroup.org/reports/2016-elections/the-five-types-trump-voters; For a roughly similar typology, Drew DeSilver, "A Closer Look at Who Identifies as Democrat and Republican," Pew Research Center, 1 June 2014, www.pewresearch.org/fact-tank/2014/07/01/a-closer-look-at-who-identifies-as-democrat-and-republican (both accessed 23 July 2019).
14 See discussion later in this chapter.
15 Robert A. Caro, *The Passage of Power, vol. IV: The Years of Lyndon Johnson* (New York: Random House, 2012), pp. 489–91.
16 Ibid., p. xv.
17 Ibid., 488–91, 498, 585.
18 Georg Franz, *Erzherzog Franz Ferdinand und die Pläne zur Reform der Habsburger Monarchie* (Vienna: G. D. W. Callwey, 1943); Samuel R. Williamson, Jr., "Influence, Power, and the Policy Process: The Case of Franz Ferdinand," *Historical Journal* 17 no. 2 (1974), pp. 417–34.
19 Karl W. Deutsch and Lewis J. Edinger, *Germany Rejoins the Powers: Mass Opinion, Interest Groups, and Elites in Contemporary German Foreign Policy* (Stanford, CA: Stanford University Press, 1959); Konrad H. Jarausch, *After Hitler: Recivilizing Germans, 1945–1995* (Oxford: Oxford University Press, 2008), pp. 147–55.
20 Robert Jervis, *Perception and Misperception in International Relations*, 2nd ed. (Princeton, NJ: Princeton University Press, 2017), ch. 4.
21 Walter M. Simon, *The Failure of the Prussian Reform Movement, 1807–1819* (Ithaca, NY: Cornell University Press, 1955); Thomas Nipperdey, *Germany from Napoleon to Bismarck, 1800–1866*, trans. Daniel Nolan (Princeton, NJ: Princeton University Press, 1996), pp. 237–80; Reinhart Koselleck, *Preussen zwischen Reform und Revolution: Allgemeines Landrecht, Verwaltung und Soziale Bewegung von 1791 bis 1848*, 3rd ed. (Stuttgart: Ernst Klett, 1981), pp. 318–32; Matthew Levinger, *Enlightened Nationalism: The Transformation of Prussian Political Culture, 1806–1848* (New York: Oxford University Press, 2000).
22 Lebow, *Rise and Fall of Political Orders*, ch. 7.
23 Guan Guihai, "The Influence of the Collapse of the Soviet Union on China's Political Choices," in Thomas P. Bernstein and Hua-yu Li, eds., *China Learns from the Soviet Union, 1949–Present* (Lanham, MD: Lexington Books, 2010),

pp. 505–15; Gilbert Rozman, "China's Concurrent Debate about the Gorbachev Era," in Bernstein and Li, eds., *China Learns from the Soviet Union*, pp. 449–76; Minglang Zhou, "The Fate of the Soviet Model of Multinational State-Building in the People's Republic of China," in Bernstein and Li, eds., *China Learns from the Soviet Union*, pp. 477–504.

24 Xincheng, "Sulian yanbian guocheng zhong"; Sarotte, "China's Fear of Contagion."

25 Richard Ned Lebow, "Generational Learning and Foreign Policy," *International Journal* 40 (Autumn 1985), pp. 556–85.

26 Ibid.

27 Alice Cooper, "When Just Causes Conflict with Acceptable Means: The German Peace Movement and Military Intervention in Bosnia," *German Politics and Society* 15 no. 3 (1997), pp. 99–118.

28 Harrison Salisbury, *The All Shook Up Generation* (New York: Harper & Row, 1958), p. 136; Simon Frith, *Sound Effects: Youth, Leisure, and the Politics of Rock and Roll* (New York: Pantheon, 1981); Glenn C. Altschuler, *All Shook Up: How Rock 'n' Roll Changed America* (New York: Oxford University Press, 2003), ch. 4.

29 Michael Crozier, Samuel Huntington, and Joji Watanuki, *Crisis of Democracy: Report on the Governability of Democracies to the Trilateral Commission* (New York: New York University Press, 1975), p. 2.

30 Arthur Herman, *The Idea of Decline in Western History* (New York: Free Press, 1997), p. 1.

31 A. G. Hopkins, *American Empire: A Global History* (Princeton, NJ: Princeton University Press, 2018), pp. 107–8, 114.

32 Joseph Roth, *The Radetzky March*, trans Joachim Neugroschel (London: Penguin, 1995); Robert Musil, *The Man Without Qualities*, trans. Sophie Wilkins (London: Picador, 1995).

33 Holger Afflerbach, "Topos of Improbable War Before 1914," in Holger Afflerbach and David Stevenson, eds., *An Improbable War: The Outbreak of World War I and European Political Culture Before 1914* (New York: Berghahn Books, 2007), pp. 161-82; Richard Ned Lebow, *Forbidden Fruit: Counterfactuals and International Relations* (Princeton, NJ: Princeton University Press, 2010), ch. 3.

34 Jacques Lésveque, *The Enigma of 1989: The USSR and the Liberation of Eastern Europe*, trans. Keith Martin (Berkeley, CA: University of California Press, 1997); Archie Brown, *The Human Factor: Gorbachev, Reagan, and Thatcher and the End of the Cold War* (Oxford: Oxford University Press, 2020), chs. 15 and 16.

35 Afflerbach, "Topos of Improbable War Before 1914;" Lebow, *Forbidden Fruit*, chs. 1 and 3.

36 Robert Tombs, *France, 1814-1914* (London: Routledge, 2014), pp. 329–53.

37 Lebow, *Rise and Fall of Political Orders*, ch. 7.

38 The French Revolution produced initial panic and the Napoleonic Wars some degree of confidence about the stability of the political order. Roy Porter, *English Society in the Eighteenth Century*, rev. ed. (London: Penguin Books, 1990), pp. 348–52; Frank O'Gorman, *The Whig Party and the French*

Revolution (London: Macmillan, 1967); Marilyn Morris, *The British Monarchy and the French Revolution* (New Haven, CT: Yale University Press, 1998); Ian R Christie, *Stress and Stability in Late Eighteenth-Century Britain* (Oxford: Oxford University Press, 1984); Mark Philip, *French Revolution and British Popular Politics* (Cambridge, MA: Cambridge University Press, 1991); Emma Vincent Macleod, "The Crisis of the French Revolution," in H. T. Dickinson, *A Companion to Eighteenth Century Britain* (Oxford: Blackwell, 2002), pp. 112–24.

39 J. C. D. Clark, *English Society 1688-1832: Ideology, Social Structure and Political Practice During the Ancien Regime* (Cambridge, MA: Cambridge University Press, 1985); Richard Price, *British Society, 1660-1880: Dynamism, Containment and Change* (Cambridge: Cambridge University Press, 1999); Hilton Boyd, *A Mad, Bad, and Dangerous People? England, 1783-1846* (Oxford: Oxford University Press, 2008), p.30; Lebow, *Rise and Fall of Political Orders*, ch. 7.

40 Kotkin, *Stalin*, p. 174.

41 Amos Tversky and Daniel Kahneman, "Extensional versus Intuitive Reason: The Conjunction Fallacy as Probability Judgment," *Psychological Review* 90 no. 2 (1983), pp. 292–315; Derek Koehler, "Explanation Imagination and Confidence in Judgment," *Psychological Bulletin* 110 no. 3 (1991), 499–519; Philip E. Tetlock and Richard Ned Lebow, "Poking Counterfactual Holes in Covering Laws: Cognitive Styles and Historical Reasoning," *American Political Science Review* 95 no. 4 (2001), pp. 829–43.

42 Jay Bergman, *The French Revolutionary Tradition in Russian and Soviet Politics, Political Thought, and Culture* (Oxford: Oxford University Press, 2019), ch. 8.

43 Irving L. Janis, and Leon Mann, *Decision Making: A Psychological Analysis of conflict, Choice, and Commitment* (New York: Free Press, 1977); Brian C. Rathbun, *Reasoning of State: Realists, Romantics and Rationality in International Relations* (Cambridge, MA: Cambridge University Press, 2019).

44 Ibid. and Mann, *Decision Making*, pp. 57–58, 74, 107–33.

45 Ibid.

46 Ibid, p. 70.

47 Ibid., pp. 55–56.

48 Ibid., pp. 56–57.

49 Ibid., pp. 57–58, 74, 107–33.

50 Ibid., pp. 59–60.

51 Ibid., pp. 62–63.

52 Rathbun, *Realists, Romantics and Rationality in International Relations*.

53 Le Roy Ladurie, *The Ancien Régime: A History of France*, 1610–1774, trans. Mark Greengrass (Oxford: Blackwell, 1991), pp. 437–69; William Doyle, *The Oxford History of the French Revolution*, 2nd ed. (Oxford: Oxford University Press, 2002), pp. 66–86; Colin Jones, *The Great Nation: France from Louis XV to Napoleon, 1715-99* (New York: Columbia University Press, 2002), pp. 364–95.

54 Douglas Dakin, *Turgot and the Ancien Régime in France* (London: Methuen, 1939).

55 Rathbun, *Realists, Romantics and Rationality in International Relations*.

56 On the Young Turks, M. Şükrü Hanioğlu, *Preparation for a Revolution: The Young Turks, 1902–1908* (Oxford: Oxford University Press, 2001).
57 Archie Brown, "Gorbachev and the End of the Cold War" in Richard K. Herrmann and Richard Ned Lebow, eds., *Ending the Cold War: Interpretations, Causation and the Study of International Relations* (New York: Palgrave-Macmillan, 2003), pp. 31–57, and *The Rise and Fall of Communism* (London: Bodley Head, 2009); Richard K. Hermann and Richard Ned Lebow, "Learning from the End of the Cold War," in Herrmann and Lebow, *Ending the Cold War*, pp. 219–38.
58 Archie Brown, *The Gorbachev Factor* (Oxford: Oxford University Press, 1997), ch. 6.
59 Interview with Mikhail Gorbachev, Moscow, May 21, 1989.
60 Brown, "Gorbachev and the End of the Cold War"; Hermann and Lebow, "Learning from the End of the Cold War"; Serhii Polkhy, *The Last Empire: The Final Days of the Soviet Union* (New York: Basic Books, 2014), pp. 29–30, 395–97.
61 Robert L. Tignor, *Anwar al-Sadat: Transforming the Middle East* (London: Oxford University Press, 2016), pp. 122–75; Thomas W. Lippmann, *Hero of the Crossing: How Anwar Sadat and the 1973 War Changed the World* (Lincoln, NE: University of Nebraska Press, 2016), chs. 2, 5.
62 Alexis de Tocqueville, *The Old Regime and the French Revolution*, trans. Stuart Gilbert (New York: Doubleday, 1955), p. 177.
63 Derek Beales, *Joseph II, vol. I: In the Shadow of Maria Theresa, 1741-1780* (Cambridge, CA: Cambridge University Press, 1987), pp. 481, 96.
64 Otto Pflanze, *Bismarck and the Development of Germany*, 3 vols. (Princeton, NJ: Princeton University Press, 1963–90).
65 Samuel R. Williamson, Jr., *Austria-Hungary and the Coming of the First World War* (London: Macmillan, 1990); Steven Beller, *Francis Joseph* (London: Longman, 1996), pp. 213-30; Richard Ned Lebow, *A Cultural Theory of International Relations* (Cambridge, MA: Cambridge University Press, 2008), ch. 7; Manfred Rauchensteiner, *Der erste Weltkrieg und das Ende der Habsburger-Monarchie* (Vienna: Böhlau Verlag, 2013); Wolfram Dornik, *Des Kaisers Falke: Wirken und Nach-Wirken von Franz Conrad von Hötzendorf* (Innsbruck: Studien Verlag, 2013); Geoffrey Wawro, *A Mad Catastrophe: The Outbreak of World War I and the Collapse of the Habsburg Empire* (New York: Basic Books, 2014).
66 Kotkin, *Stalin*, pp. 166–68.
67 Sarotte, *Collapse*.
68 Ibid.
69 George Breslauer and Richard Ned Lebow, "Leadership and the End of the Cold War: A Counterfactual Thought Experiment," in Herrmann and Lebow, *Ending the Cold War*, pp. 161–88.
70 J. C. Beckett, *The Making of Modern Ireland 1603-1923* (New York: Knopf, 1966), pp. 284–434.
71 George W. Breslauer, *Khrushchev and Brezhnev as Leaders: Building Authority in Soviet Politics* (London: Routledge, 2016 [1982]); William Taubman,

Khrushchev: The Man And His Era (New York: Simon & Schuster, 2005), esp. chs. 11 and 20.

72 Edwin Bacon and Mark Sandle, eds., *Brezhnev Reconsidered* (London: Palgrave-Macmillan, 2002), esp. chs. 2, 7, and 10; Thomas Crump, *Brezhnev and the Decline of the Soviet Union* (London: Routledge, 2016), esp. chs. 6 and 13.

73 Robert English, *Russia and the Idea of the West: Gorbachev, Intellectuals, and the End of the Cold War* (New York: Columbia University Press, 2000), chs. 1, 4; Stephen F. Cohen and Katrina Vanden Heuvel, *Voices of Glasnost: Interviews with Gorbachev's Reformers* (New York: Norton, 1989), passim; Archie Brown, *The Gorbachev Factor* (New York: Oxford University Press, 1996), chap. 2; Eduard Shevardnadze, *The Future Belongs to Freedom*, trans. Catherine A. Fitzpatrick (New York: Free Press, 1991), p. xi.

74 Lebow, "Understanding the End of the Cold War as a Non-Linear Confluence," in Herrmann and Lebow, *Ending the Cold War*, pp. 189-217.

75 Lebow, "Generational Learning and Foreign Policy."

76 Juan Linz, *The Breakdown of Democratic Regime: Crises, Breakdown, and Reequilibration. An Introduction* (Baltimore, MD: Johns Hopkins University Press, 1978), pp. 3–4, for a similar complaint.

77 On the problems of predicting the fragility of orders and their consequences, Douglas Webber, "Trends in European Political (Dis)integration. An Analysis of Postfunctionalist and other Explanations," *Journal of European Public Policy* 26 no. 8 (2019), pp. 1134–1152.

78 Richard Ned Lebow, "Evolution, Adaption, and Imitation in International Relations," in William P. Thompson, ed., *Encyclopedia of Empirical International Relations Theory* (Oxford: Oxford University Press, 2017).

79 William J. Bouswma, *The Waning of the Renaissance: 1550-1640* (New Haven: Yale University Press, 2000), pp. 246–58.

80 Afflerbach, "Topos of Improbable War Before 1914"; Lebow, *Forbidden Fruit*, ch. 3.

3   End of Democracy or Recurrent Conflict: Minimalist Democracy, Legitimacy Crisis, and Political Equality

Peter Breiner

A very significant strand of argument in political theory posits a general model of complementarity between liberal democracy and political equality.[1] Political equality, competitive party politics, and a body of liberal rights and procedures are viewed as mutually supportive. And a large body of political scientists and political theorists has viewed this process as the source of its robustness, its durability, and its appeal. However, this complementarity is under attack, especially by forces labeled alternately as populist and/or authoritarian. Many theorists wonder if liberal democracy can resist this attack and restore a harmonious relationship between liberalism and democracy.[2] This disharmony has become particularly problematic in the recent commentary that we might call "the end of democracy" argument, or what Jan-Werner Müller has facetiously called "the democracy defense industry."[3] This much discussed commentary seeks to offer ways to understand the reasons why liberal democracy (often simply referred to as "democracy") has come under attack by what these analysts see as authoritarian populism and offer ways to resist the attacks on liberal democratic political procedure. On their account, a once robust and self-sustaining model of liberal democracy has increasingly proved to be frail and vulnerable under the onslaught of antiliberal political ideologies and agents.

My argument in this chapter is very much a counter to this pessimistic commentary, though I am not arguing that liberal democracy is in fact robust where others have argued it was uniquely frail. The problem, I contend, is that this theory of democratic decline based on the fragility of liberal regimes to "populist" counterattacks takes one manifestation of a recurrent and cyclical problem of liberal democracy and treats it as a distinctly new developmental trend. It then posits this development as new and uniquely dangerous requiring restoration to a state of democratic political harmony that has never actually existed. In making this move, this commentary confronts the classic problem of political and sociological judgment of taking a cyclical recurrence as a new developmental tendency.[4] I further argue that the rather narrow and stylized account of populism used to reveal the frailty of liberal democratic regimes – especially in their minimalist Schumpeterian form – leads these theorists to offer proposals to shore up these regimes that may produce responses quite the opposite of what is intended. Specifically, these proposals reproduce the very political alienation and anti-system politics they are trying to diminish. And so the attempt to return liberal regimes to a robust state unleashes the very causes that produced their frailties. Finally, I will argue that the dichotomy of liberal democracy versus populism at the core of these arguments has a similar effect on political discourse as more recent arguments on the inevitability of the liberal democracy ceding authority to the market: They imply that there is no alternative to liberal democracy in its minimalist form. But precisely this conclusion blinds us to the weaknesses produced by the recurrent failure of this model to realize a robust form of political equality. But before I can make this argument, we must first turn to the major claims of the "end of democracy" argument and its problems.

Three Accounts of Democratic Decline

Recently we have experienced something of an ironic counterpoint to the wave of political science and political theory that embraced the consolidation of democracy in the 1990s and early twenty-first century and saw the spread of liberal democracy side-by-side with markets as a worldwide phenomenon.[5] We now see a counter-wave in which political scientists and theorists claim that "democracy" is in danger of coming to an end due to the threats of authoritarian leaders, populism, or simple complacency in the face of destructive forces beyond our control. In this section, I will argue that the proponents of this new wave of "end of democracy" commentary suffer from a series of problems stemming from their identification of "democracy" with liberal democracy, and liberal democracy with a version of the minimalist Schumpeterian model of democracy. Four problems stand out: They acknowledge but often do not engage with the historical tension between liberalism and political equality; they accept the Schumpeterian minimalist notion of democracy as the core model of liberal democracy, even when they seek to modify its most undemocratic features so as to render it more responsive to citizens or are critical of its functioning precisely because it renders citizens spectators; they oppose liberal democracy to an overly stylized notion of populism such that the latter appears as a singularly pathological form of politics when populism can take a variety of forms; and they produce a naive periodization based on a golden age of liberal democracy that was never as harmonious as they claim. By doing so they bypass a chronic and recurrent problem in the ability of liberal democracy to deliver on political equality, the very ground for judging a political order to be a democracy as such. Finally, I argue that it is precisely their polarization of a stylized notion of liberal democracy to a stylized notion of populism that prevents us from actually judging the durability and frailties of liberal democracy and the open-ended variety of consequences that flow from them.

Here I would like to focus on three of the most prominent of these commentaries, David Runciman, *How Democracy Ends*; Steven Levitsky and Daniel Ziblatt, *How Democracies Die*; and Yascha Mounk, *The People vs. Democracy*.[6] Each of these works finds that something has gone profoundly wrong in the way liberal democracy has given voice to the citizens as political equals, but they all attribute the immediate threat to liberal political institutions, whatever the internal long-run threats may be, to "populism." For each of them, "populism" represents a larger problem than simply the political alienation of citizens from political elites. But what this problem is varies from commentator to commentator.[7]

The most subtle of the three commentaries is David Runciman's. Runciman claims democracy is in a crisis, but he forcefully rejects the standard metric of political science that measures democracy on a sliding scale according to which political regimes that meet a set of functional criteria such as allowing competing parties, fair elections, and peaceful transitions of power are labeled democracies while regimes suffering the reverse of the process driven by loss of trust on the part of the citizens are labeled as "backsliding." Instead, he argues that the crisis arises from the fact that both politicians and citizens take the present-day existence of democracy for granted (if without much enthusiasm), and that as a result of this acceptance, democracy is simply suffering from a loss of energy and a wavering of attention to politics – in short, a midlife crisis.[8]

The crisis that follows from what we might call this democratic state of inertia for Runciman stems from the fact that we have grown so used to trusting political institutions to eventually correct themselves that we no longer notice they have failed to work. The senses in which, he argues, they have failed to work consist both of an internal failure of what he takes to be the standard model of "liberal democracy," and an external failure of this model to deal with several very large, long-run developments that seem to elude political control. In discussing the internal failure of democracy, Runciman immediately elides the word "democracy" with the extreme minimalist definition of democracy of Adam Przeworski: As long as there is a peaceful transfer of power from one party to another after an election, we have democracy; the liberal element is added through regular elections, representative legislative institutions, universal suffrage, free press and law courts.[9] Under this kind of democracy, Runciman argues, the people, that is the citizens at large, have become bystanders as political decisions are taken on their behalf by elected representatives who then after the fact ask for their vote during elections. The political system functions on "the public's innate passivity."[10] This passivity side-by-side with the existence of elections and decisions taken by representative institutions and driven by executives in office, according to Runciman, offers a means for the slow subversion of liberal democracy without a coup: specifically, through executive aggrandizement when office holders diminish democratic institutions piecemeal; and through strategic election manipulation by means of voter suppression or manipulating voting procedures.[11] As this silent coup takes place, the citizens do not resist because all of this is taking place under the cover of democratic procedure. The disillusionment felt by the populace simply feeds this process, more so as it gives rise to conspiracy theories that democracy is being suborned, especially if the losers outnumber the winners.[12]

This account leads Runciman to embrace the Hofstadter thesis that populism is exemplary of "the paranoid style of American politics" and declare that the recent "populist response" that democracy has been stolen by elites demonstrates that "conspiracy theory is the logic of populism."[13] This identity between paranoia and populism is exacerbated, according to Runciman, because democracy has simply run out of steam in the sense that it can no longer offer its citizens more democratic possibilities: Liberal democracy based on the minimalist model leaves no room for further democratization as it once did by expanding suffrage, incorporating labor unions, and opening the party system.[14] The citizens are disillusioned with it because – and this is the core of his argument – because the institutions are tired and have lost their dynamism.

There is an odd tension in this account between Runciman's demonstration that liberal democracy in fact allows for its own quiet subversion precisely because it is unable to respond to the citizens' demands for more democracy – in this sense we are fatalistically tied to the stasis of the minimalist model – and his claim that the reaction of citizens to this subversion in which elections are truncated and executive power increased without accountability is "paranoia." It would seem fatalism, resentment, and active indignation at unfulfilled democratic aspirations are all conflated here.

Once Runciman has established that "liberal democracy" in its minimalist form is at a standstill and citizens respond to this state of affairs by being either passive and inattentive or paranoid and angry, there are, he argues, a range of external developments to which both citizens and liberal democratic institutions will be unable control. And the reason is that the gaze of both ordinary citizens and politicians is turned inward toward the self-reinforcing circle of democratic stasis and irrational backlash. The first development, he argues is runaway technology that threatens "existential risk," such as climate change or environmental pollution, which endanger humanity's very existence. Liberal democracy, he claims, is distinctly unsuited to address such problems because to do so it would have to ask citizens to deal with risks well before their consequences were fully palpable; and even were it able to act proactively, it would require technical expertise, not citizens, to solve these problems. Citizens detached from their representatives will be even more disinclined to accept the decision-making of technical specialists to address problems that will play themselves out in the distant future.[15]

The second development Runciman references is the rise of a networked society in which essential social functions such as finance, energy provision, communication, and transportation depend on digital technology that bypasses the control of democratic politics. Large monopolies that control social networks can influence people beyond parties, elections, and government bureaucracies.[16] In turn, ordinary people can overcome the distance from representative institutions by directly communicating through networks even though this form of interaction has no appreciable influence on political decision-making. Lastly, Runciman sees a third development flowing out of the previous one, the rise of an epistocracy, an elite of individuals who simply claim they have superior political judgment based on social science, and so should be placed beyond a democratic veto through elections.[17]

Here once again we see a tension in the argument. On the one hand, Runciman is keenly aware that the failure of liberal democracy to deal with these runaway external developments directly follows from the success of the modern version of minimalist democracy in disassociating citizens from their original historical motivation for engagement in democratic politics: the struggle for inclusion and equal dignity as well as the demand for collective provision in the form of social rights.[18] On the other hand, Runciman sees this moment as having passed rather than as a recurrent conflict internal to liberal democracy. Thus, as we will see shortly, what could be a cyclical conflict within liberal democracy turns out, on Runciman's account, to be a new and irreversible phase of its development – a loss of energy in middle age while any alternative is part of its youth and long since over. Thus, everything in Runciman's argument – the slide into authoritarianism, the angry and paranoid reaction of the citizens, the loss of control over long-range developments – assumes the grim continuation of liberal democracy in its minimalist form as the only form of democracy on offer.

A more standard political science version of the "end of democracy" argument is offered by Stephen Levitsky and Daniel Ziblatt. But unlike Runciman's life-cycle account, characterized by a self-reinforcing loss of vitality and decline, Levitsky and Ziblatt look back to a static self-reinforcing ideal of liberal minimalist democracy, now under threat from populist authoritarians. Their argument rests on the standard political science view that present-day liberal democracy is in danger of "backsliding" along a continuum whose features are fixed. To Levitsky and Ziblatt, the election of Donald Trump and the rise of authoritarian leaders with populist appeals in ostensibly liberal democratic states represent a danger signal that democracy is suffering a breakdown in the functional features that sustained it in the past – here too democracy is identified with liberal democracy and liberal democracy with the minimalist model.

Similar to Runciman, Levitsky and Ziblatt argue that instead of coups, authoritarian leaders are now using a series of tactics within the procedures of liberal democratic institutions, especially mass elections, to gain power and then rule by subverting these same institutions from within. Levitsky and Ziblatt then provide a catalogue across a wide variety of cases of the ways populist authoritarian leaders have used the procedures to subvert liberal democracy. Relying on examples from a most disparate set of contexts, they argue that leaders of this type gain power by (1) attacking their opponents as subversives and the system as having been hijacked by oligarchic political elites and false media – though one should notice that even within Levitsky and Ziblatt's cases, the frustration and hostility to the governing political elites is already present to be exploited.[19] (2) Once elected to office these authoritarians slowly under the frame of legality dismantle the democratic institutions through which they were elected, packing the law enforcement agencies and the courts with loyalists. (3) They then marginalize or buy off opponents such as opposition leaders, hostile business leaders, media, and cultural figures, often giving cooperative members of the opposition benefits in the new regime and jailing those who will not go along.[20] And (4) finally, they consolidate their power by changing the rules of the political game irrevocably. In particular, they change the electoral system so as to produce a predictable majority in favor of the authoritarian ruler though appearing merely to introduce impartial measures.[21] The aim here is to produce a kind of reversal of the historical gains of universal suffrage and political inclusion by disenfranchising their opponents. A paradigm case here is Victor Orban in Hungary who used a supermajority in parliament to gerrymander electoral districts so only his party would win. However, Levitsky and Ziblatt's main concern is less Hungary than the breakdown of political institutions in the United States, as Donald Trump and the Republican Party aspire to tick all the boxes, especially the first two, even if they have not brought the process to completion.

The question they then ask is what could have allowed liberal democracy to be subverted in this way? Curiously, in giving their answer, the internal functioning of liberal democracy is not to blame. Rather, the blame lies with the collapse of two of its core components under the pressure of forces seeking to open up the political system to participation and contestation. First, there was a breakdown in the barriers, "the guardrails" and "gatekeepers" that would have prevented parvenu politicians from running for office. The main barrier in the American case were the professional operatives of the political party machines, the insiders, who decided on candidates for high office at the expense of the vast majority of ordinary voters.[22] This barrier, Levitsky and Ziblatt complain, was broken after 1968 when party insurgents demanded open primaries and inner party democracy and before that the civil rights movement demanded voting rights and an end to segregation. This, and not the failure of the party system and the representative institutions to address increasing inequality, stagnation, or citizen disempowerment, opened the way for autocratic demagogues like Trump with a weak commitment to democratic procedure to seek the presidency. No mention is made of the outside developments in economy or society or a crisis of legitimation that a parvenu authoritarian might exploit. The failure is reduced to "a story of ineffective gatekeeping."[23]

This disappearance of the "gatekeepers" and procedural barriers is not enough. Thus, Levitsky and Ziblatt offer the second and most important reason for the subversion of the competitive party system: the breakdown in liberal democracy of the norms of "forbearance" and "tolerance" among competing political parties. Mutual tolerance here means accepting one's opposition as having a legitimate claim on power and office, and "institutional forbearance" requires each party exercise restraint in using all legal (and one might add extra-legal) means at their disposal to gain power in a way that would undermine the institutions of democratic contestation and thereby the political system as such.[24]

Relying on the American model of the party system, Levitsky and Ziblatt paint a picture of a golden period pre-1990s in which the Democratic and Republican parties, both during elections and even more so in the Congress regarded one another as adversaries rather than implacable opponents. During this period, they claim, parties were heterogeneous with the Republican Party containing Northeast liberals and Midwest and Western Conservatives while the Democrats contained the New Deal coalition of liberals, organized labor, immigrants, and Afro-Americans along with racist Southern supporters of segregation – they admit the latter to be something of a problem for their ideal moment. But on balance they claim that "this internal heterogeneity defused conflict" and led each party to seek the "common ground."[25]

This harmonious state they admit was broken by the Republican Party in the 1990s when its leaders in Congress ended the practice of forbearance and sought to use every rule at their disposal to block all the Democratic legislation and appointments they could. And eventually, Levitzky and Ziblatt claim, a bit disingenuously, both parties refused to adhere to the unwritten rules of competition and compromise and came to view one another as enemies, though the two authors admit that it was the Republicans who regularly labeled their opponents as traitors.[26] As the norms of forbearance and tolerance vanish, the electoral process opens the way for a demagogue claiming to represent the disempowered people to gain executive office. The American case now becomes the paradigm for the frailties of liberal democracy, that is, for how populist authoritarianism can use liberal democracy to subvert its barriers to popular influence over politics (although it is not clear why countries not riven by race and with different structures of political opposition will necessarily follow the path of the American example).

We should note here that the ideal moment of "democracy" is identified with political competition hemmed-in by explicit barriers to entry and implicit "guardrails" to prevent clear and well-defined alternatives. The principle of political equality in the sense of equal citizens directly influencing political decisions and deciding on who should hold office seems to play no role in this account. Only hard and soft barriers to the effectual exercise of political competition and decision-making are seen as democratic. Liberal democracy, in effect requires "liberal elitism."[27] Thus, as with Runciman, there is a tension here as well. Levitsky and Ziblatt's solutions to save "liberal democracy" from authoritarians who might use elections to attack its institutions follow directly, if somewhat naively, from this fusion of democratic elections and liberal elitism. Rather than seeking alterations in liberal democracy to answer the new forms of authoritarian politics, they call for the reinstitution of guardrails in the form of barriers to participation and call upon the competing parties to recommit themselves to the norms of forbearance and tolerance. The hope is to restore the older pluralist notion of crosscutting cleavages that will attenuate political opposition[28] In effect, their proposals offer to protect democracy from the mass of citizens. The assumption underlying this solution is that their ideal of liberal democracy based on political elitism and a cartel arrangement among parties did not contribute appreciably to the very crisis they are trying to solve. But if indeed it did, their solution to the breakdown of liberal democracy becomes a significant part of the problem. Indeed, it might spawn the very populist response or at least opening for such a response that their solution is meant to prevent – the sense that the system is closed to the voice of the citizens.

Unlike Ziblatt and Levitsky and Runciman, Yascha Mounk explicitly addresses the problem that liberalism and democracy are not on the face of it complementary and may in fact have always been at odds. He further acknowledges – much like Runciman – that populism in the present appears as a political ideology and a political force precisely because it reflects a deep seated disillusionment with liberal democratic politics: "citizens have long been disillusioned with politics... party systems have long seemed frozen" and "voters have long disliked particular parties and politicians or governments." But what makes the present period different, he claims, is that "many have become fed up with liberal democracy itself."[29] The argument here seems to imply a causal nexus between citizens' disillusionment with liberal democracy and the tendency of this political form to be unresponsive to their concerns. Indeed, Mounk explicitly maintains that liberal democracy in the present spawns the very populist insurgency that challenges the claim of liberalism to be democratic in the sense of realizing something like a popular will. But then the argument moves in the direction of saving liberal democracy from the very effects it brings about, namely, "populism." Liberal democracy, for Mounk, needs to be protected against populism. And, as with other "end of democracy" writers, he defines this populism so that it invariably displays undemocratic characteristics. And yet, he also suggests that populism contains a fundamental principle that liberalism by itself fails to achieve: that democracy is coextensive with a popular will.

At the core of Mounk's approach is what I would call the complementarity argument. Democracy in the sense of the popular will of all the citizens and a government responsive to it, he argues, needs the limitations imposed by liberal institutions including impersonal institutions and individual rights. Otherwise, majorities will overrun minorities and institutional protections of individual liberties and rights will be abolished. On the other hand, liberal procedures and protection of individual liberties by themselves do not entail democracy in the sense of a popular will and a government that responds to it. While distinct, liberalism and democracy are "complementary," each reinforcing the other, but only when they are properly aligned. But for Mounk – and here he departs from the other commentators – these two principles are interdependent within liberal democracy. Popular voice depends upon constitutional restraints and protections to not impede upon minority rights and the legitimacy of these restraints and protections depend on popular voice for their legitimacy. A dysfunction in one direction of this balance can cause a dysfunction in the other.[30]

We can see this complementarity–tension already in his definition of democracy. In conceptualizing democracy, Mounk seeks to avoid attributing to liberal democracy a simple fusion of a purely minimalist Schumpterian version based on competition of parties and political elites with the liberal principles of free and fair elections, universal suffrage, civil liberties and an absence of paternalistic authority. This minimalist definition – akin to that employed by Runciman, and Levitsky and Ziblatt – fails, he argues, to acknowledge the tension between the principles of liberalism and democracy within liberal democracy itself, as well as the need to align them. Seeking to find a more robust definition that captures both the complementarity and tensions between liberalism and democracy Mounk, though without direct reference, returns to Schumpeter's stylized account of "the classical theory of democracy" defining democracy as "a set of binding electoral institutions that effectively translate popular views into public policy." [31] In effect, Mounk combines Schumpeter's model of the "classical democratic method" that seeks to transmit the popular will through elections of representatives who will seek the common good with Schumpeter's realistic "democratic method" that through "competitive struggle" was intended to overcome the impossibility of realizing the popular will and a common good of the prior model.[32]

To be sure, this definition expands political equality beyond the minimalist model by linking it to the principle of popular sovereignty, "that effectively translates popular views into public policy"; but it then diminishes the very political equality it aligns with popular sovereignty by reducing it almost exclusively to "electoral institutions" that offer equal voting presumably for parties not policies as such. Here Mounk's combination of the two opposed Schumpeterian models echoes the very tension in the two terms constituting liberal democracy that he seeks to render complementary: namely, liberal democracy here claims legitimacy based on translating the people's views in their role as citizens (not as private individuals) into public policy, but the vessel through which his definition offers to express that will consists almost exclusively of elections for politicians of competing parties offering competing programs. The popular will under this definition does not entail any standards of legitimacy based on seeking a collective good from the principle of political equality. Likewise, democracy under this definition does not demand a robust concept of political equality as an acceptance of equal dignity and equal membership or equal power to authorize decision-making. Nor does the concept of democratic citizenship require the polity to seek an equal sharing of benefits and burdens. Instead, the "people's views" are somewhat arbitrary, reflected in a majority vote limited by minority rights but only contingently connected to any principles of collective good or justice internal to the notion of a popular will.

There is a similar tension in Mounk's definition of "liberal democracy," as a political system "that both protects individual rights and translates popular views into public policy."[33] On the one hand, liberal rights may further popular voice through inclusion and influence since freedom of speech, convictions, press, and association can further political equality in the strong sense of democratic legitimation and constant participation between elections. But they can also serve to restrict that expression and influence to elections alone, thus severely limiting these political and civil rights as forms of political influence and the equal exercise of power on the part of citizens. In effect, the minimalist model so central to the political sociology of liberal democracy exercises a gravitational pull on Mounk's attempt to supersede it with a more robust version of liberal democracy as popular will combined with legal protections and individual rights. The competitive process of parties and elites for the vote of citizens is given a democratic makeover so that the popular will reflected in elections and policy complements and is furthered by liberalism.

This complementarity account of liberal democracy is not merely a potential to be realized or a regulative ideal for Mounk. On his stylized account it was more or less realized during the golden period from post-World War II to the later 1970s through a combination of liberal democracy based on stable competing parties of the right and left and a welfare state that delivered collective goods to citizens.[34] As was the case with the other two commentators, Mounk characterizes this golden age of a robust liberal regime by the willingness of losing parties to cede office after elections in the hope of future success, though he adds the claim that during this period, representatives in legislatures mirrored the lives of their constituents.[35] But according to Mounk's version of the story, this harmonious moment of complementarity has been broken in the last 25 years, and we are now entering a period democratic "deconsolidation" in which liberal states have become increasingly detached from democracy as he defines it, and democracy as popular will has increasingly become detached from liberalism.[36] And so without a popular will restrained and enabled by liberalism and a liberalism no longer responsible to a popular will, liberal democracy has split into two dysfunctional political forms.

The first, and most dangerous political form for Mounk is "populism," which he labels "illiberal democracy." On this account, populist parties, movements, and leaders reject liberalism but claim to recover democracy in the form of a genuine will of the people. They attack liberal institutions, plural associations, divided constitutions, the free press, and government, and are led by leaders with authoritarian tendencies. Ideologically these movements claim to represent simple policies to overcome inequalities. And they blame these inequalities on corrupt political elites, often acting on behalf of outside interests who have betrayed the people. In keeping with this criticism, they claim that politics in their respective states are dominated by a political cartel that has secured itself in liberal institutions. In turn, they portray themselves as the democratic alternative to this long-running oligarchy.[37] As we have seen, this is a fairly typical characterization of recent populist movements in liberal states – and the same rather diverse cast of characters are referenced, on the right Silvio Berlusconi in Italy, Marine Le Pen of the National Front in France, and on the left Podemos in Spain and Syriza in Greece, neither of which in fact is authoritarian and whose criticisms of past cartel politics in their respective countries were fairly accurate. As with the other commentators discussed earlier, Mounk characterizes populism as representing nothing less than an "existential threat" to liberal democracy – a dramatic portrayal that echoes the language of the very populists he is describing.

This said, what makes Mounk's approach somewhat different is that he views this assertion of a popular will without liberal rights as a direct response to a liberalism that has become increasingly antidemocratic, which he labels "illiberal democracy." Mounk underscores the historical fact that proponents of liberalism in its early period (the seventeenth through the nineteenth centuries) were not democratic but rather saw representative institutions as a substitute for popular rule. Only later under pressure to open up the political system does liberalism annex the rule of the people to representation by claiming representative institutions could realize popular aspirations through elections. This in effect limited popular voice to elections for competing teams of representatives but elites would control the decision-making process.[38] Given Mounk's more robust working definition of liberal democracy – as a political system "that both protects individual rights and translates popular views into public policy" – liberalism's offer to democracy was inadequate. Though implicit in his account, it would seem that the potential for liberal democracy to revert back to its antidemocratic origins has always already been available even beneath his more robust definition that liberal democracy has provided a regular means for transmitting popular views into public policies that citizens might identify as their own. This reversion back is precisely what Mounk finds to be the case for the development of liberal democracy in the last several decades.

Mounk identifies the agents and processes that have undermined his imputed harmony of democracy and liberalism both in the United States and Europe. Most are the usual suspects: bureaucratic government agencies, courts, central banks, investment banks, international organizations and international agreements, and of course corporations and special interest groups lobbying representatives, executives, and government agencies.[39] All of these agents make or influence policy decisions outside of the control of representative institutions that are formally accountable to the electorate. Worse still, increasingly policy decisions shift to the domain of technical expertise well distant from politicians and citizens.

However, the consequences as well as the causes for the loss of a popular voice of citizens in liberal democracy are more basic. For Mounk the fundamental cause for the collapse of liberal democracy into undemocratic liberalism occurs because professional politicians of all parties have formed a caste of professionals who unlike the golden age are distant from the very people they are supposed to represent. And thus, legislators do not identify with citizens but with other professional politicians as well as financial, educational, and cultural elites. In turn – and here the argument resembles Runciman's – voters are alienated, – both subjectively and objectively, from politics, professional politicians, and the decisions taken by representative institutions.[40] Thus, it is not surprising, Mounk argues, that politicians are more comfortable responding to special interests than the interest of the citizens. Mounk sums up this development of undemocratic liberalism as an "ought" that is unrealized: "Democracy should have in place a set of effective institutional mechanism for translating popular views into public policy." But countries with intensive liberal rights are "increasingly undemocratic."[41]

Echoing an argument of Runciman but quite at odds with Levitsky and Ziblatt, Mounk has captured here the very causal circle that produces the authoritarian populism that he views as such a danger to liberal democracy. That is, he acknowledges that what he calls "illiberal democracy" provokes the democratic energy of citizens to oppose this form in the name of "the people" and provides the occasion for individual leaders and parties to exploit that energy. That is, "populism" as he has stylized it, is produced by the very tendencies within liberal democracy that produce "undemocratic liberalism." But counter to Mounk's causal circle one might want also to recognize that a populism, or at least populist language opposed to undemocratic liberalism, may very well not seek the destruction of liberal rights and guarantees, but instead demand democratic institutions that enlarge citizen engagement beyond voting for representatives who form a political caste with its own norms and interests – in short, a populism that is not authoritarian. This form of populism makes no appearance in Mounk's argument though he alludes to the possibility of an "anti-system energy" that does not entail one that is antidemocratic.[42]

Toward the end of his argument in favor of liberal democracy, Mounk suggests that liberalism can avoid turning into its undemocratic variant that spawns populism by solving a series of problems that are endemic to present-day liberal states and society: economic inequality, loss of civic allegiance to a concept of the common good, and the transformation of national identity from civic loyalty into ethno-nationalism. To this end, he offers a series of imperatives that "we" must solve to ward off what he sees as a dangerous, bigoted, authoritarian populism: vastly reducing inequality of wealth and income; reconstructing civic loyalty to support a concept of a shared common good; and a shared national identity supportive of liberal rights. Were all these imperatives realized, the frailties of liberal democracy will have been overcome and the robustness it once had will have been restored. But what is left open is whether the liberal state under which these problems have gestated is the vehicle to solve these problems.

Problems of End-of-Democracy Theory

While each author has his own distinctive account of why democracy is in serious trouble, there is enough overlap in their respective arguments to point to a number of deficiencies they all share. First, their accounts of the threat to "democracy" all too easily conflate "democracy" with "liberal democracy" even when, as in the case of Mounk, they explicitly address the difference in the two principles. Typically, their pronouncements that liberal democracy is in danger from authoritarian populists and populist movements slide into statements that "democracy" as such is in danger. To be sure, the concept of liberalism is so varied that when we speak of "liberal democracy" in political theory we can be referring to a vast variety of forms ranging from a limited constitutional state that merely sets rules for society to an organic welfare state that treats all of its citizens as members of a community in which all have a stake.[43] But in the contemporary debates about liberal democracy the structure of that term tends to have a fairly consistent if mobile set of features. This version of democracy guarantees civil rights of free speech, free press, security of person, formal legal procedures and due process, and political rights of free association and equal voting, acceptance by losing parties to cede power to the party that wins elections, representative institutions, a norm not to turn opponents into implacable enemies of the political system, and tolerance of diverse interest groups.

While political theorists such as Runciman and Mounk point out that liberal democracy is a fusion of two principles often in tension with one another – a fusion of an egalitarian popular will and liberal individual rights along with impartial procedures – they also treat this version of liberal democracy as a baseline from which to measure democratic decline. The problem here is that, as Runciman and Mounk acknowledge, there is a long historical tension between liberalism and democracy. Liberal defenders of procedures and rights have not always been champions of political equality or popular sovereignty. Indeed, in the name of both meritocracy based on a copious set of conflicting criteria and more specifically market success as the metric for merit, nineteenth-century liberals argued for political inequality as the basis for representation. And the demands of citizens for political equality and popular sovereignty have often had to challenge both liberals and liberal institutions. Indeed, the demands of the working classes as well as women for the vote at the turn of the century, and more recent demands by excluded groups for equal treatment and civil and political rights have invoked the principles of equal inclusion, equal dignity, and equal power as the foundation for a socially just and legitimate political order.[44] Of course, political equality and popular sovereignty can be furthered by liberal rights. The right of association and free speech may further political associations, political mobilization, and political engagement both within and in opposition to governments. But, as is well-known, the right of voluntary contract can further economic and social inequality; and equality of political influence by citizens can be thwarted by liberal procedures and an emphasis on individual private liberty.[45]

Hence the second problem. Even when they acknowledge that liberal rights and procedures and democracy may not be in harmony, the "end of democracy" theorists treat the minimalist model of democracy – most explicitly articulated by Joseph Schumpeter – as the political-sociological core of liberal democracy. Indeed, the durability of the Schumpeterian model at the core of liberal democracy bulks large even in Mounk and Runciman, who are critical of it for being unresponsive to citizens and producing political alienation. For all three commentators it is at once the source of robustness and fragility of liberal regimes.

This model famously views the competition between parties and leaders of parties for the people's vote as the criterion for democracy: "The democratic method is that institutional arrangement for arriving at political decisions in which individuals acquire the power to decide by means of a competitive struggle for the people's vote."[46] By redefining the role of the citizens from transmitting issues to government they would seek to have acted upon to merely choosing those who will do the deciding, competition between parties and politicians becomes the defining criterion of "democracy" – Competition is meant to play the role that popular sovereignty can no longer play on this argument. The model assumes political equality and popular sovereignty to be unrealizable but retains these principles as useful fictions invoked by politicians to win over the masses and bludgeon their opponents as undemocratic.[47] Hence it is absorbed into the phraseology of political competition.

The political process itself on Schumpeter's reading aims at the selection of successful leaders with the formation of governments, policies, plural associations, and civil liberties as an unintended by-product of a kind of oligopolistic competition among parties that seek to close the political market to new entrants.[48] Indeed, Schumpeter argues, the very possibility of creating a fair, non-oligopolistic competition among parties is completely unrealistic. The notion that the competitive model of democracy based on seeking the people's vote could allow open entry to all parties and citizens, he maintains, is as unrealistic as the possibility of realizing a pure competitive market open to all entrants, or as he puts it, "it does not exclude cases that are strikingly analogous to economic phenomenon we label 'unfair or 'fraudulent' competition or restraint of competition. And we cannot exclude them because if we did, we would be left with a completely unrealistic ideal."[49] Party programs in this model are viewed as products to be offered to voters as consumption items. And this consumption needs to be stimulated through the intervention of public relations and advertising to shape the preferences of the voters for these items.[50] Schumpeter assumes "the competitive struggle for power and office" will produce a democratic consensus as a by-product of the competition itself, not as a precondition for the struggle to take place. This consensus, however, as we saw in Levitsky and Ziblatt, depends on self-restraint by which "the opposition *should* ... keep political warfare within certain rules" and the voters "*must respect*" the political division of labor between citizen and politician [my emphasis].[51] Otherwise "democracy" so defined will collapse. I will have more to say about this claim in a moment.

The problem here is that this model is one of the central causes of the very forces opposed to it. To be sure, the "end of democracy" commentators recognize that this model leaves the citizens as spectators, and often disappoints citizens because party machines serve as barriers to political influence, and political elites in representative institutions and government are necessarily distant from the populace whom they are entrusted to serve. Mounk would even like to amend it to render the democracy side of the term liberal democracy more democratic by combining Schumpeter's realist model with his stylized "classical theory of democracy."

But these commentators still treat the Schumpeterian model as the core of liberal democracy though buttressed by civil, political, and constitutional rights that they view as internal to this model – that is, not as mere functional aspects, as Schumpeter claimed when arguing that the rights of free speech, association, and majority rule are by-products of effective political competition, but as logically part of the model itself. The problem here is that while the "end of democracy" writers claim that the civil, political, and constitutional rights they associate with "democracy" are internally related to the principle of liberal democracy, these principles are in fact only contingently connected to the minimalist model once we view it as the political-sociological core of liberal democracy.

By "political sociological-core" here I mean the organization, processes, relations of power and domination, decision-making, and social influences that constitute the politics of (liberal) democracy apart from the norms, rights, and principles that are morally attached to it. That is, these latter features are additives to the simple Schumpeterian model of competitive parties seeking votes leading to elites making governing decisions and asking the people to submit to this rule between elections. The model *does not by itself* generate support for these features. Schumpeter reveals this cleft between principles and political sociology in his claim referenced earlier that this model requires "democratic self-restraint": "the opposition *should* ... keep political warfare within certain rules" and the voters "*must* respect" the political division of labor between citizen and politician [my emphasis].[52] But the force of this "must" and this "should" is not connected to any principle of legitimacy. So in effect, the model is unable to cultivate in both citizens and politicians the very principles that are meant to sustain it. It is not able to internally produce the principles of its own legitimacy. This becomes especially clear in recent defenses of the minimalist model, which I would call the "minimalist-minimalist model." According to this model, a peaceful change of government after an election is sufficient to constitute a political system as a democracy.[53] In this recent version of the Schumpterian model, civil liberties and individual rights are useful but merely instrumental to peaceful transitions of government. We will have more to say about this legitimacy problem further on.

This strategy of defending liberal rights but leaving the minimalist model intact exacerbates the tension between liberalism and democracy. To be sure, a wide basket of liberal rights may support the minimalist model of alternation of political and party elites through elections and even allow for opposition between elections. But these rights are not entailed by the minimalist model in its functioning or in its principle. The model itself is perfectly compatible with a citizenry that is politically alienated from both the election process and representative institutions but nevertheless may view them as a protection against worse alternatives. Likewise, this model is compatible with a citizenry that views it as a betrayal of democracy precisely because the political competition at best captures their preferences and aspirations only in passing, that is, as an instrument for parties and elites to attain power in government offering programs merely as an instrument to get into power. Of course, the political alienation experienced by citizens only sporadically manifests itself through active insurgent forms of political opposition.[54] Yet, it is a chronic condition of the liberal democratic model with a minimalist political-sociological core. If political alienation is a constant, then the problems raised by populism as a species of anti-system politics – sometimes absorbed by established competing parties or embraced by insurgent parties – are a recurrent feature of liberal democracy.

Thus, we arrive at the third difficulty with the "end of democracy" arguments. The "end of democracy" theorists view the threat to "democracy" through a very stylized notion of "populism." Often leaning on the Hofstadter thesis offered in the *Age of Reform*, they characterize populism as if it were an ideology at once irrational, paranoid, and authoritarian when in fact both conceptually and historically populism was part of the language of the democratic left, though often hijacked by the right or fused with images from the right.[55] This view of populism as a pathology is problematic both conceptually and historically. Conceptually, populism offers a classic democratic argument that genuine political equality means the people in the sense that all the citizens should have an effective voice on the decisions that they must obey. It does indeed assume that there is tendency for political parties to become responsive to their own organizational perpetuation and interests distinct from the demands of the citizens, that political elites are attentive to their own preservation, and that governments in the midst of implementing policy, favor the partial interests affected by the policy as well as the preservation of the will of government itself over the public interest – to use Rousseau's language. It does, as critics and commentators point out, offer a "them versus us" relationship in arguing for increased democracy, and in its attack on the influence of economic elites it does often make a distinction between a productive populace and corporate and rent-seeking elites. But the language of populism is part and parcel of the vocabulary of democratic critics and social movements opposed to the operation of the minimalist model – indeed it is internal to all political orders that claim to be democratic in the sense of uniting political equality and popular sovereignty with representative institutions and centralized governments that fail to live up to their democratic credentials. In sum, populism appeals to a fundamental principle that democratic states often fail to live up to. And it invokes principles that reform politicians *within* political parties as well as insurgents outside of established parties often use. So the claim that populism is fundamentally irrational and paranoid overlooks the logic of its appeal in a system based on minimalist democracy.

Historically, these theorists rely on the Hofstadter thesis according to which populism in the United States was a retrograde movement seeking in the face of industrialism to return to a world of the small, self-sufficient (petit-bourgeois) farmer, but under threat this movement irrationally embraced racism, xenophobia, and a paranoid view of financial elites secretly running the country.[56] Hofstadter claims that we can see the modern paranoid style of American politics as rooted in 1890s populism.[57] This characterization has been undermined by a wide variety of historical accounts that demonstrate that in fact the populists of the 1890s sought a graduated income tax, the right of unions to organize, a transference of monetary authority from the banks to the federal government, and an end to deflationary economic policy. And in their Omaha Program they argued that none of these demands could be attained unless voters rather than party bosses and political machines determined governments; governments, they claimed, could only be responsive to the citizens if the influence of corporations and large finance over the economy were ended. As an editorial in their paper *The Farmer's Alliance* put it, the goal was to "make this nation an industrial democracy" with the goal of producing a genuine democracy that up to now has been "thwarted both by the modern party system and the modern corporate economy."[58] As Charles Postel points out, the populists of the 1890s were a relentlessly modern movement.[59] Indeed, they proposed collective cooperative production and the deployment of modern production techniques as a way of attaining efficiency and profit.[60] In a curious sense, the 1890s' form of populism sought to force changes upon the competitive party model of democracy *avant la lettre* so that it would live up to its democratic credentials.

What we see then in the critics who polarize the new phase as one of liberal democracy in conflict with an authoritarian populism is an elision of a recurrent democratic criticism internal to liberal democracy with authoritarian leaders and movements making use of democratic language.[61] Once one stylizes "populism" as nascent authoritarianism, it becomes all too easy to take every statement by social movements or, for that matter mainstream political leaders, that the political system is cartelized, that it cleaves to the imperatives of finance, that it is open to corporate influence at the cost of public goods, that instead of responding to the citizens, parties and professional politicians are more interested in their own perpetuation, as an expression of irrational conspiratorial beliefs rather than a reasonable assessment of contemporary democratic politics.

Consider these two examples of claims similar to those attributed to irrational populism: Peter Mair in *Ruling the Void* has advanced an argument that political elites and parties now operate in a governing sphere separate from their constituents. When a politician loses office in an election, s/he simply moves on to another part of the governing network – s/he finds a position in a transnational organization, finance, or lobbying.[62] Likewise, Adam Tooze in his recent book *Crash* offers copious evidence that during the 2008 financial crash the US Federal Reserve behind the backs of even the parties, representative institutions, and the citizens became the conduit for replenishing European banks with dollars after the overnight money markets worldwide broke down due to a lack of dollars to back up their undercollaterized and overleveraged assets. As Tooze concludes, "Though it is hardly a secret that we inhabit a world dominated by business oligopolies, during the crisis and in its aftermath this reality and its implications for the priorities of government stood nakedly exposed. It is an unpalatable and explosive truth that democratic politics on both sides of the Atlantic has choked on."[63] Surely these well-founded claims from a most respectable political scientist and economic historian are not signs of paranoia or a submission to irrational conspiracy theories. Clearly, the use of populism by the "end of democracy" theorists is at once too broad and too narrow.

It is too narrow simply because there are multiple notions of populism of which the authoritarian version is more a deviation than a variant. As Cas Mudde and Cristobal Rovina Kaltwasser point out, populist movements within liberal democracies can be both a danger to or a corrective for representative institutions when political elites and parties in liberal democracy have lost touch with the citizens.[64] In turn, Margaret

Canovan maintains that populism fills the gap within liberal democracy between its pragmatic features of liberal day-to-day politics – bargaining, party competition, elections – and the claim that democracy must realize a political community based on popular sovereignty.[65] Hence, rather than representing a threat, it seeks to redeem the democratic claims of liberal democracy. It is thus internal to the functioning of liberal democracy, especially of the Schumpeterian variety. And famously Ernesto Laclau pushes the concept of populism further yet by claiming "populism would be just the special emphasis on a political logic, which ... is a necessary ingredient of politics tout court."[66] That is, the formation of an antagonistic front against an existing regime through a set of equivalent demands typically indicating some form of deprivation of which one demand is representative of a whole set of grievances constitutes a people. And because the people are constituted by an antagonistic frontier against an elite or regime, populism does not have a stable identity. But the antagonism of a constantly shifting relation between a people so contingently constituted and an opponent opposing the demands though occasionally absorbing some of them renders populism for Laclau part of the logic of politics rather than a special form of it.[67] There are many other concepts of populism beyond those mentioned. Viewed in this light, even if we argue as do some "end of democracy" critics, that they are merely using the word populism to refer to one distinctive authoritarian threat to contemporary liberal democratic institutions, they are collapsing a rather wide-ranging debate over the relation of populism to the logic of politics in liberal regimes into one of its many variants.

But paradoxically, their use of populism to designate either a pathology of politics or an authoritarian danger or both is also too broad, as it sweeps the vast variety of approaches to populism under a very general concept, one in which any opposition invoking the principle of the popular will against political elites – "them versus us" – invariably contains a latent authoritarianism that would manifest itself were that movement successful in entering government.[68] All other concepts of populism come to harbor this dangerous trend or are put in the category of democratic social movements willing to play by the rules of the game.

But, why the distorted characterization of "populism" as the new authoritarian antidemocratic politics of the present? This has to do with a fourth problem we might call tendentious periodization. The problem here is that the "end of democracy" critics treat a cyclical problem internal to liberal democracy with its minimalist political-sociological core as if it signaled a wholly new phase of development in the life of democracy itself. Each of the "end of democracy" arguments posit a golden time when a self-reinforcing harmony reigned between liberalism in the form of individual rights and formal procedures and democracy viewed largely as the competition among parties for the people's vote. While parties saw each other as opponents, according to the golden age argument, they did not see one another as enemies and therefore peacefully ceded power in the aftermath of elections. And both political elites and citizens of liberal democracies accepted the outcome of elections. Parties, elected representatives, and office holders in government all adhered to "the rules of the game." Focusing on the American model, Levitsky and Ziblatt argue the two parties were able to compromise on legislation, though they admit this inclination was built upon the acceptance of racial segregation in the American South. Runciman argues that once inclusion and well-being under a welfare state were won, political competition became normalized without any new impulses to make demands on liberal democracy. And Mounk claims that prior to the emergence of both populist-driven "illiberal democracy" and technocratic- and finance-driven "undemocratic liberalism," liberal rights and procedures reinforced as well as provided limits upon democracy as the expression of majority will through elections. This harmony they all argue has dissolved in the last decade or two or three, and, as we saw earlier, each offers a somewhat different diagnosis for the rise of a fusion of populism and authoritarianism.

The difficulty here is that the moment of harmony never was that harmonious. We need not go into the history of this period, one that was characterized by war, urban racial uprisings, industrial strikes, and student protests along with continuous economic growth, a stabilization of income inequality, and expansion of welfare states. If we merely confine our focus to the political theory of the golden age period, we already see theories of political crises within the very institutions that were so harmonious. Jürgen Habermas understood this period as suffering from a "legitimation crisis" in which the crisis of guaranteeing sufficient investment in the capitalist economy was now transferred to a modern interventionist social democratic welfare state, but that state lacked sufficient legitimacy to intervene in the economy to solve that problem due to its reliance on voting as acclamation rather than active consent of the citizens. And thus, for Habermas, the problems resulting from insufficient legitimation to intervene in the economy were displaced to the culture whose norms could not bear the weight of resolving an unresolved crisis of political legitimacy. The upshot was both cultural dislocation and political alienation.[69]

We have the arguments of Fred Block and Charles Lindblom to the effect that no matter which party was in power, the state managers had to induce capital to invest; and so businessmen became so to speak "unelected decision-makers" over public well-being, making decisions on investment, environment, and ordinary people's life chances without political accountability.[70] Thus, in Lindblom's language, we could see "The Market as Prison" in the sense of imposing shackles on democratic will over both decision-making in realizing public goods and in directing investment in the economy.[71]

We also have the conservative, Jacques Ellul, who in *The Political Illusion*, argues that under modern democratic states, what we view as day-to-day politics is "ephemeral" even though it preoccupies us, while "the necessary" – the decisions that deal with actual problems – are made behind the scenes or, more significantly, have already been made.[72]

And of course, we have the whole debate during this golden period over political elitism versus pluralism in which Robert Dahl famously occupied the latter position claiming the Schumpeterian model could be rendered sufficiently democratic as long as interest groups could influence decision-making between elections.[73] But he came over to the former position once he concluded that democratic systems based on plural groups and competing political parties could not live up to the simplest rudiments of political equality, especially with regard to each citizen having the equal opportunity to put questions on the agenda, to influence binding decisions, and to live in a polity that guaranteed full maximal inclusion of inhabitants enjoying these political rights.[74] Corporations, he maintained, were not just one of many plural groups, but were able to cumulate political resources, enabling them to exercise inordinate influence over both agenda-setting and binding political decisions.[75]

More recently, Colin Crouch in *Post-Democracy* updating Dahl's argument in the backdrop of neoliberalism has argued that we are living with the forms of (liberal) democracy – elections, free association and speech, the right to influence government; but public goods have been contracted out to private providers, corporations exercise inordinate influence on public decision-making, media have filled the vacuum of public discussion, parties have lost touch with their original constituents, and citizens have become spectators to the political process.[76] If these works of political science and political theory are a guide, the harmonious period preceding the breakdown as laid out by the "end of democracy" theorists is something of a political science construct that obscures the fact that liberal democracy in its minimalist form has been in a recurrent and perpetual crisis but one that has metamorphosed over time.

What I would suggest here is that what the "end of democracy" theorists view as the golden period of political compromise and of the victory of equal political rights and inclusion only to collapse – or reach an entropic endpoint in the case of Runciman – through the counter-thrust of anti-system populism against liberal democracy is part of a political cycle *internal* to the minimalist model of competitive party politics. But if this is so, what the "end of democracy" theorists claim to be a new phase is simply the result of the cyclical countermovement by the proponents of inequality against the expansive phase of democratic political equality. Some proponents of this countermovement have indeed dangerous authoritarian tendencies, some explicitly call for replacing constitutional restraints with personal rule to overcome dysfunctional legislative institutions, some defend nationality and boundaries at the cost of the relationship between political equality and equal inclusion, and some directly attack the closure of the democratic politics by a cartelized political caste or a technocratic elite, claiming all government can be run by amateurs.

On the other hand, at times, we see movements that under various demands seek to expand political equality against the limited participation of minimalist democracy. So we see demands of social movements to rein in police powers, bring finance under democratic control, make voting rights more effectual, or, more recently, provide or reinstate public services by extracting their provision from the market, or seek a citizen voice on matters handed over to technocrats.[77] These two sets of responses are at odds. But they each in their own way are able to use the deficiencies of the minimalist model of liberal democracy – especially its inability to offer a robust version of political equality and popular sovereignty – against that model itself. In short, the struggle over political equality for inclusion and equal dignity along with equality of political power and social provision as an entitlement of equal citizenship is not finished (as "end of democracy" theorists like Runciman explicitly maintain) but rather exists as a perpetual part of liberal democratic politics built into the minimalist model itself.[78] At this point I want to turn toward the other working assumption of the "end of democracy" theorists, that the form of "democracy" that is in need of renewal is liberal democracy with a minimalist political-sociological core.

The Political Logic of the Schumpeterian Model and Its Problems

Once we view the minimalist model as the political-sociological core of liberal democracy and understand that even liberal rights such as free speech, association, and individual security as well as the norms of forbearance and tolerance are contingently related to it, there is an internal logic in this model that creates a recurrent crisis of movement and countermovement such that we are always already in a crisis moment, even during periods of apparent of harmony.[79] This internal logic takes a threefold form.

First, its internal functioning leads to what I will call a horizontal crisis of liberal democracy. As we saw earlier, Schumpeter claims that political competition "presents similar difficulties as the concept of competition in the economic sphere, with which it may be usefully compared."[80] By applying this notion of economic competition to the democratic procedure, Schumpeter concluded that electoral parties would eventually become more like firms, attempting to "sell" their platforms by any means possible. And political competition would tend toward political oligopolies, monopolies, and political cartels much as do the large firms in the economy. Like large corporate firms, political parties under this model seek to close entry to the political market for themselves while subjecting smaller competitors to fierce competition and demise through predatory selection.

The dilemma this poses for the minimalist model is that with the development of political oligopolies and cartels side-by-side with economic ones, parties and leaders would be in a position to disassociate themselves from the very electoral followings whose preferences they were seeking to influence. Thus, when a party and its leaders lost the majority, instead of redoubling their efforts to win over the majority to their party program/product to use Schumpeter's analogy, they would have an incentive merely to accept the political cartel arrangement and find some office within it.[81] They could share power in the minority or move on to some large aggregation within either the business of politics or the economy. As Mark Blyth has pointed out, this has been precisely the calculation of social democratic parties from the 1980s on. As these parties can no longer deliver on continuous growth leading to expanding social rights and public goods along with inclusion of new members to enjoy the benefits of society, they choose to enter into an arrangement in which they agree to share power with their opponents to retain the votes that otherwise would threaten to render them a constant minority were they to stay outside the cartel. So as a survival strategy, they forego opposition to their right-of-center opponents over public provision and instead declare that markets and the global economy are dictating policy rather than party-driven political calculations.[82] They thus reduce their claims as to what they can accomplish. And so the very competitive dynamic of Schumpeterian party competition leads to its foreclosure, especially for parties of the left that originally pressed on the agenda an expansive notion of social citizenship through public provision: "Rather than maximizing votes as competitors, social democratic politicians may have discovered that governing less may be less risky than promising more."[83] This decision to no longer challenge cumulative inequalities of income leading to inequalities of wealth – what Piketty has labeled a return to patrimonial capitalism – or to engage in the struggle for inclusion of those left behind creates a political vacuum.

This situation leads to what I call the vertical crises of the minimalist model. This crisis occurs due to the closure of competitive party systems to outsiders and the separation of party elites from party members and followers. This condition leads to political alienation among citizens, both as an objective separation of citizens from the means of power and authority and as a subjective sense of estrangement from political institutions and politicians – more so that the established parties of the center-left have now become defenders of the political cartel against the possibilities of addressing chronic problems of inequality and inclusion. This situation is exacerbated by the fact that political elites increasingly occupy a kind of system of governing positions in which they can move from political office to transnational organizations, to high-ranking positions in finance to lobbying.[84] Not surprisingly this induces a sense among citizens that the system is rigged against them.

The result is that the cartelization of politics based on parties sharing offices and government then may lead to its very opposite. Once large portions of the citizens sense they are left out of both parties and government, the occasion is there for parties and leaders and movements to come along and claim they alone can render the system responsive by attacking both existing parties and institutions. It is particularly propitious for an insurgent political party or social movement as it can attack its establishment opponents for upholding a closed cartel of elites against the productive masses in a system in which the decision-making is closed to "the people" who have now become outsiders. There is nothing distinctly authoritarian in such an attack.[85] However, as said earlier, it can be used by authoritarians of the right, be they an established or an insurgent political party who fill the political space left by the model of liberal democratic compromise by claiming to represent the "real people" against outsiders such as migrants, immigrants, or simply indigenous ethnic groups threatening to "replace" the "genuine people" of the nation.

By the same token, this space can be filled by a left party or social movement that claims to restore political rights, membership, and power to the citizens against the elites of the cartel who monopolize the competition. In this case, cartelization can open up a space for renewal. In sum, because cartelization creates a political vacuum; these movements can claim rightly that the system has betrayed its claim to be responsive to the popular will and ceded its authority to business and financial elites as well as a governing caste.

Together, both of these tendencies lead to a legitimation crisis. Liberal democracy with its Schumpeterian core and the logic of its functioning, promises full political equality to the degree it claims to be "democratic" at all. But it fails to deliver on this principle. It defines the "democratic" features of the model by displacing equality with regard to popular sovereignty to equality with regard to voting for competing politicians and parties – though contingent liberal rights may allow for the right to voice opinions and organize political associations to try to influence decisions between elections. But as we saw, the logic of the Schumpeterian model even undermines this displacement of the full exercise of political equality to political competition through the separation of professional politicians from the electorate and the cartelization of politics leading to the decline of political opposition itself. It thus undermines two of the other central components of political equality, equal inclusion and equal political power while claiming both have already been achieved via universal suffrage. Universal suffrage claims to include equal membership and dignity and political power when in fact it is merely a precondition for realizing these other aspects of political equality. The struggle for these additional features of political equality – in particular full inclusion and the equal exercise of political power – is part of democratic politics quite apart from party competition for the popular vote.

To be sure, as argued earlier, the principles of liberal democracy such as universal suffrage, civil rights of free speech and association may further this struggle. But the logic governing the competitive process within the minimalist model along with its tendency to further the careers of elite professional politicians may thwart it. And so, given the internal logic of the minimalist model, what might have started as a period of political opposition in which parties claimed to capture the demands of society becomes a period of political cartelization, which in turn opens to a period of intense polarization and political alienation, all part of the same logic built into the minimalist model.

Viewed this way, liberal democracy with its Schumpeterian core does not merely suffer occasional crises but a chronic problem of political legitimation. And so what seems to be the very source of robust continuity – the absorption of demands from society into the demands of parties seeking office and then realizing those demands as part of the exercise of power over their opponents in representative institutions – turns into a recurrent source of frailty in liberal democratic institutions. What I mean here is that if we treat political legitimation following Max Weber simply as a *belief* in the validity of a state's claim to govern or exercise political rule by those subject to that state, then its legitimacy can wax and wane according to the subjective understanding of the citizens. But if we understand political legitimation as a justification in which the moral *principles of political order*, in this case a liberal democratic order, coincide with or are embedded in the actual *functioning* of that order, and that order nevertheless systematically thwarts those principles, we can then speak of political legitimation crises as chronic in an objective sense. In this case, liberal democracy is justified by its claim to harmonize its democratic claims and its liberal claims, but the political-sociological institution that is expected to produce this harmony – the political competition of modern parties and professional politicians to organize the preferences of the voters and form governments – in fact thwarts the realization of the democratic side of the equation: the principle of political equality.

By political equality I mean here the realization of a political society that realizes political equality with broad effectual civil and political rights, inclusion of all permanent inhabitants as equal members with equal standing and dignity, and giving citizens equal power and influence over the government of the state: in short, equality with regard to popular sovereignty. It follows then that the failure to realize the *moral* principle of political equality in these several distinctive features can *causally* lead to a systematic crises of political legitimation because it is both morally and empirically undermined by the very political system – here the minimalist model of competition among parties for the people's vote – that invokes political equality as its defining feature.[86] The political alienation of citizens is the consequence whether it becomes the driving motivation for active political voice or protest when political actors and parties mobilize citizens to reclaim what has been lost or issues in mere submission or detachment due to cynicism or fatalism. The fissure between the claim to legitimacy of the minimalist model and its displacement of this claim to party and parliamentary competition for leadership always threatens to open up a political space for parties and movements from outside to claim the political system has betrayed its democratic promise to the citizens.

But, surprisingly, this legitimacy problem is already prefigured in Schumpeter's own account of the conditions for sustaining his minimalist "democratic method." Specifically, at the beginning of his account of the democratic method, he claims that "classical democratic method" he is rejecting presupposes that "'the people' hold a definite opinion and rational opinion about every individual question and that they give effect to this opinion – in a democracy – by choosing 'representatives' who see to it that that opinion is carried out." And so the representatives are given second place in favor of giving the power to decide political issues to the "electorate" – we will ignore whether this characterization actually coincides with any major theory of democracy based on popular sovereignty. Clearly, popular sovereignty means more than merely electing representatives who act as virtual agents of the people. But then, Schumpeter in the name of "realism" proposes to reverse even this priority and "make the deciding of issues by the electorate secondary to the men who are to do the deciding."[87] The role of the people now is to produce a government that will from that point on make the decisions. It is this reversal that becomes the foundation for his famous displacement of popular sovereignty to the process of political competition "for the people's vote." What is often overlooked is that by treating the citizens as merely an instrument to produce governments, he has cut off any standard to judge the legitimacy and feasibility of the decisions that the new democratic method leads to. This problem becomes chronic to the whole account of the competitive party model despite Schumpeter's various justifications based on its feasibility.

Why might this be so? In listing the requisites for the functioning of his minimalist model of democracy, Schumpeter maintains, as discussed earlier, that certain norms must be adhered to regarding the rules of the game: "The voters outside of parliament *must* respect the division of labor between themselves and the politicians they elect. They *must not* withdraw confidence too easily between elections and they must understand that, once they have elected an individual, politics is *his business and not theirs*. This means that they must refrain from instructing him about what he is to do [my emphasis]." Likewise, "the opposition *should* ... keep political warfare within certain rules" and the voters "*must respect*" the political division of labor between citizen and politician.[88] And effective competition for leadership requires. "tolerance for difference of opinion." These are the conditions our three commentators of the end-of-democracy see endangered by "populism."

But they ignore Schumpeter's admission that the model itself cannot generate the very norms that are supposed to sustain it: "even the minimum of democratic self-control requires a national character and national habits of a certain type which not have everywhere had the opportunity to evolve and *which the democratic method itself cannot be relied on to produce* [my emphasis]."[89] But if the democratic method so central to liberal democracy relies on customs and habits that it in fact cannot cultivate, why should we assume it to be "more realistic" as well as desirable? Are we asking for a commitment to democratic principles that the model fails to realize – or possibly thwarts? It would seem that

Schumpeter's model – and liberal democracy built on it – requires a principle of legitimacy drawn from the very principles that the model requires we abandon. Or to put the problem differently, the shift to treating the electorate as merely a *means* to elect the elites and leaders of parties who will make the decisions leaves the citizens with no reason to adhere to the norms of restraint any more than it leaves the politicians with any reason to display tolerance toward their opponents rather than treat them as enemies. Unlike most political theories of republics and democracies, the minimalist model cannot cultivate in its citizens the very norms and principles that support it. It is thus not surprising that both the vertical and horizontal problems in the model should issue in a chronic and recurrent crisis of political legitimacy.

Recurrent Logic and Unpredictable Outcomes

If this argument is right, what the "end of democracy" commentators view as new and dangerous phase in the fate of liberal democracy, is in fact built into an internal logic unleashed by the minimalist model itself – a logic that is recurrent though manifests itself in a variety of unpredictable ways. Both right authoritarian movements and left democratic populism may fill this vacuum claiming that the political system has betrayed its democratic credentials, in particular its claim to realize political equality with regard to governance. Indeed, at the very end of 2019 and the beginning of 2020, pre-pandemic, we saw a wave of protest movements in the form of "civil resistance" throughout the world demanding more democracy in Hong Kong and Algeria, the end of the privatization of education and transportation in Brazil and Chile, or the combination of the Yellow Vest protest against a rise in gas prices first as a merely dislocated response but subsequently in alliance with labor unions attempting to maintain a long-established differentiated pension system in France – all of these protest movements directed against established parties and the state.[90] While these protests were aimed against an out-of-touch political establishment often in direct conflict with the state and many did not succeed, none of them could be classified simply as authoritarian populism, though perhaps populist in a nonauthoritarian sense. In the midst of the pandemic, we have seen social movements for racial justice that are not sectional but demand a society that is no longer racist as part of its definition. These social movements and new parties may fill this political space if social democracy or reform liberalism in the US case leaves it unfilled. Or alternatively, as we have seen recently with the Corona virus pandemic, the latent fragility in both liberal and social democratic political systems and their various regimes of social provision may lead either to a breakdown of the political system's capacity to control the disease and its economic effects or to collective action demanding comprehensive provision of public services such as universal health care or income supports. More recently we have seen both responses.

All of this I argue follows not from some recent abandonment of the norms of liberal democracy, inadequate barriers or guardrails to keep authoritarians out of established political parties, the failure to translate the popular will through voting for representatives into policy, complacency in seeing to democracy's survival in the face of existential threats, or patching up the severe political and economic inequalities of liberal democracy, but rather from a chronic failure of the minimalist model to deliver on its claim to political legitimacy: specifically, political equality in its full sense of equality of civil and political rights, equality of inclusion and membership, and equality of influence and power – in short, equality with respect to popular sovereignty. Thus, this legitimacy failure provides a space for political actors across the political spectrum be they right-wing authoritarian movements, left populist movements and parties, insurgent members of established political parties, new democratic social protest movements, or even social democratic parties willing to give up their participation in political cartel arrangements to make a claim to fulfill the unfilled promise of political legitimacy based on equality with regard to popular sovereignty – precisely the promise of legitimacy that liberal democracy in its minimalist variant cannot fulfill.

Conclusion

Why the Liberal Democracy–Populism Dichotomy?

The question is why does "end of democracy" commentary not capture either the recurrent legitimacy problem of liberal democratic regimes with a Schumpeterian core or the many political outcomes that may ensue in response to it? Jacques Rancière has suggested a powerful answer. He argues that the stylized version of populism employed by liberal commentators creates a logically indefensible entwinement between the democratic principles of popular sovereignty, a criticism of careerist politicians, and a militant xenophobia as if the former two principles entailed the third. The effect of tying popular sovereignty to xenophobia and authoritarian leaders who promote it, he argues, is to discredit these democratic principles of popular politics, even though they are firmly embedded in constitutions of all kinds and used by political critics across the political spectrum – a kind of moral guilt by association. The upshot then of this stylized dichotomy, liberal democracy versus "populism," for political discourse is to generate a new version of TINA, "there is no alternative," in this case, there is no alternative to liberal democracy in its Schumpeterian form.[91]

But as we have just argued, there are multiple alternatives under the principle of political equality and in opposition to political elites including multiple "populisms" that the "end of democracy" argument fails to capture. The problem thus is not merely that we are faced with a normative argument for a deficient liberal democracy under the guise of a feasibility argument – TINA. It is also that the liberal democracy–populism dichotomy blocks our understanding of the many unpredicted and unpredictable political developments that the vertical, horizontal, and legitimacy crises of liberal democratic regimes occasion. That is, it desensitizes us as to the unpredictable ways the vertical and horizontal crises of liberal democracy leading to a chronic legitimation crisis of political equality will play out. Discerning the various outcomes of these crises is a matter of political judgment in the face of chance and contingency with certainty coming only after the fact.

But what one can say with some certainty is that if we view these crises through the dichotomy of liberal democratic regimes against a vaguely defined "populism," we will most certainly misunderstand both the variety of frailties of liberal democracy produced by its minimalist political model and, equally important, the paradoxical ways these frailties may contribute to its robustness: among them, the possibility that the recurrent struggle within society to force the Schumpeterian model to realize the very political equality on which it fails to deliver may serve unintentionally as a source of political renewal, overcoming the political alienation endemic to this model; but also the counter-possibility that the competitive process of parties and politicians may absorb merely as an instrumental aspect of its functioning demands from society, while continuing to reproduce the very political alienation that spawned those demands. And this says nothing of the variety of political outcomes produced by its failures from protest movements to the differential structural breakdown of liberal democratic states produced by diseases and global economic dislocation. Indeed, whether we focus on the various authoritarian parties and leaders of late or the recent recovery of parties and movements demanding a more equal and responsive form of democracy than liberal Schumpeterian democracy can offer, the conceptual framework of the liberal democracy–populism dichotomy employed by the "end of democracy" theories as a guide to save democracy from its apparent frailties promises to produce outcomes quite at odds with its intentions. After all, the cyclical long-run legitimation crisis of liberal democracy that I have argued is built into its political-sociological Schumpeterian core may play out in multiple ways that the dichotomy of liberal democracy versus populism fails to capture.

Notes

1 For a thick version of this complementarity see John Rawls, *A Theory of Justice* (Cambridge, MA: Belknap Press of Harvard University Press, 1971), Sec. 34, 221–27. Here Rawls not only demands citizens be given an equal vote based on majority rule but effective political equality including the equality of opportunity in agenda-setting, roughly equal political resources, genuine free speech and assembly, and an equal opportunity to inform themselves about alternatives. But then he sides with a more minimal model in which only those so inclined should participate in seeking political office (228). Also see Charles R. Beitz, *Political Equality: An Essay in Democratic Theory* (Princeton, NJ: Princeton University Press, 1989), 17–23. Similar to Rawls, he defines political equality as setting the fair terms of political competition based on the degree of participation each citizen would find to be fair. For a famously thin version of complementarity based simply on majority voting and each vote counting equally see Anthony Downs, *An Economic Theory of Democracy* (New York: Harper, 1957), 23–24.
2 The central works of this strand of commentary are Steven Levitsky and Daniel Ziblatt, *How Democracies Die* (New York: Crown, 2018); David Runciman, *How Democracy Ends* (New York, NY: Basic Books, 2018); Yascha Mounk, *The People vs. Democracy: Why Our Freedom Is in Danger and How to Save It* (Cambridge, MA: Harvard University Press, 2018).
3 Jan-Werner Müller, "Is This Really How It Ends? Democracy's Midlife Crisis," May 6, 2019, www.thenation.com/article/how-democracies-dies-how-democracy-ends-book-review/.
4 For the errors of judgment deriving from mistaking recurrent cycles for evolutionary trends see W. G. Runciman, "Has British Capitalism Changed Since the First World War?," *The British Journal of Sociology* 44, no. 1 (1993): 66, https://doi.org/10.2307/591681.
5 Larry Diamond, "Universal Democracy?," July 2003, 1–25; Francis Fukuyama, *The End of History and the Last Man*, Reissue edition (New York: Free Press, 2006).
6 Runciman, *How Democracy Ends*; Levitsky and Ziblatt, *How Democracies Die*; Mounk, *The People vs. Democracy*.
7 Beyond these three authors there is a vast variety of commentators who have contributed to this "end of democracy" genre who might be worthy of discussion, but the three discussed here have spawned much discussion and are capacious enough to serve as a model for various claims of this genre of commentary. Among other authors of this genre of significance see Larry Diamond, *Ill Winds* (New York: Penguin Books, 2019); Jan-Werner Müller, *What Is Populism?* (Philadelphia, PA: University of Pennsylvania Press, 2016); William A. Galston, *Anti-Pluralism: The Populist Threat to Liberal Democracy*, 2nd ed. (New Haven; London: Yale University Press, 2020).
8 Runciman, *How Democracy Ends*, 5.
9 Runciman, 4, 14. These additions bring the Przeworski model closer to Schumpeter's minimalist model, but not a great deal beyond it except that the latter views these features such as universal suffrage, competitive

elections, and representative legislatures as functional to the efficient operation of "the democratic method."
10 Runciman, 47.
11 Runciman, 45–46.
12 Runciman, 59–61.
13 Runciman, 65, 67–68.
14 Runciman, 71–72. Runciman does admit that the struggle for civil and political rights is not over, but then insists that the space for larger battles for inclusion and democratic rights is now constrained and is no longer a collective experience. One could argue, however, the reverse: that this condition opens up the space for countermovements parties and social movements, but only if the populace has a sense of indignation at what has been lost rather than a sense of fatalism that nothing can be done. Runciman assumes only the latter response as likely.
15 Runciman, 103–12.
16 Runciman, 114–26, 131–36.
17 Runciman, 182–83.
18 Runciman, 214–15.
19 Levitsky and Ziblatt, *How Democracies Die*, 75–76.
20 Levitsky and Ziblatt, 81–87.
21 Levitsky and Ziblatt, 87–88.
22 Levitsky and Ziblatt, 41–43.
23 Levitsky and Ziblatt, 67.
24 Levitsky and Ziblatt, 102,106, 109.
25 Levitsky and Ziblatt, 168.
26 Levitsky and Ziblatt, 168.
27 See Müller, "Is This Really How It Ends? Democracy's Midlife Crisis."
28 Levitsky and Ziblatt, *How Democracies Die*, 217–20.
29 Mounk, *The People vs. Democracy*, 2.
30 Mounk, 6.
31 Mounk, 26–27.
32 Joseph Schumpeter, *Capitalism, Socialism, and Democracy*, 3d ed (New York: Harper, 1950), 250–51, 269–71.
33 Mounk, *The People vs. Democracy*, 27.
34 Mounk, 2, 32, 220–21, 236.
35 Mounk, 18, 32, 59.
36 Mounk, 124.
37 Mounk, 32–39, 46–51.
38 Mounk, 55, 57.
39 Mounk, 61–91.
40 Mounk, 59–60.
41 Mounk, 95.
42 Mounk, 123. For a more nuanced understanding of populism as an "antisystem politics" and a response to the cartelization of politics see Jonathan Hopkin, "When Polanyi Met Farage: Market Fundamentalism, Economic Nationalism, and Britain's Exit from the European Union," *British Journal of Politics & International Relations* 19, no. 3 (August 2017): 465–78, https://doi

.org/10.1177/1369148117710894. Jonathan Hopkin, *Anti-System Politics: The Crisis of Market Liberalism in Rich Democracies* (Oxford: Oxford University Press, 2020).
43 See Michael Freeden, "European Liberalisms: An Essay in Comparative Political Thought," *European Journal of Political Theory* 7, no. 1 (January 1, 2008): 9–30.
44 David Miller, "Democracy and Social Justice," *British Journal of Political Science* 8, no. 01 (1978): 1–19.
45 See Danielle Allen, "Equality and American Democracy," *Foreign Affairs*, December 14, 2015, www.foreignaffairs.com/articles/2015-12-14/equality-and-american-democracy.
46 Schumpeter, *Capitalism, Socialism, and Democracy*, 269.
47 Schumpeter, 268, 264–65.
48 Schumpeter, 282, 286–89.
49 Schumpeter, 271.
50 Schumpeter, 203, 263.
51 Schumpeter, 294–95. We will have more to say about this "should" and this "must." That parties should not engage in warfare with their opponents and voters must respect the elected politician's unrestricted room for decision-making is not based on any principle of political legitimacy. It is merely a functional need for the sustenance of the competitive party model. And yet, to the degree that we can call this model a "democracy" it requires a conception of legitimacy drawn from the very principles Schumpeter has claimed to be unrealistic. In effect, as I will argue below, these principles become part of the realist calculus precisely because the Schumpeterian minimalist model has to appeal to citizens to accept that the politicians emerging from the competition will act on their behalf. But what if the citizens do not? Is there anything in the Schumpeterian model that claims they "should"? Without a principle of political legitimacy, the "should" becomes a mere preference.
52 Schumpeter, 294–95.
53 Adam Przeworski, "Minimalist Conception of Democracy: A Defense," in *Democracy's Values*, ed. Ian Shapiro and Casiano Hacker-Cordon (Cambridge: Cambridge University Press, 1999), 44, 49.
54 See John Medearis, *Why Democracy Is Oppositional* (Cambridge, MA: Harvard University Press, 2015); Albert O. Hirschman, *Shifting Involvements: Private Interest and Public Action*, 1979 (Princeton, NJ: Princeton University Press, 1982).
55 Richard Hofstadter, *The Age of Reform* (New York: Vintage, 1960), 60–61. Hofstadter admits that the Populist demands of the 1890s prepared the way for Progressivim but then pivots immediately to claiming they suffered from nostalgia for a lost agrarian golden age.
56 Hofstadter, 70–71. Hofstadter speaks of the populists suffering from conspiratorial thinking whose leaders projected their own "psychic disturbance" onto the movement itself.
57 Hofstadter's claim that the populist demands of 1890s reflected a paranoid, xenophobic, conspiratorial view of politics populism that carried over into the politics of mass society was shattered by Michael Rogin, who showed that the

bulk of the supporters of Joseph McCarthy in the 1950s—Hofstadter's model for modern populism—were in fact small-town businessmen, and not rural farmers. Michael Rogin, *The Intellectuals and McCarthy: The Radical Specter* (Cambridge, MA: MIT Press, 1967).

58 Norman Pollack, *The Populist Response to Industrial America* (Cambridge: Harvard University Press, 1976), 162–66.
59 Michael Kazin, *The Populist Persuasion: An American History* (New York, NY: BasicBooks, 1995); Pollack, *The Populist Response to Industrial America*; Charles Postel, *The Populist Vision*, 1 edition (New York: Oxford University Press, 2009).
60 Postel, *The Populist Vision*, 16–17, 141–63.
61 For the latter see Müller, *What Is Populism?*; Jan-Werner Müller, "The People Must Be Extracted from Within the People': Reflections on Populism," *Constellations* 21, no. 4 (December 1, 2014): 483–93, https://doi.org/10.1111/1467-8675.12126; Cas Mudde and Cristobal Rovira Kaltwasser, *Populism: A Very Short Introduction*, 2nd ed. (New York: Oxford University Press, 2017); Cristóbal Rovira Kaltwasser, "The Responses of Populism to Dahl's Democratic Dilemmas," *Political Studies* 62, no. 3 (October 1, 2014): 470–87, https://doi.org/10.1111/1467-9248.12038.
62 Peter Mair, *Ruling The Void: The Hollowing Of Western Democracy* (London; New York: Verso, 2013).
63 Adam Tooze, *Crashed: How a Decade of Financial Crises Changed the World* (New York: Viking, 2018), 13.
64 Mudde and Kaltwasser, *Populism*, 83–84, 95.
65 M. Canovan, "Trust the People! Populism and the Two Faces of Democracy," *Political Studies* 47, no. 1 (March 1, 1999): 10–13, https://doi.org/10.1111/1467-9248.00184.
66 Ernesto Laclau, *On Populist Reason*, Reprint edition (London: Verso, 2007), 8.
67 Laclau, *On Populist Reason*.
68 See Nadia Urbinati, "A Political Theory of Populism," *Annual Review of Political Science* 22, no. 1 (2019): 111–27.
69 Jürgen Habermas, *Legitimation Crisis*, trans. Thomas McCarthy, 1 edition (Boston, MA: Beacon Press, 1975); Jürgen Habermas, "What Does a Crisis Mean Today? Legitimation Problems in Late Capitalism," *Social Research* 40, no. 4 (December 1, 1973): 643–67. Yes, Habermas later rejected this argument, but its validity still stands, perhaps even more so in a period when neoliberalism has disaggregated the very state provision citizens are counting on at this moment of crisis in the provision of economic supports and public health.
70 Fred Block, "The Ruling Class Does Not Rule Notes on the Marxist Theory of the State," in *The Political Economy: Readings in the Politics and Economics of American Public Policy*, ed. Thomas Ferguson and Joel Rogers (M.E. Sharpe, 1984), 32–46; Charles Lindblom, *Politics and Markets: The World's Political Economic Systems* (New York: Basic Books, 1977); Lindblom.
71 Charles Lindblom, "The Market As Prison," *The Journal of Politics* 44, no. 2 (1982): 323–36.

72 Jacques Ellul, *The Political Illusion*, trans. Konrad Kellen (New York: Vintage Books, 1972).
73 Robert A. Dahl, *A Preface to Democratic Theory* (Chicago, IL: University of Chicago Press, 1956), 145–46.
74 Robert A. Dahl, "Pluralism Revisited," *Comparative Politics* 10, no. 2 (1978): 191–203, https://doi.org/10.2307/421645; Robert Dahl, *Democracy and Its Critics* (New Haven, CT: Yale University Press, 1989).
75 Robert Dahl, *Dilemmas of Pluralist Democracy: Autonomy vs. Control*, Yale Studies in Political Science 31 (New Haven, CT: Yale University Press, 1982), 110, 184.
76 Colin Crouch, *Post-Democracy*, Themes for the 21st Century (Malden, MA: Polity, 2004).
77 For a recent argument for bringing citizen participation and contestation into the regulatory process as an alternative to the technocracy versus market debate, see K. Sabeel Rahman, *Democracy Against Domination*, Reprint edition (New York: Oxford University Press, 2018), 116–65.
78 A similar argument is made by Ned Lebow who claims that political orders in the West suffer a chronic legitimacy problem over two principles of justice spawned by disagreement between proponents of equality as shared benefits and proponents of "fairness" defined as rewarding individual merit. He suggests that serious and possibly chronic conflicts will result in democratic political orders as proponents of one side of this justice dichotomy press their principle to its conclusion politically. Richard Ned Lebow, *The Rise and Fall of Political Orders* (Cambridge: Cambridge University Press, 2018), 336–44.
79 Even Larry Diamond, a political scientist who was central to the wave of democracy interpretation, understands that liberal democracy "means more than just voting." It includes protections of basic liberties of freedom of association, press, assembly, and conscience, fair treatment of minorities, equality under the law, an independent judiciary, and a robust civil society of independent associations and social movements. But these characteristics are added on to competitive party democracy to produce "a good democracy." They are neither entailed by that model, nor are they cultivated by it. Interestingly, he now worries that the United States is failing as an exemplar of liberal democracy precisely because many of these contingent features have fallen away. See Diamond, *Ill Winds*, 19.
80 Schumpeter, *Capitalism, Socialism, and Democracy*, 271.
81 See Mair, *Ruling The Void*.
82 Mark Blyth, "Globalization and the Limits of Democratic Choice: Social Democracy and the Rise of Political Cartelization," *Internationale Politik Und Gesellschaft - International Politics and Society* 6, no. 3 (July 2003): 69–74.
83 Blyth, 74.
84 See Mair, *Ruling The Void*.
85 Jan Werner-Müller argues the opposite claiming that populism becomes authoritarian as soon as it attacks pluralism and in his words "claims that a *part* of the people *is* the people" (22). The problem with this definition is that it is at once too narrow and too capacious. Werner-Müller understands

populism always to have an authoritarian trajectory insofar as a movement or political leader claims to embody "the people" when in fact it or the leader represents only a portion of the people and excludes their opponents as enemies of the genuine people. In this sense, "populism" rejects pluralism and unfavorable electoral outcomes (101). But with this definition, movements or political leaders claiming that under the competitive party system citizens are political equals only in name but in fact are political unequals with regard to effectual political rights, membership, and political influence are not populist. Moreover, under this definition a group should not be described as populist if it claims a political party has become unresponsive to its followers or to the majority of citizens; likewise, social movements outside the party system cannot be described as populist if they seek to reverse the decision-making power in a political system dominated by party cartels or the influence of corporations and finance on fundamental economic policy. Thus, if we accept Werner-Müller's definition of populism, then either all movements claiming political equality in a liberal democratic state are potentially authoritarian or the term applies only to a small set of such movements – those with authoritarian leanings. Müller, *What Is Populism?*, 19–23, 101–2.

86 For an argument for why we can speak of a political regime's (moral) legitimacy or illegitimacy as a causal force distinct from simply the subjective belief in its validity see Alasdair Macintyre, "Is a Science of Comparative Politics Possible," in *Against the Self-Images of the Age* (Notre Dame, IN: University of Notre Dame Press, 1978), 277–78.
87 Schumpeter, *Capitalism, Socialism, and Democracy*, 269.
88 Schumpeter, 294–95.
89 Schumpeter, 293.
90 See Robin Wright, "The Story of 2019: Protests in Every Corner of the Globe," December 30, 2019, www.newyorker.com/news/our-columnists/the-story-of-2019-protests-in-every-corner-of-the-globe; Max Fisher and Amanda Taub, "The Interpreter: How Inequality Explains the World," New York Times: The Interpreter, November 7, 2019, https://messaging-custom-newsletters.nytimes.com/template/oakv2?uri=nyt://newsletter/8bf8c2a4-aac6-4e5c-9a15-975f3da0d177&te=1&nl=the-interpreter&emc=edit_int_20191107.
91 Jacques Rancière, "Attacks on 'Populism' Seek to Enshrine the Idea That There Is No Alternative," Versobooks.com, May 2, 2017, www.versobooks.com/blogs/3193-attacks-on-populism-seek-to-enshrine-the-idea-that-there-is-no-alternative.

4 Politics and the Administrative State
Perceptions of Stability and Fragility in Weimar Germany

Paul Petzschmann

Introduction

The Weimar Republic is invoked whenever democracy is ailing. The Weimar example has not only been used to diagnose problems in "young democracies" but also in some of the world's most established ones such as Britain and the United States. These comparisons are built on the assumption that "Weimar" stands for democratic fragility. Recent scholarship has shifted away from this narrative. No longer the preserve of the standard juxtaposition between "good culture and bad politics," numerous recent publications have celebrated the achievements of the fledgling Republic and its innovative constitutional design.[1] Experimentation also extended to the political sphere. This chapter will make the case that these scholarly reassessments echo the perceptions of the defenders of Weimar themselves. It is not surprising that political actors, and especially administrators, should have a high opinion with regard to their own actions as being beneficial to the stability of their regime. It is not only the contrast between their perceptions of Weimar stability and our own that is of interest here but also the way these perceptions of stability formed contextual – and necessary – background conditions for necessary if ambitious reform projects. Just because their assumptions of stability were not vindicated by the fate of the Weimar Republic does not mean that their decision-making informed by these assumptions was necessarily flawed.

To the contrary, I will argue that the assumption of robustness was an important precondition for them to engage in further stabilization efforts. Without these, the young Republic might have failed much earlier than it did. Ultimately, these administrative initiatives were unable to overcome larger structural contradictions and it can be argued that even awareness of these would not have made a difference to the overall outcome. Although mistakes can be fatal – and Weimar has become synonymous with democratic experiments "gone wrong" – this should not detract from the need for policymakers to engage in them and for observers to see them – also – in this light. Two contextual features stand out in explaining the robustness assumption made by the elites at the heart of this chapter: firstly, the relative insulation of administrators inside a civil service apparatus marked institutional conservatism and an assumption of "historical continuity" and secondly, an ideology of statism that all too easily conflated this continuity with robustness. This chapter will examine each of these features in turn.

The first part of this chapter will introduce two administrative experimenters – Hans Staudinger and Arnold Brecht and their proposals for economic and territorial reform aimed at stabilizing Weimar. The second part of this chapter will discuss the administrative ideology of "statism" that explains why administrators like them assumed the fundamental stability of administrative regimes and the political consequences that this had on their assessments of National Socialism. Statism had a very restricted view of political membership, which made mass-democracy suspect and associated it with instability in the minds of administrative elites. Associating stability with historical continuity of the state apparatus also meant that administrative rule was normalized, leading administrators and scholars of public administration alike to mis-recognize the Nazi seizure of power as radical regime change – in contrast to the German Revolution of 1919.

Arnold Brecht (1884–1977) is known to American political scientists primarily as a theorist and the author of *Political Theory: The Foundations of Twentieth-Century Political Thought*, which served as a standard textbook in many courses taught in the field during the 1960s.[2] Yet before coming to the United States as a refugee, Arnold Brecht enjoyed a long and distinguished career as a civil servant both in the dying days of the last German Empire and during the Weimar Republic.

Hans Staudinger (1889–1980), secretary of state in the Prussian trade ministry from 1929 to 1932. A card-carrying Social Democrat, he was one of the more prominent cases of Prussian Interior Minister Carl Severing's attempt of filling the upper echelons of the state civil service with Social Democrats. He was forced to flee Berlin after the Nazi seizure of power and, like his colleague Brecht, ended up lecturing and researching at the New School of Social Research in New York of which he was to become Dean in 1939. Staudinger's work in American exile was primarily that of an administrator and fundraiser for the New School and as a specialist for several New Deal agencies.[3]

While Staudinger championed a version of Weimar Keynesianism through his proposal for a "communal economy," Brecht was busy drafting ambitious plans for territorial reform that would streamline Germany's scattered state administrations into an effective unitary state.

While these reform proposals were clearly born out of desperation in the dying days of a regime under siege from anti-constitutional forces, their proponents were optimistic not only about their realization but also regarding their effectiveness in saving Weimar. Their optimism was at least partly the result of the context in which they operated – their position within a Prussian administration that, unlike the Republic as a whole, was characterized by strong pro-Republican coalitions under democratic leadership.

Brecht and Staudinger's attempts to stabilize Weimar by creating a unitary administration that would enable the carrying out of counter-cyclical spending policies were conceived of within and limited by competitive party democracy in Prussia and the Reich as well as within the context of deflationary politics of Germany's central bank. Rather than a historical "warning" or extreme case of "democracy gone wrong" the Weimar case illustrates the structural contradictions faced by representative party democracies attempting to reform themselves by administrative means and within the constraints of Schumpeterian elite competition – a dilemma that is clearly outlined by Peter Breiner's contribution to this volume. Ludvig Norman's chapter features another German émigré-administrator with a similarly "statist" mind-set. Norman demonstrates that the European Union is heavily reliant on a "militant" interpretation of democracy according to which the people cannot be trusted to decide on the correct outcome. During the 1930s, Loewenstein's functionalism already blinded him from recognizing the "rule by administrators" as part and parcel of the Nazi threat. His continued "statism" was merely a symptom of the problem he was seeking to redress, not the solution to warding off the threat extremism posed to democracy. In making a broader argument regarding the importance of the specific context in which elites make assessments about robustness and fragility, this chapter will first provide some historical background about the conditions in which "Schumpeterian" and "functionalist" conceptions of democracy first emerged.

Weimar Prussia: Bulwark and Laboratory

If any elite group could have any confidence in the robustness of the Weimar constitutional order this was especially true of members of the Prussian civil service between 1919 and 1933. Their confidence was not misplaced. Weimar Prussia has been referred to in the literature as a "bulwark"[4] and the "rock"[5] of democracy. According to the historian Rudolf von Thadden: "Prussia did not just survive into the Weimar

Republic, it actually acquired new political weight of its own. With a social-democratic government, it enjoyed a measure of stability that was in stark contrast to the upheavals typical of Reich politics at the time."[6] Both contemporaries and historians of Weimar tend to judge the stability of the two regimes in relation to one another: Prussia was a haven of stability compared to the Republic as a whole and vice versa. This could give Prussian administrators grounds to be optimistic. Just as it had dominated the politics of the German Reich before the Revolution of 1919, Prussia could do so again under very different political conditions: Rather than in the service of militarism and reaction it would act as a progressive force that through its sheer size would stabilize the Republic and force the *Reich* as a whole in a modernizing, democratic direction. In accomplishing this goal pro-Republican forces would lean heavily – and problematically – on the instruments of the state and especially of civil service.

The preeminence of the civil service had gone largely unchallenged after the 1919 Revolution. Prussia's first Social Democrat prime minister, Otto Braun regarded the principal risk to the Weimar Republic to be revolutionary instability, a reflex that became deeply embedded in the thinking of administrative elites in the years that followed. The perceived danger of revolutionary insurrection from the left meant that Social Democrats were unable to conceive of alternative forms of political membership in the Republic that included Germany's proletariat and many of its demobilized soldiers. The continued prominence of the state in the thinking of Weimar elites looms large in the way they assessed the stability of the new regime. While the counterrevolutionary reflex was especially prominent among the older generation of Germany's democratic leadership, its younger members imbibed much of it through their socialization in the civil service at the federal and the state level.

It was the move from the federal to the Prussian administration that led both Arnold Brecht and Hans Staudinger to recognize the importance of what the historian Dietrich Orlow described as the "Prussian *mentalité*" – both a commitment to service for and within the state and the firm conviction that the interests of Prussia and the Weimar Republic under Prussian leadership were synonymous.[7] As Staudinger reminisced, "the political horizon of a Prussian civil servant is wider, meaning less party-political than that of the an average politician or trade unionist … . My social democrat comrades gave priority to their service to the state."[8] Brecht recognized the identification with the common good also carried with it the risks of myopia and delusion. While Prussia as a political entity was becoming less and less important, Prussian bureaucrats still regarded themselves as all-powerful.[9] Braun could therefore describe himself as a "proud Prussian" even in 1938 and emphatically agreed with Thomas Mann's words that "Prussia had a special mission" that even in the context of the Weimar Republic had not yet been fulfilled.[10] This commitment to Prussia as a political entity survived into the war years: As late as 1943 he insisted in a memorandum to President Franklin D. Roosevelt that while the Reich government should be dissolved, he still remained acting prime minister of Prussia – and therefore presumably the right interlocutor for the allies in negotiating the terms of postwar reconstruction. In a similar display of the grandeur that Brecht had criticized elsewhere, he himself believed that through an act of self-sacrifice Prussia and its leadership could resolve the constitutional dualism between the *Reich* and its most powerful member state by dissolving itself. This quasi-Hegelian sublation of the Prussian state for the sake of saving the Republic was part of Prussia's "special mission."

The most important feature of the Prussian mentality during the Weimar period was undoubtedly a commitment to the preservation of the Weimar constitutional order and with it a shared understanding of who its enemies were. Brecht spoke for many when he pronounced that "by temperament, by sentiment, by reason, and by loyalty to my sworn duties I was positively on the side of the republican principles of the Constitution at all times, and outspokenly so."[11] The Prussian perspective allowed him and others to fuse the traditions of German and Prussian statism with support for the Weimar Constitution and its parliamentary democracy. It allowed for the mobilization of Prussia's considerable administrative resources in the service of preserving the Republic.

Yet this "Prussianism" also had something naïve about it in that it mistook all support for "the state" as an abstract entity for support of the Weimar democratic state. Moreover, in identifying themselves with the state, administrators could interpret their actions as automatically in the interest of the state and its preservation. The political stalemate that would characterize Weimar Politics heightened these tendencies because it meant that administrators acted outside of the normal legislative channels and arrogated to themselves explicitly political functions in the name of "necessity." This – perfectly understandable – reaction often went hand-in-hand with an instrumental understanding of democracy itself. Democracy may have been desirable if and only if it enabled stability.[12] Because of the ongoing political stalemate, Hans Staudinger and Arnold Brecht felt themselves called to design ambitious policy proposals.

Staudinger's proto-Keynesianism was aimed at the transformation of the German economy into a state-managed form of welfare capitalism. This approach needed to assume that political and economic actors were invested in the idea of rationally managing macroeconomic cycles along the lines of the Prussian state. But Staudinger didn't account for the party-political nature of the conflict between Prussia and the federal government even in the management of (to an economist) as technical an issue as the fallout from the Great Depression.

Brecht's proposals similarly assumed a widely shared political objective for overhauling the constitutional structure in the service of administrative centralization. Even more optimistic than Staudinger, Brecht judged the economic crisis of the early 1930s to have been dealt with effectively by political leaders whom he regarded as united in their will of preserving the constitutional order. For him, the eventual collapse was not down to systemic failings of Weimar's constitutional order but could be attributed to bad timing.

While both reform proposals were perhaps naïve regarding the assumptions they made about the extent and durability of pro-regime coalitions at the time they were not irrational *per se* and important components of them became permanent features of the West-German constitutional order after 1949. This highlights, in spite of their failures, the important historical continuities between the first two German republics.[13]

Hans Staudinger and the Promise of *Gemeinwirtschaft*

The Weimar Constitution of 1919 did not only effect a transition from monarchy to parliamentary democracy but also gestured toward a novel type of economic organization. Article 155 spelled out a number of social rights while Article 165 established the principle of worker and employee participation through a system of councils – the remains of the council democracy envisaged by the revolutionaries. Many of these provisions, progressive though they were, remained ineffectual in practice. Social rights were never to be enforceable in the courts and much of the implementing legislation for the establishment of worker and employee council was not passed by the federal legislature, the *Reichstag*.[14] Similarly to the preservation of the Civil Service, the retaining of the basic structures of Germany's economy was in itself thought to be contributing to the regime's stability as against the "destabilizing" economic designs advocated by the revolutionary councils and their supporters on the left of the Social Democratic movement.

While the constitution was an uneasy compromise between radically divergent ideas about the reorganization of the economy, the vagueness of its provisions left state governments – especially those of the left – to experiment with forms of organized capitalism. Experimentation was a response to crisis – the inflation crises of the early 1920s and in particular the fallout from the world economic crisis of 1929. In their desire for stability, German Social Democracy turned away from the full-scale socialization of the means of production. Rudolf Hilferding, the foremost theoretician of Social Democracy in Weimar, regarded state coordination as the way forward. By the mid-1920s, the view that organized capitalism was "not only the most mature variant but also the most crisis-proof, allowing for increased politicization and planning ... thus allowing for an evolutionary, steady transformation to Socialism through continued concentration, organization and planning."[15]

It was in this spirit that the social democrat Hans Staudinger joined the Prussian civil service as state secretary to the ministry of trade and commerce in 1927 to further the establishment of Prussia's communal enterprises, especially in the sectors of coal mining and electricity production but also in the creation of majority state-owned holding companies for Prussia's ports.

Staudinger regarded Prussia as an important proving ground for developing new hybrid forms of state and private ownership that can be summed up in his advocacy for the idea of *Gemeinwirtschaft*, or communal economy. While the concept was vague enough to span a wide variety of reform proposals within Social Democratic circles, Staudinger regarded the establishment of public utility companies as its central element. As he argued in his 1932 work, *The State as Entrepreneur*, the main objective of these was twofold: They were to provide public goods such as transport and electricity at reasonable and stable rates to the public and bear the capital costs of infrastructure, especially in rural areas where low revenues would never incentivize private investors.[16] Prussia offered much better preconditions for this kind of mixed economy as it had operated on a quasi-mercantilist basis throughout much of the nineteenth century.[17] As a Social Democrat, Staudinger knew only too well that this version of the Prussian "state as entrepreneur" was used as a way to support the state's military ambitions abroad and political repression at home.[18] Its rationale was territorial expansion and the maintenance of a rigid caste system based on the violent suppression of the working class and its political organization. Typical for the Weimar-Prussian "*mentalité*", Staudinger believed that under Social Democratic leadership the efficient state apparatus could be put to work in the interests of a democratic welfare capitalism. The state would assume the role of a large-scale public investor during times of economic crisis. In this prefiguration of the principles of Keynesianism and the postwar German social market economy, he echoed the work of Social Democratic unionists such as Woytinsky, Tarnow, and Baade who attempted to generate public support with the use of fiscal stimulus measures and public works programs.[19]

That this peculiar mélange of Prussianism and socialism was widespread in circles of the SPD in the late 1920s and early 1930s can be seen in the reception by the party press. Staudinger was celebrated here as a "soldier" fighting on the "economic front" for the state to finally assume its leading role in the direction of the economy.[20] Yet after 1930, even the Social Democrats had reached the conclusion that a democratic solution of the economic problems was no longer possible. Faced with the challenges they had in coming to an agreement between Unions and the party, and between the state and federal levels of the SPD, Staudinger and others contemplated and even suggested the creation of a government of national unity led by a three-person directorate.[21] Perhaps this might have allowed a better coordination of economic policies at state and federal levels as well as the taking of a much stronger line against paramilitary organizations at the same time. In the final days of the Republic, Staudinger invested his hopes for a stabilization of the Weimar economy in the formation of an emergency government to enact some of these measures by decree.[22] Chancellor Brüning refused citing his commitment to "democratic principles" and the German constitution, leading Staudinger to reason that it was in the end the lack of decisive action that allowed the National Socialists to gain in strength. Such action should have combined a strong police response to the SA by the Prussian and Reich government, a much larger countercyclical investment policy and better executive coordination between the federal and Prussian government. The lack of coordination and the failure of either government to take decisive action also resulted in a deep sense of personal responsibility for this failure. "I felt responsible as the captain of a ship who saw what was coming but who hesitated, as did so many, to use all means necessary and without scruples."[23]

The accounts of Weimar's disintegration not only overemphasized his own role but also downplayed the structural conditions necessary for the realization of his designs for a communal economy. Strong disagreements between the Federal and Prussian governments over questions of covering budget shortfalls were accompanied by disunity inside the Social Democratic movement itself as trade unions and the party leadership could not agree on a course of action to combat the economic crisis. The national government remained restricted through the terms of the

Versailles treaty and under Brüning's premiership bent on fulfilling its obligations.[24]

The Prussian government was torn between keeping Brüning's administration in office at the federal level while strongly objecting to the impact of its economic policies on the Prussian economy. It demanded to be given budgetary space to allow for deficit spending in order to be able to pay unemployment benefits and to start an expansive credit financing program for public investments. The result was a trade-off between the demands of economic and political stability – the one inevitably came at the price of the other.

Ultimately, administrative improvisation in the context of deep distrust of democratic institutions "unravelled the authority of the state"– the same authority that was needed to implement long-term economic strategies.[25] The increasing conflict between Prussia and the Reich as well as the federal government's commitment to principles of "sound money" and "fiscal stability" in the wake of the inflation crises of the early 1920s precluded these kinds of policies at the federal level.[26] "Staudinger in Weimar" illustrates not just the contradictions of administrative politics in a crisis situation but the dilemma that administrators in all democracies face: Political stalemate requires administrative improvising, which eats away at the legitimacy of the democracy the administrator is aiming to stabilize. In the case of Weimar, the risk of improvisation was heightened by the general distrust faced by Republican state governments and their administrators both from within and from without the Civil Service. Operating from within the confines of Prussia gave Staudinger, Brecht, and others an "Illusion of Strength" – to use the phrase by Dietrich Orlow – of its democracy that did not extend to the Republic as a whole. A case in point is Arnold Brecht's continued faith in the feasibility of a sweeping program of administrative centralization.

Arnold Brecht and Territorial Reform

The contradiction between long-term reform ambitions and short-lived political coalitions vexed Staudinger's ambitious designs and Arnold Brecht's territorial reform program faced similar structural obstacles. Brecht, more attuned to the short-term problems that his designs might face, was far more optimistic about their realization and regarded fortuitous timing as the most important precondition for success. If only the right political constellation at the Prussian and federal levels would align with geopolitical opportunity, the defenders of Weimar could seize the initiative and complete the trifecta of constitutional reform: economic recovery, administrative centralization, and the decisive reversal of the Versailles treaty.

Like Staudinger, Brecht had joined the Prussian Ministry of the Interior following the collapse of the last *Reich* government with Social Democratic participation in 1927. His brief was to draft proposals designed to resolve the imbalance within the federal structure of the Republic dominated by Prussia both administratively, economically and territorially. As he later observed: "In practice, the Reich legislated, but Prussia administered,"[27] indicating that he regarded the disjointed nature of German federalism as Weimar's main problem. If administrative centralization was the solution to the problem of German federalism in the eyes of Social Democrats, a political solution was difficult to come by in times when conservative coalitions increasingly dominated at the federal level. A civil servant himself, Brecht was especially concerned with "waste" and "inefficiency" resulting from the duplication of federal and Prussian agencies. His distance, he said, from "everyday politics" was not perceived as a disadvantage but "tended to increase my independence and my objectivity."[28] Described by Staudinger as a "perennial optimist," Brecht advocated the creation of a unitary state as all the essential problems of the Republic had resulted from the halfhearted move toward a unitary state by the drafters of the 1919 constitution.[29] Weimar's survival depended on the completion of territorial reform because enforcement of all measures to stabilize the Republic was a matter for the states and "unless the national government resorted to presidential emergency decrees it had to rely on the good will and the efficiency" of their governments.[30] It was this lack of federal enforcement mechanisms combined with a system of proportional representation that gave rise to anti-Republican forces in smaller states and within the federal chamber.[31]

Prussia with its pro-Republican majorities demonstrated that engineering democratic majorities within large territorial units was possible, yet paradoxically the need to strengthen federal powers at the same time demanded the dissolution of Germany's largest state. What for Brecht was an administrative and efficiency calculus proved to be a major political stumbling block as the Prussian and Reich governments were increasingly at odds over budgetary and security questions as the previous section has already pointed out. Yet in the years leading up to the most violent confrontation between the two – the "Prussian Coup" of 1932 – Brecht could still describe the Republic as being "on the threshold of salvation."[32] In contrast to Staudinger, Brecht judged the deflationary policies of the Reich government to have been a success. Not only had the federal cabinets of Müller and Brüning negotiated an end to the occupation of the Rhineland, they had also stabilized the economy to an extent that the budget was balanced and the Reich could meet its obligations. "A potent public works corporations, authorized to give self-liquidating grants-in-aid to states, provinces, counties, and municipalities for public works, had been created and functioned satisfactorily. Future financial operations on a large scale would have a sound basis. The collapse of the great financial institutions had been avoided, mainly by a system of federal outlays and guarantees rather by direct contributions."[33]

Staudinger's strategy for stabilizing the Reich lay in the long-term transformation of its economic policy that would have required both time and substantial resources. For Brecht, stability had already been achieved – thus bringing his life-long ambition of transforming the Republic into a unitary state to the verge of completion. The large structural problems – most importantly the dualism between Prussia and the Reich and the financial reparations resulting from the peace treaty – were almost resolved by the Spring of 1932. The collapse of the Republic came down to unfortunate timing.[34] Similarly, the reorganization of the Reich, masterminded by Brecht himself as the Prussian representative in the constitutional committee appointed for this purpose, was close to completion. Again, Brecht believed that his reform proposals could have been implemented peacefully in the dying days of Schleicher's chancellorship as late as January 1933.[35]

What is remarkable reading the recollections of Arnold Brecht today is how convinced he remained of both his own capacity as a Prussian official to change the course of events and of the last chancellors of Weimar to mobilize majorities for ambitious reform proposals. If it had not been for "bad timing" both Germany's political elites would have risen to the occasion and saved the Republic.

Staudinger and Brecht in their role as administrators overlooked the structural problems that weakened the hand of Prussia's pro-Republican administrations throughout the early 1930s. The decision of the Braun government to support the reelection of Hindenburg in the presidential contest of 1932 and to avoid any conflict with the conservative chancellors after 1930 for the sake of preserving Weimar's stability "left virtually all trump cards in the relationship ... in the hands of the Reich cabinet. As a result, Prussia lost the initiative and was unable to use the remaining strength of its intact political system during the final crisis years of the Weimar era ... ."[36] Like Staudinger, Brecht took personal responsibility for this turn of events. Not only was it "the most tragic event in my professional life," it was the "unsolved dualism between the Reich and Prussia over which the Weimar Republic broke down."[37] Reducing the structural instability of the Weimar Republic to questions of unfortunate timing and overestimating the efficacy of their plans for stabilizing also left both Staudinger and Brecht with feelings of personal responsibility and guilt for democracy's failure.

This perspective on regime robustness displays a number of assumptions that have been described as the peculiarly German phenomenon of "statism." Sharply delineating between state and society, statism relied on an account of political membership that gave pride of place to civil servants as "Germany's first rational political members."[38] Rather than challenging the distinction between "members" and "subjects" of the state even the republican elites of Weimar Germany preferred to change the composition of political membership to integrate the defenders of the Republic into the civil service. If rule by these "rational members" could be ensured in the Republic there was every reason to suppose that the regime was robust. Even after 1933, in his third year in American exile, Arnold Brecht could argue that the civil service was still a positive source of institutional continuity even after Germany had ceased to be a democracy and the Weimar constitutional order had been effectively destroyed. The bureaucratic state in Germany is not confined "to a particular period but to the general trend as developed for centuries and prevailing, at least as the basic system, despite all differences, *through the three regimes in this century*."[39]

Weimar administrative elites had reversed Weber's distinction between politics and administration. This reversal was partly due to the fact that Weber's theory of bureaucracy had already in his own time run counter to traditional German bureaucratic ideals. As Staudinger, who had been close to Weber, subsequently stated: "Weber had no flesh and blood in his understanding. I was an administrative bureaucrat who had a great deal of political discretion not just in the emergency... but in day to day operations as well."[40] These views were not only ex-post rationalizations but were based on a comprehensive and systematic ideology of administrative action. Originally devised to shore up the status of the administrative apparatus that saw itself under siege from elected politicians and "mass democracy," more generally it quickly morphed into a science of crisis management in the context of a new, antitotalitarian politics. After the Nazi seizure of power, exiled elites, Staudinger and Brecht among them, were quick to shape the perception of Weimar abroad as well as fashion a set of theoretical assumptions that systematically prioritized administrative action as a way of achieving stability. The equation of institutional continuity with regime stability may have been valid in the limited context of Weimar Prussia, yet it revealed a fatal flaw during and after the Nazi seizure of power in 1933. The second part of this chapter will discuss in more detail how the assumption of robustness that guided both administrative elites and scholars of public administration also led them to misrecognize Nazi rule.

Public Administration as a "Science of Stability"

At the same time that Brecht, Staudinger, and their colleagues were extolling the virtues of administrative experimentation, the Civil Service had already been in crisis for a considerable time. This was to no small extent due to the 1919 Revolution but also to social changes that had taken place since the beginning of the twentieth century. Although prior to World War I, administration had not been unproblematic, it was only after the German Revolution of 1918 that it became a widely debated and politicized problem.[41] The numerical expansion of the ranks of civil servants had swelled the size of the German bureaucracy, mostly as a result of the expansion of welfare, the transport system, the postal service, and de-mobilization after the war. This had led to a very wide variety of types of civil servants, the politicization of parts of the civil service resulting in fears regarding its elite status and the threat of "proletarianization." There were subsequent attempts to distinguish between those bureaucrats directly representing the sovereign state (*staatstragende Beamte*) and mere state employees (*Angestellte*). In order to distinguish between these two categories consistently, the *Beamte* needed to be invested with a degree of responsibility and freedom to act that would have been completely anathema to Weber.

German scholarship on public administration had already challenged the distinction between policy and administration, arguing that recourse to "rule by administrators" was nothing to be fearful of. The complexity of policymaking in the twentieth century made administrative legislation not only unavoidable but also desirable. Complexity, the extension of the remit of state activity, and time pressure generated by the number of issue areas confronting modern government, make a consistent separation between politically responsible elected officials and their non-responsible administrative agents impossible. What in Germany had always been the case due to its strong bureaucratic tradition was bound to increase equally in other politically developed nations.

Carl J. Friedrich argued that the main issue was 'to insure effective action of any sort.'[42] In the interest of achieving action, it was irresponsible to worry unduly about the destabilizing potential of emergency rule safe in the confidence that "rule by the administration" would in fact prevail. The transition from politics to administration was not as absolute as Weber had implied but was in fact a "continuous process."[43] Since policy is always inadequately framed and in need of adaptation according to circumstance, "it is the function of the administrator to do everything possible which will make the legislation work."[44] Friedrich was arguing for joint responsibility of political leaders and administrators, not just simple subordination under the authority of plebiscitary leaders based on how emergency rule in fact operated, rather than from an abstract distinction between "responsible" politics and "irresponsible" administrators. This argument was based both on the idea that technical expertise, not plebiscitary authority, legitimated the wielding of political power. Even if it was true that a permanent civil service will develop into a political pressure group in its own right, such influence would be based on superior knowledge and exercised in good faith. As such it was to be welcomed rather than rejected.[45] In any case, meddling in politics by professional bureaucrats was to be preferred to ignorant neutrality. This was quite a stark reversal of Weber's original position and betrays none of his anxieties regarding the dangers of an unlimited bureaucracy.

The flipside of this primacy of administration in defining regime stability was the delegation of democracy and its institutions to secondary importance, as pointed out earlier. An "instrumentalist" or "functionalist" view of democracy did not only reach far back into the German statist tradition of the eighteenth and nineteenth centuries, it would survive World War II virtually intact. Karl Loewenstein – whose functionalism is discussed by Ludvig Norman in this volume – and Carl J. Friedrich were two of the thinkers who carried this legacy to the United States and beyond during the 1930s and 1940s. For Friedrich and Loewenstein, Germany did not enjoy an organically grown consensus regarding the rules of the political game – unlike Great Britain. Given the lack of durable parliamentary majorities, executive leadership was made "workable" by emergency legislation or rule by emergency decree. The acceptance and indeed the welcoming of emergency rule by the executive followed from the assumption that robustness and rule by administrators were synonymous and that parliamentary institutions were a source of fragility or outright destabilizing. Such assumptions, born out of German statism, led to the misrecognition of the Nazi takeover as simply another period of emergency administration that left the vital backbone of the German state largely intact.

Constitutional Emergency Provisions:

Misrecognizing the Rise of Nazism

The Weimar Constitution is mostly remembered for the emergency provisions contained in Article 48, which is often invoked to highlight the link between emergency powers and totalitarian dictatorship.[46] This view is easily projected back onto views held by Weimar's contemporaries. Yet the relationship between emergency rule, dictatorship, and stability presented itself as far more complex to commentators at the time. They regarded constitutional emergency provisions and the rule by decree as a sort of functional equivalent of the plenitude of powers that a British prime minister enjoyed as the result of organic institutional growth. In the words of political scientist F. A. Hermens – an advocate for electoral reform – it was the job of government to "make a decision, not divide a cake."[47]

It was the pluralism of parliamentary parties, exacerbated by a system of proportional representation – or representation over decision-making – that was at the heart of the Republic's instability.[48] The view that parliament and the party system more generally were to blame for instability was widespread among observers and not reserved to opponents of the Republic. At the same time, writing on Weimar politics remained remarkably uncritical of presidential emergency powers. Whereas Bismarck's constitution with its Article 68 refers to emergency rule in a state of war (*Kriegszustand*), the Weimar Constitution, owing to the revolutionary circumstances of the time, contained emergency powers that were far more sweeping. Under its famous Article 48, the constitution stated that "If security and public order are seriously disturbed or threatened in the German Reich, the president of the Reich may take the measures necessary to re-establish security and public order, with the help of the armed forces if required. To this end he may wholly or partially suspend fundamental rights."[49]

The main factor in the extended use of emergency powers, however, was due to the failure of the *Reichstag* to pass legislation specifying the conditions under which emergency powers were to be exercised by the president. It was the practical use by successive German governments throughout the 1920s and 1930s that set the precedent for future use. Governments of all political parties, under Marx, Stresemann, as well as Brüning, made extensive use of the emergency provisions of the Constitution in order to issue decrees on more than 250 occasions for the purpose of imprisoning militants, establishing special criminal tribunals, and to stabilise the currency. This use of emergency powers thus confirmed a more general tendency to conflate economic and political emergencies.[50] From 1930 onward, government took to ruling entirely by emergency decree, effectively side-stepping parliament and normal legislative procedure. The state of the exception (*Ausnahmezustand*) had become a permanent feature of political life. The emergency provisions under Article 48 were considered sensible provisions for the safeguarding of public order and constitutional integrity and the potential for their abuse did not invalidate their utility. As Carl Friedrich argued: "Germany might well be congratulated for the wisdom of its constitution-makers, who included in their fundamental charter provisions which enable a responsible minority to tide the country over a temporary impasse ... . Truly benevolent despotism of this sort forestalls internal chaos and a complete breakdown of the government, particularly when it is placed in the hands of a man who has grown old in unswerving loyalty and service to his country."[51]

The emergency provisions of Article 48 were not only considered 'peculiarly ill adapted' for a radical transformation of the constitutional order, they were good instruments for its preservation and maintenance.[52] Emergency provisions comparable to Article 48 were widespread among all developed Western political regimes. The rise of democratic, parliamentary government with its reliance on legislation "after extensive discussion and negotiation with all interested groups, is peculiarly in need of extraordinary arrangements whenever an imminent danger requires immediate action ... Reflection will show that some provision similar to this is found in the constitutions of all popular governments."[53]

Rule by emergency decree had become a permanent feature of political life so that on this account there was little effective difference between the only theoretical limited plebiscitary leadership of the *Reichspräsident* until 1933 and Hitler's dictatorship. Far from triggering a rapid reassessment of positions regarding the stabilizing functions of executive strength and bureaucratic rationality observers of Weimar politics regarded Nazism, at least initially, as continuous with Weimar realities rather than as a radical rupture. Nor did rise of Nazism to power discredit any of the policy instruments that they had regarded as stabilizers. Karl Loewenstein could argue as late as 1938 that Nazism meant a return of Germany to its political essence: "[T]he congruity between the methods of domination and the national character may, in the long run, lead to a normalization of the regime of which there are at present no visible signs. The essential justification of any political system is that of reflecting the norm of the national traditions and of maintaining the equilibrium of social forces."[54]

Even under the Nazi dictatorship, the civil service continued to provide the "backbone of the German state" as Carl J. Friedrich had predicted in 1933.[55] If that was the case, it was then difficult to differentiate between rule by presidential decree that had been in place frequently since 1930 and Adolf Hitler's early chancellorship. Karl Loewenstein was able to argue that "the transition of power from the cabinet of von Schleicher to the cabinet of Hitler was in accordance with the actual requirements of the political situation."[56] Not only was it legal but reliance on emergency legislation made it seem normal and even rational and practical. Writing in the spring of 1933, Friedrich defended the continued use of emergency legislation – by the now National Socialist regime. Pointing to the many constitutional constraints on its exercise he argued that Hitler's rule did not represent a fundamental change in the nature of German politics.[57] The essence of the German constitutional order was constituted by the rule of the bureaucracy and the professional civil service, not by parliamentary democracy. Emergency rule enables superior decision-making not only because it reduces the number of individuals involved in the process but also because it represents a return of the nation to its culturally specific political roots. It was based on these ideas that Friedrich could argue that "it is in its best established behaviour patterns that a nation seeks its salvation" and the legislative supremacy of parliament was definitely not one of these "best established" patterns.[58]

This was only a short step away from the view of cultural conservatives who argued that democracy was inherently "un-German." If, as Friedrich argued, parliament's role in legislation was already minimal in periods of normal government due to the complexity of issues dealt with by modern governments, there was not really a need for parliamentary government at all. In any case, the president enjoyed democratic legitimacy due to his direct election. The difference of whether emergency rule was ratified by parliament or by the president could therefore be said to amount to a mere difference in emphasis and not of fundamental constitutional importance. This argument effectively subordinated considerations of constitutionality to matters of bureaucratic expediency and efficiency. National Socialist rule did not, then, constitute anything resembling a decisive break in constitutional practice per se for Carl Friedrich. He was able to proclaim confidently that Germany "will remain a constitutional, democratic state with strong socializing tendencies whose backbone will continue to be its professional civil service."[59]

The fact that Germany did not remain a *democracy* under the Nazis and nevertheless managed to preserve its political essence underlines the view held by many émigrés that public participation in politics was not an issue of inherent significance and value to the nature of the German constitutional order but merely a technical problem or *staatstechnisches Problem*.[60] In Friedrich's view it was better to recur to the rule by unelected yet competent technocrats rather than risk institutional destruction through an ill-managed democratic process.

These assessments of National Socialism as continuity rather than radical change were quite different from Franz Neumann's later "Behemoth" argument, according to which Nazi Germany had turned into an anarchic 'non-state' dominated by competing and increasingly destructive centers of power.[61] Yet both diagnoses of the Nazi state and of its continuity or discontinuity with the Weimar Republic were based on the integrity of the bureaucracy as the most important indicator of regime stability rather than on the existence of democratic forms of legitimacy. While this assessment confirms Chris Thornhill's thesis regarding the continuing centrality of "statism" in twentieth-century German political discourse, at the same time it renders the concept more complex and contradictory.[62]

Weimar administrators and scholars of administration tolerated a much expanded range of phenomena as continuous with democratic government, partly because they did not regard parliamentary democracy, at least in the – to them – unconstrained form of the first German Republic as stable. As a result, they could disregard what we today condemn as destabilizing and antidemocratic policies as indicators of radical regime change. The reasons for this myopia were manifold. In the case of Social Democrats such as Otto Braun, Hans Staudinger, and Arnold Brecht, their familiarity with Prussian politics and their service to the Prussian state led them to fall prey to what Orlow has called the "illusion of strength": the inference that Prussia's superior size and the pro-Republican majorities that its governing coalition enjoyed throughout much of the brief life of the Republic would act as a "vise" for the entire Reich.[63] The overreliance on institutional continuities with past regimes as a sign of future regime stability was as much to blame as was the hubris of the Berlin mandarins concerning their own ability to influence events in the *Reich*. Secondly, a conception of stability that relied on a balanced relationship between charismatic leaders and emotionally charged masses was at constant risk of being made self-fulfilling. The National Socialists could be understood as defenders of stability or as dangerous revolutionaries, depending on whether they were understood as forces mobilized for the purposes of establishment politics or as signs of mass-emotionality unleashed by upstart demagogues. As a system of emergency governance, the Nazi regime functions admirably well because of its legislative efficiency. As political scientist Karl Loewenstein could write from his American exile as late as 1936: "Dictatorial government facilitates the legislative process in that the legislative will of the state encounters no obstacle arising from the parliamentary deliberation and compromise involved in parties. ...

Fundamentally ... the legislative process is immensely simplified and its machinery operates rapidly and without friction."[64]

In some instances, emergency rule has led to beneficial reforms that the previous, institutionally constrained constitutional regimes were unable to enact.[65] From the point of view of administrators, the two regimes were not that different. The fact that a refugee like Loewenstein could in the end come to a remarkably balanced assessment of Nazi governance after three years of otherwise radical political change points to the great importance attached by him to the possibility of and institutional openings for swift, uniform, and decisive emergency action by the executive. Emergency powers were therefore considered an important device for the self-stabilization of democratic regimes. Friedrich and Loewenstein seemed to assume that with a concentration of executive power would come greater capacity to wield such power responsibly.

Conclusion

This chapter has attempted to demonstrate how closely interwar German views of regime robustness and fragility were tied to the ideology of "statism." In particular, statism served as a background assumption for Weimar's administrative elites, even the most outspokenly pro-Republican among them. Were the assumptions of stability made by statists counterproductive for the stability for the Weimar Republic? I have argued that – however misguided – they were also necessary in order for defenders of the regime to engage in necessary constitutional reform projects under conditions of extreme political volatility, where outward signs of regime fragility were very apparent even to the casual observer. Yet in retrospect it is obvious that "statism" also had its dark side: associating administrative continuity with regime robustness too easily identified administrative politics as stabilizing and emergency rule as merely an extension of bureaucratic normality. "Patriotic institutionalists" like Staudinger and Brecht were not simply pragmatists who wanted to "get things done." Their actions were informed by a political philosophy that identified the bureaucracy and in particular the Civil Service as national institutions. Rather than countering the stultifying effects of the bureaucratic machine, elected leaders needed to know when to step aside in order to allow professional bureaucrats to deal with emergencies using their technical expertise. Bureaucracy rather than political leadership held the key to the continuity and stability of the Weimar regime and the regime's crises gave bureaucrats the freedom to act. This freedom meant that after 1933 and the collapse of the first

German Republic, many blamed themselves for its failure. This personal sense of failure was bound up with a misrecognition of the structural contradictions that no amount of administrative experimentation could overcome: the declining role of Prussia within a federal structure dominated by increasingly conservative and anti-regime coalitions, the twin pressures of reparation payments and the global recession and, finally, the rising tide of street violence under conditions of political stalemate.

In the context of these structural crises the focus on administrative efficiency rather than the expansion of political membership was understandable in that it focused elites on what was possible and what lay in the realm of their own experience – that of the Prussian exception. In the end, the very things that had made representative democracy viable in Prussia led to its eventual downfall – the focus on strong yet ageing leaders, the stability of the governing coalitions that at the same time made them exclusive circles, the willful ignorance of the political realities at the federal level and above all the conviction that "Prussia could impose its political system on the Reich."[66] In the end, their own embrace of what Karl Loewenstein would later theorize as "militant democracy" sprang from the wish of bringing the "Prussian mission" to a successful conclusion. In fighting for political membership in the Civil Service in the most powerful state in the new Germany, they were fighting the battles of the past. Weimar Prussia was no longer the Prussia of Bismarck. Paradoxically, it may have only been by giving up the paradigm of "statism" that the conditions for their reform projects could have been created. Yet in retrospect looks like an inescapable contradiction should not lead us to an unduly fatalist account of Weimar as a whole but serve as a reminder that experimentation and therefore also failure are a necessary part of democratic politics.

Notes

1 Jochen Hung, ""Bad" Politics and "Good Culture": New Approaches to the History of the Weimar Republic," *Central European History* 49, no. 3/4 (2016), pp. This was acknowledged by the German Federal Minister for Justice, Brigitte Zypries on the occasion of the Ninetieth anniversary of the Weimar constitutional convention, cf. Brigitte Zypries, Weimar – die unterschätzte Verfassung, in: *Die Weimarer Verfassung – Wert und Wirkung für die Demokratie* (Erfurt: Friedrich-Ebert Stiftung und Bundesministerium für Justiz, 2009).
2 Arnold Brecht, *Political Theory: The Foundations of Twentieth-Century Political Thought* (Princeton, NJ: Princeton University Press, 2016).

3 For a history of the New School see Claus-Dieter Krohn, *Intelletuals in Exile: Refugee Scholars and the New School of Social Research* (Amherst, MA: University of Massachusetts Press, 1993); Judith Friedlander, *A Light in Dark Times: The New School for Social Research and its University in Exile* (New York: Columbia University Press, 2019).
4 Hagen Schulze, Otto Braun oder Preußens demokratische Sendung. Eine Biographie (Frankfurt: Propyläen, 1977), p. 856.
5 Orlow adapted the title from a Social Democratic campaign pamphlet used before the 1924 Prussian state elections that described Prussia as "the democratic ... solid rock." Dietrich Orlow, *Weimar Prussia. The Unlikely Rock of Democracy* (Pittsburgh: University of Pittsburgh Press, 1986), p. 10.
6 Rudolf von Thadden, *Prussia: The History of a Lost State* (Cambridge, MA: Cambridge University Press), p. 7.
7 Dietrich Orlow, *Weimar Prussia 1925-1933: The Illusion of Strength* (Pittsburgh: University of Pittsburgh Press, 1991), p. 5.
8 Hans Staudinger, *Wirtschaftspolitik im Weimarer Staat. Lebenserinnerungen eines politischen Beamten im Reich und in Preußen 1889 bis 1934*. Herausgegeben und eingeleitet von Hagen Schulze (Bonn: Neue Gesellschaft, 1982), p. 49.
9 Arnold Brecht, *The Political Education of Arnold Brecht: an autobiography, 1884-1970* (Princeton, NJ: Princeton University Press, 1970), p. 270.
10 Otto Braun, *Von Weimar zu Hitler* (New York: Europa Verlag 1940), p. 213.
11 Arnold Brecht, *A Prelude to Silence. The End of the German Republic* (Oxford: Oxford University Press, 1944), pp. xvi–xvii.
12 Rainer Eisfeld, "German Political Science at the Crossroads: The Ambivalent Reaction to the 1933 Nazi Seizure of Power", in Rainer Eisfeld, Michael T. Greven and Hans-Karl Rupp, eds., *Political Science and Regime Change in 20th Century Germany* (New York: Nova Science Publishers, 1996), p. 26.
13 Important for the survival of this body of administrative thought was the community of German émigré scholars in the United States as discussed most recently in Udi Greenberg *The Weimar Century: German Émigrés and the Ideological Foundations of the Cold War* (Princeton, NJ: Princeton University Press, 2013).
14 Jeff King, "Social Rights, Constitutionalism, and the German Social State Principle," *Revista Electronica de Dereito Publico* 1, no. 3 (2014), pp 19–40, p. 26.
15 Martin Höpner, Sozialdemokratie, Gewerkschaften und organisierter Kapitalismus, 1880-2002, *Max Planck Institute for the Study of Societies Discussion Paper* No. 04/10, 2002, p. 14.
16 Hans Staudinger, *Der Staat als Unternehmer* (Berlin: Gersbach und Sohn, 1932).
17 Hagen Schulze, editorial introduction to Hans Staudinger, *Wirtschaftspolitik im Weimarer Staat. Lebenserinnerungen eines politischen Beamten im Reich und in Preußen 1889 bis 1934. Edited and introduced by Hagen Schulze* (Bonn: Verlag Neue Gesellschaft, 1982), p. ixx.
18 Hagen Schulze, editorial introduction to Hans Staudinger, *Wirtschaftspolitik im Weimarer Staat*, p. ixx.

19 George Garvy, "Keynes and the Economic Activists of Pre-Hitler Germany," *Journal of Political Economy* 83, no. 2 (1975), pp. 391–405.
20 *Vorwärts* 117, March 10th 1932, quoted from: Hagen Schulze, editorial introduction to Hans Staudinger, *Wirtschaftspolitik im Weimarer Staat*, pp. xxi–xxii.
21 Ibid., p. 91.
22 Ibid., *Wirtschaftspolitik im Weimarer Staat*, pp. 90–91.
23 Ibid., *Wirtschaftspolitik im Weimarer Staat*, p. 132.
24 Schulze, editorial introduction to Hans Staudinger, *Wirtschaftspolitik im Weimarer Staat*, p. xxii.
25 David Runciman, *The Confidence Trap: A History of Democracy in Crisis from World War I to the Present* (Princeton, NJ: Princeton University Press), 2014, p. 79.
26 Knut Borchardt, "Zwangslagen und Handlungsspielräume in der großen Wirtschaftskrise der frühen dreißiger Jahre: Zur Revision des überlieferten Geschichtsbildes" in *Bayerische Akademie der Wissenschaften*, Jahrbuch 1979 (Munich 1979), pp. 87–132; Knut Borchardt, *Perspectives on Modern German Economic History and Policy* (Cambridge, MA: Cambridge University Press, 1991).
27 Dietrich Orlow, *Weimar Prussia 1925-1933: The Illusion of Strength* (Pittsburgh: University of Pittsburgh Press, 1991), p. 248.
28 Arnold Brecht, *Prelude to Silence*, p. xvii.
29 Hans Staudinger, *Wirtschaftspolitik im Weimarer Staat*, p. 89.
30 Arnold Brecht, *Prelude to Silence*, p. 39.
31 Ibid., p. 137.
32 Ibid., p. 35.
33 Ibid., p. 36
34 Ibid., p. 37.
35 Brecht, *The Political Education of Arnold Brecht*, p. 302.
36 Orlow, *Weimar Prussia*, p. 268.
37 Brecht, *Political Education of Arnold Brecht*, p. 302.
38 Gregg Kvistad, *The Rise and Demise of German Statism: Loyalty and Political Membership* (New York: Berghahn Books, 1999), p. 11.
39 Arnold Brecht, "Civil Service," *Social Research* 3, no. 1 (1936), p. 206. footnote 1, emphasis mine.
40 Interview with Hans Staudinger in Peter M. Ruttkoff and William B. Scott, *The Inner Nazi: A Critical Analysis of Mein Kampf* (Baton Rouge, LA: Louisiana State University Press, 1981), pp. 146–147.
41 Jane Caplan, *Government without Administration. State and Civil Service in Weimar and Nazi Germany* (Oxford: Clarendon Press 1988), p. 14.
42 Carl Joachim Friedrich, "Public Policy and the Nature of Administrative Responsibility," (Cambridge, MA: Harvard University Press, 1940), p. 222.
43 Carl Joachim Friedrich, "Public Policy and the Nature of Administrative Responsibility," p. 225.
44 Ibid., p. 237.
45 Arnold Brecht, "Bureaucratic Sabotage," *Annals of the American Academy of Political and Social Science*, 198, no. 1 (1937), pp. 48–57, p. 57.

46 For research into Weimar uses of emergency rule or *Notverordnungsrecht* see: Heinrich Oberreuter, Die Norm als Ausnahme. Zum Verfall des Weimarer Verfassungssystems, in Heinrich Oberreuter and Rudolf Lill, eds., *Machtverfall und Machtergreifung. Aufstieg und Herrschaft des Nationalsozialismus* (München: Bayerische Landeszentrale für politische Bildungsarbeit, 1983), pp. 39–61; Achim Kurz, *Demokratische Diktatur? Auslegung und Handhabung des Artikels 48 der Weimarer Verfassung* 1919-25 (Berlin: Duncker & Humblot, 1992).
47 Friedrich A. Hermens, "Rejoinder," *Social Research* 4, no. 1 (1937), p. 236.
48 This view was accepted among historians of the Weimar Republic well into the 1960s. For a recent overview of the development of research into Weimar political parties see Eberhard Kolb, *The Weimar Republic*, (London: Routledge, 2005), esp. pp. 164–66.
49 The Weimar Constitution, http://germanhistorydocs.ghi-dc.org/pdf/eng/ghi_wr_weimarconstitution_Eng.pdf, p. 3 (accessed 24 March 2021).
50 William E. Scheuerman, "The Economic State of Emergency," *Cardozo Law Review* 21, nos. 5–6 (2000), pp 1869 – 1894.
51 Carl J. Friedrich, "Dictatorship in Germany?" *Foreign Affairs* 9, no. 1 (1930), pp 118–132, p. 132.
52 Ibid.
53 Ibid.
54 Karl Loewenstein, "Dictatorship and the German Constitution: 1933–1937," *University of Chicago Law Review* 5, no. 4 (1938), pp 537 – 574, p 574.
55 Carl J. Friedrich, *"The Development of the Executive Power in Germany," American Political Science Review* 27, no. 2 (1933), pp 185 – 203, p. 203.
56 Loewenstein, *Dictatorship and the German Constitution*, p. 539.
57 Friedrich, *"The Development of the Executive Power in Germany,"* p. 199.
58 Ibid.
59 Ibid, p. 203. Although in his *Constitutional Government and Democracy* published in 1937, Friedrich acknowledged that this statement regarding Germany's future had "made him look like a fool" this does not mean that by that time he had changed his mind of the importance and necessity of emergency rule, cf. the chapter on emergency rule in Carl Joachim Friedrich, *Constitutional Government and Democracy* (Boston, MA: Ginn, 1950).
60 The term is used by Loewenstein and quoted by Markus Lang, *Karl Loewenstein: Transatlantischer Denker der Politik* (Stuttgart: Franz Steiner Verlag, 2007), p. 208.
61 Franz Neumann, *Behemoth. The Structure and Practice of National Socialism* (London: Victor Gollancz, 1942).
62 Chris Thornhill, *Political Theory in Modern Germany* (Cambridge, MA: Polity Press, 2000), p. 16.
63 Orlow, *Weimar Prussia*.
64 Karl Loewenstein, "Law in the Third Reich," *Yale Law Journal* 45, no. 5 (1936), p. 787.
65 Ibid., p. 793.
66 Orlow, *Weimar Prussia*, p. 268.

5 Roots in Common: The Fragility–Robustness of Democratic and Ecological Regimes

Andrew Lawrence

Introduction

What explains the behavior of putatively democratic liberal regimes that fail to protect and empower populations in the face of the climate crisis? This chapter highlights ways in which this outcome results from critical reflexivity's being trumped by instrumental reasoning. The mechanisms, as well as consequences, of this provisional and pyrrhic victory include a misframing of the ecological crisis and a progressive narrowing of the purpose and scope of liberal and democratic practice. They are manifested institutionally in colonialism, militarism, and the hegemony of neoclassical economics, and are characterized by the economic objectification of people and the environment in pursuit of wealth, markets, and growth. In each instance, they are characterized by a subordination or denial of reciprocal relations among members of a given community or between individuals and nature – or both – which together have come to constitute different manifestations of the "imperial mode of living." Political elites' objectification of nature, uncertainty, and oppressed groups has the cumulative effect of delimiting the normative scope of the nature of climate crisis in a manner that is both blinkered and self-defeating. Over the past two centuries, these tendencies have largely succeeded in coopting democratic movements worldwide.

In order to understand why most elite as well as non-elite actors do not adequately perceive the extent to which their political orders are ecologically embedded – and thus do not perceive the fragility of these political orders – the chapter first explores how perceptions and preferences came to be structured in everyday institutions, discursive tropes, and ways of seeing that collectively have come to constitute a hegemonic "common sense." The next sections argue that in order to become counter-hegemonic, critiques of the status quo need to identify collective actors as well as oppositional policies that can effectively counter this common sense. After tracing its structuring logic at the level of ideology via a brief genealogy of ideas in Descartes, Locke, Hegel, and Marx, the chapter then explores some of its current institutional and practical manifestations. The conclusion reflects upon how elite and popular forms of climate leadership differ in their epistemologies and ontologies of nature. The core logic of commodification for profit cannot be channeled or reformed in ways that strengthen the ecological, and thus also the liberal-democratic order. This necessarily implies that liberal-democratic actors need to recognize that the adequate defense of their order requires the subordination of commodification processes to the necessary goals of ecological and social well-being.

Underestimating the Challenges of Avoiding a Ghastly Subject–Object Division

A recent meta-analysis of the current ecological crisis, while correctly underscoring its scale and gravity, inadvertently perpetuates a key methodological error contributing to this crisis: that of maintaining an analytical and practical distinction between subject and object, including one between humanity and nature. Put differently, the question of *how* ecological order and fragility are (mis)perceived should not be separated from *who* (mis)perceives them, and to what ends. The report, by a multidisciplinary team of scientific leaders of various fields in the natural sciences, "Underestimating the Challenges of Avoiding a Ghastly Future," contends that "future environmental conditions will be far more dangerous than currently believed. The scale of the threats to the biosphere and all its lifeforms – including humanity – is in fact so great that it is difficult to grasp for even well-informed experts"; while "the science underlying these issues is strong," awareness of "the near certainty that these problems will worsen over the coming decades, with negative impacts for centuries to come" is weak.[1] Current negative impacts upon human well-being include at least 10 percent of the world population experiencing starvation, and a quarter, malnutrition; it anticipates that the climate crisis in future will trigger a mass environmental migration of anywhere between 25 million to 1 billion people by 2050. The fact that wild animals (all vertebrate species other than human beings and livestock) now make up only 5 percent of the living biomass of terrestrial vertebrates worldwide and that a million eukaryotic species (including all animals, plants, and fungi) – 10 percent of the total – are threatened with extinction make it "scientifically undeniable" that "we are already on the path of a sixth major extinction."

The report contends that although "the predominant paradigm is still one of pegging 'environment' against 'economy,' ... in reality, the choice is between exiting [ecological] overshoot by design or disaster – because exiting overshoot is inevitable one way or another." Doing so by design, they argue, "requires fundamental changes to global capitalism, education, and equality, which include *inter alia* the abolition of perpetual economic growth, properly pricing externalities, a rapid exit from fossil-fuel use, strict regulation of markets and property acquisition, reigning in corporate lobbying, and the empowerment of women." Without specifying actors or processes for these goals, they conclude that "a human 'optimism bias' that triggers some to underestimate the severity of a crisis and ignore expert warnings" requires of "experts in any discipline that deals with the future of the biosphere and human well-being to eschew reticence, avoid sugar-coating the overwhelming challenges ahead and 'tell it like it is'."[2]

I argue that "telling it like it is" means not merely reporting the existence of the climate crisis, but taking the materiality of nature – and society-in-nature – seriously. This in turn entails providing a historically contextualized account of the origins and institutions driving the crisis; only then can actors understand their place in these contexts and thereby successfully address and overcome this crisis.

The sheer scale of crisis, persuasively documented by the aforementioned report, readily suggests that "social order" – far from being a timeless motif or a generic discourse with a readily translatable meaning from one user and context to the next – is a rapidly changing and contingent phenomenon. Its definition depends at least in part on the subject-position of those defining it. Since at least the interwar period, when Gramsci penned his *Prison Notebooks*, political analysts have highlighted the stabilizing effects of liberal state institutions upon a country's social order.[3] Elites with a stake in their respective social orders, Gramsci argued, sought ways to recognize and as much as possible validate contending definitions of the common good via hegemonic blocs. They presume liberal democratic institutions to facilitate effective decision-making. This in turn contributes to the survival of their attendant order and, for a time, enables a collective democratic intelligence that can – short of challenging underlying structures of power – highlight problematic aspects of current policy, while also bestowing adequate time and freedom of action to achieve a dispensation both alternative and superior to the status quo. But if this view accurately describes the nature of capitalist stability over the past century, how did it come to pass that the most rapid acceleration of the climate crisis coincides exactly with the "third wave of democratization" over the past three decades, when institutions channeling collective democratic intelligence became most widespread?[4]

The following section briefly historicizes some generic reasons behind the inadequacies of collective democratic intelligence that apply to varying extents to newer as well as older democracies.

Twentieth-Century Precedents of Misperceived Ecological Fragility

Like perceptions of the threat of nuclear war – whose prior position at the center of mass existential angst has been eclipsed since the end of the Cold War – dominant framings of the climate crisis have generated muted actions that not only lag perilously behind words, but that serve to normalize an inherently unstable and unsustainable status quo. A proximate explanation points to decades of Big Oil- and Koch Industries-sponsored mass campaigns of misinformation that persist in the face of growing attention and critique.[5] Unsurprisingly, the world's biggest emitter of cumulative greenhouse gasses (GHG), the United States, is also among the top countries polling high levels of denial of the existence of human-caused climate change, with denial especially concentrated among white, male, older Americans residing in the redder counties of red states.[6] The typical posture is not one of mere ignorance but *motivated* denial: deniers have access to the facts but discount them in various ways. Their motivations include libertarian individualism, generalized mistrust in government and science (and paradoxically, a desire to defend the system-based status quo and express loyalty to an idealized national identity), and adherence to consumerist social norms.[7]

Aligning climate stability with democratic stability, in this view, would entail stronger and more far-reaching forms of scientific education, as advocated by the authors of "Underestimating the Challenges." Indeed, global surveys worldwide find that educational attainment is the single strongest predictor of climate change awareness. Improving public awareness and risk perceptions leading to support for collective climate action requires improving basic education, climate literacy, and public understanding of the local dimensions of climate change.[8]

Climate denial is by no means unique to the United States, and neither is the broad pattern of political polarization and fragmentation that it typifies and from which it largely derives. Countering it most immediately depends on tailoring climate communication strategies to specific national circumstances. For some world regions, particularly in Latin America and Europe, the strongest predictor of climate change risk perceptions is an understanding of the anthropogenic cause of climate change. For others, as in much of Africa and Asia, perception of local temperature change is the strongest predictor.[9]

Yet without properly identifying the causes of this polarization and fragmentation, education efforts are likely to prove inadequate. Indeed, increased polarization and fragmentation over the past four decades have become the norm within and beyond OECD democracies. A major contributing factor has been the growing adoption by both center-left and center-right political parties of austerity-driven fiscal policies, which increase both electoral abstention and votes for non-mainstream "populist" parties on the left and right, contributing to polarization and political destabilization.[10] As well as driving a growing sense of precarity among large segments of the working class, these policies have arguably eroded a collective capacity for autonomous opposition and critique.

Precarity was the inevitable result of the era of neoliberal monetarism and austerity that replaced the preceding accumulation regime and mode of development, whether state-led import-substitution industrialization in much of Asia, Africa, and Latin America or the Keynesian policies that fostered the growth of postwar OECD welfare states. Although highly gendered and racialized in its social norms and material effects – valorizing male head-of-household "breadwinners" to the detriment or exclusion of women and, often, a noncitizen migrant labor class – the hegemonic power of Keynesianism lay in its capacity to bestow material security and advancement. Working-class pluralities or majorities in these states demanded these material gains via adequate work and wages that for the most part had been denied them during the interwar Great Depression. Their gains in terms of mass consumption became a central component of the postwar accumulation regime centered on mass manufacturing.[11]

Paradoxically, as labor rights eroded with the onset of neoliberal monetarism and increasingly globalized chains of production and distribution, the ideological allure of consumption became accentuated. This was partly in compensation for the loss of workplace and bargaining rights, and partly as a consequence of these very processes of globalization and their extension of mass markets throughout the Global South. Major parties' capacity to educate their base and deliver meaningful reform became crippled as a consequence of these changes. The ideology of consumerism became an end in itself, as an "imperial mode of living" based on a putatively unlimited appropriation of resources, space, and labor attained global reach.[12]

A major role of climate leadership therefore is to rearticulate collective self-affirmation in sustainable, rather than consumerist terms. This is all the more important to the extent that improvements in formal educational attainment take several years even under optimal conditions, and the imperative to drastically reduce emissions among OECD states must be realized within the next decade at most.[13] Insights from critical psychology (whose theoretical basis is explored further in the next section) suggest why risk and fragility perception of both climate and political crises needs to take place at the collective level. They suggest that perception currently occurs not at the level of the individual subject but through an ensemble of social relations based on institutions of private property, ones necessarily entailing the effects of alienation, exploitation, and ideological misrecognition.[14] Although the ascendancy of the "imperial mode of living" has become increasingly apparent over the past four decades, it is never total in its effects or reach, has always been contested (e.g., by the ecological movement of the early 1970s), and has ideological roots extending back several centuries. The latter are briefly elaborated upon in the next section.

Ideological Roots of the "Imperial Mode of Living"

The origins and development of the imperial mode of living and its relation to nature and society can be traced historically and in terms of its ideological effects. Most generally, the use of concepts and language is always political, from perspectives that are always situated. Similarly, theoretical categories do not simply mimic an external nature, but are actively produced, with specific ends, and within a historically specific and contingent society and nature. Engaging such epistemological realism enables an awareness of how putatively "natural" entities are posited as ontologically real and outside us through and in terms of such categories, thereby helping to grasp the materiality of nature. Since we inevitably take concepts as givens while at the same time seeking to explain them – just as a critique of reason operates within the bounds of reason – so should critical understandings of nature simultaneously refer to both ontological realities and ideological constructs.[15]

Such critical understandings stand in contrast to the perspective of nature as both universal and external to society – one that is inherently contradictory, since the very act of positing nature requires entering into a certain relation with nature, and indeed, denying that humanity has always already been part of nature. Yet precisely this contradictory perspective was arguably the dominant one among Europe's sixteenth-century colonial outposts, whose architects were influenced by a Cartesian mind–body dualism whereby the world of nature was increasingly perceived as external and subordinate to the self. The false universalism of political rights conferred by property thereby underwrites the false perception of nature as infinite. Their worldview was perhaps most famously articulated and put into practice by Locke, whose theoretical works are entirely consonant with his identity as investor in the Royal African Company, at the time a significant corporate actor in the Triangle Trade. His *Second Treatise on Government* privileged both "perfect freedom" and a "state of equality, wherein all the power and jurisdiction is reciprocal" as foundational elements of the state of Nature – but pertaining only to a select few of the male, propertied members of the settler class. More explicitly, his *Fundamental Constitutions of Carolina* classed not only settler territory expropriated from native populations, but also slaves, as elements of Nature ("Every freeman of Carolina shall have absolute power and authority over his negro slaves, of what opinion or religion soever").[16]

It is precisely because settlers – as opposed to natives and slaves – perceived themselves (and were perceived by imperial elites) as being exclusively capable of turning previously worthless Nature into tradeable goods, thereby creating commodified value, that they became entitled to exercise such absolute sovereignty. This structured entitlement is also evident in the "optimism bias" that the Lockean proviso implicitly expresses in the *Second Treatise*, namely, that rights to Nature are circumscribed only by allowances for "enough, and as good, left" in common for others, for "he that leaves as much as another can make use of, does as good as take nothing at all."[17] From the perspective of individual investors eager to reap further profits, Africa would always appear to have had enough and as good slaves available, notwithstanding the millions lost to transit, overwork, disease, and early death. Similarly, North American settlers hunting passenger pigeons in the seventeenth to nineteenth centuries perceived infinite bounty as flocks declined from billions to millions to thousands of birds, yet none was witness to the tipping point of species collapse.

While persuasive to many among the settler populations, this perspective however had less to offer the native, female, indentured, and slave populations from Locke's day up to the present. Subaltern groups and dissenting voices have always contested it and resisted its oppressive and genocidal consequences. Whereas dominant Cartesian perspectives seek to silence or elide these struggles, critical perspectives highlight them – not merely through the important and necessary work in recovering lost or hidden transcripts of subaltern voices, but more fundamentally, through reflexive critiques of ideology that engage in both self-critique and struggles of recognition, thereby transcending the subject/object divide.[18] In this manner, they also provide a means of more radically and completely realizing the fullest extent of humanity's embeddedness within the broader biosphere.

An awareness of this embeddedness in the critical tradition is intrinsically connected to impulses toward social liberation. A central contention of Hegel's in this regard is that, as Karen Ng elucidates, "insofar as the dialectic between self-consciousness and life is the mode of all human activity, this relation in fact expresses the universal form of self-determination." His *Science of Logic* yields "the radical, methodological insight that the critique of reason ultimately rests on the ongoing determination of the relation, opposition, and necessary connection – the ongoing dialectic – between the activities of life and the activities of self-consciousness"; in other words, "*life* is the root of reason."[19] This insight centrally informs Marx's understanding of the basic essence of humanity, our "species-being," denoting the reflexive and reciprocal relation between life and self-consciousness that is the form of all human productive activity and human labor. Our fullest humanity is expressed in "a dialectic between life and consciousness of life," our ability to take our collective life-activity as an object of volition and consciousness. This sociality "irreducibly serves both the ends of life and the ends of self-consciousness at once." Self-determination is thus the necessary consequence of "taking one's life-activity as the object of further determination. ... The interest in freedom is thus not merely incidental to the reflexive self-relation, but rather, it is intrinsic to its very structure, its very form."[20]

Because this reciprocal relation extends further to relations of recognition, a sociality "that irreducibly serves both the ends of life and the ends of self-consciousness," then its perversion entails a basic denial of humanity that informs Marx's key categories of critique: alienation, reification, and exploitation.[21] Locke's delimiting of this sociality to a sphere of similarly positioned property owners, to the violent detriment of subalterns and outcasts, in this view is evidence of both his retarded humanity and his privileged position in the global capitalist order. Conflicts with subalterns are inevitable precisely because the reflexive relation of self-consciousness and life is a free activity that leads toward self-determination.

By extension, the mind-set, actors, and institutions that seek to perpetuate the "imperial mode of living" necessarily misrecognize or overlook their dependence upon and location within the web of planetary life, leading to yet further and more protracted conflicts and struggles. A Lockean and idealist insistence upon an "autonomy from the conditions of life, ... is nonetheless a philosophy that is decidedly, perhaps even necessarily, a product of the bourgeois form of life."[22] Marx uncoincidentally was among the first to identify the root causes of what came to be known as the "metabolic rift" – first associated in the early nineteenth century with the loss of soil nutrient content and thus fertility – in rent-based landholding and intensive capitalist agriculture, with geographical expression in the polarization between cities and countryside, and globally, between metropoles and colonies. He perceived the phenomenon as a further symptom of what can be termed the "value rift," the alienation or estrangement of people in capitalist societies from their ecological conditions of existence and reproduction, of workers from the products of their work, and of members of society from each other, thus generative of unequal relations within and among households, enterprises, states, and world regions, as he made clear in observing that the capitalist mode of production:

> disturbs the metabolic interaction between man and the earth, i.e., it prevents the return to the soil of its constituent elements consumed by man in the form of food and clothing; hence it hinders the operation of the eternal natural condition for the lasting fertility of the soil. Thus it destroys at the same time the physical health of the urban worker, and the intellectual life of the rural worker.[23]

Global warming thus is merely the deadliest manifestation of the centuries-old "metabolic rift," with causal links to the other forms of alienation.

Fossil fuel economies promoted the progressive widening of both of these rifts, accelerating by orders of magnitude the rate at which labor could become commodified, energy-intensive commodities produced and distributed, uncultivated land cultivated, territories and markets colonized, and greenhouse gasses emitted, leading to the outcomes detailed in the "Underestimating the Challenges" report.

This quest for imperial autonomy was for example epitomized by the US Paley Commission's 1952 report "Resources for Freedom: Foundations for Growth and Security," expressive of the postwar US orientation toward the securing and expansion of global markets for all commodities. It is noteworthy for having redefined resource scarcity from assessments of absolute scarcity to a relative, price-based definition of scarcity. A key factor facilitating this change, Timothy Mitchell has argued, was that oil had become so cheap and plentiful by this time that it could underwrite a decontextualized, "dematerialised conception of economic flows" that "made possible the idea of growth without limits," thereby deepening a perceived "divide between nature and society."[24] This perspective was succinctly expressed by the 1987 Nobel Economics prize winner Robert Solow's claim that "the world can, in effect, get along without natural resources."[25]

Objectifying Uncertainty, Misrecognizing Risk, Shortchanging the Future

In order to "unthink" the prevailing common sense of instrumental reason that sees nature and labor as infinite resources for maximizing wealth and external to identity, interest, and subjectivity, it is of course necessary not only to highlight its fundamental unreason, but also to transform the material, institutional, and temporal underpinnings of this view. Among them are the still-dominant set of discourses and practices seeking to assess a numerical value to nature in order to more efficiently exploit its use in pursuit of "natural capitalism." Corporate actors engaging in these practices thereby short-circuit both critical reflexivity and practical alternatives in a manner that renders coming to terms with the climate crisis less possible. They include the Big Four accounting firms and The International Organization for Standardization (ISO), the leading international standard-setting body composed of representatives from various national standards organizations and "perhaps the most influential private organization in the contemporary world, with a vast and largely invisible influence over most aspects of how we live."[26]

As with environmental economics more generally, the mandate of natural capitalism is to attempt to calculate marginal utility and thereby internalize externalities that arise from the inevitable uncertainties of the contemporary world. Costs and benefits that transpire in future are given a current valuation, dependent upon an assigned discount rate. Thus, the key issue of environmental economics at present is "how to balance costs and benefits of global emissions reductions."[27] Nordhaus prefers to strongly discount the future in order to permit current emissions in the name of growth; his 2007 intervention maintained that the "optimal" warming target is about 3.5°C Celsius over preindustrial levels – vastly in excess of the 1.5°C Celsius threshold that the IPCC insists is needed to prevent climate catastrophe. More recently, he allowed that 3°C of warming would reduce global GDP – but only by 2.1%, compared to an absence of climate change; even a 6°C increase, he claimed, would incur only an 8.5% decrease in GDP.[28] Extraordinarily, Nordhaus arrives at this conclusion by excluding the great majority (87% of GDP) of economic sectors that – because they are not directly exposed to the weather and elements (such as office work, services, underground mining, manufacturing, communications, and finance) – "are undertaken in carefully controlled environments that will not be directly affected by climate change." He thereby erroneously equates weather and climate change, and overlooks the possibility that office workers could be (indeed, the reality that they have been) directly affected by droughts, flooding, hurricanes, and increased food and water insecurity.[29]

The ethics of avoiding discounting the future in fact had been demonstrated by Frank Ramsey eight decades previously (earlier and more decisively than by his former teacher, then colleague, J.M. Keynes had expressed in his *General Theory*), long before widespread awareness of global warming.[30] By now, the dangers entailed in confusing or conflating (calculable) risk with (intrinsically incalculable, Knightian) uncertainty should be readily apparent. Increased warming resulting from the exponential increase of atmospheric CO_2 levels and consequent climate extremities of flooding and drought are of course entirely certain elements of the "ontology of nature"; but how effective will current "crisis management" institutions, social practices, and assumptions remain in the event that the natural and social worlds collide at scales and with consequences that have not been anticipated, let alone accounted for?

It is worth recalling that average warming temperatures mask considerable geographical variation, and that the actual warming in tropical zones is likely to be (and indeed is already manifesting itself as) twice as great. Even a 3° average Celsius increase would mean in southern Africa, for example, a total collapse of the maize crop and the livestock industry, and thus the near-certainty of mass starvation.[31] Such a steep discount level seemingly implicitly presumes that "if climate breakdown ends up starving and displacing a few hundred million impoverished Africans and Asians, that will register as only a tiny blip in GDP. After all, poor people don't add much 'value' to the global economy. The same goes for things like insects and birds and wildlife, so it doesn't matter if global warming continues to accelerate mass extinction."[32]

Even within the literature of political ecology, while highlighting the ineffectiveness of current measures to address the climate crisis, there remains a depoliticized, functionalist bias focusing on regime complexes and governance mechanisms designed to "solve" emissions "collective action problems." The identities, interests, and strategies of corporate, financial and government actors most responsible for the climate crisis – and even more, of those who would benefit from ending it – go mostly unexplored. The same is true of corporate actors' specific hegemonic interpretations of this crisis (beyond the misinformation campaigns alluded to at the outset) that highlight some policy solutions (e.g., carbon capture and storage, carbon trading and "offsets," or more recently, small modular nuclear reactors) designed to maintain as much of the fossil fuel status quo as possible, while marginalizing or ignoring others (decommodification of public goods, services, transport, food; reducing inequality and harmful advertising as a means of minimizing consumerism, etc.).

Hegemonic deployments have both "material-concrete" as well as "cultural-symbolic" dimensions, which must both be identified if for example the privileging of certain technologies and commodities (such as privately owned vehicles, let alone the rise of SUVs among them) is to be adequately understood and countered.[33] Both aspects are evident in corporate and managerial approaches to commodifying collectively created knowledge. These include the imposition of rent-generating artificial scarcity via the separation of intellectual from manual labor, or its integration into a networked, digitized production–consumption process that is controlled by capital, or by means of patent and copyright law as a basis of revenue generation.[34] Both dimensions, however, betray the constant tension between capital's inherent drive to commodification and its dependence on non-commodity forms of social relations, a contradiction that rests on the (both "cultural-symbolic" ideological and "material-concrete" institutional) separation of the economic and extra-economic.[35]

Above all, the mechanisms of what David Harvey terms "spatial" and "temporal" fixes (playing on the double meaning of fix as "solution" and "predicament") that are inevitable to processes of capitalist accumulation play a role in misperceiving social and ecological degradation.[36] He defines "spatial fixes" as capital's flexible *geographic* strategies such as globalized commodity chains, outsourcing of work, etc., and *temporal* fixes, by contrast, as responding to capital's crises related to, for example, discounting rates, currency, commodity, and growth swings, not to mention fossil fuel reliance. The "fixes" by definition adopt partial, provisional, short-term responses to crises generated by capitalist development that merely exacerbate these problems over the longer term. By taking place elsewhere or subsequently, these fixes' negative externalities are removed from the perception of those with the most power to alter or prevent them.

A War of All against All of Nature?

A failure to adopt a more temporally and spatially far-reaching perspective on the climate crisis is evident among contemporary elites who readily acknowledge its links to political instability and illegal immigration, for example, without at the same time theorizing their own role in producing these outcomes. The problem in such cases lies not without, but within. For example, the 2019 Report on Effects of a Changing Climate to the US Department of Defense, recently mandated by US

Congress, identified several of these links and other climate threats to its operations.[37] It readily acknowledged that "flooding, drought and wildfires driven by climate change pose threats to two-thirds of the U.S. military's installations," and that climate change was a "threat multiplier" contributing to "country instability issues" and likely to spur increasing mass migration and humanitarian aid missions fueled by extreme weather events.

Yet the report was strangely silent regarding adequate mitigation plans to address these vulnerabilities – let alone their underlying causes, in which case it would need to be prefaced *Quid rides? Mutato nomine et de nobis fabula narrator.*[38] Notwithstanding its PR about "solar powered soldiers," the US military remains the single largest institutional consumer of hydrocarbons in the world, consuming roughly 270,000 barrels of oil a day in 2017 and thereby emitting more than 25 million tons of CO_2: more than the annual emissions of 140 countries combined, and more than twice the annual emissions of all cars on US roads.[39] Since it was inaugurated in 2001, the Global War on Terror that has caused the deaths of hundreds of thousands of civilians has also emitted 1.2 billion tons of greenhouse gasses.[40] Embarrassment at this carbon footprint may have induced the Clinton administration to demand that it be exempt from reporting its military emissions in the 1997 Kyoto Protocol. Once the Paris Accord removed this exemption, the Trump administration wasted little time in abandoning these commitments.[41]

Although the amount of US military expenditure dwarfs that of all other countries – greater than the next ten biggest military spenders combined, more than the combined military budgets of the remaining 144 countries, and twice the GDP percentage average of the other G7 countries – its relation to emissions is however a matter of degree, not kind. The most comprehensive study of the relation between militarism and carbon emissions finds that from 1960 to 2014, "countries that allocate relatively higher percentages of their total GDP to the military have higher average per capita CO2 emissions, even after controlling for the size of the economy, urbanization, and adult population."[42] For low-income countries, and for Africa as a whole – that is, those least responsible for, yet most affected by, global warming – the arms race that increased military expenditure comes at the detriment of economic and social well-being, rendering them more likely to become wellsprings of mass emigration.[43]

The Struggles to Replace Gross Distortions of Perception

The reasons why elites worldwide – but those in the global metropoles of the OECD in particular – underestimate the fragility of their political systems and the broader world order are multiple, but they all relate in various ways to a misperception, or denial, of individuals' dependence upon the societies of which they are a part and the dependence of these societies, in turn, upon planetary life systems. More fundamentally, there is a misperception of the asymmetry of this dependence, betrayed as well by the ecological rallying cry of "save the planet." If by "the planet" is meant life in general, then there is little uncertainty that life – in the form of bacteria or even more complex multicellular organisms – will survive the sixth mass extinction event, even if it is further hastened by nuclear war. What needs saving – or perhaps, creating for the first time – is the durable chance of a decent life for all.

As we have seen, numerous factors contribute to this pattern of misperception, including imperial tropes of autonomy from reciprocal relations with society and nature; historical amnesia and denial of past injustices; and geographies of globalized commodity production that exacerbate these tendencies. Each, in turn, constitutes a source of fragility of the current political order: These include inadequate or utterly absent consideration of historical antecedents of a given policy or of political consequences for the public good; and a tacit or explicit reference to "value free" or "market-based, pragmatic" approaches.

Indeed, so long as GDP, the progeny of Kuznets and Keynes during the age of "carbon democracy," remains the golden bull worshipped by bean-counters the world over as the best or only relevant indicator of social well-being and progress, the global political and social order remains imperiled. But even among this economic elite, the Bank of England's former Chief Economist and Deputy Governor for Monetary Policy Professor Sir Charles Bean, observed in his 2015 Independent review of UK economic statistics that "the growth rate of GDP is often viewed" erroneously "as a 'summary statistic' for the health of the economy." Although often conflated with wealth or welfare, it is only a monetary measure of market activity over a given period, not accounting for "unpaid activities, home production and other non-market services. ... Importantly, GDP... does not reflect economic inequality or sustainability (environmental, financial or other[wise])." Relevant factors such as depreciation or depletion rates, percentage of the population engaged in economic activity (let alone essential leisure, play, and cultural activities), job quality, emissions, and physical and mental health, remain excluded. He went on to observe that its former modest utility has been further eroded by the rise of the service sector and of equally valid, but incommensurate, methods of assessing economic activity.[44]

This erosiin is exacerbated by the digital economy, which both extends the commodification of the knowledge economy and erodes its calculability, leading to often seemingly deflationary outcomes. The deficits are magnified through a partial reliance upon GDP by other, supposedly more accurate or encompassing, measures of well-being or development, such as the UN's Human Development Index (HDI). Even indices that are in principle divorced from GDP assessments, such as those measuring happiness, remain shackled to strictures of national accounting, despite abundant evidence that (like global finance) institutions and processes increasing or detracting from these accounts know no borders.

It is one thing to repeat these increasingly familiar critiques of GDP at the level of ideas, however, and quite another to transform its materiality in terms of institutions and processes that continue to decisively shape the global economy, including international organizations such as the World Bank, IMF, BIS, and WTO, and the global system of banking, credit and accounting more generally. Their profit- and growth-centric habits of mind are so deeply ingrained that it is difficult to imagine a force or actor capable of delivering an "exogenous shock" sufficient to achieve a change of course commensurate to the current threat. Indeed, it is all too easy to infer an inevitably dystopian future from the above vicious cycle of capitalist accumulation, climate devastation, refugee crises, and war – particularly if political partisanship yields only gridlocked tweaks to the status quo – above all, in the United States. The power of US capitalist interests, its culture and global dominance, all conspire to make its institutions, political culture, and leadership incommensurate to the challenges the world confronts. As Rawls put it on the eve of the Global War on Terror,

Germany between 1870 and 1945 is an example of a country where reasonably favorable conditions existed – economic, technological and no lack of resources, an educated citizenry and more – but where the political will for a democratic regime was altogether lacking. One might say the same of the United States today, if one decides our constitutional regime is largely democratic in form only.[45]

Yet the neo-Kantian approach for which Rawls is best known is itself incapable of adequately elucidating where requisite "political will" comes from. Such an insufficiently contextualized analytical focus paradoxically risks *both* neglecting or unnecessarily minimizing the significance of democratic institutions, processes, and actors in achieving "steady-state" stability, *and* insufficiently understanding the sources of their persistent underdevelopment.

Indeed, political elites and ordinary citizens alike are rarely inclined – or even able – to perceive the extent to which and ways in which their alienation from control over production processes is unsustainable. On the one hand, as Harry Dahms argues,

> the illusory nature of the superiority of the West is most evident in its unwillingness to conceive of strategies to confront the challenges that are contingent on recognizing the actual gravity and contradictory character of social structures and practices. ... Perhaps the most conspicuous case in point is ... the assumption that the Earth provides limitless resources, even though it has been evident since the beginning of modern capitalism, if not earlier, that resources are in fact limited, and that "production" is not possible without "destruction" – socially, ecologically, and organizationally.[46]

At the same time, however, he goes on to argue that this unwillingness is bound up with the extent to which we, individually and socially, are reluctant to perceive the normative dimensions of our order's sources of supposed stability, as distinct from its true robustness:

> The stability and security of social order may be contingent to a high degree on the willingness of individuals (including social scientists) to entertain as germane to understanding modern social reality, the representations a specific social order produces of itself – *precisely in order to limit transparency, as a precondition of stability* – not the social order of stability in general, but the stability of a social order in its specificity.[47]

In short, the blinkered, repressive and illusory sense of stability that capital confers systemically is itself symptomatic of humanity's most profound source of unstable fragility.

How then to break out of the prison house of collectively blinding and unsustainable misperceptions of illusory social order? Although endogenous to global systems of production and distribution, and thus entirely predictable, the Covid-19 crisis as it is now unfolding may have the effect of an "exogenous shock" potentially sufficient to this task. Functioning indeed as a preview of intensified manifestations of the climate crisis, including the likelihood of future pandemics, it has entailed seemingly unprecedented levels of disruption and reveals an immense lack of societal preparedness, as well as the manifold inequalities of government consultation, attention, and assistance (or lack thereof). Both crises underscore the importance of scientific awareness of their respective threats to wellbeing. Above all, they demonstrate the need for large-scale scientific, social, and institutional transformation in realizing a globally coordinated response with an extraordinary level of government action and societal coordination to achieve systemic change that not only abates the current threat but also builds resilience toward future threats.

Both crises are indiscriminately transboundary, with huge cross-sectoral economic impacts that affect the most vulnerable (and, typically, also the least responsible) the worst. For both, fossil fuel consumption links cause and effect. Studies link populations most severely affected by Covid-19 to areas with the worst levels of air pollution (responsible for one fifth of all deaths, or nearly 9 million, worldwide in 2018), not only because hearts and lungs are weakened by polluted air, leading to higher death rates among exposed populations, but also because dirty air makes catching the virus more likely, as pollution inflames the lungs, and could help to carry the virus further.[48] The World Health Organisation observed that localities with high levels of pollution require heightened preparation for future outbreaks.[49] Finally, both demonstrate the need for policy responses to be polyvalent in addressing both crises simultaneously.

The response to the Covid crisis by President of the Council on Foreign Relations Richard Haass furnishes a good example of an individual endorsement of a social order's specific representation of itself. More inclined to see structures of continuity than change, he argues that the Covid-19 crisis will leave the pre-pandemic world order not only remarkably intact, but with its crisis tendencies intensified in the post-pandemic period.[50] These include "waning American leadership, faltering global cooperation, [and] great-power discord" that "are likely to be even more prominent features of the world that follows." He defines leadership in military terms; although many Americans will disregard the ways in which "domestic well-being is affected by the rest of the world" and argue that the United States should "devote resources to needs at home rather than abroad, to butter rather than guns," this "is a false choice, as the country needs and can afford both."

At the same time, the "federal government's slow, … ineffective response to the pandemic will reinforce the already widespread view that the United States has lost its way," while "the near irrelevance of the World Health Organization, which should be central to meeting the threat at hand, speaks volumes to the poor state of global governance." This judgment includes CoP multilateral action on climate change – "once the crisis passes, the emphasis will shift to national recovery. In this context, it is hard to see much enthusiasm for, say, tackling climate change" – and multilateral cooperation more generally. Instead, he foresees increased support for inward investment in manufacturing, together with decreased support for US–Chinese economic investment and trade, and growing hostility to immigration and the growing ranks of refugees. The "economic toll of the pandemic will create even more weak or failing states … exacerbated by a mounting debt problem … . The developing world in particular will face enormous requirements it cannot meet," further inhibiting global economic recovery. With economic nationalism must come an erosion of civil liberties and democratic norms. Above all, multilateral progress is unlikely because "the world today is simply not conducive to being shaped. Power is distributed in more hands, both state and nonstate, than ever before. Consensus is mostly absent."[51]

By contrast, *Financial Times* journalist Simon Kuper argues that the Covid crisis has revealed hidden realms of agency for nonelites to transform their lives for the better. He cites as examples white-collar workers working from home; patients adapting to telemedicine; millions of leisure hours devoted to volunteering and care for the elderly, isolated, or vulnerable; millions of nonviolent prisoners released from prison before their punitive sentences are served; housing millions of homeless people; and improving hygiene across the board, all of which demonstrate how everyday life can, has, and should change.[52] The list can be extended indefinitely, including the capacity for the global scientific community to engage in collaboration of unprecedented breadth and speed toward the goal of developing Covid vaccines. But it should also underscore the ongoing injustices wrought by the continued imposition of the imperial mode of living upon local and global Covid responses, from police brutalization and systemic oppression of communities of color, women, and the poor, to vaccine imperialism, pointing to the need to subordinate debt and intellectual property considerations to maximizing vaccine access.[53] A rapidly globalizing awareness that health and sickness, fragility and robust solidarity, are no less global in scope, informs the imperative for climate leaders from the broadest cross section of society to build upon provisional successes and address failures in order to promote an alternative vision of social order.

The guiding thread in this vision constantly reconnects struggles against historic and ongoing social harms with those against harms to the broader biosphere: it perceives fragility and harm in the one sphere as creating fragility and harm in the other. This dual struggle toward affirming humanity's fullest realization within the most fully restored environment, by way of the most rapid and equitable decarbonization of the atmosphere possible, is not the same as viewing the environment or nature as pristine or external, but as indispensably integral to a good life for all.

This vision is and should remain inimical to the ever-present threat posed by neo-Malthusian assumptions insisting either that ever-increasing consumption of commodities is indispensable to well-being, or that universal access to decent work, food, and living conditions is impossible, or both. Nothing better exemplifies perverse and futile jeopardy than repeated denials that limiting warming to 1.5°C is possible;

nonetheless, a neo-Malthusian posture is probably the most common variant of the "rhetoric of reaction" so aptly dissected by A. O. Hirschman.[54] It is also entirely consonant with the "imperial mode of living" discussed above in its view of the intractability of warming, the externality of nature to society, and by extension, the externality of peasants and working classes to the subject position of the reactionary in question. Malthus's baseless argument that it was inevitable that the sexes, being subject to "natural passions," would cause geometric population increases in the face of an immutable nature able to yield food at only an arithmetic rate, was far from despairing. Rather, he celebrated the inequality and poverty created by scarcity, because the ensuing proletarianization of workers (denied access to lands previously used in common by centuries of enclosures) provided "the foundation of industry" leading "not to despair but activity."[55] It exemplifies what Ted Benton has termed an "epistemic conservatism" that celebrates the heteronomous subjugations of the status quo and resists "emancipatory projects on broadly cognitive grounds"; or, in Adorno's trenchant phrase, a "bourgeois love of people as they are stems from [its] hatred of what they might be."[56]

This posture is in full evidence in Haas's insistence that "faltering global cooperation, great-power discord," and lack of collective will to "tackle global warming" are inevitable, no less than his presumption that increased US militarism is necessary, desirable, and separate from global warming concerns. It is also discernable in the "Underestimating the Challenges" report's disproportionate concern over population growth as opposed to corporate control over resources and labor for profit. It highlights how "large population size and continued growth are implicated in many societal problems," and when "combined with an imperfect distribution of resources, leads to massive food insecurity." But rather than elaborate upon the ways in which resources are imperfectly distributed, it goes on to detail overpopulation as a driver of "soil degradation and biodiversity loss, ... dangerous throw-away plastics," increased "chances of pandemics," "ever-more desperate hunts for scarce resources," "crowding and joblessness," "deteriorating infrastructure, bad governance ... and war".[57] The authors never ask themselves why, for example, they perceive a Malian fertility rate less than four times that of the United States to be more alarming – or more of a causal factor in all these negative outcomes – than a US CO_2 per capita emissions rate 100 times that of Mali's.[58] For democratic and ecological orders to become more robust than at present, the inverse perspective needs to become part of a hegemonic common-sense.

Conclusion

These instances of epistemic conservatism bear a family resemblance, ironically, to the motivated climate denialism discussed earlier in their reluctance to question and move beyond epistemological frames of reference such as those equating GDP with well-being and development. There are doubtless more such frames relevant to the entwined ecological and democratic crises than can be enumerated here. The question of the subject-position of those perceiving fragility or robustness is clearly bound up with their chosen criteria and means of assessment of a complex totality that will always remain contested. Those who own, manage, and control the industrial and financial order – proprietors of the imperial mode of living and thus prime agents of its further colonization of life-worlds and biospheres – are, if not monolithic in outlook, then at best, tendentially disinclined to take steps to reverse this colonization, and with it, global warming and mass extinction.

Those most squarely in the crosshairs of these agents and thus, in a sense, their polar opposites, are humanity's most radical conservatives, consigned to eradication by capitalist modernity's grand narrative of progress, yet still tenaciously surviving: the global communities of the peasantry and indigenous peoples. Typically marginalized by liberal democratic institutions, these communities do better than all others at minimizing harmful impacts upon their biomes, precisely because their lives, livelihoods, and ways of life are so deeply dependent upon them.[59]

Although more numerous than the proprietors of the imperial mode of living, these marginalized communities need allies among the nonindigenous, non-owning global majority in order to survive, no less than the rest of humanity needs these communities to continue as vanguards of ecological stewardship. The limitations of dominant representations of nature relate as well to those of political representation: blinkered framings of stability premised on growth and hierarchies of power separate human nature from nature and deny the interdependence of humanity with all forms of life exemplified by these vanguards.

As Joel Wainwright and Geoff Mann convincingly argue, such allies are most likely to be found not among blocs of states, but rather among grassroots participants of what they term "Climate X" – an assemblage of mutually recognized movements of "disruptive countersovereignty" whose participants advocate universal equality, the inclusion and dignity of all in struggles for self-determination, and pluralistic solidarity.[60]

With reference to this volume's leitmotif concerning ways of seeing and knowing fragility and robustness, Wainwright and Mann's vision of a

Realism beyond states poses several urgent questions. To the question of how this assemblage can reliably recognize these vanguard communities, a "first-order" answer is relatively straightforward: The indigenous communities are those that foster ecological robustness most completely, and as a consequence, typically suffer the greatest levels of existential fragility.

A more difficult question is how this assemblage recognizes its fellow members – those who guard the guardians of our fragile ecological order while seeking to strengthen it through disruptive countersovereignty. How can they reestablish the immanence of critical theory, refusing to take at face value the tasks that dominant powers assign to contemporary society, but instead brings struggles and contradictions to the fore?[61]

One approach to an answer is suggested by one of Adorno's best-known aphorisms, "The splinter in your eye is the best magnifying glass."[62] An intact and unbroken magnifying glass might be said to widen a Cartesian subject–object duality, while missing the burning rainforest for the subset of healthy trees. Riffing on the injunction against judging in the Gospel of Matthew 7:3, the "splinter" is suggestive of both a painful shard that inhibits normal sight, as well as a prism that enlarges perception of the world's pain and suffering, precisely by enabling a sympathetic and empathetic community of suffering.[63] This latter meaning thus amplifies Adorno's contention elsewhere that "the need to lend a voice to suffering is a condition for all truth."[64] Suffering here becomes a condition for the need to lend a voice to others' suffering, not least when others – whether human (including dead victims of past injustices) or animal, as Bentham reminds us – have no voice of their own.[65] In this context, the coal miner's canary is both a metaphor for social fragility and emblematic of ecological fragility.[66] Communities of suffering can thus reinscribe human nature in both history and nature, as well as provide a further means of reconnecting collective self-determination with reflexive self-relation.

A splintered magnifying glass cannot reveal all sufferings and struggles in a single panoptic sweep; but it can reanimate all prior struggles, however faltering or compromised they have become over time, including the labor, women's, peace, and anticolonial movements and struggles, among others. The video of a single act of police brutality can retrospectively illuminate and connect thousands of others that had all but vanished in the prevailing order's solitary confinement. The momentary shattering of this order affords the chance to reimagine a world in which all can safely breathe.

Notes

1 Corey Bradshaw, Ehrlich, P.R., Beattie, A., Ceballos, G., Crist, E., Diamond, J., Dirzo, R., Ehrlich, A.H., Harte, J., Harte, M.E. and Pyke, G., Underestimating the Challenges of Avoiding a Ghastly Future. *Frontiers in Conservation Science* 2, no. 1 (2021), pp. 1–9. Accessible at: https://doi.org/10.3389/fcosc.2020.615419
2 Bradshaw, Underestimating, p. 8.
3 Antonio Gramsci, *Prison Notebooks*, v. 1–3. Edited and translated by Joseph A. Buttigieg with Antonio Callari. (New York: Columbia University Press, 2011).
4 Samuel Huntington, *The Third Wave: Democratization in the Late Twentieth Century* (Norman, OK: University of Oklahoma Press, 1993).
5 Justin Farrell, Corporate Funding and Ideological Polarization about Climate Change. *Proceedings of the National Academy of Sciences*, 113(1), (2016) pp. 92–97.
6 Oliver Milman, US is Hotbed of Climate Change Denial, Major Global Survey Finds. *The Guardian*, 09 May 2019. Accessible at: www.theguardian.com/environment/2019/may/07/us-hotbed-climate-change-denial-international-poll; Peter Howe, Mildenberger, M., Marlon, J.R. and Leiserowitz, A., Geographic Variation in Opinions on Climate Change at State and Local Scales in the USA. *Nature Climate Change*, 5(6), (2015), pp. 596–603.
7 Gabriela Wong-Parodi and Irena Feygina, Understanding and Countering the Motivated Roots of Climate Change Denial. *Current Opinion in Environmental Sustainability* 42, (2020), pp. 60–64.
8 Tien Ming Lee, Ezra Markowitz, Peter Howe, Chia-Ying Ko, and Anthony Leiserowitz, Predictors of Public Climate Change Awareness and Risk Perception around the World. *Nature Climate Change* 5, no. 11 (2015), pp. 1014–1020.
9 Lee, *Predictors*, p. 1015.
10 Hübscher, Evelyne, Thomas Sattler, and Markus Wagner. Does Austerity Cause Political Polarization and Fragmentation? SSRN 3541546. DOI: 10.2139/ssrn.3541546
11 Michel Aglietta, *A Theory of Capitalist Regulation: The US Experience* (London: New Left Books, 1979).
12 Ulrich Brand and Markus Wissen, Global Environmental Politics and the Imperial Mode of Living: Articulations of State–Capital Relations in the Multiple Crisis. *Globalizations*, 9, 4 (2012), pp. 547–556: 550; Ulrich Brand and Markus Wissen, Crisis and continuity of capitalist society-nature relationships: The imperial mode of living and the limits to environmental governance. *Review of International Political Economy*, 20, 4 (2013), pp. 687–711.
13 According to calculations by the Mercator Institute on Global Commons and Climate Change, for example, 2029 is the year in which the remaining CO_2 budget (i.e., the amount of fossil fuel consumption at current rates until the IPCC's 1.5°C warming target is reached) gets used up – underscoring the inadequacy of virtually all "carbon neutral" targets set any later. Mercator Institute, Remaining Carbon Budget: That's how fast the carbon clock is

ticking. Mercator Institute on Global Commons and Climate Change (2020). Accessible at: www.mcc-berlin.net/en/research/co2-budget.html
14 Ian Parker, Critical Psychology and Revolutionary Marxism. *Theory & Psychology* 19, no. 1 (2009), pp. 71–92.
15 Noel Castree, The Nature of Produced Nature: Materiality and Knowledge Construction in Marxism. *Antipode* 271, (1995), pp. 12–48.
16 John Locke, *Political Writings*. Wooton, D., ed. (New York: Mentor, 1993), pp. 262, 230.
17 Locke, *Political Writings*, p. 277.
18 James Scott, *Decoding Subaltern Politics: Ideology, Disguise, and Resistance in Agrarian Politics* (London: Routledge, 2012).
19 Karen Ng, Ideology Critique from Hegel and Marx to Critical Theory. *Constellations*, 22, 3 (September 2015), pp. 393–404: 395–96 (emphasis in text).
20 Ng, "Ideology Critique," p. 397.
21 Ng, "Ideology Critique," p. 397.
22 Ng, "Ideology Critique," p. 399.
23 Karl Marx, *Capital*, vol. I (New York: Vintage, 1976), pp. 637–638; John Bellamy Foster, *Marx's Ecology: Materialism and Nature* (New York: Monthly Review Press, 2000): pp. 155–64; 170–73; Kohei Saito, *Karl Marx's Ecosocialism: Capital, Nature, and the Unfinished Critique of Political Economy* (New York: NYU Press, 2017).
24 Timothy Mitchell, *Carbon Democracy: Political Power in the Age of Oil.* (London: Verso, 2011), pp. 247, 241.
25 Robert Solow, The Economics of Resources or the Resources of Economics. *American Economics Review* 64, no. 2 (1974), pp. 1–14: p. 11; Richard Lane, The American Anthropocene: Economic Scarcity and Growth during the Great Acceleration. *Geoforum* 99 (2019), pp. 11–21: p. 17.
26 Mark Mazower, *Governing the World: The History of an Idea, 1815 to the Present* (New York: Penguin Books, 2013), p. 102. Two of the ISO's more recent codified standards – ISO 14007 (Environmental management: Determining environmental costs and benefits) and ISO 14008 (Monetary valuation of environmental impacts and related environmental aspects) – aim to put a price tag on environmental impacts resulting from organizations' economic activities (ISO 14008) and supporting an environmental cost/benefit analysis to relate such impacts to decision-making processes (ISO 14007), with the mutual goal of enabling putatively "sustainable" decision-making by governments and firms, as well as competing with alternative accounting approaches. Sylvain Maechler and Jean-Christophe Graz, The Standardisation of Natural Capital Accounting Methodologies, in Kai Jakobs, K. (ed.), *Shaping the Future Through Standardization* (Hershey, PA: IGI Global, 2020), Chapter 2, pp. 27–53.
27 William D. Nordhaus, To Tax or Not to Tax: Alternative Approaches to Slowing Global Warming. *Review of Environmental Economics and Policy* 1(1) (2007), pp. 26–44; p. 30. DOI:10.1093/reep/rem008.
28 William Nordhaus, Projections and uncertainties about climate change in an era of minimal climate policies. *American Economic Journal: Economic Policy* 10, no. 3 (2018), pp. 333–60.

29 Nordhaus, Projections and uncertainties. This erroneous supposition was previously asserted by Nordhaus in William D. Nordhaus, To Slow or Not to Slow: The Economics of The Greenhouse Effect, *The Economic Journal* 101, no 407, 1 July 1991, pp. 920–37. Evidence of its far-reaching influence is found in its being reproduced intact in the IPCC's Report, Climate Change 2014: Impacts, Adaptation, and Vulnerability. Part A: Global and Sectoral Aspects, p. 688, accessible at: www.ipcc.ch/site/assets/uploads/2018/02/WGIIAR5-PartA_FINAL.pdf . See Steve Keen, The appallingly bad neoclassical economics of climate change. *Globalizations*, (2020), pp. 1–29.

30 Orazio P. Attanasio, Frank P. Ramsey, Frank Ramsey's A Mathematical Theory of Saving. *The Economic Journal* 125, no. 583, (2015), pp. 269–94.

31 Kevin Bloom, Interview: South Africa, climate change "hot spot." *Daily Maverick*, 07 November 2018. Accessible at: www.dailymaverick.co.za/article/2018-11-07-interview-south-africa-climate-change-hot-spot/

32 Jason Hickel, The Nobel Prize for Climate Catastrophe, *Foreign Policy*, 06 December 2018, accessible at: https://foreignpolicy.com/2018/12/06/the-nobel-prize-for-climate-catastrophe/

33 Brand and Wissen, Crisis and continuity, p. 601.

34 Bob Jessop, The State and the Contradictions of the Knowledge-Driven Economy. In Bryson, J., Daniels, P., Henry, N., and Pollard, J. (eds.) *Knowledge, Space, Economy*, (London: Routledge, 2000), pp. 63–78.

35 Jessop, The State and the Contradictions, p. 77.

36 David Harvey, *Spaces of Capital: Towards a Critical Geography* (New York: Routledge, 2001).

37 Department of Defense, Report on Effects of a Changing Climate to the Department of Defense, January 2019. (RefID: 9-D30BE5A. Washington, DC: Office of the Under Secretary of Defense for Acquisition and Sustainment). Accessible at: https://climateandsecurity.org/wp-content/uploads/2019/01/sec_335_ndaa-report_effects_of_a_changing_climate_to_dod.pdf

38 "Why do you laugh? Change but the name and this story is about us" (in the original, "about you"). Horatius, *The Satires of Horace*, A.M. Juster, trans. (Philadelphia, PA: University of Pennsylvania Press, 2012).

39 Oliver Belcher, Patrick Bigger, Ben Neimark, and Cara Kennelly, Hidden carbon costs of the "everywhere war": Logistics, geopolitical ecology, and the carbon boot-print of the US military. *Transactions of the Institute of British Geographers* 45(1), (2020), pp. 65–80.

40 Neta C. Crawford, *Pentagon Fuel Use, Climate Change, and the Costs of War* (Providence, RI: Watson Institute, Brown University, 2019). Accessible at: https://watson.brown.edu/costsofwar/files/cow/imce/papers/Pentagon%20Fuel%20Use%2C%20Climate%20Change%20and%20the%20Costs%20of%20War%20Revised%20November%202019%20Crawford.pdf

41 Arthur Nelsen, Why the U.S. Military Is Losing Its Carbon-Emissions Exemption. *The Atlantic*, 15 December 2015. Accessible at: www.theatlantic.com/science/archive/2015/12/paris-climate-deal-military-carbon-emissions-exemption/420399/

42 John Hamilton Bradford and Alexander M. Stoner, The Treadmill of Destruction in Comparative Perspective: A Panel Study of Military Spending and Carbon Emissions, 1960–2014. *Journal of World-Systems Research* 23 no. 2, (2017), pp. 298–325.
43 Charles Shaaba and Nicholas Ngepah, Empirical Analysis of Military Expenditure and Industrialisation Nexus: A Regional Approach for Africa. *International Economic Journal* 34 no. 1, (2020), pp. 58–84.
44 Charles Bean, Independent review of UK economic statistics: interim report (2015), p. 9. Accessible at: https://assets.publishing.service.gov.uk/government/uploads/system/uploads/attachment_data/file/481452/Bean_review_Interim_Report_web.pdf
45 John Rawls, *Justice as Fairness* (Cambridge, MA: Belknap/Harvard University Press, 2001), p. 101.
46 Harry Dahms, *No Social Science without Critical Theory* (Bingley, UK: Emerald Group Publishing, 2008), p. 5.
47 Dahms, *No Social Science*, p. 15.
48 Frontera, Antonio, Lorenzo Cianfanelli, Konstantinos Vlachos, Giovanni Landoni, and George Cremona, Severe Air Pollution Links to Higher Mortality in COVID-19 Patients: The "double-hit" Hypothesis. *Journal of Infection* 81, no. 2 (2020), pp. 255–59; Karn Vohra et al., Global Mortality from Outdoor Fine Particle Pollution Generated by Fossil Fuel Combustion: Results from GEOS-Chem. *Environmental Research*, (2021), p. 110754.
49 Surinder Suthar, et al., Epidemiology and Diagnosis, Environmental Resources Quality and Socio-Economic Perspectives for COVID-19 Pandemic. *Journal of Environmental Management* (2020), 1–14.
50 Richard Haass, The Pandemic Will Accelerate History Rather than Reshape It. *Foreign Affairs*, 07 April 2020. Accessible at: www.foreignaffairs.com/articles/united-states/2020-04-07/pandemic-will-accelerate-history-rather-reshape-it
51 Haass, The Pandemic Will Accelerate.
52 Simon Kuper, The Pandemic Will Forever Transform How We Live, *Financial Times*, 09 April 2020, accessible at: www.ft.com/content/06647198-77b9-11ea-9840-1b8019d9a987
53 See e.g. the Gates Foundation's role in thwarting universal, decommodified access to the vaccine developed by Oxford University's Jenner Institute, leading to artificial scarcities: Achal Prabhala and Leena Menghaney, The World's Poorest Countries Are at India's Mercy for Vaccines. It's Unsustainable, *The Guardian*, 02 April 2021; accessible at www.theguardian.com/commentisfree/2021/apr/02/india-in-charge-of-developing-world-covid-vaccine-supply-unsustainable
54 Albert O. Hirschman, *The Rhetoric of Reaction: Perversity, Futility, Jeopardy*. Cambridge, MA: Belknap/Harvard University Press, 1991.
55 Thomas Robert Malthus, *Essay on the Principle of Population* (London: J. Johnson, 1798), pp. 19–20. Giorgos Kallis persuasively counterposes a Malthusian, heteronomous understanding of limits of nature – celebrated by defenders of the capitalist status quo and abstracted from politically imposed inequalities in a manner characteristic of much contemporary

ecological thought – with an older, autonomous understanding of limits that understands nature and the world as abundant because it is sufficient, deriving from collective practices of self-limitation, such as the precapitalist agricultural commoning once prevalent in Britain and throughout the world. See Giorgos Kallis, *Limits: Why Malthus Was Wrong and Why Environmentalists Should Care* (Stanford, CA: Stanford University Press, 2019).

56 Ted Benton, The Malthusian Challenge: Ecology, Natural Limits and Human Emancipation. In Osborne, P. (Ed.)(1991). *Socialism and the Limits of Liberalism* (London: Verso, 1991), pp. 241–69: p. 241; Theodor Adorno, *Minima Moralia*, trans. E. F. N. Jephcott (London: Verso, 1978), p. 25.
57 Bradshaw, Underestimating.
58 World Bank, CO_2 emissions (metric tons per capita), (2021). Accessible at: https://data.worldbank.org/indicator/EN.ATM.CO2E.PC?locations=1W
59 Stephen T. Garnett, Neil D. Burgess, et al. A Spatial Overview of the Global Importance of Indigenous Lands for Conservation. *Nature Sustainability* 1, no. 7 (2018), pp. 369–74.
60 Joel Wainwright and Geoff Mann, *Climate Leviathan: A Political Theory of Our Planetary Future* (London: Verso Books, 2018), pp. 175–95.
61 For an account of how the Frankfurt School's attempt to realize this goal faltered, see Stathis Kouvelakis, *La critique défaite: Emergence et domestication de la Théorie Critique: Horkheimer, Habermas, Honneth* (Paris: Éditions Amsterdam, 2019).
62 Adorno, *Minima Moralia*, p. 26.
63 This theme is further elaborated in Martin Jay, *Splinters in the Eye: Frankfurt School Provocations* (London: Verso, London, 2020).
64 Theodor Adorno, *Negative Dialectics*, trans. E. B. Ashton (London: Routledge, 1973), pp. 17–18.
65 Bentham's key question remains pertinent, beyond a discourse of rights: "The question is not, Can they reason? nor Can they talk? but, Can they suffer?" Jeremy Bentham, *An Introduction to the Principles of Morals and Legislation* (Oxford: Clarendon, [1789], 1907).
66 Lani Guinier and Gerald Torres, *The Miner's Canary: Enlisting Race, Resisting Power, Transforming Democracy* (Cambridge, MA: Harvard University Press, 2003).

6 The End of Communist Rule in Europe: A Comparative Perspective on the Fragility and Robustness of Regimes

Archie Brown

To speak of a "robust regime" is another way of saying that the regime – or political system – is unlikely to collapse or be overturned. Robustness may flow from long and respected tradition, severe and effective coercion, or democratic legitimacy – or a combination of two of the three. In the first of these categories, citizens obey laws and accept the decisions of their rulers largely because they have known no other form of government. Habit and lack of experience of alternatives are conducive to compliance. A tradition of autocratic government or a tradition of democratic governance makes for a political culture more accepting of authoritarian norms in the former case and fosters expectations of adherence to democratic values in the latter.

Tradition, however, is not destiny. Every country that today counts as democratic was at one time authoritarian, for democracy at a country-wide level is a relatively modern development.[1] At least half of the world's population lives under a greater or lesser degree of authoritarian rule. Furthermore, in the twenty-first century there have been serious violations of democratic norms and manifestations of authoritarianism not only in recently democratized countries (including several post-Communist states) but also in the land that has long regarded itself as the world's leading democracy – the United States. Donald Trump's disregard for constitutional convention, his undermining of democratic institutions, and his willful and groundless refusal to accept the outcome of the 2020 American presidential election impaired trust in the rules of the game of accountable government. His conduct was a reminder that democracy should never be taken for granted; it is always a work in progress. As the Nigerian writer Chimamanda Ngozi Adichie lamented, "Trump showed me how fragile democracy is, how fragile what we consider the norms are."[2]

That was before a Trump-incited mob forced their way into the Capitol building on 6 January 2021, a last straw that led to Trump's second impeachment by the House of Representatives. Fiona Hill, who served as Deputy Assistant to the President and Senior Director for European and Russian Affairs on the National Security Council from 2017 to 2019, was in no doubt that Trump was "trying to stage a coup." His warm words to his followers who were about to march on the Capitol building, she suggested, could be seen as but a substitute for a still more serious attempt to implement his rejection of the electoral outcome – thwarted, Hill observed, by the unprecedented open letter signed by all ten living American former Defense Secretaries.[3] Trump's attempt to overturn the result of the November 2020 election, and thus subvert American democracy, was abetted by the support of a substantial minority of Republican members of both Houses of Congress.[4] Their postelection antics were a reminder that democracy, like liberty, requires constant vigilance as well as politicians who value it in word and deed. Attempts to nullify democracy, the more especially when they are the actions of elected legislators, call for both legal and political accountability. The United States has shown how easily democracy can degenerate into nepotism, plutocracy, and potentially dictatorship, abetted by the personality cult of a would-be "strongman."[5] Although Trump was repudiated by a clear majority of citizens and the Electoral College in the presidential election and by still larger numbers after his anticonstitutional attempt to hang on to power, the level of support he could, nevertheless, command leaves no room for complacency about the robustness of American democracy.[6] In his inclusive and generally optimistic inauguration speech, America's forty-sixth president Joe Biden did not shirk the issue of the precariousness of democracy, even in the United States. He noted that recent events meant that they had "learned again" that "democracy is fragile," but "at this hour," democracy had prevailed.[7]

In authoritarian states where the rulers have powers that Trump envied but did not possess, a robust stability rests in part on long experience of such rule. No government, as David Hume observed long ago, relies on coercion or raw power alone in order to gain compliance.[8] Nevertheless, the dire consequences of challenging particular decisions of autocratic or oligarchical rulers (never mind questioning their *right* to rule) have been a large part of the explanation of conformist behavior in most authoritarian states. Naked power and the willingness to deploy it ruthlessly buttress authoritarian regimes. Perceptions, however, matter, and perceptions can alter. If people perceive that hundreds of thousands of their fellow-citizens are likely to come on to the streets in defiance of a despotic regime, they will be much more willing to join the resistance than if the likeliest result of overt opposition is deemed to be isolation, arrest, and imprisonment. The large-scale and sustained peaceful protests in Belarus against Alexander Lukashenko's rigged reelection in 2020 and against the seizure of absolute power by the military in Myanmar in 2021 (even though the army was already a powerful force within the coalition led by Aung San Suu Kwi) are recent examples of courageous opposition to dictatorship. Enough people believed that weight of numbers gave protest at least a chance of success against a brutal autocrat in the one instance and an even more brutal junta in the other.

The third main alternative foundation of robust stability is democratic legitimacy. As Robert Dahl noted, throughout the twentieth century many critics believed democracy to be doomed. Yet, "experience revealed that once democratic institutions were firmly established in a democracy, they would prove to be remarkably sturdy and resilient."[9] Consolidated democracies do not, as a rule, revert to authoritarianism, even if developments in the twenty-first century have underlined that it would be most unwise to see that generalization as an iron law. In an important study of democratization, Juan Linz and Alfred Stepan noted that "Constitutionally, democracy becomes the only game in town when all the actors in the polity become habituated to the fact that political conflict will be resolved according to the established norms and that violations of these norms are likely to be both ineffective and costly."[10] But they are careful to note that when they say "a regime is a consolidated democracy, we do not preclude the possibility that at some future time it could break down."[11]

Shifts from robustness of regimes to fragility can occur quite quickly (as Ned Lebow notes in Chapter 2). The underlying sources of change may be relatively dormant for decades, suppressed by coercion and bolstered by the perception that to rebel would ruin the individual's own life while producing no useful outcome for the broader society. But aspirations that seem more of an indulgent dream than practical prospect can quite suddenly appear realizable when new facilitating conditions or stimuli emerge. For all the Washington rhetoric of the 1950s about "rolling back" Communism in Eastern Europe, those regimes rolled on until the late 1980s. So long as the Soviet leadership had the political will to maintain their hegemony over Eastern Europe, they had the military power to enforce it. The facilitating conditions for the end of Communist rule in Eastern Europe were radical reform of the Soviet political system and the transformation of Soviet foreign policy. During the first term of Ronald Reagan's American presidency, neither political elites nor citizens in the United States, the Soviet Union, Western Europe or (most pertinently) Eastern Europe had any expectation of this happening.

Moreover, the West as a whole and the United States in particular ("rollback" rhetoric notwithstanding) accepted that there was a Soviet sphere of influence – indeed, a "Soviet bloc." Much though governments in the United States or Western Europe might deplore the crushing of the Hungarian revolution in 1956, the military intervention in Czechoslovakia in 1968 that put an end to the "Prague Spring," and the imposition of martial law in Poland in December 1981 (pressed on the Polish Communist leadership by the Kremlin), they were not able to do anything to prevent those outcomes. In the last case mentioned, Solidarity was reduced from mass political movement to small underground organization, and its leaders were imprisoned. The dramatic resurgence of Solidarity in 1988–89 was far less reflective of change in the aspirations of Poles, a majority of whom in *all* postwar decades aspired to national independence and an end to Communist rule, than of political change in Moscow.

An important factor over the long term in the robustness or fragility of Communist states was the extent to which national sentiment could be mobilized in support of the regime or whether, on the contrary, Communist rule felt like a foreign imposition. In the latter case, matching the regime's institutional domination with popular acceptance of its ideology and values was more difficult. In contrast, it is not accidental that four of the five surviving Communist states are in Asia – China, North Korea, Vietnam, and Laos – and that the fifth is Cuba. When those four parties came to power in Asia, they were surfing a strong anti-imperialist, anticolonial tide. The Chinese Communists fought a bitter civil war with Chiang Kai-shek's Nationalists, but they, too, appealed to national pride, with their stress on ending humiliation at the hands of imperialist states and on China becoming a great power to be reckoned with.

Anti-Americanism specifically was a powerful sentiment advantageous for the Communist leadership in North Korea, especially during and after the Korean War. In Vietnam, the United States took the place of the French as the main imperialist enemy. The United States fought an unsuccessful war that, as David Elliott observed, "was never about Vietnam, but always about some larger abstraction of concern to the United States – containing China, dominos, credibility."[12] American bombing of Laos during the Vietnam War did not prevent Communists seizing the whole of Laos by the mid-1970s, but it did help to ensure that in Laos, too, hostility to the United States became a rallying cry. Anti-imperialism and resentment of the US was significant also in Cuba. Although there had been American help in the liberation of the island from Spanish rule at the end of the nineteenth century, the

United States was widely regarded by Cubans as Spain's successor colonial power. Hostility to the island's giant northern neighbor was stoked by the links between the corrupt Batista regime and disreputable American business interests and later intensified by US attempts to remove Fidel Castro from power.

A Communist state was more robust if the ruling group or party had made their own revolution rather than being placed in power through foreign agency. Of the five currently remaining Communist states, this was most clearly true of China, Vietnam, and Cuba. In the Cuban case, it was not initially a *Communist* revolution, but it *was* indigenous. In the Eastern half of the European continent only the Soviet Union, Yugoslavia, and Albania are reasonably clear-cut cases of indigenous revolution. It is more than a coincidence, therefore, that it was the Yugoslav and Albanian leaderships that had the self-confidence to break (for quite different reasons) with the Soviet leadership and yet to survive for decades longer as Communist states without being members of the Warsaw Pact. Among the Soviet Union's Warsaw Pact allies, Czechoslovakia's Communist leadership had the strongest claim to have seized power indigenously, although it was more of a coup than a revolution. The Soviet army was not present in the country when the Czech Communists, who had become the largest single party in free elections in 1946 and were part of a coalition government, seized full power in February 1948.

The Czech and Slovak Communists (the latter fewer in number even in proportion to the smaller population of Slovakia) did not, however, question Stalin's position at the head of the international Communist movement, and before long Soviet "advisers" were influencing their choice of people to be arrested, which in some cases led to execution. The victims were not just political opponents but included prominent members of the Communist Party of Czechoslovakia. The last years of Stalin saw anti-Semitic purges in the Soviet Union and in countries of the Soviet bloc. The most prominent Communists to be arrested in Czechoslovakia were disproportionately of Jewish origin and they included none other than the party' general secretary from 1945 to 1951, Rudolf Slansky. Following a show trial, he was hanged in late 1952. Czechoslovakia had been largely free of anti-Semitism until Stalin's malign influence was brought to bear. Yet, compared with Poland, Hungary, or the GDR (East Germany), Communism in Czechoslovakia in the early postwar years, and even after the power grab of 1948, had substantial indigenous support.

Communists rarely constituted a majority in the countries in which they came to power at the time they seized the reins of government.

Lenin's party did not even have a majority among Russian socialists at the time of the October Revolution (as the Bolsheviks termed their seizure of power), but they did capture power indigenously. Their takeover was not orchestrated by forces outside Russia, though Lenin benefitted from German complicity in his return to Russia from exile, since this was in 1917 and his opposition to Russian participation in the war was helpful for Germany.

The Soviet Union was, indeed, a prime example of a country in which Leninists not only came to power as a result of their own revolutionary efforts but subsequently acquired a form of patriotic legitimacy, especially as a result of the country's immense suffering and ultimate triumphs in World War II. The wartime tribulations of the people, with civilian and military casualties jointly amounting to approximately twenty-seven million dead, along with the Soviet army's decisive role in winning the ground war in Europe over Nazi Germany, added a patriotic weight to the robustness of the regime. Memories of the war, real and embellished, were used effectively by the Soviet leadership, especially in the years (1964–82) in which Leonid Brezhnev headed the Communist Party of the Soviet Union (CPSU).

Institutional controls, nevertheless, remained extremely important for securing compliance with the edicts of the party-state. The permeation of the society by the Communist Party, to which about one in ten members of the adult population belonged, and the presence of the KGB and their informers within every place of employment and of education made forcing change from below unthinkable over many decades. Alongside party and police permeation of society, a significant contribution to the longevity of the regime was played by a more subtle system of graduated rewards for conformist behavior and a hierarchy of sanctions, of varying severity over time, for heterodoxy (with the punishments becoming draconian for overt opposition).

Any regime that does not accord its own people the right to hold it to account and to change the government of the day through democratic elections is *potentially* fragile. It may last for many decades, but it can collapse quickly in a crisis, if it is faced by nonviolent mass protest or violent unrest, especially when this is accompanied by splits within the ruling elite. Yet, authoritarian regimes led by a ruling party tend to be more stable than autocracies that lack such a buttress, for "ruling parties underpin durable authoritarianism by providing a political setting for mediating elite disputes and preventing elite defections to the opposition."[13] And even among ruling-party regimes, the relative robustness of Communist systems is especially striking. In addition to the sophisticated system of institutional controls, including the censorship and strict oversight of the mass media, there was (and, to a much more limited extent, still is in the surviving Communist regimes) a comprehensive ideology that purported to explain all political and social phenomena. Communism also provided and imposed a language of politics that determined the way in which public political discourse was conducted and, in the case of long-lasting regimes, influenced the categories in which many people thought.[14] That was more the case with those Communist systems that had been established indigenously than those that existed only as a result of foreign imposition. Such a conceptual hegemony was especially to be found in systems that had lasted over many decades – much truer, in other words, of the Soviet Union (the Russian republic in particular) than of Poland.

The keys to understanding both the relative robustness of East European Communist regimes, which lasted between forty and fifty years, *and* their fragility lie in the history and politics of their relationship with Russia and the Soviet Union, where Communist rule lasted for approximately seventy years. In every central and east European country there were local Communists who were happy to assume a monopoly of power. Yet, with the partial exceptions of Yugoslavia, Albania, and Czechoslovakia, they were able to form a government only because the Soviet leadership had determined that every East European country liberated from Nazi domination by Soviet forces must adopt a Soviet-style system in which that country's Communist rulers would accept Moscow as the ultimate source of authority. Compliance of the population was to be secured by the usual Communist controls and policies. The latter produced winners as well as losers. Industrialization turned many peasants into workers, some workers became officials in the service of the party-state, and children of workers were given preferential treatment for admission to higher educational institutions, making for substantial upward (and, in the case of the displaced bourgeoisie, downward) mobility.

For most of the postwar decades, reliable political opinion polling data were lacking in the East European countries, for it was only on rare occasions – such as Czechoslovakia in 1968 – that questions could be asked on the most sensitive issues and respondents could feel secure in answering honestly. Nevertheless, there is every reason to suppose that East European citizens – notwithstanding the political socialization carried out by each Communist party-state, with varying degrees of success – would have opted in any one of the postwar decades to reject their Moscow-subservient rulers, had they felt (which, with good reason, they did not) that they could do so with impunity. Yet the stability of the East European Communist states was far from absolute, even in the decades before it ceased to exist altogether. There were worker uprisings in Pilsen (Czechoslovakia) and in East Berlin in 1953, a revolution in Hungary in 1956 (crushed by Soviet tanks), massive protests in Poland in the same year, the "Prague Spring" of 1968 (ended by a Soviet-led intervention of Warsaw Pact forces) and the challenge to the Polish Communist regime posed by "Solidarity" – the labor union that became a socio-political mass movement – in 1980–81 (outlawed with the imposition of martial law in December 1981). What all the various crackdowns underlined for the citizens of the East-Central European states was that behind their local Communist rulers stood the formidable coercive force of the Soviet Union. They concluded – just as Western governments had – that for the Kremlin the preservation of these Soviet-style regimes, with governments loyal to Moscow, was nonnegotiable. Until the mid-1980s that was a well-founded assumption.

Three Popular but Misleading Conceptions

If far-reaching change in the Soviet Union was the facilitating condition for what happened in East-Central Europe in 1989, it matters all the more to clear away popular misconceptions about why that change occurred. Three assumptions or propositions often voiced by Western politicians and commentators are (1) that the Soviet Union was in crisis in the mid-1980s; (2) that reform was an unavoidable response to that crisis; and (3) that any reform was doomed to fail since Communism was unreformable. These propositions were not much aired in advance of the transformation and disintegration of the USSR, but they became increasingly popular once the dramatic changes had occurred. Even though they result from hindsight rather than foresight, the first two assumptions are wrong and the third is an oversimplification. The Soviet Union had problems in the mid-1980s, but it was *not* in crisis. Lack of freedom and democracy was nothing new, and there were no public demonstrations demanding either the one or the other. This was a thoroughly consolidated highly authoritarian regime. Economic growth had slowed to a trickle, and that was a substantial problem, especially when it was accompanied by a low price on world markets for Soviet oil and gas. But if the existence of significant problems were to be synonymous with crisis, few states would be exempt from that predicament. An authoritarian regime *is* in crisis when its laws and commands are no longer obeyed, when there is persistent mass protest, and especially when such societal unrest is accompanied by open splits within the ruling elite.[15] Nothing of the kind was to be found in the Soviet Union in the first half of the 1980s or at the mid-decade point when Gorbachev became Soviet leader. Even during the totally uninspiring leadership of the ageing oligarchy, headed by Konstantin Chernenko, overt dissidence was negligible in quantity, even if impressive in moral quality. In the society as a whole, the hegemony of the Communist Party and the ubiquity of the KGB were taken for granted.

For Gorbachev, the economic slowdown was one of the stimuli to reform, but there were large and powerful institutional interests within the system committed to the command economy in which they enjoyed positions of power and privilege. They included Gosplan (the State Planning Committee), the numerous economic and branch-industrial ministries, the military-industrial complex, and a large section of the party apparatus. In that last category were not only the economic departments of the Central Committee of the CPSU but also provincial party secretaries, whose most significant tasks included acting as economic facilitators within their region. Doing that effectively did more for their political standing than the ideological leadership they were meant to provide.[16] Furthermore, a Western economic analyst, Marshall Goldman, who, prior to Gorbachev coming to power, held that the USSR *was* in crisis, also appositely observed that "attempts to introduce economic and industrial reform to revitalize the economy could set off uncontrollable political and economic forces" and that, while the "present situation is bad," the consequences of reform "may be even worse."[17]

Far from being unavoidable, fundamental reform was a nettle that would be grasped only by an unusually bold Soviet leader. Gorbachev was such a leader, but even he allowed economic policy during the first five years of his leadership to remain largely within the technocratic hands of the Chairman of the Council of Ministers, Nikolay Ryzhkov. It was as late as 1990 that Gorbachev embraced a market economy in principle. Even then he did not actively pursue movement to market prices. Over and above the opposition of powerful institutional interests, he faced a serious dilemma. In the absence of market pricing, continued shortages were unavoidable, but moving to them would raise the prices of hitherto subsidized foodstuffs, fuel already growing discontent, and – in the short run, at any rate – make millions of Soviet citizens still worse off. Economic reform became a lower priority for Gorbachev than increasingly fundamental domestic political reform, on the one hand, and the transformation of Soviet foreign policy, on the other hand. Instead, therefore, of slowdown in growth making economic reform inescapable, the toughest economic choices were avoided. And the bold political change Gorbachev did foster is incompatible with an economic determinist interpretation of the Soviet perestroika. The liberalization and partial democratization of the Soviet state, far from ameliorating economic difficulties, exacerbated them. The command economy, which had worked after a fashion, now worked still less well, for commands could be ignored with impunity, and the new tolerance and political freedoms meant that citizens could give voice to their anger about queues and shortages.

The idea that Communism was unreformable – the third of the three widespread assumptions mentioned above – was an oversimplification. Khrushchev's reforms were both inconsistent and incomplete, but they were real enough. They removed some of the worst cruelty and most extreme arbitrariness from the system. In contrast with the years of "high Stalinism," there were no longer mass arrests, scooping up even loyal and uncritical Soviet citizens because the security police had to find enough "saboteurs" or "enemies of the people" to fill their quotas. Under Khrushchev and Brezhnev, a Soviet citizen was liable to be arrested for something that would not be a crime in a democracy – such as possessing or, worse, distributing prohibited political literature – but there were rules of the game that enabled more conformist or cautious citizens to live with little fear of incarceration. Significant partial reforms took place in several Communist systems and had some success. Thus, limited concessions to the market in Hungary under its Communist leader János Kádár produced a much better supply of foodstuffs in Hungarian shops than was available in the Soviet Union. More fundamentally, the renunciation of Maoism, the substantial marketization of the Chinese economy, and the opening of China to the world under the leadership of Deng Xiaoping dramatically improved living standards in China. That was real and successful reform. Yet, politically, the system remained essentially Leninist, with the hegemony of the ruling Communist Party firmly in place.

Gorbachev, however, took greater risks than even Deng Xiaoping was prepared to contemplate. The Soviet leader moved rapidly from espousing a glasnost (transparency) that broadened the flow of information and the scope for debate to endorsing a freedom of speech that by 1989 had become a freedom of publication. In that year, even such hitherto banned works, deemed to be incorrigibly anti-Soviet, as Alexander Solzhenitsyn's *Gulag Archipelago* and George Orwell's *Nineteen Eighty-Four*, were published in large editions. The first seriously contested elections for a new legislature endowed with real power took place not in an East European country but in the Soviet Union. Addressing a closed meeting of regional party secretaries in April 1988, Gorbachev said that it was not only in the West that the question was asked, "On what basis do 20 million" (party members) "rule 200 million?."

Answering the question, Gorbachev said, "We conferred on ourselves the right to rule the people!."[18]

Two and a half months later he pushed through the Nineteenth Party Conference a decision to move to contested elections for a new legislature, to be held not later than the spring of the following year. In March 1989, the first such elections were held. They were not yet multiparty, but in most electoral districts they were multi-candidate, and they resulted not only in the defeat of some senior party officials but also in the victory of deputies, especially from the three Baltic republics of Estonia, Latvia, and Lithuania, who were supportive of greater national autonomy. Fatefully, they also enabled Boris Yeltsin, who had fallen foul of the party leadership in October 1987, to return to the political fray with a resounding win in a seat in the second chamber for which the entire adult population of Moscow constituted the electorate. The American ambassador Jack Matlock observed that he "found Yeltsin's victory less astonishing than the fact that *the votes had been counted honestly*" (italics Matlock's).[19] This was a sign of how much the Soviet Union had evolved by 1989. As Matlock commented, "An important milestone on the road to Russian democracy had been passed."[20]

Soviet Transformation and East European Liberation

The political will of the Soviet leadership and the military might at their disposal had been the essential determinants of Communist rule throughout the region ever since the Soviet army played the most decisive part in liberating Eastern Europe from Nazi rule in World War II. At times in the postwar era, elements of relaxation in Moscow raised expectations in one or more of the East European countries that they could achieve greater autonomy. That occurred even during the mild "Thaw" following Stalin's death in 1953 and, more seriously, in the wake of Nikita Khrushchev's "Secret Speech" to the Twentieth Congress of the CPSU in 1956, in which the Soviet leader attacked the hitherto sacrosanct Stalin. Whenever, however, the pre-Gorbachev Soviet leadership inadvertently damaged the robustness of their client regimes, they used their political and, to the extent they deemed necessary, military resources, to put a stop to events that were getting out of hand or threatening to do so.

The key to systemic change in Eastern Europe was held in Moscow, and until the second half of the 1980s it was used to keep the door to such transformation firmly locked. Political innovation in the Soviet capital between 1945 and 1985 was never system-transformative at home or supportive of fundamental change within what was euphemistically called the "Socialist Commonwealth." That is not to say the changes in degree of repression, in policy preferences and of political style during the Stalin, Khrushchev, and Brezhnev eras were inconsequential. But among the things those very different Soviet leaders had in common – as did their successors, Yury Andropov and Chernenko – was a firm commitment to preserving the Communist regimes in Eastern Europe.

When Gorbachev became general secretary, he had given his Politburo colleagues no reason to doubt his readiness to defend the pillars of Communist power within Eastern Europe and in the USSR itself.[21] It was clearly no part of his intention to promote the breakup of Comecon (as the Council for Mutual Economic Assistance of the USSR and Eastern Europe was known in the West) or the Warsaw Pact, not to speak of the Soviet Union itself. The editors of this volume correctly note that change can enhance or reduce robustness depending on its nature, timing, and reception. The nature of the change Gorbachev espoused moved from reform he believed would improve life in the Union through economic innovation, cultural relaxation, and a widening of the limits of the politically possible – thereby supposedly strengthening the system – to something radically different.

After being in power for just a little over three years, he began to dismantle the pillars of the Communist system by instituting competitive elections, supporting a wide range of political freedoms, and by embracing, both in theory and practice, political pluralism. From the summer of 1988 onward not only Gorbachev's priorities but also his goals had changed. The holder of the highest political office in the Soviet Union, far from seeking to make Communist institutions more robust, had decided that the system needed to be democratized and equipped with a qualitatively different set of institutions. As Gorbachev himself put it, speaking in 1996, "Until 1988 I had the same illusions as previous reformers. I believed that the system could be improved. In 1988 I realized we needed systemic reform. The system had to be replaced."[22]

Gorbachev was a leader exceptionally open to new ideas and to learning from others and from experience. Thus, generalizations about his aims and ultimate goals should specify the stage of his leadership they are talking about. If there is no time dimension to the generalization, there is every likelihood it will be misleading. Gorbachev's response to growing criticism from intra-party conservative forces, especially in the first half of 1988, was to embrace more radical goals and means of achieving them. Thus, it would be quite wrong to say that he *inadvertently* made the Soviet political system more fragile. From the run-up to the Nineteenth Party Conference in mid-1988 onwards, he was *not trying to preserve the Communist system*, he was seeking something qualitatively different. As general secretary of the Central Committee of the CPSU, Gorbachev could hardly, of course, issue a public statement to that effect, since this would have provided rich ammunition for his conservative Communist opponents. It is what, however (as he later readily acknowledged), the conceptual and institutional changes he introduced added up to.

At no stage, obviously, did Gorbachev wish to dismantle the Soviet *state*, as distinct from the *system*. But as he noted some years after the USSR had ceased to exist, that country had been a "party state" and as "the CPSU and state institutions were ineluctably interwoven," it followed that a "weakening of the party" entailed a "weakening of the state."[23] It is crucial that Gorbachev's attitude to the party also changed greatly during his general secretaryship. He believed when he became Soviet leader, and continued to believe after he had lost office, that any attempts to begin change from below were "doomed to failure," for "the system had the capacity to suppress such attempts and to effectively combat them." Reform could only "begin from the top down."[24] The CPSU was strictly hierarchical and so Gorbachev was able to use the power and authority of his office as general secretary at the apex of the organization to striking effect. Over time, however, the limitations of the party as an instrument of change became clear.

Notwithstanding Gorbachev's skilful manoeuvring, the systemic changes he espoused gradually undermined his own authority as party leader, and the powers he acquired as President of the USSR in 1990 did not replicate the unquestioning obedience to the general secretary in the unreformed Soviet Union, nor were they intended to. Contested elections from 1989 onwards gave other political actors a power base and a novel source of legitimacy in the Soviet context. An especially important moment was Gorbachev's acceptance that those members of the new legislature, the Congress of People's Deputies of the USSR, who belonged to the CPSU (and they constituted the overwhelming majority of deputies) were not obliged to speak and vote along strictly party lines. That not only diminished the deference accorded him as party leader; more fundamentally it signalled the end of "democratic centralism." In other words, Gorbachev broke one of the foundation blocks of the party Lenin built, for no longer was there a strictly disciplined, highly centralized organization, with decisions at the top of the party structure unquestioningly implemented lower down the hierarchy.

In the earliest years of his leadership, Gorbachev believed that he could use the party as an instrument of reform and, indeed, for several years he succeeded in doing so – most notably with the breakthrough represented by the changes he persuaded the Nineteenth Conference of the CPSU in 1988 to accept.[25] From the outset, he was well aware of serious opposition to far-reaching reform from within the party apparatus, but he believed that, with skilful use of the authority of his office, he could overcome it. The more radical Gorbachev's changes became, the more overt was intra-party opposition to them. With the creation of a new legislature, endowed with real power, in 1989 and the executive presidency, to which that legislature elected him, in 1990, he shifted power from party to state institutions. By the summer of 1991, when he was under severe criticism from many different quarters, he was ready to go further. He persuaded the CPSU Central Committee (some of whose leading members were already planning a coup against him) to agree to holding an extraordinary Party Congress in November or December 1991 to adopt a new party programme. Gorbachev's expectation was that the party would then split between those ready to accept the social democratic content of that programme and those who would not. The Congress was never held, for by then there was no longer a Communist Party of the Soviet Union. The August coup that put Gorbachev under house arrest in his holiday home on the Crimean coast, and the coup's failure, led to the winding up of the CPSU, mainly at the instigation of Russian President Boris Yeltsin. Gorbachev himself was shocked when he learned of the extent to which party officials both at the center and in the regions had gone along with the putsch and its aim of restoring authoritarian rule.[26]

The Fourth Wave of Democratization

A substantial body of scholarly writing has classified the changes in the Soviet Union and Eastern Europe in the second half of the 1980s as part of the "Third Wave" of democracy, a notion that had hitherto referred especially to the 1970s democratization in southern Europe (Greece, Portugal, Spain) and in Latin America.[27] I have argued elsewhere that it is misleading to embrace the dramatic Soviet and East European democratizations in that Third Wave.[28] The notion of a "wave," in its figurative meaning of a movement or groundswell, as applied to the acquisition of democracy, makes most sense when there is interconnection among the different cases of democratization and evidence of transnational influences. The southern European examples of democratization had no real impact within the USSR or Eastern Europe when they occurred in the 1970s and the Latin American cases even less. Both seemed too far removed from everyday realities and political feasibility in the region. The Soviet oligarchy, headed by Leonid Brezhnev, was firmly opposed to the pluralization of their own regime or that of any East European country, and Moscow's hegemony in the region was taken for granted. The election of a Polish Pope in 1978 was a huge stimulus to the rise of Solidarity in the years that immediately followed. But not even Pope John Paul II could do anything to prevent the imposition of martial law in Poland in December 1981, the arrest of Solidarity's leaders and the outlawing of the organization. It maintained a slender, underground existence, but was able to reengage in the political process, and to spectacular effect in 1989, only following democratizing political change in Moscow and the transformation of Soviet foreign policy. Even in the Polish case, it was change of occupancy of the Kremlin, rather than change of occupancy of the Vatican, that made democratic transition and independent statehood possible.

The coming to power of Gorbachev in 1985, and his replacement of the entire top Soviet foreign policymaking team within a year of becoming general secretary was the essential facilitating condition for the democratization of Eastern Europe as a whole.[29] The clearest signal, even if many in Eastern Europe doubted whether it could be taken entirely at face value, came in Gorbachev's speech at the United Nations in New York on 7 December 1988, when he declared that the people of every country had the right to choose for themselves their form of government. Freedom of choice is "a universal principle," Gorbachev told his UN audience, and there must be no exceptions.[30] Stressing the importance of "all-human" values, ideas, and interests (transcending class and national interests), he insisted that this did not mean decrying the variety and legitimacy of different sociopolitical systems.[31] The times, he said, demanded a "deideologization of inter-state relationships."[32] "Re-reading that speech today," Pavel Palazhchenko (Gorbachev's long-standing interpreter and the man who simultaneously translated his 1988 UN speech into English) reflected in December 2020, "it is difficult to find even traces of "Marxism-Leninism."[33]

The change in Soviet foreign policy, and of the ideas that underpinned it, facilitated the rapid acquisition of national autonomy in Eastern Europe. The dependence of the Warsaw Pact countries' Communist regimes on the USSR meant they had an underlying fragility. Any robustness they had enjoyed was reliant on the support of the regional hegemonic power in Moscow. The overwhelming majority of East-Central European party officials, and many of the party members, viewed that as unexceptionable rather than neo-imperialist, for they recognized the Soviet Union's leadership of the International Communist Movement. Thus, the Marxist-Leninist version of "socialism," as purveyed by its Soviet guardians in ex cathedra pronouncements, was generally accepted by Communists in Eastern Europe. The party leaders, in particular, had every reason to be loyal to Moscow, for without Soviet support their hold on power would be tenuous. But from 1987–88 onward, official doctrine as well as past policies were being openly questioned and criticized in the Soviet Union itself. This led to heightened awareness within the East European regimes of the potential fragility of their rule and a nervousness among the most conformist leaders and ideologues in these countries about their future.

Liberalization in the USSR, involving a vast expansion of freedom of speech and of publication, developed into a process of democratization with the decision at the 1988 Nineteenth Party Conference to move to competitive elections for a new legislature. That prospect, and especially the reality, of those elections in early 1989 further raised expectations of the peoples of Eastern Europe. These Soviet national elections of March 1989 were the first in any of the Communist states to lead to the defeat of senior party officials. They accelerated the process of democratization but gave impetus also to fissiparous tendencies, which were a wholly unintended consequence of the pluralization. Elections in Poland in June of the same year had still more dramatic immediate consequences. In a compromise between the reemergent and now legalized Solidarity and the Polish Communist authorities, it had been accepted that the former would be allowed to contest approximately half of the seats in the election. Solidarity won almost all of them, surprising even themselves by the scale of their success. By the end of 1989, the "leading role" of the Communist Party had been taken out of the Polish Constitution, a few months ahead of its removal from the Soviet Constitution in March 1990. It was not only the new atmosphere and policies in Moscow that accelerated change in Eastern Europe, but also influence from one East European country on another. When one country's citizens were able to end Communist rule, and to get away with such apostasy, their example had profound repercussions throughout the region.

The reaction of Communist leaders varied from one Warsaw Pact country to another, with Hungary, whose political elite included some serious reformers, ahead even of Poland. In February 1989 the Hungarian parliament passed laws permitting a multiparty system and in that same month the Central Committee voted to give up the party's "leading role." Three months later, roundtable talks between the Communists (with a reformist group prevailing over harder-liners) and the democratic opposition led to free elections for a new and powerful parliament and a directly elected presidency. By October, Hungary was no longer a Communist state.[34] Democratizing pressures were felt in all of the remaining Warsaw Pact countries. The process got underway later in 1989 in Bulgaria, with its long-standing leader, Todor Zhivkov, deposed a day after the still more dramatic event of the fall of the

Berlin Wall on 9 November without a shot being fired. The breaching of the wall with impunity led to accelerated change in Germany, pushed by Chancellor Helmut Kohl, supported by President Bush, but negotiated mainly by Kohl and Gorbachev.[35] Less than half a year after the fall of the wall, the Christian Democrats emerged as the largest grouping in East German elections of March 1990, and within a year of the wall coming down, Germany was united (and as a full-fledged democracy) on 3 October 1990.[36]

The Communist leadership in Czechoslovakia was well aware of the precariousness of its power. If the ruling party had the confidence prior to the Prague Spring and during it – up until the moment when Warsaw Pact forces invaded – that came from attaining power indigenously, those who neither left the party after the Soviet-led invasion nor were expelled from it were conscious, from that point onward, of the essential fragility of their rule. They were dependent on the ultimate support of the Soviet Union which, until the late 1980s, they felt no reason to doubt. With their memories of the arrival of Soviet tanks in 1968, the Czech and Slovak peoples were understandably cautious about openly demonstrating against their Communist rulers. It was only in the last months of 1989 that the opposition became a mass movement, but then events moved very fast. Before the end of the year, the country's most eminent dissident, playwright Václav Havel, became President of Czechoslovakia, and the Communists ceded power, as a result of what Havel called the "Velvet Revolution." The last East European country to rebel against Communist rule was Romania where the autocratic Nicolae Ceauşescu resorted to violent repression in a vain effort to stem the tide of revolt. He and his wife, who was no less brutally hard-line, paid the ultimate price for years of repression and the killing of hundreds of demonstrators in December 1989 when they were executed by firing squad on Christmas Day, as a new coalition of democrats and only partly reconstructed Communists assumed power.[37]

The changes in the Soviet Union and Eastern Europe at the end of the 1980s belong to a discrete Fourth Wave of Democratization. Transnational influences, which began but did not end in Moscow, were crucial to the transformation. There was a circular flow of influence in which the liberalization that evolved into democratization in the Soviet Union acted as a stimulus to pressure from below in Eastern Europe. The Communist regimes in those countries were stable only for so long as their rulers could rely on the Soviet leadership to come to their aid in times of stress, but at risk from the moment it appeared to citizens and rulers that Soviet political support for the Communist order could not be taken for granted. When it became a reasonable hypothesis that there would be no backing from Moscow for any East European regime that instituted a violent crackdown on oppositional elements – and still less likelihood of Soviet military assistance to reinforce that country's domestic repressive organs – this undermined the confidence of the Communist rulers and emboldened the many in each East European country who aspired to a different kind of political and economic order.

South African democratization was also very much part of the Fourth Wave. The changes in Moscow and Gorbachev's transformation of Soviet foreign policy, especially when they led to the fall of Communism in Eastern Europe, totally changed South African political calculations. As Adrian Guelke noted, "the National Party government" had become "increasingly reliant on anti-communism to justify its policies internationally, particularly as any residual sympathy for racial oligarchy in the Western world faded."[38] When East European countries, in the course of 1989, became independent and non-Communist without a shot being fired by a Soviet soldier, the notion of the minority South African government being a bastion against the encroachment of Communism began to be seen as the absurdity it was even by the conservative but pragmatic President F.W. de Klerk. On the other side of the South African standoff, the change of Soviet policy had implications for the African National Congress (ANC). The "New Thinking" in foreign policy emanating from Moscow was supportive of peaceful change and negotiated transitions and averse to violent insurrection. Thus, the ANC was encouraged to enter into dialogue with the apartheid regime to negotiate the transition to full democratic rights for the majority of the population.[39]

The flow of influence from Moscow to Eastern Europe and among the Warsaw Pact states came full circle when the spectacle of one East European country after another successfully pushing for an end to Communist rule, and achieving independent statehood, emboldened the most disaffected nations within the multinational Soviet state. In the Baltic republics, ethnic nationalism flourished as democratization proceeded further and faster than in most Soviet republics. That, however, was a threat to the further democratization of the Soviet political system, for it led conservative Communists to call for a crackdown not only on the fissiparous forces but also on the new political pluralism. The speed of the East European transition from Communism, once it got seriously underway in 1989, and the removal of leaders who had long been reliable partners of their Soviet overlords, was as alarming for unreconstructed Communists in Russia as it was encouraging for the most disaffected of Soviet citizens, especially in the Baltic republics and Ukraine. In the Ukrainian case, the Polish influence on Rukh, which began as a movement in support of perestroika and developed into one in favor of independent statehood, was direct. A delegation from Solidarity traveled to Ukraine to participate in Rukh's founding congress in September 1989 where the long-standing critic of the Polish Communist regime and leading Solidarity intellectual Adam Michnik acknowledged that Gorbachev's reforms had been "the key to democratization throughout the region." Though he did not call for separate Ukrainian statehood, he got a prolonged ovation when he finished his speech with "Long live a free, democratic, and just Ukraine!."[40]

End of the USSR and Yugoslavia

By definition the multinational Soviet state was not a "nation-state." It was the successor regime to Imperial Russia, and it could be perceived as a Greater Russia. Yet, it is an oversimplification to regard it as a Russian Empire, even though the USSR was sometimes referred to as the "Inner Empire," as distinct from the "Outer Empire" in eastern and central Europe. There were, indeed, periods of aggressive russification, as well as suppression at all times prior to the perestroika era of those elements in the country's variety of national cultures, which were seriously at odds with Soviet norms. But it is unsurprising that Russian was the lingua franca of the USSR, given that the state included as many Russians as all other nationalities put together. Moreover, Union Republican status conferred a degree of protection for the language and culture of the other fourteen republics, not only for the Russian Republic. Indeed, some Russian nationalists complained that Russia was discriminated *against*, for unlike the other republics, it did not have its own Russian Central Committee of the CPSU or its own Russian Academy of Sciences (whereas in Ukraine, Georgia, Lithuania, and the other republics these organizations existed) and had to settle for being the dominant nationality within the all-Union party organization and the Academy of Sciences of the USSR. More significantly at odds with the idea that the Soviet Union was no more than a Russian empire is the awkward fact that Josef Stalin, its longest-lasting top leader, ruled the country for three decades, and he was a Georgian. One of the most influential Politburo members over a still longer period was the Armenian Anastas Mikoyan. At various times in Soviet history, Georgians, Armenians, and Ukrainians were particularly well represented in the higher party echelons. Within the ruling party's membership as a whole, it was not Russians but Jews (who were counted as a nationality in the USSR) who were the most over-represented group.[41]

Stalin's well-known description of the Soviet pseudo-federal state as "national in form, socialist in content" was studiously vague.[42] In essence, "socialist" meant that, however federal the forms of the Soviet state structure might appear on paper, the highly centralized Communist party organs would call the shots. Real political power was not devolved. The party rules (which were a better guide to Soviet realities than successive Constitutions of the USSR) stipulated the subordination of lower party bodies to higher party organs. That included the subordination of republican Central Committee organizations to the departments of the all-Union Central Committee in Moscow. The federal forms were, however, not unimportant, even before they acquired vastly more substance during the perestroika years. They helped to institutionally entrench national consciousness, even among some of the peoples for whom it barely existed before the revolution. The historian Terry Martin makes the point that what Stalin called *natsional'naya kul'tura* is best captured in English not by "national culture" but by "national identity" or "symbolic ethnicity."[43] That consciousness of national identity coexisted with a sense of Soviet identity and in the very last years of the USSR the former trumped the latter.

The Soviet Union is better understood as a state-nation than as an empire. The concept of "state-nation" was introduced by Juan Linz and Alfred Stepan when they were trying "to think anew about how polities that aspire to be democracies can accommodate great sociocultural, even multinational, diversity within one state."[44] But there is no need to restrict the use of the term, state-nation, to democracies, and Stepan and Linz do not do so.[45] An external enemy can be very important in generating or consolidating a state-wide identity, such as a sense of Soviet or Yugoslav identity that went along with consciousness of being Russian or Georgian, Serb, or Croat. For the USSR, World War II, with its losses and triumphs, reinforced Soviet identity (though there was a minority of citizens for whom the Soviet state was so hated that they welcomed the Nazi invasion). The Cold War, too, fostered a Soviet patriotism in the face of an external potential enemy. As one of the world's leading specialists on the Soviet economy and society Alec Nove observed, "The arms race doubtless contributed to economic overstrain, but paradoxically the Cold War may have helped the system to survive, by providing a *raison d"être* for its continuance" and for "the dominant role of the military-industrial complex." Nove added: "The centralized economy, Party control, censorship, and the KGB were justified in the eyes of the leaders, and of many of the led, by the need to combat enemies, internal and external."[46]

A majority of citizens took pride in Soviet achievements, above all the huge part played by the Red Army in victory in World War II, followed by pride in Soviet pioneering space exploration (including the first cosmonaut Yuri Gagarin), as well as Olympic and other sporting successes. Feeling Russian and Soviet may have been the easiest combination, but citizens could feel themselves to be Kazakh and Soviet, Georgian and Soviet, Armenian and Soviet, and so on, accepting both the state-nation (Soviet) and ethno-national identity into which they were born and had been socialized. Even among the most disaffected of Soviet peoples, notably the Balts and Western Ukrainians, the Soviet identity was very real, however much many of those citizens resented it. Moreover, among the more than one hundred nations within the vast USSR, there were many smaller nationalities who welcomed the supranational Soviet state as a counterweight to the hegemony of the titular nationality of their Union Republic. Soviet identity was, of course, manipulated by the party-state authorities. What would have been legitimate dissent within a democracy was stigmatized as anti-Soviet, with the implication that this was a betrayal of the Soviet motherland. Over many decades, Soviet propaganda successfully linked criticism of party policy or of the system with lack of patriotism. Even overt dissidents (until the vastly freer atmosphere of the final years of the USSR) tried to avoid being characterized as anti-Soviet. They would call, for example, for the authorities to obey their own Soviet Constitution and abide by the 1975 Helsinki Agreement, of which the Soviet government was itself a signatory.

The implications of what happened in East Europe in 1989 for the nations of the USSR and for Soviet statehood were profound. The completion of this circular flow of influence saw Estonians, Latvians, Lithuanians, Georgians, and Western Ukrainians, and other Soviet nations in their wake, inspired to greater boldness in their demands for national self-determination. Increasingly, they saw no reason why they should be any less entitled to independent statehood than Poles, Czechs, or Hungarians. The move from seeking greater autonomy within a radically reformed Soviet federation, in a process of negotiation with "the centre," became a more radical demand for separate statehood. Gorbachev's agency in this lay in a tolerance and liberalization that provided political space for national movements to develop and democratization, which created institutional mechanisms for their advancement.

Boris Yeltsin was much more directly an agent of the Soviet Union's disintegration. No-one played a larger part in ensuring that even a radically reformed federal Union, with extensive powers devolved to the republics, would not survive. Yeltsin used the authority he gained by election to a series of political offices, culminating with his election as President of Russia in June 1991, to assert Russian interests, as he interpreted them, against those of the Union. After becoming Chairman of the Congress of People's Deputies of the Russian republic in May 1990, he steered through that body a declaration of Russian sovereignty on 12 June, and then proceeded to transfer by fiat rights and resources from the USSR to the RSFSR in what became known as the "War of Laws."[47]

Whether provoking the breakup of a Union in which Russia had been the dominant nation was in Russia's national interest is extremely doubtful, but it was unquestionably in Yeltsin's short-term interest as he sought to supplant Gorbachev. He was able to exploit Russians' growing dissatisfaction, especially in the last two years of the Soviet Union's existence, both with deteriorating economic conditions and with what many felt were other republics' interests taking precedence over theirs. Yeltsin asserted that he was standing up for Russia against a Union central authority that was a "cruel exploiter" and "miserly benefactor," and this appealed to his followers.[48] When, in the spring of 1990 Yeltsin insisted on Russian law's supremacy over Soviet law, this was more momentous for the fate of the Union than even massive pro-independence demonstrations in the Baltic republics. A viable Union could have continued without Estonia, Latvia, and Lithuania, and Gorbachev was slower than were some of his advisers to regard them as having a special case for secession (conscious, as he was, that the loss of any Soviet territory would enrage large sections of the party and state apparatus and the military-industrial complex). Since Russia contained half the population of the USSR and three-quarters of its territory, it was in a uniquely significant category. Clearly there could be no Union without it.[49]

The Soviet multinational state was always potentially fragile, for the administrative boundaries of what had been largely a nominal federal system (since power was highly centralized in Moscow) were based on national homelands. Over the years the Soviet leadership had contained ethno-nationalism with a combination of concessions to national languages and heritage and crackdown on the slightest manifestation of ethno-national deviation (with the partial exception of Russian nationalism, which at times was shown a greater tolerance, so long as it was accompanied by acceptance of and loyalty to the Soviet state). Administration in the union republics was mainly in the hands of members of the titular nationality of that republic, although the extent to which that was true varied over time and from one republic to another.

The End of Communist Rule in Europe 163

Until the late 1980s, however, ultimate control had remained in the CPSU Central Committee building in Moscow. Nationalism only became an actively disintegrating force in the Soviet Union after fundamental reforms had taken place in the political system. Before that, nationalist sentiments could be harbored but not publicly expressed, still less acted upon.

Yugoslavia was another state-nation in which identification with the state and the idea of being Yugoslav accompanied the sense of national identity of Serbs, Croats, Slovenes, and of the other ethno-national groups. It had been reinforced by loyalty to, and a cult of, Tito, who was born in Croatia to a Slovene mother and Croat father, yet was highly regarded by the especially numerous Serbian members of the Yugoslav League of Communists.[50] This multinational party, and the Communist system it had created, kept national separatist movements from emerging for as long as Josip Broz Tito, the man who had led the Partisan resistance to Nazi Germany and the Communists to power, was alive. Tito, the Yugoslav state, and its citizens' sense of Yugoslav identity all benefited from their country's defiance of Stalin and the Soviet Union. Refusing to be dictated to by Moscow, the Yugoslavs were expelled in 1948 from the Soviet-dominated Cominform, the organization of the main European Communist parties that existed from 1947 until its dissolution in 1956. Thereafter, Yugoslavia carved out a leading role among "non-aligned countries" and acquired an international political significance much greater than its economic or military strength would have indicated.

Yugoslavia had a more genuinely federal system than that of the pre-perestroika Soviet Union, and though the Communists were the only legal party, each republican party organization tried to defend and advance the interests of that national republic. Extreme interregional inequalities led to tensions over the distribution of resources, but so long as Tito was alive, these were kept within bounds. Following his death in 1980, the inter-republican differences became sharper, and with the advent of the Soviet perestroika and the winding down of the Cold War, Yugoslavia's position as a prominent nonaligned state lost some of its relevance. By the end of the 1980s, Yugoslavia was held together neither by ideology nor by a united Communist Party, and what happened in the rest of Europe in 1989 had its effect in Yugoslavia, too, even though it had been outside the Soviet bloc for more than four decades. Yugoslavia, like the Soviet Union, had been not only a state-nation but also a party-state and, as in the Soviet case, the pluralization and subsequent disintegration of the party presaged the disintegration of the state. By the end of 1991, the Yugoslav state had ceased to exist. In the process and especially the aftermath of its dissolution, parts of the country descended into bitter civil war. The willingness of the Serbian leader Slobodan Milošević and his Croat counterpart Franjo Tuđman to exploit ethno-nationalism and sponsor violent ethnic cleansing in pursuit of territorial dominance made a grim contrast with the breakup of the Soviet Union, which, during Gorbachev's leadership, was comparatively peaceful. The dissolution of the Soviet and Yugoslav states starkly illustrated how destructive of Communist statehood nationalism could be (although, as noted earlier in this chapter, in some more ethnically homogeneous Asian Communist states it could be turned into a bulwark). The very different ways in which the Soviet Union, Yugoslavia, and, indeed, Czechoslovakia broke up highlighted also the significance of the personalities, values, and political choices of the leading political actors in these countries.

Institutions also mattered greatly. The only three Communist states which had federal forms, the Soviet Union, Yugoslavia and Czechoslovakia, were the three "state-nations" which broke up into their "nation-state" component parts. Nationalists were able to use the institutional resources of their republics, especially when "democratic centralism" gave way to political pluralism.[51]

Conclusion

Regimes that were viewed by their citizens as robust in 1985 were anything but robust by the end of that decade. Changing perceptions of what had become possible produced changed realities. "New Thinking" and dramatically new policies in the Soviet Union, once East Europeans realized that they were for real, were more welcome to a majority of the population in those countries than they were to their leaders. Over the years, the Communist leaderships in the East and Central European states had generally been content to cooperate with their ultimate Soviet overlords and accept "limited sovereignty." They were aware that without Soviet support, they were highly likely to be removed from office by their own people. Understanding how transformative change occurred in Eastern Europe involves, accordingly, understanding how it came about in the Soviet Union. That, in turn, involves recognizing how greatly the aims of its Soviet progenitors – and of Gorbachev in the first instance – evolved within a few short years.[52]

The categories of "robustness" and "fragility" do little to illuminate the relationship between the leader and the *system* during the Soviet perestroika, since Gorbachev moved from political reformer in 1985–86 to systemic transformer by 1988–89, and the agency of the leader in those years was of decisive importance. In the late 1980s, Gorbachev did not misunderstand the fragility of the Communist *system*, since he was consciously engaged in dismantling it. He did, however, underestimate how much more fragile the Soviet *state* would become in the absence of the monopoly of power of a highly disciplined Communist Party. The new tolerance, competitive elections, and the secularization of ideology whereby Marxism-Leninism was deprived of its hitherto untouchable authority provided novel opportunities for ethno-nationalism to make headway in the multinational USSR and to call into question the future of Soviet statehood. And the notion of fragility is of especial relevance to the East-Central European systems and, in some instances, their states. Whereas Communist rule disappeared within the same few years in all the East-Central European countries in which it had prevailed, in only three of them was this accompanied by the dissolution of the state. The German Democratic Republic (East Germany) became part of the Federal Republic of Germany, Yugoslavia broke up into its main ethno-national parts, and Czechoslovakia gave way to the Czech Republic and Slovakia. That "velvet divorce" to match Czechoslovakia's "velvet revolution" contrasted benignly with the Yugoslav experience.

An emphasis on the decisive importance of change in Moscow should not lead to neglect of the influence of the West. Even during the Cold War, all the more so when tensions eased, Western countries were objects of fascination and attraction in Eastern Europe. Western products were prized by their peoples, as well as by Soviet citizens, and visits to the West were a still more special privilege, available only to a few. To be allowed Western travel was one of the most attractive of the various rewards for conformist political behavior that existed alongside the hierarchy of sanctions for nonconformity and dissidence. Notwithstanding the regimes' control over their own mass media, there was a wide awareness in the eastern half of the European continent of the higher standard of living and political freedoms of Western Europe and North America. Over the long term, this example of free, democratic, and relatively prosperous societies was more of a factor conducive to change within Communist states than was the West's formidable military capacity. The Soviet Union found it easier to match the might of the latter than the appeal of the former. Indeed, as already noted, fear of war and the military threat from external enemies were manipulated by pre-perestroika Soviet leaders, and their East European acolytes, to justify party control, the centralized economy, the bloated military-industrial complex, secret police surveillance, and the need for ideological vigilance.

Neither the attraction of the West nor the threat it supposedly posed was, however, new. It does not explain why the collapse of Communism in Europe occurred when it did. Prior to Gorbachev becoming general secretary of the CPSU – embracing new ideas and appointing a likeminded and innovative top foreign policymaking team – Communist leaders reacted to Western military buildup, including President Ronald Reagan's in his first term, in a traditional, intransigent way.[53] The change of Soviet leadership in 1985, the institutional resources of the party general secretaryship, and the contrast between Gorbachev's values and open-mindedness, on the one hand, and the beliefs and attributes of his predecessors, on the other hand, are fundamental to understanding why the liberalization, pluralization, and democratization of the political system developed alongside transformation of Soviet foreign policy between 1985 and 1990.

Gorbachev's espousal of ever more radical political change illustrated the adage, familiar from de Tocqueville onward, that the most dangerous time for an authoritarian regime is when it begins to reform itself. But, to reiterate, that should not obfuscate the important distinction between the disintegration of the Soviet state, which Gorbachev strove to avoid (but without resorting to repression) and the pluralization and substantial democratization of the Soviet political system. From 1988 onward, that was a Gorbachev goal, even though it was a more root-and-branch change than he sought or envisaged when he entered the Kremlin. He also accepted calmly the de-Communization of Eastern Europe, not least because he was by then doing the same in the Soviet Union, being already well advanced in his evolution from Communist reformer to socialist of a social democratic type.[54]

The end of Communist rule in Europe owed much to contingency and the agency of particular leaders, especially a leader of the Communist Party of the Soviet Union unlike any of his predecessors. If a high value is placed on democracy and a wide range of freedoms, then this period in the history of Russia, and not only that of Eastern Europe, can be seen as one in which the gains greatly exceeded the losses. It cannot be fully encapsulated by the dichotomy between fragility and robustness. Whether a smaller but genuinely federal Union could have survived will remain a matter for debate,[55] but to the extent that the Soviet state was democratized, it was a logical consequence that some of its component parts, the Baltic republics in the first instance, would become separate states. Democratization had the same logic for the countries of Eastern Europe. It went hand-in-hand with movement to a more independent statehood. Since Communist rule in the region was linked in popular perception with Russian domination, national independence also involved the dissolution of Comecon and the Warsaw Pact and movement away from the Russian orbit.

The unaccountable power of the party elite, economic slowdown, and rank injustices were part of the Soviet legacy Gorbachev attempted to address through reform and, subsequently, systemic change. But radical reform turned out to be less effective for preserving the state within its existing boundaries than highly authoritarian, single-party rule. In the long run, relative economic failure, combined with severe political and social problems, is likely to result in crisis. That point had *not* been reached in the Soviet Union in 1985. Gorbachev and his allies were bold enough to tackle the problems before they reached crisis point. They succeeded in transforming the political system, as well as relations with the Western world, but in doing so, they opened the way to the crisis of Soviet statehood. That does not mean they were mistaken to embark on reform and then move on to systemic political change. Nor does it mean that Gorbachev was wrong to try to hold together a Union by voluntary agreement – which he came to accept might have a different name and lose several of its existing components – in a process of negotiation with the leaders of the Soviet republics.

If, as a counterfactual, we were to suppose that Gorbachev, rather than Defence Minister Dmitry Ustinov, had died in 1984, we know enough about the remaining surviving members of Chernenko's Politburo (the narrow group from whom the general secretary had to be chosen) to be confident that none of them would have dreamt of endorsing a pluralization of the political system, abandoning "democratic centralism" and the monopoly of power of the party. Change on that scale exceeded the expectations in the mid-1980s of even the most optimistic Soviet and East European intelligentsia supporters of reform. If Gorbachev had restricted reforms to those that did not touch the fundamentals of the political system or of Soviet foreign policy, he could have ruled the country for very much longer and expectations at home and abroad would have remained modest.

Had a crisis, accompanied by open unrest, erupted several decades later, under a very different Soviet leader from Gorbachev, it would be rash to assume it would not have been brutally suppressed. However, if expectations had not been aroused in the first place, Tiananmen Square-type repression would scarcely have been required. Estonians, Latvians, Lithuanians, and Western Ukrainians put up with their lot under Stalin, Khrushchev, Brezhnev, Andropov, and Chernenko, since to challenge the status quo offered no prospect of success. The transformation of the Soviet political system, together with the decisive role the Soviet Union played in ending the Cold War, owed much to the agency of

Gorbachev – his values, the rapid evolution of his political outlook, and the institutional power he possessed as leader of the CPSU.[56] These changes were intended by the Soviet leader. They also opened pathways to the entirely unintended outcome of the disintegration of the Soviet state. That this breakup was so complete, with Russia playing a decisive role in bringing it about (whereas Russia had been a prime beneficiary of the Union state), owed a great deal to the agency of Yeltsin. Even as late as the immediate aftermath of the August 1991 coup, Yeltsin, although ambivalent, was inclined to support the preservation of some kind of Union that would include many of the Soviet republics, Ukraine among them. However, at every stage between 1989 (when he won a seat in the Soviet legislature) and the end of the USSR, Yeltsin's "instinct for power" prevailed.[57] Demanding ever greater devolution of power to Russia and, ultimately, supporting Russian separate statehood served that purpose.[58]

To ignore severe problems and injustices does not mean they go away. At some point real and widespread grievances have to be addressed or forcibly repressed. Thus, democracies, too – some much more than others - remain potentially fragile. This chapter opened with a brief discussion of what it is not unreasonable to call a crisis of American democracy – when an outgoing president refused to accept the legitimacy of a fair election.[59] As Alfred Stepan and Juan Linz observed in 2011, the United States has too often been studied in "glorious isolation," distanced from the study of comparative politics, even though a comparative perspective highlights its democratic shortcomings. As Stepan and Linz point out, the United States has the highest incidence of inequality among long-standing democracies and an unusually large number of anti-majoritarian constraints for a country priding itself on its exemplary democratic credentials.[60] Between 2017 and 2020, a narcissistic president, with authoritarian instincts, played upon and exacerbated these already existing deep-seated problems. If, however, among his many disservices to democracy, Trump performed one useful service, it may be through dispelling complacency and demonstrating that even the most prestigious of democracies can be fragile and in need of far-reaching reform. It may, after all, be as much of an error to imagine that the United States is immune to authoritarian capture as to believe that absolutism is Russia's eternal destiny.

If, however, we return to where this chapter began, it is clear that changing the Russian political order was a task for more than one generation of political leaders. Institutional controls and curbs on political freedoms were long taken for granted and belonged to a much longer, predominantly authoritarian Russian political tradition. The robustness of the Soviet system over almost seven decades rested not only on the institutional controls – including censorship, a rigidly hierarchical and strictly disciplined Communist Party, secret police surveillance, and elections without choice – but on low expectations of political change and the weak sense of political efficacy of its citizens. That a vibrant political society emerged, and substantial measures of democratization were enacted, in the late 1980s and beginning of the 1990s, strongly suggest that a cultural determinism (like economic determinism) should be resisted. Nevertheless, Russia's transition to democracy remained incomplete and liable to regress. A creeping authoritarianism during three post-Soviet decades became a galloping authoritarianism from February 2022, with domestic crackdown accompanying the start of the Russian war against Ukraine.

Political changes that were widely welcomed by Soviet citizens at the end of the 1980s lost their lustre when they became linked in the public mind with worsening economic conditions.[61] The breakup of the Soviet Union, which, apart from a brief moment in December 1991 when Yeltsin succeeded in persuading a majority that this was granting Russia an independence it did not have hitherto, was also a source of regret for most Russians. Indeed, nostalgia for the Soviet Union (which is not the same as wanting a Communist system) has been growing.[62] And far from being consolidated, democracy was discredited under Yeltsin's crony capitalism, and democratic institutions have been more comprehensively hollowed out during Vladimir Putin's presidency.

Yet the six and a half years of perestroika – indeed, their first four – turned out to be time enough for the transformation of Eastern Europe. Much commentary on the end of Communist government in the USSR and Eastern Europe, and discussion of the analytically distinct but politically connected issue of the end of the Cold War, is colored by "retrospective determinism."[63] Even with the benefit of hindsight, the assumptions discussed earlier in the chapter – that the Soviet Union was in crisis in 1985, that any Soviet leadership had, accordingly, no option but to reform, and that this was bound to fail because Communism was "unreformable" – have been distinctly unhelpful. Contingency, the agency of particular leaders (Gorbachev for the transformation of the political system and of Soviet foreign policy, Yeltsin for the complete breakup of the USSR), and rapidly evolving ideas (which, in Gorbachev's case, were different in 1988, and still more different in 1990, from what they were in 1985) are essential components of an explanation of the dramatic change of the second half of the 1980s. In Eastern Europe, as distinct from the Soviet Union, there had always been quite a fine line between the "robustness" of the regimes and their fragility. Every "thaw" or element of liberalization in Moscow had knock-on effects within the other Warsaw Pact countries that were, however, held in check by Soviet coercive power or the perception that it would be deployed. The fundamental Soviet change of the perestroika years, which included an abjuring of the use of force to impose a system on a country against the wishes of its citizens, had a correspondingly momentous effect in Eastern Europe – the end of Communist rule.

Notes

1 A rule of law, political pluralism, and some curbs on executive power have existed for centuries in several countries, including Britain and the United States. But when more than half the adult population was not granted the right to vote, this did not amount to democracy. Except in New Zealand, where full adult suffrage was extended to women in 1893, women's right to vote was granted as recently as the twentieth century (with Scandinavian countries characteristically in the vanguard of progress). The right to vote in free and fair elections, unrestricted by gender, social group, ethnicity, or religion should be seen as one of the defining characteristics of democracy. By the eighteenth century, Britain was as far removed from ideal-typical authoritarianism as from democracy, but just a few centuries earlier England (and the separate state of Scotland) fully meet our criteria of authoritarianism, be that the rule of an absolute monarch or of local lords and chieftains.

2 Chimamanda Ngozi Adichie, interviewed by Lisa Allardice, *Guardian Review*, 14 November 2020, pp. 6–9, at p. 8. The alarm was raised earlier and explored in Cass R. Sunstein (ed.), *Can it Happen Here? Authoritarianism in America* (New York: Harper Collins, 2018), the title echoing Sinclair Lewis's 1935 novel, *It Can't Happen Here* (Penguin Classic edition, London, 2017), warning of the rise of an authoritarian populist leader to dictatorial power in America.

3 See, for example, "Trump was deliberately "trying to stage a coup," a former White House national-security official says," https://uk.finance.yahoo.com/news/trump-deliberately-trying-stage-coup-1303333264.html; and "Fiona Hill: This was 'an attempted coup'," https://edition-cnn-com/videos/tv/2021/01/11/Amanpour-fiona-hill-capitol-hill-russia.cnn. The term "coup" was used also by Arnold Schwarzenegger in an impressive 7-minute statement in which he compared the Washington events of 6 January 2021 to the Nazi Kristallnacht of 1938: www.cnet.com/news/arnold-schwarzenegger-compares-capitol-attack-to-kristallnacht-in-viral-video/.

4 Noting that "some 147 members of Congress, including eight senators, voted to reject the states' votes," Martin Wolf, describes Trump's "attempted coup" as "a very bad moment for the credibility of the US republic, to the delight of despots everywhere": Martin Wolf, "American republic's near-death experience," *Financial Times*, 20 January 202 (www.ft.com/content/c085e962-f27c-4c34-a0f1-5cf2bd813fbc).

The End of Communist Rule in Europe 171

5 For a much fuller discussion, see Archie Brown, *The Myth of the Strong Leader: Political Leadership in the Modern Age* (Basic Books, New York, 2014; paperback with updated Foreword, Vintage, London, 2018); and Brown, "Against the *Führerprinzip*: For Collective Leadership," *Daedalus* 145, no. 3, (2016), pp. 109–123.
6 A CNN poll conducted between the invasion of the Capitol on 6 January and Trump's departure from the White House found that, overall, 34 percent of Americans approved of Trump's handling of the presidency, down from a preelection 42 percent, and that 23 percent of respondents, but 58 percent of Republicans, believed the conspiracy story that "Biden did not legitimately win enough votes to become president," "CNN Poll: Trump's approval rating reaches new low as term ends" (https://edition.cnn.com/2021/01/17/politics/cnn-poll-trump-lowest-approval-of-his-presidency/index.html).
7 "Full transcript of Joe Biden's inauguration speech," 20 January, 2021, www.bbc.co.uk/news/world-us-canada-55656824.
8 David Hume, "Of the First Principles of Government" in *Essays Moral, Political, and Literary: A New Edition* Cadell, London, 1788, pp. 37–39.
9 Robert A. Dahl, *On Democracy* (New Haven, CT: Yale University Press, 1998), p. 188.
10 Juan Linz and Alfred Stepan, *Problems of Democratic Transition and Consolidation: Southern Europe, South America, and Post-Communist Europe* (Baltimore and London: Johns Hopkins University Press, 1996), p. 5.
11 Ibid., p. 6.
12 David W.P. Elliott, "Official History, Revisionist History, and Wild History," in Mark Philip Bradley and Marilyn B. Young (eds), *Making Sense of the Vietnam Wars: Local, National, and Transnational Perspectives* (New York: Oxford University Press, 2008), p.295.
13 Jason Brownlee, *Authoritarianism in an Age of Democratization* (New York: Cambridge University Press, 2007), p. 42.
14 These points are elaborated in Archie Brown, *The Rise and Fall of Communism* (New York: Ecco, and Bodley Head, London, 2009), esp. ch. 28, "Why Did Communism Last So Long?," pp. 574–86,
15 The point is expanded in Archie Brown, "Leadership and Crisis: The last years of the Soviet Union, 1985-91," *APSA-CP Newsletter* 30, no. 2, (2020), pp. 73–80.
16 On the last point, see Jerry F. Hough, *The Soviet Prefects: The Local Party Organs in Industrial Decision-Making* (Cambridge, MA: Harvard University Press, 1969).
17 Marshall L. Goldman, *U.S.S.R. in Crisis: The Failure of an Economic System* (New York: Norton, 1983), p. 182.
18 "Vstrecha Gorbacheva s tret'ey gruppoy sekretarey obkomov, 18 aprelya 1988," in *V Politbyuro TsK KPSS...po zapisyam Anatoliya Chernyaeva, Vadima Medvedeva, Georgiya Shakhnazarova (1985–1991)*, 2nd ed. (Gorbachev Foundation, Moscow, 2008), pp. 336–47, at p. 342; and Archie Brown, *The Human Factor: Gorbachev, Reagan, and Thatcher, and the End of the Cold War* (Oxford and New York: Oxford University Press, 2020), p. 225.

19 Jack F. Matlock, Jr., *Autopsy on an Empire: The American Ambassador's Account of the Collapse of the Soviet Union* (New York: Random House, 1995), p. 210.
20 Ibid.
21 For discussion of Gorbachev's rise to power and the reasons for his speedy selection as Soviet leader in succession to Chernenko, see Archie Brown, *The Gorbachev Factor* (Oxford: Oxford University Press, 1996), pp. 69–88; and William Taubman, *Gorbachev: His Life and Times* (New York: Norton, 2017), pp. 192–213.
22 Archie Brown, "The Gorbachev Factor Revisited," *Problems of Post-Communism* 58, no. 4–5 (2011), pp. 56–65, at p. 66; and Brown, *The Rise and Fall of Communism*, pp. 101–114 and 503–521.
23 Mikhail Gorbachev, *Ponyat' perestroyku ...pochemu eto vazhno seychas* (Moscow: Al'pina, 2006), p. 373.
24 Gorbachev in Mikhail Gorbachev and Zdeněk Mlynář, *Conversations with Gorbachev: On Perestroika, the Prague Spring, and the Crossroads of Socialism*, translated by George Shriver (New York: Columbia University Press, 2002), p. 201.
25 Brown, *The Gorbachev Factor*, pp. 175–84; Taubman, *Gorbachev*, pp. 359–65; and Vadim Medvedev, *V komande Gorbacheva: Vzglyad iznutri* (Bylina, Moscow, 1994), pp. 71–78.
26 Gorbachev and Mlynář, *Conversations with Gorbachev*, pp. 123–27.
27 For example, Samuel P. Huntington, *The Third Wave: Democratization in the Late Twentieth Century* (Norman, OK and London: University of Oklahoma Press, 1993); and Larry Diamond, *Developing Democracy: Toward Consolidation* (Baltimore and London: Johns Hopkins University Press, 1999).
28 Cf. the section, "The Fourth Wave," pp. 181–186, of Archie Brown, "Transnational Influences in the Transition from Communism," *Post-Soviet Affairs* 16, no. 2 (2000), pp. 177–200. See also Michael McFaul, "The Fourth Wave of Democracy and Dictatorship: Noncooperative Transitions in the Postcommunist World," *World Politics* 54, no. 2 (2002), pp. 212–44.
29 For discussion of the new top foreign policymaking team, see Brown, *The Gorbachev Factor*, pp. 97–111 and 212–20.
30 "Vystuplenie v organizatsii ob"edinnenykh natsiy, 7 dekabrya 1988 goda," in M.S. Gorbachev, *Izbrannye rech'i i stat'i*, Vol. VII (Politizdat, Moscow, 1990), pp. 184–202, at pp. 188–89.
31 Ibid., p. 189.
32 Ibid.
33 Pavel Palazhchenko, "On khotel vnedrit' v politiku moral'," *Mir peremen* (Moscow), No. 4, 2020, pp. 119–24, at p. 122.
34 For an illuminating analysis of the Hungarian transition from Communist rule, see Rudolf L. Tőkés, *Hungary's Negotiated Revolution: Economic Reform, Social Change, and Political Succession* (Cambridge: Cambridge University Press, 1996).
35 Aleksandr Galkin and Anatoliy Chernyaev (eds), *Mikhail Gorbachev i Germanskiy vopros: Sbornik dokumentov 1986-1991* (Ves' mir, Moscow, 2006).
36 On the fall of the Berlin Wall and the political process leading to the unification of Germany, see especially Mary Elise Sarotte, *The Collapse: The*

Accidental Opening of the Berlin Wall (New York: Basic Books, 2014); Galkin and Chernyaev (eds), *Mikhail Gorbachev i Germanskiy vopros*, op.cit.; Helga Haftendorn, "The unification of Germany, 1985-1991," in Melvyn P. Leffler and Odd Arne Westad (eds), *The Cambridge History of the Cold War, Volume III: Endings* (Cambridge: Cambridge University Press, 2010), pp. 333–55; Svetlana Savranskaya and Thomas Blanton, *The Last Superpower Summits: Gorbachev, Reagan and Bush. Conversations that Ended the Cold War* (Budapest and New York: Central European University Press, 2016), esp. pp. 573–86; and Philip Zelikow and Condoleezza Rice, *Germany Unified and Europe Transformed: A Study in Statecraft* (Cambridge, MA: Harvard University Press, 1995).

37 For vivid and more detailed accounts of the transformation of Eastern Europe in 1989–90, see Timothy Garton Ash, *We the People* (Cambridge: Granta, 1990); Jacques Lévesque, *The Enigma of 1989: The USSR and the Liberation of Eastern Europe* (Berkeley, CA: University of California Press, 1997); and Gale Stokes, *The Walls Came Tumbling Down: The Collapse of Communism in Eastern Europe* (New York: Oxford University Press, 1993). For more recent analyses of the transition from Communism, as well as a resurgence of authoritarian trends in several post-Communist countries, see Martin K. Dmitrov (ed.), *Why Communism Did Not Collapse: Understanding Authoritarian Regime Resilience in Asia and Europe* (New York: Cambridge University Press, 2013), a work concerned with the surviving Asian Communist states as well as with the former Warsaw Pact countries; and Ivan Krastev and Stephen Holmes, *The Light that Failed: A Reckoning* (London: Allen Lane, 2019).

38 Adrian Guelke, "The Impact of the End of the Cold War on the South African Transition," *Journal of Contemporary African Studies* 14, no. 1 (1996), pp. 87–100, at p. 97.

39 Brown, "Transnational Influences in the Transition from Communism," op. cit., p. 182.

40 Mark Kramer, "The Collapse of East European Communism and the Repercussions within the Soviet Union" (Part 1), *Journal of Cold War Studies* 5, no. 4, (2003), pp. 218–19.

41 That was certainly not because of discrimination in their favor, whereas some positive discrimination was employed at times within the party and in Soviet cultural policy to advance citizens from the Central Asian republics. The reason why there was a disproportionately high representation of Jews in the membership of the CPSU is that the party recruited a much larger percentage of the population with higher educational qualifications than of those with basic education and a greater proportion of urban than of rural residents. It was because Soviet Jews were predominantly to be found in the cities, were disproportionately well educated, and were occupying the kind of jobs associated with CPSU membership that their incidence of party membership was high. In the early Soviet years, Jews were prominent in the revolutionary movement.

42 Terry Martin, *The Affirmative Action Empire: Nations and Nationalism in the Soviet Union, 1923-1939* (Ithaca, NY: Cornell University Press, 2001), p. 12.

43 Ibid., p. 13. As Martin puts it succinctly: "The Soviet Union was not a federation and certainly not a nation-state. Its distinctive feature was the systematic support of national forms: territory, culture, language, and elites" (ibid., p. 15).
44 Linz and Stepan first used the term in *Problems of Democratic Transition and Consolidation*, p. 34; but they developed it in Alfred Stepan, Juan J. Linz, and Yogendra Yadav, *Crafting State-Nations: India and Other Multinational Democracies* (Baltimore, MD: Johns Hopkins University Press, 2011), p. 1 for the passage quoted.
45 Stepan, Linz, and Yadav, *Crafting State-Nations*, pp. 14–17.
46 Alec Nove, *The Soviet System in Retrospect: An Obituary Notice*, the Fourth Averell Harriman Lecture, 17 February 17 1993 (New York: Harriman Institute, Columbia University, 1993), pp. 30–31.
47 Russian Soviet Federative Socialist Republic – the official name of the Russian Republic. Jeffrey Kahn, *Federalization, Democratization, and the Rule of Law in Russia* (Oxford: Oxford University Press, 2002), p. 94.
48 Ibid., p. 95.
49 Mark R. Beissinger, *Nationalist Mobilization and the Collapse of the Soviet State* (Cambridge and New York: Cambridge University Press, 2002); Brown, *The Rise and Fall of Communism*, esp. ch. 27, "The Break-up of the Soviet State," pp. 549–73; Andrei Grachev, *Final Days: The Inside Story of the Collapse of the Soviet Union* (Boulder, CO: Westview Press, 1995); Serhii Plokhy, *The Last Empire: The Final Days of the Soviet Union* (New York: Basic Books, 2014); and Vladislav Zubok, *Collapse: The Fall of the Soviet Union* (New Haven and London: Yale University Press, 2021).
50 Brown, *The Rise and Fall of Communism*, pp. 11–153.
51 Valerie Bunce, *Subversive Institutions: The Design and Destruction of Socialism and the State* (Cambridge: Cambridge University Press, 1999).
52 I have explored this at much greater length elsewhere, especially in Archie Brown, *Seven Years that Changed the World: Perestroika in Perspective* (Oxford: Oxford University Press, 2007) and *The Gorbachev Factor*. See also Alexander Dallin and Gail W. Lapidus (eds), *The Soviet System: From Crisis to Collapse* (revised edition, Boulder, CO: Westview Press, 1995); Mark Sandle, *Gorbachev: Man of the Twentieth Century?* (Hodder, London, 2008); and Taubman, *Gorbachev: Life and Times*. There is a rich and illuminating memoir literature in Russian, most of which has not been translated into English. One which does exist in an excellent translation is the highly informative book by Gorbachev's close aide and principal adviser on foreign policy, Anatoly Chernyaev, *My Six Years with Gorbachev*, translated and edited by Robert D. English and Elizabeth Tucker (University Park, PA: Pennsylvania State University Press, 2000).
53 Brown, *The Human Factor*, pp. 288–309; and Beth A. Fischer, *The Myth of Triumphalism: Rethinking President Reagan's Cold War Legacy* (Lexington, KY: University Press of Kentucky, 2020).
54 Archie Brown, "Did Gorbachev as General Secretary Become a Social Democrat?" *Europe- Studies* 65, no. 2, (2013), pp. 198–220.
55 If Boris Yeltsin had stuck to his earlier professed commitment to bring Russia into a loosely federal multinational union, a majority of the fifteen republics of

the USSR would probably have joined this new and voluntary successor to the Soviet state. Gorbachev remained convinced that a Union (not the *Soviet Union*) could have been preserved and published a book of documents from the perestroika period to make the point: *Soyuz mozhno bylo sokhranit': dokumenty i fakty o politike M.S. Gorbacheva po reformirovaniyu i sokhraneniy mnogonatsional'nogo gosudarstava* (Aprel' 85, Moscow, 1995).

56 That argument is made at length, and documented, in Brown, *The Human Factor*.
57 "Like most Russians," wrote Gorbachev's interpreter and adviser Pavel Palazhchenko, "Yeltsin was, I believe, inwardly dubious about the breakup of the country." In the period up the end of 1991, Palazhchenko added, Yeltsin took "little interest in foreign policy" and even less in theoretical concepts. However, "Yeltsin's main political strength is his *unfailing instinct for power*" (*My Years with Gorbachev and Shevardnadze: The Memoir of a Soviet Interpreter*, University Park, PA: Pennsylvania State University Press, 1997, pp. 360 and 372, italics added).
58 Plokhy, *The Last Empire*, pp. 172–88; and Grachev, *Final Days*, pp. 87–96 and 106–110.
59 Or, more precisely, to the extent it was unfair, it was through the rigging of electoral precinct boundaries and by voter suppression, leading to the disenfranchisement of a disproportionately large number of African-Americans, whose votes would have contributed to Trump losing still more heavily.
60 Alfred Stepan and Juan J. Linz, "Comparative Perspectives on Inequality and the Quality of Democracy in the United States," *Perspectives on Politics* 9, no. 4, (2011), pp. 841–56.
61 As late as December 1989 more than 80 percent of Soviet citizens wholly or partly supported Gorbachev's political changes, according to the survey data of the most professional of Russian polling organizations at that time, led by sociologists Tatiana Zaslavskaya and Yuriy Levada (*V kakoy mere vy odobryaete deyatel'nost" M.S. Gorbacheva*, VTsIOM, Moscow, 1990).
62 The well-respected survey researchers of the Levada Center have polled Russian attitudes to the breakup of the USSR throughout the post-Soviet era. Regret about the end of the Soviet Union was expressed by 66 percent of respondents in 2018. That was the highest proportion of support for the USSR for seventeen years. The end of the Yeltsin era and beginning of the Putin presidency was the only time when nostalgia for the Soviet Union was even higher – 74 percent in 1999, 75 percent in 2000, and 72 percent in 2001 (www.levada.ru/2018/12/19/nostalgiya-po-sssr-2/?fromtg=1), pp. 1-5, at p. 2.
63 The phrase, "the fallacy of retrospective determinism," comes from Reinhard Bendix, *Nation-Building and Citizenship* (New York: John Wiley, 1964), p. 13. As early as 1992, Alexander Dallin noted its applicability to many explanations of the end of Soviet Communism and of the Soviet state (Dallin, "Causes of the Collapse of the USSR," *Post-Soviet Affairs* [formerly *Soviet Economy*] 8, no. 4, pp. 279–302, at p. 297).

7 Democracy's Fragility and the European Political Order
Functionalism, Militant Democracy, and Crisis

Ludvig Norman

Introduction

Standard accounts of the beginnings of the postwar European political order tend to focus on how cooperative arrangements were put in place to prevent further wars, by creating interdependencies between, in particular, France and Germany.[1] What is less often explored is how the ideas that shaped the specific design of these institutional beginnings emerged in tandem with widely held perceptions of the inherent weaknesses of liberal representative democracy. I explore these interconnections by focusing specifically on functionalist ideas of international cooperation that came to fundamentally shape the first concrete steps toward the new European political order.[2] By doing so, I hope to highlight assumptions regarding robustness and fragility that were built into this institutional architecture. I also seek to show how aspects of these ideas have resurfaced in our contemporary setting as a reaction to crises that face this political order.

The link between functionalist ideas and European political cooperation in the context of the European Community (EC), and later on the European Union (EU), are well-documented.[3] Functionalism won the first battle over how to organize postwar European political cooperation.[4] On the losing side stood constitutional federalist ideas of international cooperation that shaped the formation of the increasingly sidelined Council of Europe. In popular and academic debates the EU has become a symbol of technocratic rule, and functionalism is regarded as the strategy that enabled European integration "by stealth."[5] While not necessarily inaccurate, this characterization hides from view important assumptions regarding democratic politics at the basis of the functionalist program. Perceptions of democracy's fragility informed functionalist notions of international organization that shaped the early stages of postwar European cooperation. Insufficient attention has also been paid to the significant overlaps between assumptions that informed functionalism, on the one hand, and theories of democratic self-preservation and militant democracy, on the other hand. As I discuss below, strikingly similar assumptions regarding democracy's fragility form the basis for their respective analyses of what is required for creating stable international cooperation. This is especially notable since these ideas emerged from rather different traditions.

The functionalist project was perhaps most clearly articulated in the work of Romanian-born political scientist David Mitrany, by many regarded as the chief proponent of functionalist ideas in the first half of the twentieth century.[6] Mitrany's functionalism grew out of a British pluralist tradition and was part of a broader project of displacing the power of the state by supplanting it with international functional arrangements.[7] The theory of militant democracy was rooted in a Weberian tradition and its most notable exponent, the German constitutional lawyer Karl Löwenstein, drew heavily on Weber's sociology of the state in some of his writings.[8] These thinkers, however, ended up in very similar conclusions regarding what robustness of international political orders requires. From the perspective of our understanding of European postwar cooperation, the chapter thus brings together two lines of political thought, the interconnections of which have rarely been explored in this context. I revisit their ideas and underlying assumptions regarding robustness and fragility of liberal democracy and the extensions of these ideas to the international realm.

The conceptual connections that I highlight are then tied to a discussion on how similar assumptions play out in a more contemporary setting, especially in the context of the European Union. A key argument here is thus that, rather than being limited to this particular historical juncture, these ideas have continued to play an important role in the institutional evolution of the European political order, especially when faced with crises and at times when the order is perceived to be under threat. This yields a peculiar relation between politicization and democratization in the EU. Heightened politicization of issues seems to have an inverse relationship with democratization of the political order. In times when political issues become increasingly salient and the object of debate and contestation, mechanisms that work to constrain opportunities for broad participation, effective representation, and accountability are introduced.

This last point is concretized through a set of illustrative contemporary examples where the perceived fragility of democratic institutions has shaped the EU's actions. These include the EU's response to the euro crisis as well as its response to the political crisis born out by the rise of far-right populism as a political force to be reckoned with in the 2010s.

Functionalism and Democracy's Fragility

Functionalism emerged as one of the most prominent ideas on how to rethink international cooperation in the first half the twentieth century. It was inspired by the failure of the League of Nations and its inability to prevent violent interstate conflict. Functionalist ideas questioned the reliance on state sovereignty as the fundamental organizational principle of international political orders. David Mitrany, in identifying what he thought was the main "historical problem" in the 1940s, relied on assumptions in polar opposition to contemporary realist and liberal understandings of international cooperation. The problem for Mitrany was not how to explain international cooperation in an anarchical world system of states. Rather, he started out from what he considered "the baffling division between peoples of the world."[9] In spite of the humanistic universalism that Mitrany argued could be found in the main traditions of ethics as well as in doctrines of the major world religions, division and conflict dominated the international sphere. The "natural" point of departure for a global system was not, for Mitrany, interstate relations but rather organically generated forms of cooperation on well-defined problems of common concern. Indeed, the emergence of such functional cooperative forms was thwarted by the system of states.

This perspective on how to rethink international cooperation along functionalist lines was intimately associated to a more general argument regarding the decline of the state as the locus for modern politics. It is important to note, however, that Mitrany's claims regarding the decline of the modern state in the first half of the twentieth century did not rest on the state's actual lack of relevance nationally or internationally. Rather than implying that the state was powerless in terms of its efforts to shape social and economic life, the functionalist argument relied on the idea that the state had become progressively *inappropriate* to deal with an increasingly interconnected world and that it actually worked as a hindrance for the development of more apt ways to organize the world system.[10] In Mitrany, this prompted a reconceptualization of the organization of political life and with it a reconceptualization of the primary unit of representation in democratic decision-making.

What the state does, in Mitrany's characterization, is, on the one hand, to feed expectations for the provision of welfare to the point where it cannot be sustained and, on the other hand, to work toward the control of all aspects of economic and social life. The state is at once brought to the breaking point of its capacities while also becoming more and more intrusive in terms of its societal control. The organization of the state in this way thus had far-reaching negative consequences for society. Equally important for Mitrany, from this perspective, state-bound political orders are caught up in path-dependent processes that work to distort "natural" transnational connections and interdependencies. As Mitrany argued, "our social activities are cut off arbitrarily at the limit of the state and, if at all, are allowed to be linked to the same activities across the border only by means of uncertain and cramping political ligatures."[11] At the forefront of the functionalist approach lies the idea that loyalty to the nation-state can be lessened by "the experience of fruitful international co-operation."[12] This in turn serves as an avenue away from the destructive conflicts of the twentieth century's first half.

The functionalist notion of international cooperation identified state-bound organization of politics as associated with a set of mechanisms that work to limit individual freedoms and that impede peaceful transnational cooperation. These mechanisms contributed to the undesirable robustness of national political orders, while simultaneously preventing robust international orders to emerge, indeed contributing to the fragility and breakdown of an order like the League of Nations. A crucial point here is that Mitrany identified this drive toward ever-greater state control as a feature of democratic *as well as* totalitarian states. This rather controversial claim meant that the totalitarian state is merely an extreme manifestation of this fundamental force that tends toward state intervention in all spheres of society.[13] The opposition between democracy and totalitarian government, Mitrany argues, does not adequately capture what is at stake.[14] Rather, from Mitrany's point of view there is a totalitarian element in democratic political orders that works through a set of concrete mechanisms both to further state control, but which also impedes international cooperation.

First, Mitrany identified the double-edged sword of mass communication. Politicians who are wedded to the idea of the state's primacy will tend to mislead and deceive the public to embrace nationalist ideologies while making suspect "natural" connections and interdependencies on the international arena. The way that politicians interact with the masses is thus less conducive to serving public interests than to reinforce the state as the taken-for-granted unit of modern politics. Second, Mitrany argued that there is a self-reinforcing mechanism inherent in the way in which welfare states create mounting public expectations for more welfare. Thus, while national politicians stand ready to fan commitments to nationalist ideologies, the public also becomes a willing participant in giving up individual freedoms. The state will always frame the provision of public goods as necessarily correlated to heightened state control. Finally, rising demands on more welfare means that the state is tasked with dealing with an ever-growing catalogue of issues. Parliaments are overburdened and decisions are increasingly taken without public insight in committees where experts and interest groups, rather than elected politicians, dominate. The public expecting more welfare, nationally minded politicians, experts, and special interests are colluding to erode democracy, increase the state's control of all aspects of social and economic life and at the same time sever international connections.

The arguments supporting this critical position on the state are illuminating in the sense of speaking to the more specific question of democracy's perceived fragility. Key to Mitrany's functionalism is the focus on concretion and the need for practical action as the foundations for political order. At first glance, this might seem to be an argument against democracy as such. The identification of the functionalist program as merely an argument for technocratic international governance, however, constitutes an overly simplified perspective. Here I join others who have highlighted the complexity of Mitrany's position, not least on democratic politics.[15] Steffek and Holthaus point to how, rather than being a proponent of technocratic governance at the international level, he could instead be seen as a forerunner in terms of rethinking democracy from a cosmopolitan perspective.[16] For Mitrany, a lack of international social policy, and an inability to modernize liberal democratic theory in the face of "recent social transformations" allowed for fascism.[17] Key to this perspective is the tensions that Mitrany sees in what he considered the greatest problematic legacy of the French revolution. This concerned the tension between, on the one hand, universalist democratic ideals of equality based on being a member of humanity and, on the other hand, democracy articulated in terms of membership of a specific group tied to the territorial state. Mitrany's obsession with international cooperation was thus in important parts based on a wish to create a world system better equipped to realize those ideals. However, while Mitrany was a committed democrat his functionalist view is also infused with a suspicion regarding democratic *principles* as the fundaments on which political orders can be built.

At the basis of this understanding of democracy lies Mitrany's identification of the reasons behind the breakdown of the democratic political order in Weimar Germany, which he outlines in his short text *A Working Peace System*. As much as this text outlines the foundations of international cooperation along functionalist lines, it is also an account of how formal democracy disintegrates under the pressures of the great depression. Totalitarianism is a result of a breakdown in democracy's ability to deliver on human needs. The failure to do this, dramatically manifested through the depression, makes people open to surrender all liberties for the promise of the provision of those needs, but this time through fascist centralized planning wedded to the extreme nationalist notion of the racist state. The failures of the state to deliver on material needs were somewhat paradoxically seen by Mitrany to have fed and strengthened the totalitarian aspects of the state. In the words of Mitrany: "Now the masses are demanding social action without regard to 'rights', and the totalitarian dictators are playing the strong card of pragmatic socialism against constitutional democracy."[18] The functionalist perspective thus relies on the added assumption that mass politics is fundamentally volatile and that formal democracy at the state level is likely to collapse when the state is unable to live up to the expectations of the masses.

The assumptions that fed into functionalist ideas on international cooperation were intimately bound up with an assessment of the problems facing political orders at the state level. While the functionalist perspective on the decline of the state preceded the rise of European fascism, it became part of a broader set of ideas that identified weaknesses at the heart of liberal democracy. Functionalism emerges here as a school of thought that draws certain implications from democracy's demise in the interwar years for how international political orders should be structured. With that, Mitrany joins a line of postwar criticism aimed at conceptions of democracy perceived as overly formalistic and prone to ideological dogmatism coupled with a deep skepticism toward democracy as a form of mass politics.[19]

Democracy's Fragility and European Cooperation

A frequently reiterated idea among observers of democracy's downfall before World War II was, and remains, that "totalitarian movements use and abuse democratic freedoms in order to abolish them."[20] In contemporary discussions on militant democracy a quote accredited to Joseph Goebbels, taunting democrats for how democracy provided its most mortal enemies with the means for its own destruction, is often mobilized to underline the necessity of protective measures to safeguard democratic institutions from internal threats.[21] The fundamental lesson learned from the fall of the Weimar Republic was that liberal democracy lacked the means for its own self-preservation. It thus became the paradigmatic case exposing democracy's fragility.

Faced with movements that sought its downfall, it was unable to put in place safeguards to keep these forces out. Here the work of constitutional lawyer and political scientist Karl Löwenstein is emblematic. While his ideas resonate with many in the postwar context, his thinking was perhaps the most explicit on the need to reconfigure and constrain democratic politics in light of such threats. He famously wrote on these themes already before the war, exiled from Germany to the United States, in his two essays on 'militant democracy' and continued, after the war, to also apply these ideas to possible forms for cooperative structures in the European political space.[22] For Löwenstein, a democracy needed to use defensive efforts to protect its core and should not back away from such measures due to "democratic fundamentalism."[23] "Constitutional scruples can no longer restrain from restrictions on democratic fundamentals, for the sake of ultimately preserving these very fundamentals."[24] Indeed, for Löwenstein it was the dogmatic interpretation of fundamental democratic rights that bore part of the responsibility for democracy's fall.[25] What is interesting for the present discussion is not primarily the more concrete protective measures that Löwenstein suggested to ward off fascists. Rather, it is the extent to which his assumptions regarding the fundamental conditions of democratic politics overlap with functionalist notions.

Mitrany's functionalist project did obviously not position itself as a tool to protect nationally based democracies, as Löwenstein's did. However, there is a striking overlap between some of the core assumptions underlying functionalism and those that shape the notion of militant democracy. As discussed elsewhere, the militant democratic idea relied fundamentally on distrust of the notion of popular self-government and introduced an elitist logic at the heart of democracy.[26] The fault, it seems, lies primarily with the people, its emotionalism and susceptibility to the spectacle of fascist politics. The role of the media in supplying new opportunities to aestheticize politics and providing rulers with an unfettered line of communication to the masses in the 1930s was also highlighted as an important condition for fascism; especially, at a time when new possibilities for political communication were made available through the introduction of radio and film. Democracy, being built around abstract procedures and formal rules, could never compete with the emotionalism of fascist rhetoric.[27] The symbiotic links between politicians and the masses needed to be, if not cut, then at least severely weakened. Rather than a democracy of the masses, democracy had to be redefined and a more restrictive notion of democracy introduced. This diagnosis of the fragility of democratic politics was at the heart of Löwenstein's vision of democratic politics, and several of its key ideas overlapped to a considerable degree with functionalism.

Functionalism, like Löwenstein's protective notion of democratic politics, can in many ways be seen as a turn away from ideology. Whether totalitarian or not, ideologies have according to the functionalist perspective not been useful when employed to structure economic and social activities. Ideologies turn actors away from practical knowledge and take politics into the realm of contests between abstract principles on which there is little hope to find common ground. Thus, democratic representation based on the articulation of interests bound together by ideologies to form political programs that could be expressed through political parties, which then compete for votes in contested elections, does not figure prominently in Mitrany's work.

Representation from the functionalist perspective was not about mass voting but about involvement, epistemic contributions, and funding. Mass voting in elections, especially among what Mitrany refers to as "illiterate inexperienced populations," is a spurious "democratic tool."[28] Mitrany identifies such "inexperienced populations" as dominating in former African colonies and also in Latin America and South-Eastern Europe. This highly hierarchical, and at times racist, view of political development, was based on the notion that such populations were particularly "easily tempted by emotional appeals" and could not be expected to wisely choose their parliamentarians.[29] This elitism also resounds with Löwenstein's perspective that sees liberal democracy as only fitting for the most evolved among nations.[30] That said, neither Löwenstein nor Mitrany placed too much faith in the publics of Western democracies either. Instead, focus must be put on practical matters. Such matters, Mitrany argued, were of the kind that "everywhere the simple peasant is apt to be a shrewd judge."[31] Mitrany's ideals were thus characterized by an emphasis on practical knowledge and functional cooperation. Here he contributed to a line of thinking that saw constitutional politics as a nonstarter for international cooperation.

Constitutional principles are inherently about how to distribute power. From a functionalist perspective, to initiate a process of international cooperation by first establishing optimal ways to distribute power makes it likely that cooperative arrangements will be both ineffective and difficult to get off the ground in the first place. This was an important aspect of why Mitrany saw fundamental flaws in models of international cooperation based on ideas of constitutional federalism. Federal systems depend on constitutionalizing at which level decision-making powers are located. This makes the creation of such orders difficult and makes them inflexible in terms of their ability adapt to new needs. In relation to these discussions, Mitrany also pointed out that there was no basis at that point in time for a common constitutional bond and thus that "any prearranged constitutional framework would be taken wholly out of the air."[32] It is in these discussions that we approach key aspects of the functionalist diagnosis of democratic fragility, especially in times of turmoil. Here Mitrany refers to the conservative political thinker

Edmund Burke and states that "if it is 'always dangerous to meddle with foundations' it is doubly dangerous now. Our political problems are obscure, while the political passions of the time are blinding."[33] Here Mitrany's ideas were also taken up by other prominent international theorists such as E.H. Carr and Hans Morgenthau, both portal figures of realist thinking on international relations.[34] In particular, functionalist forms of organization and its focus on concretion were seen to offer attractive ways to bypass antagonistic and conflictual politics.

Similar to these thinkers, and for similar reasons, Löwenstein was entirely committed to the functionalist route to European cooperation. His reasons for this clearly highlight the connections between these two lines of thinking. In a piece published in 1952, he analyzes and compares the federalist approach to international cooperation with that of the functionalist, highlighting how the idealistic dogmatism of the federalists makes international cooperation impossible.[35] As an illustration of the problems with a federalist approach, Löwenstein supplies an analysis of the workings of the Council of Europe, an organization set up in 1949 and which in large parts followed a model through which national institutions were extended and used as the basis for international cooperation. Löwenstein's account is an almost parodical study in political paralysis, with procedural issues at every turn taking precedence over substance and concrete problem-solving. As such, it serves as an illustration of his views on the problems associated with organizing international cooperation by taking constitutional issues as a point of departure. Löwenstein caps the discussion on the issue, stating that "European unification is too serious a business to be left to politicians."[36]

Indeed, according to the functionalist perspective, cooperative arrangements should not take actors and their responsibilities as their point of departure. Instead, power could be distributed through a clear-headed assessment of practical requirements associated with different functions and objects. As Mitrany states:

Instead (...) of asking by *whom* should sovereignty and power be exercised, we should rather ask upon what objects they should be exercised(...) [T]he real question is not "who are the rightful authorities" but rather "what are the rightful ends -and what are the proper means for them?"[37]

As long as people with practical knowledge and experience sit down and seek solutions to concrete problems, chances are that those solutions will better fit the needs of those concerned. Constitutional issues, then, are not of primary concern for such arrangements. These arguments are also tied to Mitrany's perceptions of the factors that are likely to generate robust cooperative arrangements. The robustness of political order is chiefly a function of whether they deliver on the needs of its members, and it is that which must guide the construction of cooperative arrangements. Mitrany captures this view succinctly by saying, that "the peoples may applaud declarations of rights, but they will call for the satisfaction of needs."[38] What complicates Mitrany's views here is also that he identifies the expectations on democracies to deliver the goods as one of its chief weaknesses since it will inevitably push it to become overburdened. It is not entirely clear why these kinds of mechanisms would not reappear in functionalist arrangements, albeit at the international level.

From Mitrany's view, functional arrangements would be decoupled from the politicians that have a vested interest in safeguarding the dominance of the state as the locus of sovereign power. This would also mean that functional cooperation would not be subjected to the same risks that he and Löwenstein had identified as being associated with new technologies of mass communication. This ties into Mitrany's functional view of representation inspired in part by guild socialism, where tasks of functional organizations are to correspond with specific human needs. For Mitrany, the International Labour Organization (ILO) represented an ideal in this respect.[39] The critique of the political and constitutional view of international cooperation is thus informed both by the limited success of previous international arrangements, in particular the League of Nations, and the social diagnosis of the factors that had brought about fascism and communism, and the destruction of democracy.

Functionalist as well as the overtly protective notions of politics became influential in shaping the emerging European political order, the European Community and later the European Union. However, functionalism as developed in Mitrany's work was only implemented selectively in shaping this order. A key idea of functionalism was to organize international cooperation, not along territorial lines but around functional lines of common interest. The creation of a regional organization like the EC was thus vehemently opposed by Mitrany as he argued that such an order would inevitably reproduce exclusionary and nationalist logics, but at the level of a regional political order instead of at the level of the state.[40] However, ideas on how to organize international cooperation that in effect removed core issues from the grasp of elected politicians where central to both functionalism and theories of militant democracy and became an important part of the EC and later the EU. Key actors, like Jean Monnet, a French diplomat who helped draft a key document for postwar European cooperation, the "Schuman plan", exhibits a more pragmatic view on functionalist ideas.[41] The Schuman Plan that established the main direction of the European Coal and Steel Community (ECSC) clearly echoed functionalist ideas in setting out the rationale for its design. In particular, it steered clearly away from the constitutional federalist model of international cooperation, instead stating that "Europe will not be made all at once, or according to a single plane. It will be built through concrete achievements which first create de facto solidarity."[42]

The creation and the institutional design of the High Authority put in place to oversee and implement the pooling of coal and steel production also drew on functionalist ideals in the sense of depoliticizing its decision-making processes. Its operation would be led by independent officials who "in the performance of these duties [should] neither seek nor take instructions from any Government or from any other body."[43] Functionalism as tool to protect Europe, and by extension democracy, from itself, along the lines discussed by Löwenstein, created the organizational logics around the European political order was reconstructed in the postwar period. The radical nature of this piecemeal and practical approach to international cooperation emerges more clearly when considering the contrast of the intergovernmental federalist approach that characterized the setting up of the Council of Europe as a result of the 1949 Hague conference, only a year prior.[44] While ambitions were far higher in terms of its statement of ideals and scope of its actions, it amounted to far less in terms of concrete mechanisms that would tie its member countries together.

The functionalist theory of international cooperation was underpinned by assumptions regarding the fragility of democratic politics. Those assumptions were informed by the fundamental crises that beset Europe in the first half of the twentieth century, two wars, the destruction of democracy and the rise of totalitarian government. These ideas shaped the early history of postwar European cooperation in far-reaching ways. The question is to what extent these ideas supply a useful lens through which more contemporary dynamics of the European political order can be understood.

Tensions in Democratization of the EU

While my focus in this chapter is on how functionalist ideas shaped the design of the European political order, it is also important to nuance this view and to acknowledge how European postwar cooperation evolved in parallel with broad social and cultural shifts that reshaped democratic institutions in many countries. In the second half of the twentieth century, parallel to the creation of this political order, broad social and political movements calling for more inclusive democratic reforms gained in strength. At the national level, far less restrictive notions of democratic political orders emerged in many places in Western Europe. These developments were accelerated in the mid- to late twentieth century through the coming of age of the postwar generation, which had to a lesser extent experienced totalitarianism and war firsthand, and through sweeping cultural transformations entailing the gradual erosion of many traditional societal institutions. Democracy was eventually also introduced and consolidated in Southern European states previously under authoritarian rule. While proceeding through different routes, Western European states in general, and Northern European states in particular, extended their welfare states, increasingly facilitating the inclusion of women in the workforce and also, although in a much more gradual fashion, in the realm of politics.[45] It was also in the northern European countries that variants of workplace and industrial democracy were most pronounced with legislation that would introduce worker representation in company boards discussed in the 1970s and early 1980s.[46] Defensive notions of democratic politics most clearly exemplified in the provisions of the German constitution thus coexisted with a movement toward more open and participatory organizational forms of democratic politics.

These developments meant that claims based on more inclusive and democratic ideals became increasingly directed at the European Community. As totalitarian ideologies were increasingly viewed as part of the past in Western Europe, the European political order became perceived in contra-distinction to its neighbors on the other side of the iron curtain. Efforts to democratize the EC, and further on the EU, can thus partly be understood as part of defining a self-understanding separate from that of the Soviet political sphere. With the end of the Cold War, there was a new push to further democratize the EU, in particular by giving its directly elected parliament more influence on EU legislation. Furthermore, the process of European political integration unfolding in the 1980s and picking up speed in the 1990s entailed that legislation taken at the European level was affecting states and citizens in increasingly far-reaching ways. The gap between the growing decision-making competences of the EU and the absence of mechanisms for democratic accountability was by many deemed untenable. The functionalist basis of the institutions was increasingly viewed as technocratic and came to be seen as a possible challenge to the order's robustness. This was seen by some to require both a common European identity to underpin the order and also addressing the EU's 'democratic deficit'.[47]

This pushed political elites to introduce reforms of the EU which would strengthen its democratic aspects. The post-iron-curtain European political environment also presented political elites with pressures to further expand the European political order and include the Eastern and Central European states. This was framed very much as a natural step in terms of welcoming these states into the liberal democratic club.[48] Indeed, if history, as some argued, had come to an end, the EU could hardly stand in its way. Liberal democracy became intimately associated to the core identity of the European political order.

These various pressures amount to an ambivalent and tension-ridden relationship to democratic politics in the EU. On the one hand, through successive treaty revisions from the 1990s and upon until the Lisbon Treaty of 2009, the EU incrementally added democratic elements to its institutional setup. Indeed, as of the entry into force of the Lisbon Treaty, the EU is explicitly committed to representative democracy.[49] Recent institutional developments have included strengthening participatory procedures such as the so-called EU Citizens' Initiative, through which a specified number of EU citizens distributed across a certain number of member states can prompt the Commission to table a policy proposal. Political parties that organize themselves at the European level can receive funding from the EU budget for their political work and for campaigns in the European elections to the European Parliament. The Parliament itself has also been rather radically transformed from its early days as an advisory body supplying opinions on legislative proposals to a decision-making body formally carrying equal weight to the Council in the majority of policy areas.[50] In almost every revision of the EU treaties since the 1992 Maastricht Treaty the European Parliament have been awarded with greater influence. In this sense, post-Cold War European cooperation veered further toward the constitutional federal model. However, a competing set of examples seems to indicate that when under pressure the EU exhibits reflexes among its decision-makers that highlight a fundamental distrust in democratic procedures, treating it as a form of governance too fragile and indeed unable to deal with difficult decisions in a way that would also ensure the project's robustness.

Democratic Mistrust in a European Union under Pressure

The observation that the EU has been beset by crises in recent years has become commonplace. The optimism created by the end of the cold war manifested in the Eastward expansion of the European political order in the 2000s and the deepening of the EU's democratic aspects came to an abrupt halt in the 2010s. Two crises in particular helped foment this shift. The first was the economic and financial crisis of the late 2000s and the second, the more creeping political crisis of the rise of far-right populists across Europe. The aftermath of the global financial and economic crisis, along with rising support across Europe for populist movements resulted in the deepening of political fault lines among EU member states. In this sense, these crises politicized EU politics to an unparalleled degree. However, they also sparked institutional reforms as well as less formal institutional practices that in many ways undercut the stated democratic aims of previous Treaty revisions, and instead demonstrate a resurging mistrust in democratic solutions to the problems facing the European political order.

Reactions from the EU to recent crises point to important similarities in terms of the underlying ideas that informed early institutional discussions on European cooperation. They reverberate with the mistrust in democratic procedures as a basis for cooperation that can be found at the heart of the functionalist project. These perceptions of democracy's fragility seem thus to reemerge when the European political order is under pressure. However, in contrast to the immediate postwar period, today's expectations on the EU to operate in a more democratic fashion are higher. These crisis reactions thus clash with well-institutionalized narratives of the EU as founded on the tenets of representative democracy and active participation of its citizens.

The institutional reforms introduced in the wake of the economic and financial crisis has been the most widely publicized. For members of the Euro zone, they are far-reaching in the control afforded to European institutions over how member states regulate their economies and over their national budgets. In 2007–2008, the economic and financial crisis that had started in the US financial sector was unleashed on European economies, triggering the deepest recession in decades. The EU response consisted in a mix of different measures. As a general characterization, the response and the way in which this response was adopted and was made a permanent part of European institutions further removed control over economic policies from political influence. Member states of the single currency, the Euro, committed to a regime of close monitoring and coordination of their budgets in ways that considerably constrained their ability to shape politics at the national level. Many have highlighted how those effects have led to an erosion of the already weak mechanisms for democratic accountability at the European level.[51] Some have even characterized it as the institutionalization of an authoritarian element in EU governance.[52] Others saw the reforms as a necessary implication of the cooperative regime which the members had committed to. Not least, representatives of the Commission's Directorate-General of Economic and Financial Affairs asked members to accept a more 'constrained' form of sovereignty.

The main underlying rationale for this 'constrained sovereignty' approach was, and remains, straightforward: in a monetary union, while a clear mandate and safeguards from political interference bring the central bank credibility, common provisions for budgetary discipline are justified to the extent that unsustainable fiscal dynamics in one country may eventually entail costs borne by all EMU participants.[53]

According to this image, the EU should proceed with a greater acceptance of these imperatives. Similar to functionalist ideas, 'politics' appears as that which will risk leading to the failure of the system, allowing only limited room for dissent and political opposition.

Concretely, unparalleled powers were shifted to nonelected bodies, and procedures were put in place that radically diminished the ability of citizens to collectively shape economic policies and hold decision-makers accountable. The increasing removal of policy areas such as financial and economic policies from democratic control did not originate in the EU's crisis response but has a longer history associated to the shift of financial institutions such as central banks away from political control, Germany serving as a model in this domain. However, the economic crisis demonstrated an important point that highlights links to the postwar debates on the reconfiguration of democratic politics: When the stakes are high, people cannot be trusted to decide on the correct outcome. Perhaps more accurately, national politicians cannot be trusted to put long-term financial stability over short-term electoral goals. The functionalist notion of the dangers with the opportunistic politician pandering to the uninformed masses, thus skewing the possibilities for functioning cooperative arrangements, appears as a central component of the crisis response. Thus, as Sánches-Cuenca also notes, at a time where the political significance of economic and financial governance were at their height, a point at which publics around Europe were feeling the far-reaching consequences of failing economies and a financial system spinning out of control, unprecedented authority was handed over to non-majoritarian institutions.[54]

In parallel to the aftermath of the euro crisis, radical right and extremist political movements and parties have garnered increasing electoral support in many EU member states. While once considered a marginal phenomenon in European politics, such parties have moved closer to the political center stage. In several countries such as Austria, Italy, the

Netherlands, Denmark, Belgium, and Sweden, the political landscapes have shifted considerably, in some cases leading to government coalitions with far-right parties. In Hungary and Poland, two European states where radical right parties have gained government power, liberal democratic institutions such as the independent media, judiciary, as well as opportunities for civil society organizations to organize political opposition have been seriously eroded. While far less openly publicized than the EU's response to the economic and financial crisis, the response to these political developments also indicate the influence of ideas related to democracy's fragility.

From the point of view of the European Union and the scholarly literature that has focused on developments related to the rise of the far-right in European politics, the emphasis was long placed on 'Euroskepticism' as key concept.[55] These perspectives thus focused primarily on the dimension capturing varying degrees of support or skepticism toward the EU as the key drivers of these developments.

A change, however, has occurred, in particular as a consequence of the emergence of political parties shifting from opposition of the current organization of the EU to implicitly or explicitly challenging previously taken-for-granted democratic norms and political institutions. It is clearly the case that these parties tend to have a skeptic view of the EU, the prime example being the United Kingdom Independence Party (and later on the Brexit party), which had the UK's withdrawal from the EU as its primary political question. However, the "anti-system" quality of these parties is also associated to their questioning of core values of liberal democracy, such as the protection of rights of minorities and commitment to gender equality, and increasingly, the rule of law. It is thus important to not only understand these political movements as Euroskeptics. Rather, their challenge is a more far-reaching one and points to an authoritarian turn in European politics, evidenced in particular by democratic backsliding in Hungary and Poland.[56]

As these movements have become more influential, reactions from the EU have entered both public and academic debate. One of the more high-profile and visible aspects of this response concerns the triggering of Article 7 of the Treaty of the European Union in relation to Poland and Hungary. The article focuses specifically on the functioning of the rule of law in the member states and can, in theory, lead to the loss of voting rights of an EU member state in the Council. There are, however, less publicized aspects of the tendency toward a protective notion of democracy that are reshaping institutional developments and decision-making procedures at the European level. This part of the response to anti-system developments are illuminating in the sense of connections with the protective ideas of democracy proposed by Löwenstein, and the functionalist view on democracy as argued by Mitrany.

Increasingly, defensive practices are enacted within the context of the EU's institutions to shield the political order from the influence of the populist far-right. Such efforts include both the revision of formal rules and less formal practices. A notable example includes the introduction of so-called *cordons sanitaires* aimed at the far-right in the European Parliament. This means the formalization of principled positions on noncooperation with non-desirable parties. For instance, the French delegation to the social democratic group in the European Parliament insisted on such measures aimed at the parliamentary group dominated by the French *Rassemblement Nationale* (formerly the *Front Nationale*). To this end, an internal strategy was devised in 2016 that mandated members of the social democratic group to vote against any amendments to proposed legislation tabled by MEPs from the far-right political group Europe of Nations and Freedom (ENF).[57] The purpose was both to ensure that the group was unable to get any political influence but it was also deemed an important symbolic measure that would clearly signal that the social democrats wanted nothing to with the radical-right. These measures thus go further than merely agreeing on an internal political program and then allow those ideas to clash with whatever political perspectives are presented by other groups, trusting that their ideas will prevail.[58]

A similar logic informed changes to the European Parliaments rules of procedures enacted around the European elections in 2019. These rules regulate the internal governance of the European Parliament and specify, for instance, the voting procedures of the plenary, the responsibilities of the EP's substantive committees and how chairmanship for committees and other posts are appointed. In 2019, just months before the elections to the European parliament, the EP's constitutional affairs committee (AFCO) drew up a new interpretation of the rules according to which political groups in the EP could be formed. The addition states:

The political declaration of a group shall set out the values that the group stands for and the main political objectives which its members intend to pursue together in the framework of the exercise of their mandate. The declaration shall describe the common political orientation of the group in a substantial, distinctive and genuine way.[59]

This seemingly innocuous specification of the rules sparked intensive reactions from representatives from, in particular, the far-right.[60] To understand why, this change needs to be understood in the context of broader efforts to respond to the rise of the far-right populism in the EU.

As I have demonstrated elsewhere, many of the recent changes to regulations governing the EU's emergent transnational party system have been specifically aimed toward this goal, with policy discussions and formal legislation being increasingly motored by perceptions of the need to put in place protective measures against the far-right.[61] Similarly, in this case, the new interpretation added to the existing rules more restrictive criteria for setting up parliamentary groups and protecting the system from 'fake groups' opportunistically looking for the privileges that are afforded to political groups in the European Parliament.[62]

These revisions of the rules form part of an increasingly clear pattern through which mainstream political groupings in the European Parliament seek to limit the influence of the far-right through institutional mechanisms. While it is also commonly asserted that these types of rule changes are not aimed at any particular actor, it is clear that their enactment is almost always sparked by perceived threats to the political order by far-right groups. Recurring negotiations on how to divide the chairmanship of the European Parliament's issue specific committees have also been increasingly shaped by these types of concerns. After the European elections of 2014, the main political groups successfully kept representatives from the far-right out of such positions.[63] Political maneuvering after the 2019 elections mirrored these practices, the difference at this juncture being that the far-right had now secured more voter support, making their exclusion more controversial, something which was also echoed in the attention given to these practices by the EU media.[64]

Considered separately, these measures, often concerning seemingly technical institutional developments, are not necessarily controversial. It should also be clear that the point here is not to level a critique on the substantive contents of the measures. That is, it is beyond the scope of this chapter to assess the merits of the different responses and it is also beyond the scope of the discussions here to treat them from a more carefully elaborated normative perspective. Rather, the brief engagement with some of these measures serves to highlight a pattern by which institutional developments initiated as a result of crises, whether economic or political, seem to almost without fail, take institutional developments in a direction that works to further restrict efficient mechanisms of accountability, representation, and participation, rather than to make such mechanisms more inclusive. Democracy as an open, pluralistic, and experimental set of ideas and procedures is recurrently placed on the backburner, deemed inappropriate to deal with hard times. The implications is that when the stakes are high, democracy is perceived as too fragile, as the citizens and the politicians representing them cannot, in the last instance, be trusted. In Europe, fragilities viewed as inherent to the liberal democratic state informed the creation of the institutions that would later develop into the European political order, the EU. By taking these perspectives to the more contemporary setting it seems as fundamental elements of similar ideas continue to shape political thinking, in this context.

The EU is now a political order that is increasingly expected to operate on the basis of democratic procedures, not least due to its considerable influence on many areas of policymaking that affect its member states in far-reaching ways. However, this democratic identity also places reactions to various crises in rather stark relief. The EU's response to the economic and financial crisis, and in particular how the creditor countries portrayed debtor countries, appeared as an almost textbook example of the type mistrust in elected politicians that motored the functionalist project. The EU's reactions to the resurgence of the European far-right come into new light through the discussion on how the concerns underpinning functionalism overlapped with those that sought to formulate defensive, even militant measures, to protect democracy.

It is difficult to veer from the notion that the functionalist beginnings of the European political order helped inform the creation of cooperative arrangements that, although at times shaky, is arguably the most highly integrated on the globe. In this case then, functionalist assessments regarding the impossibility of building international organizations on the basis of a constitutional consensus seems to have some currency. That is, its mistrust in the proceduralism of constitutional federalism and the use of functional integration to circumvent political stumbling blocks made the EU possible. Its member states, of course, remain adamant about the principle that the only decision-making competences that they accept are those explicitly conferred to the EU through its treaty revisions to which the member states have agreed. However, those treaties in fact mirror in large parts adaptations to established practices that have evolved not by formal treaty revisions but by a combination of evolving jurisprudence of Court of Justice of the European Union and pragmatic and incremental institutional developments.[65] As the politicization of the EU has increased in terms of the degree to which the organization and substantive policies are contested, the order's collective reactions seem to work to constrain avenues for effective citizen participation and political accountability. The institutional reflexes of the EU seem to reproduce the notion of democracy's fragility that we find at the basis of Mitrany's functionalism and Löwenstein's notion of militant democracy.

Robustness and Fragility of Regional Political Orders

What are the analytical lessons that can be drawn from this analysis of functionalism, militant democracy, and the EU? While approaching truism, it bears underscoring that paying close attention to the historical circumstances in which international political orders emerge is crucial for understanding the perceptions of fragility and robustness that political elites bring to concrete architecture of such orders. This is certainly true for the EU and is often accepted due to the recognition of its *sui generis* status among current regional orders. However, this is a point less often emphasized in contemporary studies of international organizations or international political orders more generally: Decisions on how political institutions should operate are informed by actors' assumptions regarding what is likely to make those institutions robust and what will make them fragile. For the EU this meant, and still means to an extent, balancing the democratization of its institutions with mechanisms that are seen as safeguarding its robustness.

For other regional orders, those assumptions will appear differently. To take an example, for the Association of South Asian Nations (ASEAN), a regional organization founded in 1967 presently including ten South Asian states, a different set of concerns shaped its institutions and its way of working. First, the democratic qualities of its member states have from its inception been a secondary (if that) issue. What instead was assumed as being of crucial importance for stable cooperation between these states were the mutual respect for cultural differences and the principle of noninterference. This fomented institutional solutions that enable its members to engage in discussions away from the public eye, allowing leaders to make concessions without the risk of public humiliation. It also led to the construction of a set of institutions lacking a formalized conflict resolution mechanism, as such mechanisms were seen as an admission of adversarial relations.[66] It was thought that they would endanger the robustness of the cooperative regime built on quiet diplomacy, consensus decision-making, and allowing leaders to not lose face in public.[67]

In the EU, perceptions of what robustness requires have constrained democratic procedures while balancing demands for increasing transparency and strengthened mechanisms for representation and accountability. These efforts to maintain the order's robustness have also helped produce key conditions for far-reaching criticism against its current organizational setup. The charge against the EU as exhibiting democratic flaws in light of the significant impact of its legislation on member states, as well as on individual citizens, has helped fuel disintegrative pressures in recent years. The extent to which Brexit was fueled by a broad yearning for more democracy is highly debatable. However, what seems clear is that the diffuse decision-making structures of the EU have supplied ample opportunities for national political leaders to avoid blame for their own policy failures, while underplaying any role EU legislation might have had in improving the lives of their citizens. Nowhere was this game played more efficiently or with more far-reaching consequences than in the UK. Thus, what was devised as a way to create a robust order in line with functionalist tenets, contributed to the conditions that ended up making it more fragile.

This also points to the fact that while particular perceptions of fragility and robustness acquire a dominating position at various junctures, it is important to retain a sensitivity to the contested aspects of such ideas. Perceptions, whether of fragility or robustness, are not monolithic. The interaction between different conceptions of the role, function, and form of a particular order can create pressures that contribute to further strengthening the resilience of political orders or for loosening the glue that binds the order together. As the EU moved farther from its war-torn beginnings, the functionalist core of its institutions emerged in tension with increasing demands for democratization. These tensions appeared in particularly stark form during the crises of the late 2000's and 2010's as protective reflexes associated to perceptions of democracy's fragility were revived.

With European countries facing, with much of the rest of the world, the combined knock-on effects of the COVID-19 pandemic and Russia's full-scale invasion of Ukraine, it is uncertain which conclusions regarding political organization will be drawn by politicians and broader public. Perhaps, the precise democratic qualities of a political order like the EU will play less of a role for crisis-ridden publics and politicians. In this sense, perhaps Mitrany's notion that what is important, both in general and for the robustness of international political orders, are in the final instance concrete achievements related to the delivery of the people's needs. Or, perhaps, publics and politicians will recognize that we have in some sense always inhabited a world of recurring crises and that we are best served by dealing with them through procedures that work to approximate democratic ideals.

Notes

1 Desmond Dinan, *Europe Recast: A History of the European Union* (Boulder: Lynne Reiner, 2014); Philomena Murray and Paul Rich, eds. *Visions of European Unity* (Boulder: Westview Press, 1996).
2 Waqar Zaidi, "David Mitrany and Ernst Haas: Theorizing a United Europe," in Alexander Badenoch and Andreas Fickers, eds. *Materializing Europe:*

Transnational Infrastructures and the Project of Europe (Basingstoke: Palgrave Macmillan, 2010), pp. 78–81.
3 Alisdair Blair, *The European Union since 1945* (Harlow: Pearson, 2010); Martin Holland, "Jean Monnet and the Federal Functionalist Approach to the European Union," in Philomena Murray and Paul Rich, eds. *Visions of European Unity* (Boulder: Westview Press, 1996), pp. 93–108. Giandomenico Majone, *Dilemmas of Integration: Pitfalls of Integration by Stealth* (Oxford: Oxford University Press, 2005).
4 Cornelia Navari, "Functionalism Versus Federalism: Alternative Visions of European Unity," in Philomena Murray and Paul Rich, eds. *Visions of European Unity* (Boulder: Westview Press, 1996), pp. 63–92.
5 Majone, *Dilemmas of European Integration* p. 42.
6 Ernst B. Haas, *Beyond the Nations State: Functionalism and International Organization* (Colchester: ECPR Press; (2008 [1964]), p. 29; Navari, "Functionalism Versus Federalism." The discussion here is primarily based on Mitrany's discussion of functionalist ideas in David Mitrany, *A Working Peace System* (Oxford: Oxford University Press, 1943) and David Mitrany, *The Functional Theory of Politics* (London: London School of Economics, 1975).
7 For a discussion, see in particular Leonie Holthaus, *Pluralist Democracy in International Relations: L.T. Hobhouse, G.D.H. Cole and David Mitrany* (Cham: Palgrave Macmillan, 2018).
8 Löwenstein had himself frequented Weber's circles as a student in Heidelberg. In his discussions on militant democracy, while not citing Weber directly, the strong opposition between rationality and emotionalism as key to fascist techniques of government seems to echo key tenets of Weber's sociology of the state. See Karl Löwenstein, "Militant Democracy and Fundamental Rights I," *American Political Science Review*, 31 no. 3 (1937a) pp. 417–32. Löwenstein later published a monograph on Weber's political thought, Karl Löwenstein, *Max Weber's Political Ideas in the Perspective of our Time* (Amherst: University of Massachusetts Press, 1966).
9 Mitrany, *Functional Theory of Politics*, p. 123.
10 Per Hammarlund, *Liberal Internationalism and the Decline of the State: The Thought of Richard Cobden, David Mitrany, and Kenichi Ohmae* (Basingstoke: Palgrave Macmillan, 2005).
11 Mitrany, *A Working Peace System*, p. 42.
12 Paul Taylor, *Introduction to Mitrany, A Functional Theory of Politics*, p. x.
13 Hammarlund, *Liberal Internationalism and the Decline of the State*, pp. 38–39.
14 Mitrany, *A Working Peace System*, p. 56.
15 Jens Steffek, "The Cosmopolitanism of David Mitrany: Equality, Devolution and Functional Democracy Beyond the State," *International Relations* 29, no. 1 (2015), pp. 23–44; Jens Steffek and Leonie Holthaus "The Social-Democratic Roots of Global Governance: Welfare Internationalism from the 19th Century to the United Nations," *European Journal of International Relations* 24, no. 1 (2018), pp. 106–29.
16 Steffek and Holthaus, "The Social-Democratic Roots of Global Governance."
17 Holthaus, *Pluralist Democracy in International Relations*, p. 192.

18 Mitrany, *A Functional Theory of Politics*, p. 107.
19 An important target of such criticism was the procedural conception of democracy defended most prominently by Hans Kelsen who argued forcefully for the central role of political parties and constitutional arrangements for democratic political orders. See Hans Kelsen, "Foundations of Democracy," *Ethics*, 66, no. 1 (1955), pp. 1–101; Hans Kelsen, *The Essence and Value of Democracy* (Lanham: Rowman & Littlefield, 2013 [1920]).
20 Hanna Arendt, *The Origins of Totalitarianism* (New York: Harvest Books, 1951), p. 312.
21 The translated quote from Goebbels reads "This will always remain one of the best jokes of democracy, that it gave its deadly enemies the means by which it was destroyed" ('Das wird immer einer der besten Witze der Demokratie bleiben, dass sie ihren Todfeinden die Mittel selber stellte, dutch die sie vernichret wurde.'), quoted in Gregory H. Fox, and Georg Nolte "Intolerant Democracies," *Harvard International Law Review* 36, no. 1 (1995), p. 1.
22 Karl Löwenstein, "Militant Democracy and Fundamental Rights I," *American Political Science Review* 31, no. 3 (1937a), pp. 417–32; Karl Löwenstein, "Militant Democracy and Fundamental Rights II,' *American Political Science Review* 31, no. 4 (1937b) pp. 638–58; Karl Löwenstein, "The Union of Western Europe: Illusion and Reality: An Appraisal of the Methods," *Columbia Law Review* 52, no. 1 (1952), pp. 55–99; Karl Löwenstein, *Political Power and the Governmental Process* (Chicago: The University of Chicago Press, 1957).
23 Protective measures suggested by Löwenstein included among other things, the banning of anti-democratic parties and restrictions on the freedom of opinion and assembly. See Löwenstein, "Militant Democracy and Fundamental Rights II,"
24 Löwenstein, "Militant Democracy and Fundamental Rights I," p. 432.
25 *Ibid.*, p. 424.
26 Anthoula Malkopoulou and Ludvig Norman, "Three Models of Democratic Self-Defence: Militant Democracy and its Alternatives," *Political Studies* 66, no. 2 (2018), pp. 442–58.
27 Löwenstein, "Militant Democracy and Fundamental Rights I."
28 Mitrany, *A Functional Theory of Politics*, p.33.
29 *Ibid.*, p. 214.
30 Löwenstein, "Militant Democracy and Fundamental Rights I," p. 657. For a discussion on the elitism informing Löwenstein's notion of militant democracy, see Norman and Malkopoulou, "Three Models of Democratic Self-Defence."
31 Mitrany, *A Functional Theory of Politics*, p. 214.
32 Mitrany, *A Working Peace System*, p. 21.
33 Ibid.
34 For discussions on these links see William E. Scheuerman, *Morgenthau* (London: Polity Press, 2009) and William E. Scheuerman, "The (Classical) Realist Vision of Global Reform," *International Theory* 2, no. 2 (2010), pp. 246–82; Daniel Kenealy and Konstantinos Kostagiannis, "Realist

Visions of European Union: E.H. Carr and Integration," *Millennium: Journal of International Studies* 41, no. 2 (2013), pp, 221–46.
35 Löwenstein, "The Union of Western Europe." See also discussion in Ludvig Norman (2017) "Defending the European Political Order: Visions of Politics in Response to the Radical Right," *European Journal Social Theory* 20, no. 4, pp. 531–49 at pp. 543–44. For an extended discussion on the links between militant democracy and epistemic democracy see Anthoula Malkopoulou, "What Militant Democrats and Technocrats Share," *Critical Review of International Social and Political Philosophy*, (2020) Published online. https://doi.org/10.1080/13698230.2020.1782047
36 Löwenstein, "The Union of Western Europe," p. 79.
37 Mitrany, *A Working Peace System*, p. 44.
38 *Ibid.*, p. 21.
39 Leonie Holthaus, *Pluralist Democracy in International Relations*. (London: Palgrave, 2018), p. 196.
40 David Mitrany, "Delusion of Regional Integration," in *Limits and Problems of European Integration* (Dordrecht: Springer, 1963), pp. 37–46; David Mitrany, "The Prospect of Integration: Federal or Functional," *Journal of Common Market Studies* 4, no. 2 (1965), pp. 119–49. See also the imaginary interview performed by Steffek in which Mitrany laments the turn taken by the EU, Jens Steffek, "Functionalism in Uncommon Places: Electrifying the Hades with David Mitrany (1888-1975)," in Richard Ned Lebow, Peer Schouten and Hidemi Suganami eds. *The Return of the Theorists Dialogues with Great Thinkers in International Relations* (Houndmills: Palgrave, 2016), pp. 193–200.
41 Martin Holland, "Jean Monnet and the Federal Functionalist Approach"; Cornelia Navari, "Functionalism Versus Federalism."
42 *Schuman Plan*, 9 May 1950, Available at https://europa.eu/european-union/about-eu/symbols/europe-day/schuman-declaration_en
43 *Treaty Establishing the European Coal and Steel Community*. Available at https://eur-lex.europa.eu/LexUriServ/LexUriServ.do?uri=CELEX:11951K:EN:PDF
44 Blair, *The European Union since 1945*, p. 19.
45 Birte Siim, *Gender and Citizenship: Politics and Agency in France, Britain and Denmark*. (Cambridge, MA: Cambridge University Press, 2000).
46 Jorgen Anderson and Jens Hoff, *Democracy and Citizenship in Scandinavia* (Houndmills: Palgrave, 2001).
47 Joseph H. H. Weiler, Ulrich, R. Haltern, Franz Mayer, "European Democracy and its Critique," *West European Politics* 18, no. 3 (1995), pp. 4–39; Anthony D. Smith, "National Identity and the Idea of European Unity," *International Affairs* 68, no. 1 (1992), pp. 55–76.
48 Frank Schimmelfennig, "The Community Trap: Liberal Norms, Rhetorical Action, and the Eastern Enlargement of the European Union," *International Organization*, 55 (2001), pp. 47–80.
49 Article 10, *Treaty on the European Union*.
50 However, in contrast to most national parliaments, it does not have the right to initiate legislation by itself.
51 Magnus Ryner, "Europe's Ordo-liberal Iron Cage: Critical Political Economy, the Euro area crisis and its management," *Journal of European*

Public Policy 22, no. 2 (2015), pp. 275–94. Olaf Cramme and Sara B. Hobolt, *Democratic Politics in a European Union under Stress* (Oxford: Oxford University Press, 2014).

52 Christian Kreuder-Sonnen, "An Authoritarian turn in Europe and European Studies?" *Journal of European Public Policy* 25, no. 3 (2018), pp. 542-64; Jonathan White, "Emergency Europe," *Political Studies*, 63 no. 2 (2015), pp. 300–18.

53 Marco Buti and Nicolas Carnot, "The EMU Debt Crisis: Early Lessons and Reform," *JCMS:* Journal of Common Market Studies 50, no. 6 (2012), 899–911. p. 900. Both Buti and Carnot were at the time of the article's publication officials at the European Commission, DG ECFIN.

54 Ignacio Sánches-Cuenca, "From a Deficit of Democracy to a Technocratic Order: The Post-Crisis Debate on Europe," *Annual Review of Political Science* 20 (2017), pp. 351–69. Recent contributions have similarly focused on how different actors within the EU react to bottom-up pressures by seeking to politicize and depoliticize issues. See Edoardo Bressanelli, Christel Koop and Christine Reh, "EU Actors under pressure: politicisation and depoliticisation as strategic responses," *Journal of European Public Policy* 27 no. 3, (2020), pp. 329–41; Frank Schimmelfennig, "Politicisation Management in the European Union," *Journal of European Public Policy*, 27 no. 3 (2020), pp. 342–61.

55 Oliver Treib, "Euroscepticism is Here to Stay: What Cleavage Theory can Teach Us about the 2019 European Parliament Elections," *Journal of European Public Policy* (2020) (published online) https://doi.org/10.1080/13501763.2020.1737881

56 R. Daniel Kelemen, "Europe's Other Democratic Deficit: National Authoritarianism in Europe's Democratic Union," *Government and Opposition* 52, no. 2 (2017), pp. 211–38.

57 The ENF reformed after the 2019 European elections as Identity and Democracy (ID).

58 The strategy, however, ran into trouble as a representative from the *Front Nationale* proposed an amendment to a list of pesticides. The Social Democrats found themselves in the slightly awkward position of having to vote against an amendment that they found perfectly reasonable. The final solution was instead to abstain. Interview with Official of the European Parliament (S&D group).

59 European Parliament "Political declaration for the establishment of a political group," 2019/2019 REG. 19.04.17. Available at www.europarl.europa.eu/doceo/document/TA-8-2019-0393_EN.html (accessed 5 August, 2020).

60 European Parliament Committee for Constitutional Affairs "Debate of the Committee for Constitutional Affairs," 7 March, 2019, https://multimedia.europarl.europa.eu/en/committee-on-constitutional-affairs-ordinary-meeting-ordinary-meeting_20190307–0900-COMMITTEE-AFCO_vd?EPV_REPLAY=true&EPV_PHOTO=true&EPV_AUDIO=true&EPV_EDITED_VIDEOS=false (accessed 3 August, 2020); European Parliament Committee for Constitutional Affairs "Debate of the Committee for Constitutional Affairs," April 2, 2019, (2019b). Available

at: https://multimedia.europarl.europa.eu/en/committee-on-constitutional-affairs-ordinary-meeting-ordinary-meeting_20190402-1400-COMMITTEE-AFCO_vd?EPV_REPLAY=true&EPV_PHOTO=true&EPV_AUDIO=true&EPV_EDITED_VIDEOS=false (accessed 3 August, 2020).
61 Ludvig Norman, "To Democratize or to Protect? How the Response to Anti-System Parties Reshapes the EU's Transnational Party System," *Journal of Common Market Studies* (published online) https://doi.org/10.1111/jcms.13128.
62 Statement by MEP Jo Leinen, "Debate of the Committee for Constitutional Affairs," 2 April, 2019.
63 Norman, "Defending the European Political Order," pp. 534–35
64 Euractive "The costs of a cordon sanitaire, 4 July 2019," (2019) Available at www.euractiv.com/section/future-eu/news/the-brief-the-costs-of-a-cordon-sanitaire/ (Accessed 10 August 2020); Politico 'Parliament Groups Vow to Stop Far-Right MEPs Chairing Committees', 2 July, 2019. Available at www.politico.eu/article/parliament-groups-vow-to-stop-far-right-meps-chairing-committees/ (Accessed 10 August, 2020). Recently, discussions arose as to whether the Commission is actually obliged to present proposals as a response to European citizen's initiatives that have met the required level of support when such initiatives can be perceived to contradict the political order's fundamental values (CJEU 2018). These discussions were brought to the surface in a judgment by the Court of Justice of the European Union Judgment in Case T-561/14, *European Citizens' Initiative One of Us and others v Commission* (2018).
65 See, for instance, Karen Alter, *The European Court's Political Power* (Oxford: Oxford University Press, 2009).
66 Amitav Acharyam, "Collective Identity and Conflict Management in Southeast Asia," in Emmanuel Adler, Michael Barnett, eds. *Security Communities* pp. 198-227; Karin M Fierke *Critical Approaches to Security Studies* (London: Polity press, YEAR).
67 This institutional culture is sometimes referred to as the "ASEAN way." See, for instance, Logan Masilamani and Jimmy Peterson, "The 'ASEAN Way': The Structural Underpinnings of Constructive Engagement," *Foreign Policy Journal*, 15 October 2014, pp. 1–21.

8 The American Fragility–Robustness Nexus

Ariane Chebel d'Appollonia

When examining American democracy in the early 1830s, Tocqueville expressed concerns about cultural and social tendencies – such as materialism, individualism, and anti-intellectualism – that he thought would potentially weaken the American experiment in democracy. He remained, however, highly impressed with Americans and their expectations of equality and participation in politics. Tocqueville related the strengths of America's nascent democracy to the vitality of the country's political culture by noting that the former was more about values, national character, and social customs than any specific form of government.[1] Almost two centuries after the publication of *Democracy in America*, the Tocquevillian conception of American exceptionalism still sustains the oft-cited assumption that US democracy differs qualitatively from other liberal democracies because of its unique origins, national credo, and distinctive political institutions.

Certainly, a major challenge in assessing the robustness and/or fragility of democracy in the United States is to deal with how Americans perceive the meaning of democracy in a multidimensional way: as a unique set of values and principles, a political regime, a form of government, an ideology, a sense of destiny, and an expression of national character, if not a "God-given destiny," as a model for humanity. This explains why political leaders' estimates of the state of democracy have never been just context-dependent; they have also been ideologically contingent, framed by beliefs in US exceptionalism that are often disconnected from reality. Furthermore, as I discuss, US scholars have occasionally contributed to this celebration of the American democratic experiment by focusing on the peculiarities and virtues of US democratic politics and political ideals.

Consistent with the framework of Lebow and Norman's introduction, I examine the perspective of both America's political and intellectual leadership over time. Also including the perspective of the general public provides an additive dimension and possible insight. Historically, at least since the end of the Civil War, as I discuss, these three groups have largely been in sync (at least rhetorically and publicly) only when all three have expressed optimism about the state of American democracy. Politicians in power have always preferred to do so for electoral purposes, even in America's darkest moments, such as FDR's famed wartime speeches.[2] The exception to this general rule was Jimmy Carter's 1979 famed "malaise" speech, which electorally contrasted with Ronald Reagan's "morning in America" campaign and led to his crushing electoral defeat, serving as a warning to all presiding politicians.[3]

Yet what is notable now, and arguably exceptional, at least in recent decades, is the way in which America's political leadership and opposition, leading academics writing on democracy, and the general public *all* generally share a pessimistic view of democracy's prospects. Biden's "dagger at the throat" speech was unprecedented in recent times, issuing a clarion call to action, but only in the most alarmist terms, warning that the United States could become a nation that "accepts political violence as a norm" and allows "partisan election officials to overturn the legally expressed will of the people."[4] As I assess in the conclusion, this very unity (if only in terms of concerns about the threat) may be the very factor that, ambivalently, accelerates that democratic decline or corrects it. Drawing any conclusion, as so many do, seems premature in early January of 2022 with so many key elements in motion, stretching from the Congressional investigation in the events of 6 January to debates about voting rights legislation. But, as I demonstrate in this chapter, America has never historically been as robust nor as fragile as proponents of both views contend. If history is any guide, the pendulum will swing in favor of preventative action that will sustain American democracy within those guardrails.

I begin my analysis of this robustness–fragility nexus by presenting the main components of US exceptionalism. I do so for two reasons. First, perceptions of this exceptionalism have framed – and still biases – the evaluation of US democracy by both America's elites and its mass public. In reality, however, the objective uniqueness of US democracy is relative, subject to change over time. Yet the subjective foundational narrative about the exceptional character of US democracy remains absolute. Examining this tension reveals its character and the key factors that play into that variance. Second, the particular features of US exceptionalism provide sources of both strength and weakness. Attachment to those cluster of values and customs, loosely labeled as a "creed," for example, consolidates the unity of the American people by providing benchmarks for any groups seeking to assimilate into mainstream America. Paradoxically, perhaps, it also stimulates nativist feelings and exclusionary practices. The sanctity of the constitution therefore provides guardrails against the violation of fundamental rights. Yet, it also leads to the infringement of civil liberties, the perpetuation of hate speech based on the abuse of the First Amendment, and a widespread culture of violence legitimized by the Second Amendment. The institutional system of checks and balances stabilizes the regime, except when the dynamic it affords generates gridlock and polarization.

As Richard Ned Lebow and Ludvig Norman note in this volume's introduction, it is often tempting to frame robustness and fragility as polar opposites that anchor two ends of a continuum. Yet, I contend that the case of the United States illustrates how robustness and fragility may actually be interrelated, in fact sharing the same catalysts: The constitutional mechanisms that consolidate US democracy thus also facilitate its failures. The ideological stability of democratic values, for example, is counterbalanced by an intense political polarization over the meaning and scope of those values. External shocks (such as the 9/11 terrorist attacks), and internal conflicts (such as the riots at the Capitol in January 2021) have energized efforts to secure national unity while simultaneously providing further motives for political division and societal fragmentation.

Furthermore, perceptions of US democracy by political and intellectual elites actually reinforce this robustness–fragility nexus. Overconfidence in the excellence of US democracy often leads to domestic and international disasters, as I demonstrate in the second part of my analysis devoted to the "weakness of robustness." It fuels the denial of the immediate and underlying causes of fragility. American history, I can regrettably only briefly demonstrate in the context of a single chapter, is replete with examples of political leaders who have overestimated the normative power of US democracy, and engaged the country in democratic crusades that have turned into catastrophes (as illustrated by the wars in Vietnam, Iraq, and Afghanistan). Overconfidence has blinded political leaders to America's underlying systemic flaws such as the resilience of socioeconomic inequalities, suspicion toward the federal government, class tensions, and institutional racism. Such a blinkered vision has rendered them incapable of addressing the root causes of democratic disenchantment – and still does so today.

Yet US democracy was and is remarkably flexible. Unlike its peers, like France, which has been transformed by five republics, the American system's capacity to survive crises over time illustrates the "strength of fragility" that I analyze in the third section. Its response to crises has been reformist, not revolutionary. The Great Depression, for example, provoked New Deal reforms. Concerns about institutional dysfunction and fear of decline have often invigorated efforts to strengthen democratic guardrails – from the Watergate scandal to the current attempts to restore US democracy in the aftermath of the events of 6 January 2021 at the Capitol.

It is premature to evaluate the impact of the latter in early 2020. Many crucial questions await effective answers in the form of the Biden administration's policies, the Congressional investigation into events that day, and the US Supreme Court's decisions about issues relating to voter suppression and gerrymandering. I conclude, however, that the past and present state of US democracy runs against the common assumption that robustness is always good and fragility bad. Not only is US democracy both strong and fragile, but robustness and weakness are intertwined, indeed organically related, for better or worse. What therefore poses an existential threat? Addressing this question in my conclusion, I identify two main corrosive trends. The first relates to attempts by leaders to exaggerate various threats in order to justify undemocratic practices allegedly designed to protect democracy – as illustrated by the "lesser evil perspective" that has been advocated by proponents of the most controversial aspects of the war on terror since 9/11. The second relates to the popularity of declinist arguments and predictions of an imminent conflagration of US democracy. In the triumph of perception, these diagnoses and strident forewarnings can actually contribute to hastening a political collapse.

American Exceptionalism

The sustained belief in the exemplary character of the US model of democracy has been a core element of the national psyche since the colonial era, predating the creation of the Republic itself. One of the first expressions of American exceptionalism, according to the traditional iconic account, was the 1630 sermon by John Winthrop in which he proclaimed that "we shall be as a city upon the hill" – as a model of Christian charity, a concept of a fellowship united in a common dedication, and a monument intended to guide the rest of the nations to God.[5] Winthrop characterized the colonists' endeavor as part of a special pact with God to create a model state, a process that started on the shores of Massachusetts Bay and later expanded to thirteen disparate colonies. Underlying this biblical imagery was the belief among America's political leadership that America would distinguish itself as a moral, democratic country from the instrumental power politics and often antidemocratic forces that prevailed in much of Europe. This desire to protect the American project in democracy-building moved to the forefront when the colonies began to view themselves as autonomous political communities. For the generation that became America's constitutional founders, a stable political system required unity around key values, such as freedom, equality, and the various civil liberties (at least for white male property owners) listed in the Articles of Confederation that named the new nation "The United States of America."[6] From the beginning of the American Revolution, the founders wanted to emphasize the republican character of the new constitutional order, an intent manifest in the ratification of the Constitution in 1788, and the adoption of the Bill of Rights in 1791.[7] The resulting institutional architecture of American democracy – a federal government with an intricate, then novel, system of checks and balances – led to heated domestic debates about the centralization of power and the national government's power to tax. The legitimacy of the new regime, however, was strengthened by its revolutionary origins, by the canonic significance of the Federalist Papers, and by the popular perception of the Founding Fathers as creators of a unique constitutional democracy based on fundamental freedoms (such as freedom of speech, religion, and the press, along with the right to bear arms and entitlement of due process before the law).

Despite the rhetoric of democracy, America nonetheless remained divided by the foundational issue of slavery – essentially between a bourgeois capitalist state and a feudal aristocratic one – until resolved by the unprecedented violence of the American Civil War that began in 1861. Since the Civil War's conclusion, both constitutional patriotism and civic nationalism have continued to fuel a broad thematic understanding and rhetorical usage of American exceptionalism by political leaders and influential scholars. Among the former, examples include President Harding who regularly invoked the Founding Fathers, notably in his 1921 inaugural address by praising their "divine inspiration" in the making of this "new-world Republic."[8] Furthermore, "A City on a Hill" sermon was quoted by almost every president to hold office (from John F. Kennedy to Barack Obama). President Reagan invoked it when, after eight years in office, in his last address to the nation, he praised the superiority and robustness of American democracy. Possibly appending the word "shining" for the first time, Reagan noted, "I've spoken of the shining city all my political life, but I don't know if I ever quite communicated what I saw when I said it. But in my mind, it was a tall proud city built on rocks stronger than oceans, wind-swept, God-blessed, and teeming with people of all kinds living in harmony and peace, a city with free ports that hummed with commerce and creativity, and if there had to be city walls, the walls had doors and the doors were open to anyone with the will and the heart to get here. That's how I saw it, and see it still." Reagan insisted on the robustness of a city that still "stand[s] strong and true on the granite ridge ...still a beacon, still a magnet for all who must have freedom," a "proud city built on rocks stronger than oceans, God-blessed, and teeming with people of all kinds living in harmony and peace."[9] A review of the major speeches of subsequent American presidents provides plentiful examples of political statements invoking the excellence of American democracy as an exemplary political regime, as an expression of national identity (We, the People), and as a culture of individual rights.

The glorification of US democracy, however, has always included two ambivalent trends. The first relates to the preservation of the original purity of the "American creed" as the product of the distinct Anglo-Protestant culture of the founding settlers. This perspective has been reflected in the views of various nativist groups, from the anti-Catholic crusade in the mid-nineteenth century to anti-immigrant discourse and practices that gained currency in the late nineteenth century – and persist today. The second trend is illustrated by political leaders who, like John F. Kennedy in this 1958 book (*A Nation of Immigrants*), have praised the ability of the United States to assimilate immigrants of all races, ethnicities, and religions into the enduring, if mythical, American "melting pot."

Attempts to promote US exceptionalism must be understood in relation to its broader political and global context. Possibly originating in Jefferson's Farewell Address (1796), where he laid the foundation for America's isolationist foreign policy that largely dominated until its entry into World War I, it has endured under the slogan of "America first" – one used by a succession of both Democratic and Republican politicians over time such as President Woodrow Wilson, Harding during the 1920 presidential election, Pat Buchanan, and latterly Donald Trump who revived Charles Lindbergh's America Firstism. From this perspective, the greatness of the American model doesn't stem from its values. It is about sovereignty and power. Indeed, an initial invocation of US exceptionalism has often resulted in recourse to exemptionalism, as illustrated by the resilient tendency to reject any international commitment that may even potentially contradict the US constitution or undermine state sovereignty. Constraints imposed by this peculiar "constitutional culture" on US policy were at the core of the Bricker amendment controversy of the early 1950s, and have persisted over time. This culture includes a rejection of international treaties stretching from the rights of the child and discrimination against women to the rights of persons with disabilities, the International Convention for the Protection of All Persons from Enforced Disappearance or the Optional Protocol to the Convention against Torture.[10] All have been undermined by Senate

Republicans on the grounds that ratification may subvert American legislation or sovereignty.

Conversely, a sense of superiority of the US model fuels the belief in America's manifest destiny to promote democracy globally. This view is thought to have originated with Theodore Roosevelt who expanded the Monroe Doctrine to Puerto Rico and the Philippines. Rudyard Kipling penned his famous poem, "White Man's Burden," in 1899 as an ironic satire on Roosevelt's efforts at nation-building, only to have it seized upon by Roosevelt as an endorsement of his policies. Woodrow Wilson followed suit when he led the United States into World War I to make the "world safe for democracy" and many of his successors invoked the same logic. This "American destiny," a term coined by Democratic Party politician John L. Sullivan during the debate over the annexation of Texas, has been pursued multilaterally through international organizations such as the United Nations or by force, stretching from Franklin D. Roosevelt's crusade for the "four freedoms" in World War II to G.W Bush's Freedom Agenda designed to "end tyranny in the world" in Afghanistan and Iraq.[11]

Alongside politicians, scholars and intellectuals have contributed to the celebration of American exceptionalism, notably during the "American Century" – a term coined by Henry Luce, the powerful editor of *Life* magazine, to characterize the United States' political, cultural, and military hegemony after World War II. The Cold War marked the golden age of patriotic history. Publisher Bennett Cerf of Random House, for example, created the Landmark series in 1948 in order to publish books about epic American events and personalities, while avoiding the dark aspects of its history. Winthrop's "city on the hill" incantation was popularized by Harvard historian Perry Miller in *Errand into the Wilderness* (1956). According to Perry, highly influential among American scholars until the early 1960s, the uniqueness of what he called "American civilization" was based on the intrinsic qualities of the Puritans and their commitment to communal solidarity. Perry's conception of the somewhat nostalgic "meaning of America" echoed the scholarship that defined the early years of American Studies, with its focus on democracy's superior historical legacy. Scholars in other academic disciplines tried to explain the uniqueness of the US model in less sentimental terms. Political scientists, following Alexis de Tocqueville's path, endorsed the idea of American exceptionalism. Seymour Martin Lipset argued, the United States is "the first new nation" – the first nation to be created at a specific time and place, in a specific act of political invention, having at its core not shared ethnicity or language or religion but rather shared commitment to a set of defining principles as a national "political creed" or "civil religion."[12] American exceptionalism, Lipset added, entails the United States being perceived both domestically and internationally as superior to other nations.[13] Lipset's more rigorous formulations became a precursor to modernization theory, a supposed architecture for development whose celebration of the United States as a model could not authentically be characterized as even thinly veiled.[14]

Harvard professor Louis Hartz added another unique feature to the profile of American exceptionalism in *The Liberal Tradition* (1955): the strength of a Lockean liberal consensus, which, by precluding the spread of socialism and other disruptive ideologies, fueled the unwarranted assumption that there was no need to protect domestic democratic institutions from left- or right-wing authoritarianism. Hartz drew upon the work of Tocqueville and Sombart to argue that the United States was wedded to a liberal ethos.[15] As a result, political and institutional stability was ensured by the lack of an existential threat to the social order. Yet, the "tyranny of unanimity" was paradoxically a potential source of fragility, Hartz argued, by encouraging political leaders to take the liberal tradition for granted and therefore underestimate ideological threats.

Hartz's concerns were largely rejected by other influential political scientists. The United States actually recovered from the threat posed by McCarthyism, and scholars spent the next two decades analyzing the "essence" of US democratic values, the exceptional stability of its democratic governance, as well as celebrating the United States' providential mission to transform the rest of the world in the image of the United States. Daniel Bell and other end-of-ideologists diagnosed the failure of old political ideologies (such as Marxian socialism and other secular religions) and their replacement by surrogates that were adaptions of the "American scene." These surrogates include the "cult of efficiency" central to US management theory, liberal forms of capitalism, and the embrace of consumerism.[16] Together, they were perceived as consolidating the stability of US democracy, in addition to a robust system of domestic judicial review. Two classic defenses of judicial review – *The Least Dangerous Branch: The Supreme Court at the Bar of Politics* (1962) by Alexander Bickel, and *Democracy and Distrust: A Theory of Judicial Review* (1981) by John Ely – therefore linked the excellence of US political culture to domestic trust in the rule of law.

This confidence in US democracy was historically shared by the American public. Polls confirmed their attachment to the civic nationalism promoted by political and intellectual elites. It translated into an exceptional pride in American political institutions, and the tendency to evaluate these institutions far more favorably than publics in other liberal democracies. When the National Election Study began asking questions about trust in government in 1958, approximately three-quarters of Americans trusted the federal government to do the right thing almost always or most of the time. That trust, however, began eroding in the 1970s with the Watergate scandal. By 1974, the trust percentage had precipitously dropped to 36 percent. Yet, in the early 1990s, a vast majority of Americans still believed in the superiority of the US democratic model, despite this increasing distrust of the government. In 1995, about 75 percent of Americans were satisfied with the state of their democratic polity – although only 21 percent trusted the government.[17]

In *American Politics: The Promise of Disharmony* (1981), Samuel Huntington characterized this paradoxical democratic nationalism as a result of a recurrent, historical, cyclical gap between the actual performance of American political institutions and the promise of American ideals. He argued that when the gap between the ideals and the functioning of the institutions becomes too attenuated – when governmental elites ignore the underlying Jeffersonian commitment to liberty, equality, democracy, and popular sovereignty – distrust in government generates a period of sustained creedal passion. The objective, whether coming from social forces from the political Right or Left, is to restore a resonance between the institutions and their underlying principles. Order and stability thus prevail at the end of each cycle, characteristically involving a set of political reforms and the operation of institutions in a manner consistent with their constitutional values. Viewed through Huntington's optic, the Tea Party, Occupy Wall Street, Black Lives Matter and the MeToo movements – and, most importantly, the election of Donald Trump – suggest that America is in the midst of a periodic cycle of creedal passion.

Before 2016, an increasing distrust in the operation of political institutions among the mass public has remained balanced by a resilient faith in democracy. Indeed, the increasing discontent about politics among Americans has contrasted with the cheerful invocation of US democracy by political elites. George H. W. Bush constantly defended the promise of US democracy at home and abroad. Bill Clinton, while facing a declining popularity, persistently invoked both the strength of US democracy at home and exemplar American leadership abroad. From his perspective, the primary responsibility of America's leaders and government was to make America strong at home, by creating a "more perfect union" and providing "more opportunity to obtain the American Dream," in order to perpetuate America's exceptional global status and promote liberal versions of capitalism and democracy.[18]

Clinton's optimistic allegiance to US internal and external exceptionalism was reinforced by intellectuals who saw the Soviet capitulation as a vindication. From their perspective, the idea of liberal democracy had won – marking what Francis Fukuyama called the "End of History." Triumphalists rallied around this famous paean to the hegemony of US values. Communism and socialism had lost to the forces of free markets and democracy. The superiority of the American Dream would secure the exportation of the American conception of capitalism and democracy. Fukuyama acknowledged significant domestic limitations to US exceptionalism, but he remained confident of its influence. The fate of US democracy, he argued, would not be determined by material circumstances because beliefs matter more than realities in America. Furthermore, American people are able to adapt their beliefs to circumstances. This flexibility has helped US democracy to survive anything; it will continue to secure the stability of democracy – as long as people do not believe it is doomed. This triumphalism ran against the vision of influential intellectuals like Robert Kaplan who depicted the post-Cold War arena as the "coming anarchy" abroad.[19] The hubris of a Cold War victory was subsequently punctured by a series of policy failures abroad (notably Afghanistan and Iraq) and the abrogation of basic democratic values at home (such as the treatment of Muslims in the aftermath of 9/11) that set in train a process of polarization and declining trust in government.

The Weakness of Robustness

By the decade of the 2010s, confidence in democracy had begun to decline. For the first time on record, by 2019 polls showed that a majority of Americans (55 percent) were dissatisfied with the state of their democratic system. Approximately, 39 percent believed that democracy was "in crisis," while another 42 percent said it faced "serious challenges."[20] Distrust in pivotal governmental institutions has reached its highest level in history. Only 20 percent of Americans today trusted the government to "do the right thing" most of the time.[21]

This sentiment can be attributed to a growing list of daunting problems – socioeconomic inequality, deteriorating public services, persistent racist violence, dysfunctional government, decline in voter turnout, political polarization, and congressional gridlock that sabotaged efforts to pass comprehensive legislation. This worrisome trend illustrates how idealistic visions of America can actually mingle with nativist impulses (such as populism) and can be fatal to the American democratic experiment at home and abroad. The "American destiny" has now a new meaning: The United States is no longer perceived as the bastion of global democracy. Rather, it is depicted as facing the kind of existential crisis that preordains what could happen in other liberal democracies such as in Europe, for example, where many states face similar socio-economic issues, a comparable level of political distrust, and the growing influence of Trump's avatars.

A few hours before the attack on the US Capitol on 6 January 2021, while pro-Trump lawyers were trying to challenge the certification of electoral votes confirming President-elect Joe Biden's victory, Sen. Charles E. Schumer (D-NY) stated: "As we speak, the eyes of the world are on this chamber, questioning whether America is still the shining example of democracy, the shining city on the hill." The riposte was a mob of far-right Trump supporters who stormed the building, raided congressional offices, and attacked a few armed security guards – with four people dying in the tumult. For many commentators and politicians this event constituted a watershed, exposing the fragility of US democracy. "So much for American exceptionalism, for our being a shining city on a hill," tweeted Richard Haass, president of the Council on Foreign Relations, and Ishaan Tharoor likewise noted that, "far from the city on a hill, America has become a harbinger of darker days to come."[22] And the implications of Trump's antidemocratic legacy have indeed not simply been domestic. According to the International IDEA's Global State of Democracy Index, the United States has fallen victim to authoritarian tendencies and has therefore been added to a list of "backsliding democracies" such as Brazil, India, Hungary, and Poland. Trump's efforts to undermine a "fundamental trust in the electoral process had spill-over effects" globally.[23]

This assumption that American democracy is not only sullied but in fact on the verge of collapse is gaining currency among scholars who, like Benjamin Page and Martin Gilens, ask: "Democracy in America? What has gone wrong?"[24] They analyze how the most positive aspects of US democracy (such as fundamental freedoms and open competition between political parties) have been undermined by a combination of the activities of lobbyists, mega party donors, and electoral misinformation. In their analysis of "how democracies die," Steven Levitsky and Daniel Ziblatt provide a long list of symptoms, including the erosion of democratic norms, the decline of mutual toleration, undemocratic polarization, and the dysfunctional aspects of America's system of checks and balances.[25] Other scholars assign responsibility to different perpetrators. Political scientists Amy Fried and Douglas B. Harris, for example, blame the Republican Party, notably the intentional cultivation and weaponization of political distrust stretching from Barry Goldwater's

1960 campaign to Donald Trump's presidency.[26] Conversely, historian Paul Sabin suggests that much of the blame lies with liberal reformers who promote unrealistic goals (thereby enhancing a belief in the failings of government) and campaigns built on divisive identity politics.[27] Political leaders engage in a similar cycle of counteraccusations: Conservatives blame Liberals for being elitist and ignoring the needs of poor white voters; Liberals accuse Conservatives of denying people's rights by endorsing gerrymandering and voter suppression. In the electoral arena, Democrats and Republicans defame each other as posing a threat to democracy. According to a 2016 Pew Survey, 49 percent of Republicans and 55 percent of Democrats said the other party makes them "afraid."[28]

Despite countless claims that this situation is novel, most aspects of the current crisis, however, are not unprecedented. Democracy in the United States was under siege in one form or another during the 1790s, the Civil War, the Gilded Age, the Depression, and the Watergate era. Differing contextual factors mattered in each period. Yet a broad conclusion can be drawn: The structural sources of democratic fragility suggest that US exceptionalism comes at a price. It blinds the United States to underlying systemic flaws – and to the enduring threats it faces. The main peculiarities of the American model – such as the unifying power of the creed, the sanctity of the Constitution preserved by the US Supreme Court, and the presidential nature of a regime based on checks and balances – are praised for sustaining the robustness of democracy; yet, they have also generated enduring ideological, legal, political, and procedural weaknesses.

The main historical lesson we can draw is that the consensus about US exceptionalism has fueled overconfidence, arguably arrogance, about the legitimacy of the American creed and the robustness of the regime. When analyzing the ideological stability of American democratic values, we should remember that even its arch proponent Robert Dahl acknowledged that: "It would be folly to construct democracies on the assumption that civic virtue will steadily prevail."[29] Indeed, proponents of US exceptionalism subscribe to a moralistic conception of US democracy that overestimates the homogeneity of democratic values. Yet, those creedal values include but extend beyond basic freedoms associated with democracy to elements such as social equity that are associated with social justice. They uneasily cluster, orthogonally but not organically related. In reality, not only may these values conflict in any specific context, but their legitimacy has varied over time. The alleged consensus about ideals, reinforced by their characterization as part of the same creed, has actually never existed. It was challenged during the

Jacksonian period, the progressive era, the New Deal era, and – more latterly – the 1960s and 1970s. When Lipset reevaluated the American creed in *American Exceptionalism: A Two-Edged Sword* (1996), he offered a nuance analysis of its strengths (such as providing a stable regime and a prosperous capitalist economy), as well as the drawbacks of these strengths (such as high crime rate and a wasteful litigiousness).

Lipset emphasized the core paradox of US democracy: Based on high ideals, it fuels unrealistic democratic expectations. As a result, the American polity is more likely to be damaged by the inevitable discrepancy between ideals and realities than other liberal democracies. Echoing the concerns raised by Gunnar Myrdal in *An American Dilemma* (1944), American scholars and political leaders have increasingly questioned the moral status of a nation torn between an allegiance to its highest ideals and the base realities of racial exclusion. Many hoped that the election of President Obama presaged America's movement toward a post-racial society but the persistence of racism and ethno-racial inequalities runs against this optimistic vision. Furthermore, as Michael Tessler argued, Obama's presidency actually further racialized American politics, despite his administration's concerted efforts to neutralize the political impact of race.[30] GOP leaders and the Tea Party movement embraced a racial polarization fueled by a white backlash, as well – conversely – as liberals who denounced the pernicious effect of a "color-blind" ideology.[31]

The conventional glorification of the mythical "melting pot" is severely flawed. The historic capacity of the United States to turn immigrants into Americans illustrates the powerful ability of the creed to frame the assimilation of new arrivals. Yet the assimilation of new minorities changes the very nature of that "pot" in the process. Some scholars like assimilation theorists Richard Alba and Victor Nee believe that the assimilation of new groups into mainstream society signals a revitalization of US democracy.[32] Conversely, for others, like Huntington, aspects of pluralist assimilation (such as bilingualism, hyphenated identities, and multiculturalism) pose a threat to national identity.[33] Paradoxically, the assumption that the American political system is the most notable example of pluralist democracy fuels concerns about the purity of that system, one threatened by ethno-racial and ideological pluralism. For some self-declared protectors of the nation's motto, *E Pluribus unum*, the defense of American democracy actually requires limiting ethno-racial diversity and fighting liberal political beliefs promoted by "deconstructionists" (a term popularized by Huntington, as well as philosopher Allan Bloom).[34] From the debates concerning multiculturalism in the 1990s to the current intellectual and political controversies about identity politics, the assumption that the robustness of US democracy relies on a creedal identity has thus been used to justify democratic exclusion as much as for inclusion.

Overconfidence in the inviolability of the "rights culture" constitutes another source of weakness. There is plentiful evidence that the sanctity of the constitution anchors the stability of US democracy. A rights tradition, based on the Bill of Rights, defines American identity, strengthens institutions, and does provide strong democratic guardrails. Yet, constitutional patriotism does not in itself protect democracy, especially when it fuels a culture of distrust. Freedom of expression, for example, is sanctified by the First Amendment, which defines this freedom more broadly than in other democracies. It has historically protected the media, as well as social, legal, and political activists, now ranging from the leftist supporters of political wokism to Trumpists. Yet, the libertarian interpretation of the First Amendment makes it difficult to combat hate speech, and encourages Americans to believe that the government has no right to define which ideas are pernicious. The US Supreme Court legitimized this interpretation in a defamation case in 1974 when suggesting that "Under the First Amendment, there is no such thing as a false idea."[35] Controversies about freedom of expression have multiplied in recent decades – leading to the poisoning of political debates by fake news, and an inability to make reasoned moral judgements, as illustrated by Trump's statement in 2017 (that there were "very fine people on both sides") after the violent clashes between KKK supporters and antiracist activists in Charlottesville. Trump's comments illustrate, as former Vice President Joe Biden declared in his 2020 candidacy for the Democratic nomination, a tendency to "assign a moral equivalence between those spreading hate and those with the courage to stand against it." More generally, freedom of speech means that incivility is constitutionally protected in America. This may strengthen democracy; but it incurs collateral damages including discursive and sometimes physical violence, racist propaganda, and a damaging propensity toward moral relativism.

Furthermore, any assessment of the role of the US Supreme Court as the guardian of democracy is questionable for at least two reasons. The first relates to a stream of undemocratic practices upheld by the Court, such as the internment of Japanese Americans during World War II. Less extreme but nonetheless deeply problematic examples include the interference of the US Supreme Court in the election process, notably in 2000 with its Bush v. Gore decision. The larger impact of this decision was to increase distrust in the voting process, culminating with Trump's efforts to overturn the results of the presidential election in 2020. The 2000 decision also affected the Supreme Court's image as an independent judicial body, exposing it to accusations of partisanship. Relatedly, a second limitation concerns an idealistic vision of the US Supreme Court that relies on the naïve assumption that the law is above politics. Far from being politically neutral, the Court has actually become more polarized in recent decades, fueled by the spread of "originalist" legal interpretations, mostly designed to limit the influence of liberal initiatives. For example, invocations of the Federalist Papers by US Supreme Court justices have mushroomed, partly as a result of the appointment of "originalists" such as Antonin Scalia and Clarence Thomas.[36] Polarization intensified during the Trump administration, with the nominations of Neil Gorsuch, Brett Kavanaugh, and Amy Coney Barrett. This has raised concerns about the emergence of a judicial tyranny based on judicial populism, as illustrated by a series of lawsuits involving the US Supreme Court and federal appeals courts that have denigrated the decisions of the President, legislatures, and administrative agencies. Furthermore, the US Supreme Court has greatly weakened the Voting Rights Act in recent years, cutting deeply into the Justice Department's authority over voting and giving states new latitude to impose restrictions and/or gerrymander.

It is worth noting that judicial tyranny is the unexpected consequence of institutional mechanisms designed to prevent the domination of any one branch, and subsequently secure the regime's stability. The American constitutional system of checks and balances has been conceived as a perfect equilibrium to ensure that no one branch of government would become too powerful. However, a separation of powers between three coequal branches of government intended to check-and-balance each other has never been harmonious, as illustrated by the consistent tension between the US Supreme Court and the Executive, and between the Executive and Congress. From the 1870s to the late 1920s, the US Supreme Court consolidated its power, dominating both the presidency and Congress. Franklin D. Roosevelt had to threaten to add more seats to the Supreme Court in order to discourage the Justices from overturning his New Deal Policies. The idea of increasing the number of justices, as well as limiting their tenure, was revived by the Biden administration. As former federal judge Nancy Gertner argued, "the court has been effectively packed by one party and will remain packed for years, with serious consequences to democracy."[37]

The relationship between the Presidency and Congress has fluctuated over time but is generally characterized by a consistent tension. Andrew Jackson, for example, used his veto power extensively, leading to the Senate censuring him. Johnson was subsequently impeached. During the twentieth century, some presidents restored their office's authority.

Theodore Roosevelt introduced the practice of issuing executive orders. Franklin D. Roosevelt was given unprecedented powers during the Great Depression, and retained most of them after 1937. After his death, the Republican majority in Congress passed the Twenty-second Amendment, limiting presidential tenures to two terms of office. Nonetheless, presidential powers remained strong between the 1950s and the mid-1970s, when Richard Nixon had to resign because of the Watergate Scandal. Confrontations over the constitutional limits of presidential authority have intensified since the 1980s – especially when different parties controlled the presidency and Congress. During the last two decades, confrontations have turned into political fights, notably illustrated by the Senate's refusal to take up President Obama's nomination of Merrick Garland as a justice to the Supreme Court, as well as the trench warfare that erupted during Trump's impeachment. Furthermore, Arthur Vandenberg's famous dictum, that politics "stops at the water's edge" clearly no longer applies. Even foreign policy, which historically was considered the one area of government where bipartite principles predominated, is now a forum for partisan political bickering. As of October 2021, for example, Joe Biden still could only get six of his sixty-nine nominees for ambassadorships confirmed because one senator, Ted Cruz of Texas, objected to Biden's acquiescence to Germany's Nord Stream 2 pipeline deal with Russia.[38] Doing so effectively undermined one of Biden's professed chief foreign policy goals – democracy promotion.

The problem is not only the resilient competition between the three branches. It is also that mechanisms designed to stabilize US democracy are actually used in undemocratic ways. The many "veto points" in this complex political system are increasingly activated to prevent the enactment of policies that most Americans support. The separation of powers, together with highly polarized parties having "veto points," has led to repeated institutional gridlock. This gridlock is exacerbated by procedures such as the Senate's filibuster and supermajoritarian voting rules, as well as the House majority's effective disenfranchisement of the minority party. The ability of elected officials to address key societal problems (such as voting rights, health care, and social benefits) is consequently contingent on convoluted procedural rules or the preferences of a very small number of senators or congressman willing to ignore their party's edicts for their own political purposes.[39] The fear that deadlock would become a permanent feature of US democracy was first expressed in the 1960s.[40] Today, it fuels public resentment, if not anger. Americans' disapproval of Congress has reached record levels, with a poll revealing that only 12 percent expressed confidence in this body in 2021.[41]

These feelings are exacerbated by the fact that American democracy was conceived, and has remained, incomplete despite the idealistic belief that the foundation of the Constitution is the will of "we the people of the United States." The fundamental value of political equality, reaffirmed by the Declaration of Independence, inspired Abraham Lincoln's motto: "of the people, by the people, and for the people." Since then, however, any semblance of the popular control of government espoused by Lincoln has remained a myth. First, the electoral system is riddled with alarming inconsistencies when it comes to the question of representation. The Senate, for example, represents territorial states, not proportions of people. It was originally meant to ensure that new states would be fairly represented as they were incorporated. As a consequence, people (notably minorities) living in urban areas are severely underrepresented while those in sparsely populated (mostly small and/or often agricultural and geographically western) states are grossly overrepresented. Wyoming (population, 578,803) has the same number of Senators as New York (19.8 million). Second, primary elections often involve the participation of a small percentage of eligible voters in selecting party candidate for Congress.[42] This has become a key problem in a growing number of gerrymandered Congressional districts where the primary essentially determines the outcome of the elections. Third, the Electoral College, the formal body that elects the President and Vice President, has increasingly become a source of criticism and was a sustained target of Trump's efforts to overturn the 2020 election. This is because when voters go to the polls in a Presidential election, they actually vote for a slate of electors who will cast their ballots. Related to this third point, again small states are overrepresented (people in Wyoming, for example, have nearly four times the power of people in California). The machinery of elections subsequently aggravates the vulnerability of US democracy, especially when there is a gap between popular vote and election results – as illustrated by the 2000 and 2016 elections, Republicans have won the presidency while losing the popular vote. This vulnerability was on full display in the run up to the 2021 insurrection, as Trump pressured state electoral offices to organize a recount or declare the results fraudulent.

The Strength of Fragility

A question now captivates the attention of scholars, politicians, and the media: Will 2024 be the year American democracy dies? According to law professor Richard Hasen, the United States faces a serious risk – that the next presidential election, and ensuing US elections, will not be conducted in accordance with conventional rules. The means may be insidious. "Lawyers in fine suits" rather than rioters could try to overturn results, as illustrated by recent laws adopted by Republican-controlled legislatures to increase their control over how elections are run and strip secretaries of state of their powers. Ironically, Hasen adds, "the conduct of former President Trump in repeatedly and falsely claiming that the 2000 election was stolen has markedly raised the potential for an actual stolen election in the United States." [43] "The stage is thus being set for chaos," Robert Kagan argues in the *Washington Post*. US democracy is "heading into its greatest political and constitutional crisis since the Civil War, with a reasonable chance of mass violence, a breakdown of federal authority, and the division of the country into red and blue enclaves."[44] Most Democrats, and some Republicans, worry that Trump's die-hard supporters are prepared to defy constitutional and democratic norms, with the support of newly elected state officials who espouse election conspiracy theories and state legislatures controlled by Trumpists.

A more optimistic scenario is envisaged by scholars who, focusing on the *longue durée*, note that US democracy has survived numerous external shocks (such as the Pearl Harbor attack or events in the aftermath of 9/11), internal conflicts (from the Civil War to the riots at the Capitol in January 2021), socioeconomic collapse (from the Great Depression to the 2008 financial crisis), military failures (from Vietnam to Afghanistan), and political violence (including that which followed the assassination of four presidents). Furthermore, the prestige of the office of the Presidency has been restored many times after being undermined by demagogues (such as Andrew Jackson) and corrupt presidents (such as Richard Nixon). As David Runciman argues in *The Confidence Trap*, US democracy has been poor at avoiding crises, but good at recovering from them.[45] In *Four Threats*, Suzanne Mettler and Robert C. Lieberman explore various moments in history when US democracy was in crisis, such as the Depression, and Watergate.[46] These episodes have risked profound – even fatal – damage to America's democratic experiment. They have revealed, according to Mettler and Lieberman, four distinct characteristics of disruption seemingly endemic to American politics: Political polarization, racism and nativism, economic inequality, and excessive executive power. Alone or in combination, these characteristics have threatened the survival of the republic. But it has survived – so far.

The cumulative lesson is that the history of democracy is bumpy: crises build over time but they have provided ameliorative opportunities. During the Gilded Age, for example, extreme socioeconomic inequality empowered the wealthy and undermined democracy. Yet it provoked protests that engendered significant electoral reforms, such as the direct election of US senators, the right of women to vote, and the federal regulation of business monopolies. The Great Depression likewise provoked New Deal reforms. Blatant institutional racism (such as the Jim Crow regime) fueled the Civil Rights Movement and the Voting Rights Act of 1965, which significantly improved the quality of US democracy. The Watergate scandal led to a Supreme Court pronouncement that presidents were not above the law.

What are the appropriate contemporary catalysts that can produce a major counterreaction? Interestingly, many of the weaknesses revealed or intensified by Trump era politics have produced initiatives designed to protect US democracy. For the first time, the Department of Homeland and FBI now prioritize white supremacists and vigilante groups as domestic terrorists and a threat to democracy. As a result of the 6 January attack on the Capitol, political leaders are now fully aware of the threat posed by conspiracy theories spread by social media: how abusing freedom of expression can easily presage physical violence. They have held the leadership of digital corporations such as Facebook and Twitter to account for their unabashed tolerance of misinformation, warning of prospective regulation if curbs are not installed.[47] The consequence has been that a number of high-profile figures, including Trump himself, have been banned from these platforms. Beyond short-term remedial measures against perpetrators, the Committee investigating the attack intends to address institutional weaknesses (including intelligence failures and the lack of adequate resources to protect the Capitol) in order to recommend legislative and administrative reforms.[48] Members of the Committee, for example, have begun reviewing the Electoral Count Act, the nineteenth-century law that dictates the procedure for counting electoral votes during a joint session of Congress that the lead up to 6 January suggests may be subject to abuse.

Tensions between the US Supreme Court, the federal courts and the Presidency have increased due to efforts by the judicial branch to block or delay the implementation of key parts of the Biden administration's agenda. President Biden has subsequently assembled a commission designed to restore the ideological balance of the Court (now with three liberals and six conservatives, including Trump's three nominations). Among the proposals the commission is considering are term limits for justices, an increase in their number, and varied suggestions designed to enhance transparency and procedural consistency. Other potential proposed changes include a reform of the Electoral College, rescinding the Senate's filibuster, and a new Voting Rights Act aimed at stemming the tide of restrictive new election laws from Republican state legislatures. These proposals face strong resistance from both GOP leaders and some constitutional experts.[49] However, they have generated a fruitful debate about the evident institutional flaws in US democracy.

Most of the current debate surrounding the decline of US democracy focuses on federal and state government. There is, however, beyond institutional and electoral dysfunction, some reason for optimism. The current record low level of political trust, for example, is undoubtedly disconcerting. Yet, a lack of trust has often stimulated democratic political participation, as illustrated by the antiwar protesters in the Vietnam period. Pro-Trump activism energized various peaceful social movements – like Black Lives Matter and MeToo – and a variety of civic action. Furthermore, initiatives in the furtherance of local democratic governance, an enduring feature of American politics since the Dillon's Rule of 186 that contrasts with many other liberal democracies, are now plentiful. Indeed, deadlock at the federal level often stimulates improved participatory local governance and enhances the local influence of civil society actors (such as the National Civil League). Fully aware of the different character of national, state, and local governance, Americans have a more favorable opinion of their state and local governments. In 2018, 67 percent of Americans viewed their local government favorably, and 58 percent had a positive view of their state government – compared to only 35 percent who reported a favorable opinion of the federal government.[50]

Pointedly, while Americans express a high level of distrust in their democratic institutions, a majority also believe that the current crisis can be resolved. Fully, 84 percent believe their level of confidence in the federal government can improve, and 86 percent think improvement is feasible when it comes to the confidence Americans have in each other.[51] Americans are critical of how the government handles several issues. Only 34 percent think the government is doing is good job of managing the immigration system, and 36 percent in how public policies address poverty. However, majorities believe the government does a very good job keeping the country safe from terrorism (72 percent), ensuring the provision of food and medicine (62 percent), and strengthening the economy (54 percent). Furthermore, despite the grim national mood, a majority (57 percent) continue to say that "as Americans, we can always find ways to solve our problems."[52]

Conclusion

After all, it seems that Henry Kissinger had a point. Reflecting on the impact of the Vietnam experience on US democracy, he argued that "surely no other society would have had comparable confidence in its ultimate robustness to thus rip itself apart, certain that it would put itself back together. No other people would have been so cavalier about risking breakdown in order to spark renewal."[53] Kissinger, a man of great self-confidence who played a major role in one of the most deceptive administrations in American history, accurately described the pendulum between American Cassandras and Pollyannas: US democracy does not moderate from triumphalism to a more circumspect level of confidence in what it can achieve. Instead, it lurches to a crisis of confidence and declinism. There is no stable equilibrium between these two positions.

Assessments of US democracy are predictably oscillating between these two poles. It is premature to evaluate what the state of US democracy will be in the coming years – especially for the reasons Richard Ned Lebow emphasizes in his contribution to this book. First, "assessments of stability made by political actors and analysts are largely hit or miss;" and second, "leader responses to fear of fragility or confidence in robustness are unpredictable in their consequences."[54] Examining historical evidence, however, we can draw two lessons about how democracy is eventually weakened when intellectual and political elites exaggerate domestic threats intent on attracting an audience and securing their electoral support.

First, obsessively declinist ideologies unleash nativist impulses and legitimize undemocratic practices. Historic examples include Samuel F.B. Morse's propaganda pamphlet (*Imminent Dangers to the Free Institutions of the United States Through Immigration*, 1835) and Madison Grant's racialist attack against the "enemy inside" (*The Passing of the Great Race*, 1916). The specter of degeneracy inspired racial immigration laws (such as the Chinese Exclusion Act of 1882 and the eventual quota immigration system introduced in 1921), as well as eugenics experiments in the United States that predated Nazi atrocities in Germany. Furthermore, as Josef Joffe (German editor of *Der Zeit*) argued, "declinism markets a self-defeating prophecy." Politicians claim the "sky is falling" only so they can then be seen as saving the day.[55] False prophecies have been issued in the past, although the United States has not – so far - experienced a Weimar-style implosion. However, it may be prescient to note that 34 percent of Americans now believe that violent action against the government is sometimes justified.[56] Declinist arguments can generate self-fulfilling prophecies: Electoral conspiracy theories, for example, both fuel and are fueled by jaundiced assessments of US democracy – leading to efforts to actually rig the election process in order to "stop the steal." Predictions of an imminent and inevitable

The American Fragility–Robustness Nexus

conflagration are broadcast by MAGA activists on social media, as well as politicians from both parties. They also inspire prognosis, as illustrated by the burgeoning literature on the coming next civil war in America.[57] Commenting on what he characterizes as these "fear-mongering" predictions, Fintan O'Toole argues that apocalyptic narratives are "flammable and corrosive," making people so fearful of one another that "the logic of the pre-emptive strike sets in."[58]

Second, in times of emergency, US democracy can be damaged by even its most ardent champions. Actual emergencies entail the extraordinary use of executive prerogatives, defined by John Locke as the "power to act according to discretion for the public good, without the prescription of the law and sometimes even against it."[59] President Lincoln, for example, suspended the writ of habeas corpus during the Civil War without congressional approval. Habeas corpus, however, was robustly reinstituted after the war. Yet notably, in the current context of a "permanent state of exception," there is plentiful evidence of the undemocratic outcomes from the "lesser evil" perspective, defined by Michael Ignatieff as "the moral hazard of using doubtful means to defend praiseworthy goals."[60] At its core, it assumes that the fight against existential threats requires exceptions to, and derogations from, constitutional principles and civil liberties. Clearly a righteous cause, such as protecting America against terrorism, has justified undemocratic coercive measures – as illustrated by measures such as the Patriot Act taken by the United States (and other democracies) in the aftermath of 9/11. The fight against terrorism has deeply affected the exercise of fundamental democratic principles, notably the application of the rule of law, the separation of powers, the independence of judicial authority, and the accountability of government.

The most eloquent defenses of US democracy are today used to challenge the legitimacy of political institutions, discredit political opponents, and damage fundamental civil rights. In 2021, eighteen states in America enacted thirty laws that restrict voting access. These laws made mail voting and early voting more difficult, imposed more stringent voter ID requirements, and make faulty voter purges from electoral rolls more likely. Their supporters have justified them as a means to protect democracy. In Texas, for example, in September 2021 Governor Greg Abbott (R) signed into law Senate Bill 1. He declared that the purpose of this law, which restricts how and when voters cast ballots, was to protect democratic elections against fraudulent voters: "One thing that all Texans can agree on is that we must have trust and confidence in our elections."[61]

Any exaggeration of a vulnerability to threats, as well as overconfidence in the US exceptionalism, has dire consequences. Conversely, denial of actual problems by leaders can exacerbate fragility. Both Democrat and Republican leaders now agree that America is falling apart. But they diagnose this condition for different, if not opposing, reasons focusing on the role of government and the question of states' right versus the need for a federal assurance of equity.[62] Not surprisingly, this dominant narrative has an impact on public opinion. Nearly a year after the 6 January events at the Capitol, 64 percent of Americans specifically believe that American democracy is in crisis and even more, 70 percent, feel the same about America more broadly.[63]

US democracy has never lived up to Tocqueville's idealistic characterization. His vision of America as a robust democracy now appears a pallid ideal, rather than an accurate reflection of current American political norms and institutions. If he returned to contemporary America, he would surely have to revisit some of his original remarks. Yet, he might still reaffirm what he wrote in 1852: "American democracy has nothing more to fear than from itself, from the abuse of democracy, from the sense and exaggerated pride in its strength."[64]

Notes

1 Alexis de Tocqueville, *Democracy in America* (Chicago, IL: University of Chicago Press, 2000).
2 See, for example, Franklin Delano Roosevelt, "The Four Freedoms," 6 January, 1941, available in text and video at www.americanrhetoric.com/speeches/fdrthefourfreedoms.htm
3 For a video of the speech delivered 15 July 1979 see www.americanrhetoric.com/speeches/jimmycartercrisisofconfidence.htm
4 See www.npr.org/2022/01/06/1071063375/a-dagger-at-the-throat-of-democracy-president-biden-decries-election-lies
5 John Winthrop, A Model of Christian Charity (1630) quoted by Abram C. Van Engen, *City on a Hill: A History of American Exceptionalism* (New Haven: Yale University Press, 2020). Some historians have doubted these words were ever spoken.
6 The Articles of Confederation were written in 1777 but were not ratified until 1781.
7 It is worth noting that all immigrants, at the end of the naturalization process, are required to take a public oath of allegiance – not to the United States per se, but to the Constitution. This act illustrates the power of "constitutional patriotism" as newly citizens pledge to the abstract concepts of liberty, equality and justice for all.
8 Quoted by R.B Bernstein, *The Founding Fathers Reconsidered* (New York: Oxford University Press, 2009), p. 4.

The American Fragility–Robustness Nexus 225

9 Quoted by Evita Duffy, "Why We Must Preserve John Winthrop's Vision," *The Federalist*, 17 December 2020. https://thefederalist.com/2020/12/17/why-we-must-preserve-john-winthrops-vision-of-america-as-a-shining-city-upon-a-hill/ . John F. Kennedy had alluded to similar sentiments, but it was before he assumed office as President-elect. See *Congressional Record*, 10 January, 1961, vol. 107, Appendix, p. A169.

10 See Simon Reich, "Congress' Walk of Shame on International Deals," *The New Republic*, 12 March 2015, https://newrepublic.com/article/121281/republicans-have-been-stalling-bills-years.

11 See https://georgewbush-whitehouse.archives.gov/infocus/bushrecord/factsheets/freedomagenda.html. US Vice President Dick Cheney also argued the case for American exceptionalism (including the war in Iraq) by writing: "We are, as Lincoln said, the last, best hope of earth. We are not just one more nation, one more same entity on the world stage. We have been essential to the preservation and progress," in his 2015 book *Exceptional: Why the World Need a Powerful America* (New York: Threshold Editions, 2015), p. 259.

12 Seymour Martin Lipset, *The First New Nation* (New York: Basic Books, 1963).

13 Seymour Martin Lipset, *American Exceptionalism: A Double-Edged Sword* (New York: W.W. Norton, 1996). See also Byron Schafer (ed.), *Is America Different? A New Look at American Exceptionalism* (Oxford: Clarendon Press, 1991); Anders Stephanson, *Manifest Destiny; American Expansion and the Empire of Right* (New York: Hill and Wang, 1994); John W. Kingdon, *America the Unusual* (1999).

14 See, for example, Seymour Martin Lipset, "Some Social Requisites of Democracy: Economic Development and Political Legitimacy," *American Political Science Review*, 53, No. 1 (March, 1959), pp. 69–105.

15 Hartz was preceded by the German political theorist Werner Sombart who asked the question in his 1906 essay (Why is There no Socialism in the United States?). He underlined the role of the white working class, the "bourgeois nature" of American society, and the sanctity of private property.

16 Daniel Bell, *The End of Ideology: On the Exhaustion of Political Ideas in the 1950s* (Glencoe, IL.: Free Press, 1960).

17 Pew Research Center, "Public Trust in Government: 1958-2021," 17 May 2021. www.pewresearch.org/politics/2021/05/17/public-trust-in-government-1958-2021/.

18 Quoted by Jason Edwards, "Foreign Policy Rhetoric in the 1992 Presidential Campaign: Bill Clinton's Exceptional Jeremiad," *Communication Studies Faculty Publication*, 50 (2015), p. 42.

19 Robert Kaplan, "The Coming Anarchy," *Atlantic Monthly*, 273: 44–76.

20 David Schleifer and Antonio Diep, *Strengthening Democracy: What Do Americans Think?* The 2019 Yankelovich Democracy Monitor Report (Public Agenda, August 2019): www.publicagenda.org/wp-content/uploads/2019/08/Strengthening_Democracy_WhatDoAmericansThinkFINAL.pdf.

21 Pew Research Center, "Americans' Views of Government: Low Trust but Some Positive Performance Ratings," 14 September 2020. www.pewresearch

.org/politics/2020/09/14/americans-views-of-government-low-trust-but-some-positive-performance-ratings/.
22 Ishaan Tharoor, "The End of the Road for American Exceptionalism," *The Washington Post*, 7 January 2021. www.washingtonpost.com/world/2021/01/07/american-exceptionalism-end-capitol-mob/.
23 International IDEA's Global State of Democracy. 2021. *Global State of Democracy Report 2021*. www.idea.int/gsod/global-report#chapter-2-democracy-health-check:-an-overview-of-global-tre.
24 Benjamin I. Page and Martin Gilens, *Democracy in America? What has Gone Wrong and What We Can Do* (Chicago: University of Chicago Press, 2020).
25 Steven Levitsky and Daniel Ziblatt, *How Democracies Die* (New York: Viking, 2018).
26 Amy Fried and Douglas B. Harris, *At War with Government* (New York: Columbia University Press, 2021).
27 Paul Sabin, *Public Citizens* (W.W.Norton, 1990).
28 Pew Research Center, "Partisanship and Political Animosity in 2016," 22 June 2016. www.people-press.org/wp-content/uploads/sites/4/2016/06/06-22-16.
29 Robert A. Dahl, *Dilemmas of Pluralist Democracy* (New Haven: Yale University Press,1982), p. 150.
30 Michael Tesler, *Post-Racial or Most Racial? Race and Politics in the Obama Era* (Chicago, IL: The University of Chicago Press, 2016).
31 See, for example, Eduardo Bonilla-Silva, *Racism without Racists: Color Blind Racism and the Persistence of Racial Inequalities* (Boulder, CO: Rowman & Littlefield, 2013).
32 Richard Alba and Victor Nee, *Remaking the American Mainstream* (Cambridge, MA: Harvard University Press, 2003).
33 Huntington, *Who are We? America's Great Debate* (London: The Free Press, 2004).
34 Allan Bloom, *The Closing of the American Mind* (New York: Simon & Schuster, 1987).
35 Quoted by Frederick Schauer, "The Exceptional First Amendment," in *American Exceptionalism and Human Rights* edited by Michael Ignatieff (Princeton: Princeton University Press, 2005), p. 46.
36 Dan T. Coenen, 2007, "Fifteen Curious Facts about The Federalist Papers," *Popular Media*, 2. https://digitalcommons.law.uga.edu/cgi/viewcontent.cgi?article=1001&context=fac_pm.
37 Quoted by Ann Marimow, "Biden's Supreme Court Commission Endorse Final Report Noting Bipartisan Public Support for Term Limits," *The Washington Post*, 7 December 2021. www.washingtonpost.com/politics/courts_law/supreme-court-commission-term-limits/2021/12/07/eb0ef982-5767-11ec-9a18-a506cf3aa31d_story.html.
38 Josh Lederman, "Ted Cruz holding up all State Department nominees over Russian pipeline," NBC News, 2 July 2021. www.nbcnews.com/politics/congress/ted-cruz-holding-all-state-department-nominees-over-russian-pipeline-n1273009; Dan Spinelli, "Biden Is Taking Forever to Get His Ambassadors Confirmed. You Can Thank Ted Cruz for That," Mother Jones, 28 October

2021. www.motherjones.com/politics/2021/10/joe-biden-ambassadors-ted-cruz-donald-trump-obama-flake-mccain/
39 Sen. Manchin, for example, ignored 77 million voters who favored Biden, and even his own state's preferences, in rejecting in December 2021 the Build Back Better legislation that was unfavorable to the coal industry.
40 See, for example, James Burns, *The Deadlock of Democracy: Four-Party Politics in America* (Englewood Cliffs, NJ: Prentice-Hall, 1963).
41 Megan Brenan, 2021. "Americans' Confidence in Major US Institutions Dips," *Politics*, 14 July (Gallup). https://news.gallup.com/poll/352316/americans-confidence-major-institutions-dips.aspx.
42 See "How Maps Reshape American Politics," *New York Times*, 7 November 2021. www.nytimes.com/interactive/2021/11/07/us/politics/redistricting-maps-explained.html
43 Rick Hasen, "Identifying, and Minimizing the Risk of Election Subversion and Stolen Elections in the Contemporary United States," *Election Law Blog*, 20 September 2021. https://electionlawblog.org/?p=124686. See also William Howell and Terry Moe, *Presidents, Populism, and the Crisis of Democracy* (Chicago, IL: University of Chicago Press, 2020).
44 Robert Kagan, "Our Constitutional Crisis is Already Here," *The Washington Post*, 23 September, 2021. www.washingtonpost.com/opinions/2021/09/23/robert-kagan-constitutional-crisis/.
45 David Runciman, *The Confidence Trap: A History of Democracy in Crisis from WWI to the Present* ((Princeton: Princeton University Press, 2015).
46 Suzanne Mettler and Robert C. Lieberman, *Four Threats: The Recurring Crises of American Democracy* (London: Macmillan, 2020).
47 Shannon Bond, "Facebook, Twitter, Google CEOs Testify Before Congress," *NPR*, 25 March 2021. www.npr.org/2021/03/25/980510388/facebook-twitter-google-ceos-testify-before-congress-4-things-to-know.
48 See https://january6th.house.gov/about.
49 See, for example, Rosalind Dixon, "Why the Supreme Court Needs (Short) Term Limits," *The New York Times*, 31 December 2021 (www.nytimes.com/2021/12/31/opinion/supreme-court-term-limits.html?referringSource=articleShare); Thomas Griffith and David Levi, "The Supreme Court Isn't Broken. Even If It Were, Adding Justices Would Be a Bad Idea," *The Washington Post*, 12 December 2021. www.nytimes.com/2021/12/31/opinion/supreme-court-term-limits.html?referringSource=articleShare.
50 Pew Research Center, "The Public, the Political System and American Democracy," 26 April 2018. www.pewresearch.org/politics/2018/04/26/1-democracy-and-government-the-u-s-political-system-elected-officials-and-governmental-institutions/.
51 Lee Rainie, Scott Keeter, and Andrew Perrin, *Trust and Distrust in America* (Pew Research Center, 2019). www.pewresearch.org/politics/2019/07/22/trust-and-distrust-in-america/.
52 Pew Research Center, "Americans' Views of Government: Low Trust but Some Positive Performance Ratings," 14 September 2020.
53 Henry Kissinger, *Diplomacy* (New York: Simon & Schuster, 1994).
54 See Chapter 2 in this volume.

55 Josef Joffe, *The Myth of America's Decline: Politics, Economics, and a Half Century of False Prophecies* (New York: Liveright Publishing Corporation, 2013).
56 Washington Post-University of Maryland poll, *The Washington Post*, 1 January 2022.
57 See, for example, Stephen Marche, *The Next Civil War* (New York: Simon & Schuster, 2021); Barbara F. Walter, *How Civil Wars Start (2018)*; Alexander Laban Hinton, *It Can Happen Here: White Power and the Rising Threat of Genocide in the US* (NYU Press, 2021).
58 Fintan O'Toole, "Beware Prophecies of Civil War," *The Atlantic*, 16 December 2021. www.theatlantic.com/magazine/archive/2022/01/america-civil-war-prophecies/620850/.
59 John Locke, *Second Treatise on Government* (Indianapolis: Hackett, 1980), p. 160.
60 Michael Ignatieff, *The Lesser Evil: Political Ethics in an Age of Terror* (Princeton: Princeton University Press, 2004), p. xiii.
61 www.texastribune.org/2021/09/01/texas-voting-bill-greg-abbott/
62 For Democrats, the attack of 6 January was an attempted coup by far-right Trump supporters. For most Republicans, the election of Joe Biden was a coup, and his administration is a fascist regime.
63 NPR/IPSOS poll, "Seven in Ten Americans Say the Country Is in Crisis, at Risk of Failing," 3 January 2022. www.ipsos.com/en-us/seven-ten-americans-say-country-crisis-risk-failing.
64 In *Tocqueville on America after 1840: Letters and Other Writings*, eds. and trans. by Aurelian Craiutu and Jeremy Jennings (Cambridge, MA: Cambridge University Press), p. 183.

9 The Perils of Choice: Structure and Agency in EU Crisis Management

Douglas Webber

This chapter explores how the EU (European Union) managed the multiple crises that it traversed from 2010 onward, the extent to which these crises provoked its disintegration or collapse, why crisis outcomes diverged and how far the EU's crisis management policies were structurally determined or shaped by agency.

Following Lebow's definition of order as a "hierarchical arrangement" that produces "legible, predictable behavior in accord with recognized norms," the EU is a political order comprising a majority of European states and a majority of the citizens of European states.[1] It is by far the most important source of the laws, rules, regulations, and norms governing their mutual interactions. "International society," according to Lebow, is "not as robust as domestic orders because actors share fewer values and interact at more social remove."[2] Among international orders, however, the EU is arguably the most robust of all.[3] Up until 2015 at least, despite having confronted numerous crises, it had never experienced any political *dis*integration. The number of member states grew continually: from six to twenty-eight. There was no issue-area in which the member states had taken back competences they had previously granted to the EU. And there had been no reduction in the powers of the EU organs – the European Commission, the EP (European Parliament), and the ECJ (European Court of Justice – vis-à-vis the member states. Crises came and went without derailing closer political integration. In the famous dictum of the EU's intellectual founder, Jean Monnet – that Europe would be "forged in crises and will be the sum of the solutions adopted" for them – crises served not to weaken the EU but rather to strengthen it.

The crises that hit the EU from 2010 onward tested its robustness – and the validity of Monnet's dictum – like no previous ones.[4] Whilst they did not provoke the EU's complete collapse, the EU did not survive them entirely unscathed. In this paper, political (dis)integration is conceived as comprising three dimensions. The first dimension, which may be labeled *sectoral* (dis)integration, concerns the expansion or reduction of the range of issue-areas in which the EU exercises policymaking competences. The second dimension, *vertical* (dis)integration, refers to the expansion or reduction of the authority of the EU's supranational organs (such as the European Commission, the ECJ, the EP, and the ECB – European Central Bank) vis-à-vis its intergovernmental organs (the Council and the European Council) and those of the member states. The third dimension, *horizontal* (dis)integration, comprises the expansion or reduction of the number of member states. To be sure, the Eurozone and coronavirus crises culminated in higher levels of monetary and fiscal political integration, respectively. However, the refugee crisis resulted in a reduction in the level of integration of refugee policy, in the scope of borderless travel in the Schengen zone, and in the authority of EU organs such as the Commission and the ECJ vis-à-vis the member states. Above all, the Brexit crisis led to the secession of the UK. Never had a member state left the EU. A decade of crises produced a divergent pattern of simultaneous political integration and disintegration that could not be easily explained by either "optimistic" or "pessimistic" European integration theories.[5]

The principal objective of this chapter is to analyze the extent to which this pattern of crisis outcomes was structurally determined or the product of agency, that is, of choices made by key political actors that could have been different. The chapter comprises four (more) sections. The first discusses competing theoretical perspectives relating to the conditions of the survival of international orders and explores the concepts of structure and agency and the criteria by which their respective impacts on decisions and outcomes can be assessed and determined. The second section focuses on the nature of the political order of the EU, the extent of the structural constraints it imposes on the exercise of agency and the implications that this has for its crisis management capacity. The third and longest section compares the ways in which the EU managed the Eurozone, refugee, Brexit, and coronavirus crises and the degree to which key decisions were structurally determined or the product of agency. The concluding section ties together the threads from the previous sections. It argues that the decisions made by the EU in the Eurozone and coronavirus crises – decisions that forged or promised to forge political integration – were primarily structurally determined, whereas those made in the refugee crisis involved a combination of structural and agency-related variables, and Brexit was the result of a sequence of decisions, several of which could well have been different. Thus, while, at the one end of the integration spectrum, the critical decisions in the Eurozone and coronavirus crises were mainly structurally determined,

Brexit, at the other end, was precipitated by choices by actors who could well have decided differently.

International Political Orders

Competing international relations theories identify numerous, divergent preconditions for the robustness of international political orders – at least if the latter is viewed as synonymous with the maintenance of peace. Different variants of liberal theories emphasize the respective significance of democratic domestic political orders, (high) levels of economic interdependence, and international institutions. Different strands of realism focus, in contrast, on the stabilizing impact of bipolarity (structural realism) or the existence of a (benign/benevolent) dominant power (hegemonic stability theory) or on the destabilizing effect of shifting distributions of power between big powers (power transition theory).[6] Constructivist theories underline the importance of beliefs, ideas, and identities, which may or may not be conducive to the maintenance of an existing international order.

Common to all these theoretical perspectives is that (to varying extents) they leave no room in their explanation of the collapse or survival of orders for *agency*, that is, for the capacity of political actors to make free and autonomous choices. In these perspectives, preexisting *structures* ("the arrangement of or relations between the parts or elements of something complex") so constrain political actors that their scope for making autonomous choices is very limited. For the purposes of this chapter, I will distinguish between four kinds of structural constraints, all of which, to varying extents, play a role in analyzing the robustness or fragility of the EU.

The first kind are *economic-financial*. Economic-financial constraints may, for example, include the country's (or region's) role or position in the international division of labor, its level of integration in the world economy, the (degree of) freedom of movement of capital, the government's fiscal position and dependence on international bond markets, etc. The second kind are *political*. These may encompass the country's constitution (how, for example, it distributes policymaking powers between different levels of government or provides for judicial review), informal decision-making practices (such as whether it is customary to integrate organized economic or other interests into policymaking processes), the electoral system, and elections. The third kind are *legal*. To what extent, for example, is the range of feasible political responses to crises limited by the need to conform with existing (European as well as national) laws, rules, regulations, or treaty obligations or constitutional provisions? The fourth kind are *ideational-normative*. By this I mean constraints that are rooted in long-standing patterns of norms and expectations of behavior in a country (or group of countries) that limit the range of possible courses of action that are condoned or considered appropriate or "acceptable." In contrast to the "hard" others, ideational-normative constraints may be categorized as "soft," at least to the extent that they are not imposed on an actor by the external environment, but rather can change alone as a consequence of an actor's own reappraisal of what kinds of norms and ideas should guide their political action.

Structures, however, do not create only constraints. Whilst they may restrict the range of choices available to some actors, they may empower others. In this sense, we may speak of structural *opportunities*. In as far as crises loosen the tightness of preexisting structural constraints, they can expand the scope for the exercise of agency by political actors. This is what is implied by Monnet's adage that crises would advance European integration or by Churchill's – reputed – remark that one should "never let a good crisis go to waste."

International relations theories tend to take the power of structural constraints for granted. Structural constraints, however, do not impose themselves automatically on decision-makers. Their impact is always mediated by political actors' perceptions. A structure whose constraining effects are not recognized by political actors does not constrain or limit their freedom of choice or action – although the fallout from their choices may of course subsequently remind them of their significance and force them to change course.

Also, notably in crises, political actors often confront situations characterized by high levels of uncertainty and intense time pressure in which careful calculations as to which course of action is preferable are very difficult to make. Explaining her initial choice to keep Germany's borders open to refugees in September 2015, the German Chancellor Angela Merkel thus said: "I could not have waited for twelve hours and contemplated the issues."[7] Similarly she described managing the Eurozone crisis as "like being in a dark room, so dark that you couldn't see your hand in front of your face and you have to grope your way forward."[8] Hence it is not certain whether, even if they accept that they must defer to the structural constraints that they perceive, political actors will make the decisions that best translate these into ("structure-obedient") policies. In any case, structural constraints, where they exist, do not always prescribe a single course of action that political actors feel compelled to follow. Moreover, whether whatever policy is ultimately pursued will achieve its ostensible purpose is also uncertain.

The Political Order of the EU

The European continent experienced a variety of international political orders in the centuries preceding World War II. In the era of nation-states following the Treaty of Westphalia (1648), they were characterized by an unstable multipolar distribution of power, interspersed by attempts by a single state (France in the early C19 and Germany in the middle of the C20) to achieve and maintain continental domination by military force. The most durable of these was the Concert of Powers, which was born at the Congress of Vienna in 1815 but undermined by the first German unification before collapsing with the outbreak of World War I. European integration represented a collective effort, within the context of the bipolar international system of the Cold War, to supersede this disastrous historical legacy of balance-of-power politics by forging such close – especially material-economic – ties between participating states that it would be unthinkable or at least infeasible for them again to go to war against each other.

Described once by a former Commission president (Jacques Delors) as an "unidentified political object," the EU arguably constitutes a hybrid of a state and an international intergovernmental organization. In its history that now stretches back almost seven decades, the EU has developed several traits that are relevant for assessing its prospective robustness.

The first of these is that it is a consensual democracy.[9] Thus, the formal decision-making rules contained in the EU treaties requires super-majorities for decisions taken by the Council and consensus in the European Council, the EU's chief crisis-managing organ comprising the heads of the member states' governments. The effect of these rules is reinforced by the prevalence of strong norms of consensus and compromise that favor the broadest possible accommodation of member states' interests. For the EU's robustness, the implications of its consensual policymaking processes are ambivalent. On the one hand, by reducing the likelihood that especially small member states will be outvoted and marginalized, it diminishes the risk of exacerbation of interstate cleavages, increases the legitimacy of EU decisions and counters possible threats to the EU's cohesion. On the other hand, this trait militates against fast decision-making and radical changes of policy direction, such as may be required to stabilize an order in times of crisis.[10]

The second is that the EU has no means of "coercive control" of the member states – there is no European army or police force.[11] For the enforcement of EU law, rules, and regulations, the EU thus relies on the voluntary compliance of the governments and courts of the member states and their acceptance of the primacy of European over national jurisprudence. This means that, unlike states, the EU cannot deploy military force to prevent secession, explicit provision for which was made in article 50 of the Lisbon Treaty, according to which Brexit was negotiated after the UK referendum in 2016.

The third is that, whilst the EU enjoys broad, although variable, support among the publics of the member states, the integration process has failed hitherto to generate a very strong common identity (and hence a strong sense of solidarity) among member states' citizens. The EU's enlargement, especially that to include the post-Communist Central and East European states, has militated against such a process. The EU is consequently more exposed to political backlashes than most states when (especially zero-sum) distributional or deep values-related conflicts break out and the EU begins to be perceived as a motor of deteriorating rather than rising living standards or as a growing threat to national identities or dominant national norms.

Other things being equal, a consensual democracy that has no organs of "coercive control" and is not underpinned by a strong common identity may be expected to be severely constrained in how decisively it can react to crises. Consequently these – mainly political – constraints could be expected to heighten the risk of the EU collapsing in crises such as those it had to manage after 2010. However, several of the EU's other, offsetting traits arguably serve as a counterweight to any tendencies toward disintegration that crises might otherwise fuel.

The first of these is the fact that the member states are linked by high levels of economic and financial interdependence – still higher than those of any other region. This applies especially to the nineteen member states of the Eurozone. During most of the Eurozone crisis (see below), the heads of government of the member states shared a common analysis that the collapse of the Eurozone would be economically and financially damaging for them all. International bond markets exerted overwhelming pressures on them to impose financial austerity on Eurozone members running the highest budget deficits. One might argue that, for better or for worse, the strategy of the EU's founders – to tie the member states materially irrevocably to one another – has worked, at least in the Eurozone.

Second, there has long been a "pro-European" consensus among the political elites of the member states. Since the integration process was launched, their political landscapes have mostly been dominated by moderate right (Christian Democratic), centrist (Liberal) and moderate left (Social Democratic) political parties fundamentally supportive of political integration.[12] This elite consensus – which has nonetheless begun to fray and erode during the last decade - has mitigated the risk of the EU's consensual political system becoming deadlocked in crises, as it limits the degree of political polarization between governments. Judging by the statements they made at the time, most political leaders in the member states were genuinely deeply worried that these crises jeopardized the EU's very survival. Given their political-ideological orientation, they were correspondingly inclined ultimately to subordinate the achievement of any specific policy or other political objective to the overriding priority of staving off the EU's collapse.

Third, at least in times of crisis such as during the last decade, the EU's decision-making capacity is facilitated and expedited by the assertion of hierarchy, which cuts through and temporarily sets aside the normally strong consensual EU decision-making norms. In any given crisis, the most powerful actors in any international – or other – order or organization are those whose participation is most indispensable for its resolution and that can best live with no agreement as to how it should be managed. These states consequently have greater scope for the exercise of agency than the others. The former are decision-*makers*, the latter are decision-*takers*. In the history of European integration, crises are typically the hour of the Franco-German tandem (variously also described as motor, engine, vanguard, entente, couple, partnership, or axis). Pre-negotiated, bilateral Franco-German bargains have often formed the basis of multilateral, EU-wide agreements on major issues and conflicts.[13] This pattern has been facilitated not only by the superior power resources and hence bargaining power that these two states possess vis-à-vis their 'smaller' counterparts, but also by the fact that, in as far as they constitute "opposed poles" in the EU, even after successive enlargements, a Franco-German accord may broadly accommodate and reconcile the interests of the member states as a whole.[14]

Historically, France and Germany have generally managed to provide the EU with a form of stabilizing *collective* hegemonic leadership, in the sense of Kindleberger.[15] Over time and especially during the post-2010 crisis, however, the balance of power in this relationship has shifted decisively from the initial "senior" partner, France, towards Germany. France's capacity to play this role was weakened by its relatively mediocre economic performance, chronic high government budget deficits and the mounting domestic opposition to closer political integration that was reflected in the "no" referendum vote on the proposed EU Constitutional Treaty in 2005. In brief, France was no longer "what it used to be."[16] With the UK drifting further and further away from the "heart of Europe" at the same time, the task of providing leadership in the EU's crises increasingly fell to Germany alone.[17] Combined with its relative political stability and the broad "pro-European" consensus among its elites, Germany's economic and financial size and strength increasingly made it, in the words of the then Polish Foreign Minister, the EU's "indispensable" member state.[18] The fate of the EU depended significantly more heavily on Germany's choices – how it exercised its broader scope for agency – than on those of other member states or of most of the EU's supranational organs.

Fortuitously for the EU, Germany had strong geopolitical as well as economic interests in maintaining a politically highly integrated Europe. Not only was unhindered access to the markets of other EU member states provided by the EU's single market enormously important for Germany's export-oriented manufacturing industry and prosperity. Not least after German reunification in 1990, the country's integration into Europe was also important – and considered by its political elite to be critical – to avert a resurgence of coalitions aiming to balance Germany's new power and thus the country's prospective diplomatic isolation, with, from the elite's perspective at any rate, worrisome implications for European stability and peace.[19] Support for European integration became something akin to a 'state religion' in the Federal Republic, while the prospect of Germany being cut loose from international organizations and alliances in an increasingly turbulent world and Europe in which every state had to fend for itself became a nightmare.[20] The post-Cold War shift in the international balance of power away from Europe also heightened their attachment to the EU, which Merkel saw as Germany's "life insurance" in a world in which Germany is "far too small to exert geopolitical influence on its own."[21]

Other things being equal, Germany could thus be expected to exercise its power to try to hold the EU together. However, first, domestic political variables occasionally if not often generated counterpressures that the government could ill afford to ignore if it did not want to be rejected in Parliament or in (federal or state) elections. The federal government's choices could not be tailored exclusively toward the objective of preventing the EU unraveling. Second, although Germany was certainly *primus inter pares* in the EU, its power varied by issue-area and did not always suffice for it to mobilize the requisite support among other member states. Where, as in the Ukraine crisis, Germany was both willing *and* able to act as a hegemonic power in Kindleberger's sense, the EU was able to maintain preexisting levels of political integration.[22] Where, as in the refugee and Brexit crises, it was not and there was no other hegemonic actor, the EU experienced some political disintegration, whether more limited or more far-reaching. In the Eurozone and coronavirus crises, in contrast, political disintegration could be averted and closer integration forged, in the former case because, exceptionally, a powerful supranational actor (the ECB) played a functionally equivalent role to that of a stabilizing hegemon and in the latter because collective Franco-German leadership succeeded in containing the centrifugal tendencies between the member states. Last, it was not always unequivocally clear during the crisis period which policies would best further this end. In some cases at least (see above), the context in which decisions had to be taken also made it difficult if not impossible for decision-makers to weigh up carefully and prudently the implications of competing options before deciding. In other words, there was ample scope – in some crises more than others – for "mistakes" of judgment that contributed to political disintegration.

Structure and Agency

In respect of political integration as defined in this chapter, the multiple crises that the EU had to manage from 2010 onward culminated in divergent outcomes. In the following, I analyze comparatively how these crises were managed, why their outcomes diverged, and the extent to which these outcomes were the products of decisions that were dictated by the structural constraints bearing down on key decision-makers or that the latter took autonomously and which therefore could have been different.

Eurozone

Many of the most influential scholars of the EU were convinced of the Eurozone's and EU's invulnerability to crisis. Moravcsik argued, for example, that EU member states inhabited the world's most economically interdependent continent and therefore had "no choice but to cooperate."[23] Key EU decision-makers, however, were much less sanguine about the Euro's and the EU's survival prospects as the crisis intensified. At several points during the crisis they feared that the Eurozone might collapse and that if it did, this would simultaneously destroy the EU itself. During the crisis, German Chancellor Angela Merkel thus often cited the mantra "If the euro fails, Europe fails."[24] They did not seem at all certain that they would be able to agree to take action to avert the Eurozone's collapse or that the action they decided to take would suffice for this purpose. But they did recognize the enormous pressure they were under to act from international financial markets. As European Council president van Rompuy explained:[25]

The financial markets obliged us to change our policies dramatically in order to regain the confidence of the financial markets – not because we loved them, but [because] without restoring confidence the interest rates would go up, and especially the interest rates between the German bund interest rates and other national interest rates. There was really no alternative. There was no alternative for the countries which we called the "countries under programme": Greece, Ireland, Portugal, and to some extent Spain. It was clear that they had to convince the markets about the sustainability of their public finances – call it austerity but there was no other option. Other countries also had to take measures on decreasing the level of deficit and debt, in order to avoid a similar situation as in those three or four countries. There was a huge pressure from the financial markets. It was not really a free choice: we had no other option.

The Eurozone crisis in fact comprised several crises that unfolded between 2010 and 2015: conflicts over the rescue packages for the crisis-stricken member states Greece (on three occasions), Cyprus, Ireland, Portugal, and Spain, over the creation of a bailout fund, over fiscal policy coordination and integration, and over banking regulation. The issue of whether or on which terms Eurozone member states should be rescued financially arose as an indirect consequence of the Global Financial Crisis. These states were running big budget deficits relative to GDP, either because government spending relative to revenues had already been high prior to the crisis (Greece) or because governments had spent large sums of money to rescue banks that had financed a rapid growth in real-estate borrowing. Actors in international bond markets began to worry that the ECB would not serve as a lender of last resort to these governments and that their loans to these states would be lost. They therefore demanded a higher risk premium on the bonds of these governments, exacerbating the governments' already critical fiscal situation and the spread between the yields on different government bonds in the Eurozone. Bond market actors' worries were fueled by uncertainty as to whether, under the terms of the Maastricht Treaty, it would be legal for the ECB to support them.

In the crisis-afflicted states, these economic-financial constraints imposed by international bond markets invariably overrode domestic political ones related to public opinion and elections. Under the terms of the rescue agreements, the governments receiving financial aid were forced to accept conditions of varying degrees of toughness that required them to impose fiscal austerity on their citizens. These policies were normally highly unpopular and contested, often provoking strikes and violent demonstrations and protests. Only those (few) governments that had very recently been elected and therefore could escape political responsibility for the dire circumstances in which these countries found themselves were not voted out of office at the next legislative elections.[26] Governments nonetheless acquiesced in politically highly unpopular austerity measures because their leaders believed that the economic and political consequences of any alternative courses of action would have been more negative. States would have gone bankrupt, they would have had to leave the Eurozone and reintroduce a new national currency that would almost certainly have depreciated severely against the Euro and fueled inflation, banks would have collapsed, the economy would have contracted severely, and the rise of unemployment would have accelerated. Among the governments of the crisis-stricken Eurozone member states, only the radical leftist government in Greece in 2015 gave any serious consideration to this alternative. Its finance minister Varoufakis favored this policy over the acceptance of the bailout terms offered to Greece by the other member states. For him, "a new bail-out would be worse than Grexit, however painful Grexit might be."[27] But he could not convince Prime Minister Tsipras and most other members of the government that this was the better option. Tsipras judged the finance minister's proposals in this regard to be "so vague, it wasn't worth talking about."[28] The government called a public referendum to legitimize its rejection of the initial terms of financial aid offered by the EU and won it. But this ploy did not work, as the implicit threat to proceed with Grexit did not carry much weight with its negotiating partners. The finance ministers of many of the other member states, headed by the German finance minister, Schäuble, wanted Grexit, whilst, despite their opposition to austerity, most Greeks did not want to abandon the Euro.[29] Tsipras's government finally accepted a deal that was tougher for Greece than the one it had refused before the referendum. Tsipras said that his government had been "put in a corner from which there was no way out. I had no choice."[30]

For the leaders of the Eurozone member governments that did not need to be bailed out, the calculations were different. On the one hand, they were exposed to strong domestic political pressures *not* to grant financial aid to the crisis-stricken states, as this was unpopular among their citizens. On the other hand, they too had to weigh up the prospective – political as well as economic – consequences of a collapse of the Eurozone. The economic consequences were perceived to be highly uncertain and depended in part on whether the internal market and the EU would survive such a scenario. According to van Rompuy:[31]

We [the heads of the Eurozone governments – DW] were all convinced that a collapse of the Eurozone would or could also be the end of the European Union. Can you have a common market without a common currency? In theory, yes, but a crisis that could provoke a dislocation of the Eurozone would also put in danger the common market. We knew perfectly well what was at stake.

For the management of the Eurozone crisis, the calculations of German political leaders were of paramount importance. Without Germany, given the relative size of its economy and the (relatively low) level of its public debt, no credible bailout aid or fund could be provided or mounted. Most other net-contributing Eurozone members, including France, therefore took their cue from Berlin.

During the greater part of the crisis, the key German decision-makers considered that the economic and financial risks of allowing any member state to go bankrupt and exit the Eurozone were too high for this scenario to be contemplated. They were uncertain as to whether, in such a scenario, the prospective economic fallout could be contained and the collapse of Euro as such could be averted. Thus, as the second Greek bailout was being negotiated in 2012, and she was told by her advisers that Cyprus too would probably exit the Eurozone if Greece had to, Merkel asked them how many other dominoes would fall. When they told her that there was no way of knowing this, she said that this was "too uncertain."[32] Hence Germany agreed to the bailout. A German Finance Ministry study from the same year estimated that if the Eurozone should collapse and Germany have to reintroduce its own national currency, German GDP would fall by 10 per cent and unemployment would rise to five million.[33] The German finance minister Schäuble defended the bailout of Cyprus in 2013 with the argument that even the bankruptcy of this tiny member state (with barely a million citizens) could jeopardize the survival of the Eurozone.[34] Apart from the prospectively very negative macro-economic consequences of a Grexit or the withdrawal or expulsion of any other member state from the Eurozone, such events would also have caused heavy losses for German banks that had lent heavily to southern European Eurozone states prior to the Global Financial Crisis. However, once, by 2015, the Eurozone's crisis-resistance capacity had been strengthened, the German government was less fearful of the dangers of contagion and more indifferent to or even enthusiastic about a "Grexit," such that it could afford to adopt an even tougher stance in negotiations with the new Syriza government than it had done hitherto.

In any case, in case of doubt or conflict, perceived German *geopolitical* interests in the survival of the Eurozone (see above) took precedence over economic or financial ones.[35] Berlin was also nudged in this direction by the Obama administration in the United States, which was keen to avoid a Grexit and collapse of the Eurozone. Its worries related to the impact of such an outcome not only on the world economy, but also to its (geopolitical) concerns that, in this strategically important region, an economically depressed Greece with a radical leftist government could drift away from the west and into Russia's sphere of influence.[36]

German political leaders had, however, to square off the economic, financial, and geopolitical interests they perceived Germany had in keeping the Eurozone and the EU on the rails with opposed domestic political pressures. Although the EU as such enjoyed broad public support in Germany, bailing out other Eurozone member states was extremely unpopular throughout the crisis (irrespective of the fact that the aid was in the form of loans that had to be repaid). More than four-fifths of Germans, for example, opposed granting financial aid to Greece at the outset of the crisis in 2010. The imminent prospect of the first Greek bailout provoked a large decline in voter support for Merkel's CDU (Christian Democratic Union) in a critical election of Germany's most populous state, North Rhine-Westphalia.[37] Public hostility to financial aid was reflected in growing opposition to bailouts and to anything that resembled a fiscally redistributive "transfer union" in the German Parliament, which had a veto power over the successive rescue packages. This opposition and the risk of losing a Parliamentary vote compelled Merkel and the government to limit the volume of aid and to insist that it be granted only under strict conditions. Domestic political constraints tightly circumscribed the range of choice enjoyed by the federal government.

Domestic political constraints pushing the federal government toward a tough stance on Eurozone bailouts were reinforced by its ideational-normative orientation. Especially on the political Right, Ordoliberalism, which prioritized fiscal prudence and emphasized the dangers of moral hazard involved in granting financial aid, was the dominant school of economic thought in Germany after World War II. It had experienced a renaissance in early twenty-first-century Germany, as indicated by the adoption, backed by the Social as well as Christian Democrats, of an amendment to the Basic Law requiring governments to maintain a balanced budget. In the Eurozone crisis, two fundamental goals of German policy – the promotion of European integration and "sound money" – came into mutual conflict for the first time.[38] Ordoliberalism implied that financial aid should be granted to other states only under strict conditions that obliged them to pursue fiscal austerity.

Not only domestic political and ideational-normative, but also legal constraints limited the German government's room for maneuver in the Eurozone crisis. Articles 123 to 125 of the Maastricht Treaty ban any monetary financing of member state governments by the ECB. Any rescue or other measures taken by the EU had to be designed in such a way as to minimize the danger that they would be declared illegal by the

German Constitutional Court, in which case the issue of whether Germany must withdraw from the Euro could have been posed. Some 37,000 Germans contested the creation of the ESM in the "biggest protest ever brought before the court."[39] The court rejected the suit, but in its judgment strengthened the veto powers of the German Parliament.[40]

At every new phase of the Eurozone crisis, the terms of a trade-off between "debtor" and "creditor" states – how much financial aid was to be offered under which conditions – had to be freshly negotiated in the shadow of the pressures generated by international financial markets. It was by no means preordained that the maximum that was politically and legally possible, especially for Germany, was the minimum that would be required to keep the Euro on the rails. This danger was at its most acute in summer 2012, when the crisis threatened to spread and engulf Spain and Italy, two members that, given the size of their economies, would have been much more expensive to bail out than the far smaller members that had so far been rescued. The Eurozone members had just agreed the banking union and created scope for Spanish banks to be rescued directly by the bailout fund, the ESM (European Stability Mechanism). Despite this accord, the interest-rates that the Italian and Spanish governments had to pay on their bonds continued to climb, heightening the danger that they too would need to be bailed out, but that, especially on account of German resistance, the Eurozone could or would not mobilize enough financial aid to stave off their bankruptcy – and with this the implosion of the Euro.

The "absolutely decisive moment" in the Eurozone crisis, the one that brought it back from the brink of collapse, came when, in July 2012, the ECB president Mario Draghi made a speech in which he pledged that, within its mandate, the bank would do "whatever it takes" to preserve the Euro.[41] Draghi acted unilaterally. He did not coordinate his remarks with the EU heads of government or with anybody at the ECB, save for a few members of its executive board.[42] Nor were they included in the prepared text of his speech. For Draghi, the ground for his initiative had been laid by the European Council's accord the previous month to create a banking union, which foresaw the transfer of the supervision of Eurozone banks from national agencies to the ECB – a measure that he described as a "game-changer," enabling the ECB to intervene more boldly in the crisis.[43]

In responding to the Eurozone crisis, Draghi and the ECB had a major advantage over other actors. Under the European treaties, the ECB had unlimited financial resources (a monopoly of the capacity to print money in the Eurozone) and extensive legal powers. It was also politically independent. Although it had to take care to act within its treaty mandate and took care to shore up support for its policies among the member governments by consulting them extensively during the crisis, it was "not only formally, but also de facto independent in its decision-making."[44]

Draghi thus could and did act genuinely autonomously of *other actors* in the Eurozone. This is not to say, however, that he was altogether unconstrained and free in his action. First, to have let the Eurozone collapse would have dealt a heavy, conceivably mortal blow to the cause of European integration. Such an omission would have constituted a major transgression against the "pro-European" consensus of the politico-economic elite of which Draghi was a member. This consensus was not all-embracing – notably it was not shared by the German Bundesbank – but it was nonetheless very broad. At no stage was there within this elite any serious debate as to whether the crisis showed that a single currency linking member states with divergent economic structures could not work to their mutual advantage.[45] The ECB president was thus subject to a strong ideational-normative constraint to "do whatever it takes" to save the Euro. Second, if the Euro had collapsed, so too would have the ECB, which thus had a strong institutional self-interest in the Euro's survival.[46] Draghi had nonetheless to proceed very cautiously. He had to minimize the danger that the ECB's intervention would run afoul of EU treaty provisions banning the monetary financing of governments (hence his pledge to intervene *within* the ECB's mandate). And before intervening he had to wait until the last possible moment, when it was increasingly clear that the member governments themselves would not be able to reach an accord that could stabilize the international bond markets but that they would support or, at worst, acquiesce in his initiative (which conveniently enabled the German government to avoid having to decide whether to increase the volume of financial aid to southern Europe).

The ECB was thus structurally more empowered and advantaged and a much more autonomous actor than any others in the Eurozone crisis, the German government included. The nature and timing of the intervention in July 2012 was shaped by and took account of legal and EU-internal political constraints. Draghi, though, was not entirely free in deciding whether to try to save the Euro. When he weighed up his options, the ideational-normative elite consensus in (at least continental) Europe in favor of European integration and the ECB's institutional self-interest in survival probably tilted the balance strongly in favor of his intervention.

Refugees

For key EU decision-makers, the refugee crisis in 2015–16 was no less acute and no less of a threat to the EU's cohesion than the Eurozone crisis. Passport-free, borderless travel between the twenty-six member states of the Schengen Area was widely regarded as one of the EU's principal achievements. At different stages, several of them expressed their fear that the crisis would destroy Schengen or even that if Schengen were to collapse, then so too would the Euro and the EU itself.[47] Even more than in the Eurozone, critical decisions had to be taken under intense time pressures (see above). Contrary to the widely shared fear of its imminent collapse, the Schengen system largely survived the crisis – albeit not without suffering some limited political disintegration. Several member states erected and retained controls on some of their borders with other Schengen members, undermining the authority of the European Commission that requested that they be dismantled. A handful of Central European member states similarly undermined the authority of the EU's legislative organs by refusing to implement an EU decision to relocate some of the refugees that entered the Schengen Area in 2015 and that of the ECJ by refusing to accept its judgment on this issue. All efforts to negotiate and implement a common EU refugee policy failed. All in all, in contrast to the Eurozone crisis, from which the EU emerged politically more closely integrated, in the refugee crisis the preexisting level of political integration was partially eroded.

One – the biggest – difference between the Eurozone and refugee crises was that in the latter there was no powerful supranational (or other) actor, comparable to the ECB that could impose a largely unilateral solution to the crisis. In the absence of such an actor, the crisis had to be managed in an intergovernmental fashion – that is to say, in negotiations between the governments of (often subsets of) the member states. Among these, Germany was the central actor, but its power did not normally suffice for it to be able to persuade or coerce other members to tow its line on how to manage the crisis.

The EU and its member states had been warned in the first half of 2015 about a likely big increase in the influx of refugees from war zones in the Middle East. The exponential growth in the number in the summer nonetheless took it by surprise and found it ill-prepared to respond. As the number of refugees on the Balkans route began to surge, the Hungarian government of Viktor Orbán decided to close the country to any new refugees and expel those still in Hungary toward Austria and Germany. After a day in which she had traversed Germany fulfilling several political engagements, Chancellor Merkel and her Austrian counterpart, Werner Faymann, decided around midnight, in what she termed a "humanitarian" gesture, to allow refugees heading westwards to enter Austria and Germany.[48] Both leaders were motivated by a concern to avert any violence being used against the refugees to prevent them crossing the Austro-Hungarian border.[49] But for a few very limited exceptions, attempts by Merkel and her advisers to persuade other member states to take in a share of the refugees failed.[50]

The arrival of a rapidly growing number of refugees in Germany in the following days was greeted enthusiastically by many Germans. The impact of this spontaneously generated *Willkommenskultur* (literally "welcome culture") was evident in a Parliamentary debate in which there was a cross-party consensus backing Merkel's decision.[51] However, the influx of refugees rapidly began to exhaust the capacity of state and local governments to accommodate them. They ramped up the pressure on the federal government to stem the influx. A week after Merkel's initial decision, the leaders of the coalition parties decided to close German borders to the refugees and turn them back. The federal police force was told to be ready to carry out this decision within 24 hours. However, the formal order for them to close the borders – which the federal interior minister had to sign – never came. Different divisions in the interior ministry disagreed over whether these steps would be legal in terms of EU law. With the support, explicit or tacit, of Merkel and the Christian Democrats' coalition partner, the SPD (German Social Democratic Party), the interior minister decided that whilst border controls should be introduced (on this Schengen-internal border), anybody wanting to claim political asylum should be allowed to enter Germany. Whilst uncertainty about the legality of closing the border to refugees may have influenced the stance taken by the government, two other considerations were also important. First, Merkel was worried about the prospective chain reaction that such a decision might provoke. If, one after another, the states between Germany and Greece were to close their borders to refugees, the burden of coping with the influx would have been shifted progressively southwards, potentially fomenting violent unrest and political instability in the countries concerned. Merkel said that she sought a solution to the crisis for "all Europe," not for Germany alone.[52] Above all, however, Merkel and her interior minister from the same party feared that images of German police using physical force to prevent refugees, including women and children, from entering Germany would be politically too damaging and that efforts by the police to seal the border would in any case fairly quickly fail.[53]

This unilateral decision by the German government was the single most important one made in the refugee crisis. During 2015, some 1.8

million migrants or refugees entered the EU, most of them via the Balkans route from Turkey and Greece. It led to major political polarization in the EU and was highly likely the most important contributor to the subsequent rapid rise of support for anti-immigration, anti-Muslim, and "anti-European" political parties in the member states, including Germany itself, where at Parliamentary elections in 2017 an extreme right-wing party won almost 13 percent of the vote and entered the Bundestag as the largest opposition group. Some other Schengen member states introduced border controls to prevent refugees entering their territory via Germany. Whilst the government was constrained to react to the growing stream of refugees, it cannot be argued, since it had taken the opposite (provisional) decision the day before, that this was the *only* feasible choice that it could make in this context, that it could not have decided differently. This choice was thus the genuine product of agency, not a reaction to inexorable structural constraints.

Supported by the European Commission, the German government subsequently launched an initiative to redistribute (a relatively small proportion of) the refugees across the EU, aiming thereby to diminish the pressure on the "frontline" states – Greece and, to a lesser extent, Italy – through which most refugees were entering the Schengen zone. Vehemently opposed by several Central and Eastern European states, this initiative found a qualified majority in the Council of Interior Ministers but was then implemented only very partially and haphazardly by the member states. Three of them – Hungary, Poland, and the Czech Republic – refused outright to implement it, defying the Commission and a judgment of the ECJ that their stance was illegal. The threat of a reduction in the volume of financial transfers from the EU budget did not suffice to break their opposition to taking in refugees. Particularly in Central and Eastern Europe, but also in most of the older EU member states, public opinion toward taking in large numbers of refugees was predominantly hostile and hence an important constraint on their governments. As a Czech diplomat explained: "We were either with Orbán or we were with the Germans. And the public were with Orbán, so we had no choice."[54] In some of the Central and Eastern European states, which bordered historically on the Ottoman Turkish empire, the refugee crisis – as most of the refugees were from majority Muslim societies – was conceived or framed as a threat to the survival of traditional (i.e., Christian) European civilization. Domestic political motives for their governments' opposition to taking in refugees were thus underpinned and reinforced by ideational-normative reservations or objections.

Other than in the Eurozone crisis, no actor in the refugee crisis was unilaterally capable of resolving the conflict within the EU over the distribution of refugees between the member states. On this issue the EU was (and remained) paralyzed. In early 2016, the president of the European Council, Donald Tusk, warned that if the influx of refugees was not brought under control rapidly ("within two months"), the Schengen Area would collapse.[55] This risk was averted within this time frame by an Austrian-coordinated closure of the Balkans route and a German-initiated and driven negotiation by the EU of an accord with Turkey whereby, in exchange for financial aid, the Turkish government undertook to prevent refugees crossing from the coast in western Turkey to nearby Greek islands. The drastic limitation of the number of refugees entering the Schengen Area at its external border by the provision of side-payments to a third country was the only solution to the crisis on which member governments with otherwise divergent interests could converge.

The breadth and depth of the public backlash against a growing influx of refugees into the EU was so strong by early 2016 that the EU and the member governments probably had to be seen to be doing something – or, at any rate, more than they had been doing – to stem it. To the extent that there was no other policy to manage the refugee crisis around which they could all rally, the EU had little choice but to choose and pursue this option. Overall therefore the path taken by the EU and its member governments in the refugee crisis comprised a combination of, on the one hand, a unilateral choice made by Germany that could have been different and was therefore the product of agency and, on the other hand, a structurally determined collective choice that effectively reversed the one made by the government in Berlin a few months earlier.

Brexit

The Brexit crisis differed from the other three crises in four significant respects relating respectively to the causes, outcomes, how political elites perceived them and the extent to which the ways in which they were managed were structurally determined or a matter of agency. First, unlike the other three, whose roots lay in external events and processes (the Syrian civil war, the Global Financial Crisis, and the coronavirus that originated in China), this crisis was precipitated by a calculated and by no means inexorable political choice made by the UK Prime Minister, David Cameron. Second, whereas the Eurozone crisis produced greater monetary and fiscal policy integration and some (limited) political disintegration occurred in the refugee crisis, the outcome of the Brexit crisis, with the secession from the EU of one of its three biggest member states, constituted a more far-reaching case of disintegration. Third, whilst EU political elites regularly expressed their fear that the Euro or the Schengen zone and, conceivably, the entire EU would collapse, the referendum vote in favor of leaving the EU was not widely anticipated. For EU elites, Brexit in this sense came rather as a shock. Fourth, the balance between structure and agency in the shaping of the EU's management of the Brexit crisis differed markedly from that in the other three crises. In the Brexit crisis, compared with them, agency played a far greater – and structural constraints a much more limited – role in shaping how the crisis was handled, both by the British government and, to a lesser extent, the governments of the other member states. Numerous critical choices were made that increased the likelihood of Brexit but could have been different.

The first of these choices was the one made by the Labour government in the early 2000s to open the British labor market immediately to citizens of the ten, mostly post-Communist Central and Eastern European, states that joined the EU in 2004. Among the fifteen member states of the time, the UK was one of only three that did not opt to keep their labor markets closed to citizens of the new members until 2011. Official forecasts that no more than 5000 to 13,000 Central and Eastern Europeans would move to the UK to work grossly underestimated the number who did so.[56] By 2015, about one million Central and Eastern Europeans were working and one and a half million living in the UK. During the decade before the referendum, immigration and immigrants – around half of whom, however, came from non-EU countries – became one of the two or three most salient political issues in the UK.[57]

The second choice, the most critical, was the one made by the Prime Minister David Cameron in 2013 to pledge a referendum on the UK's continued EU membership if he were to win the 2015 Parliamentary election. The British political system gave him wide scope to launch such an initiative. No law or constitutional provision prevented him from calling a referendum or prescribed any rules as to how it should be conducted. Although he had had to govern since 2010 with a coalition partner, the Liberal Democrats, the first-past-the-post electoral system favored single-party government and was to enable Cameron to win a majority of seats in Parliament with only 37 percent of the vote in 2015. British public opinion toward the EU had grown more critical during the preceding two decades, a trend that the Eurozone crisis exacerbated.[58] Cameron's Conservative Party had also grown more Euroskeptic and a new political party, the UKIP (United Kingdom Independence Party), had been founded to campaign for Brexit. Early in his term as Conservative leader he had warned his party not to keep "banging on about Europe," as this was not an issue that preoccupied many Britons.[59]

By 2013, however, his analysis had shifted. To the leader of his then Liberal Democratic coalition partner, Nick Clegg, he justified his referendum pledge by saying that this was a "party management issue. I am under a lot of pressure on this. I need to recalibrate."[60] When Clegg warned him that he was pledging something that would put the 'international position of the UK for the next few decades' at risk, Cameron is said to have replied: "You may be right. But what else can I do? My backbenchers are unbelievably Euro-sceptic and UKIP are breathing down my neck."[61]

It is questionable, however, whether the domestic political pressures pushing Cameron toward calling a referendum were quite as strong or unequivocal as he reputedly described them, let alone whether the referendum pledge was the most effective means to respond to them. Euroskeptic MPs did not threaten his position as party leader and Prime Minister at the time. The referendum pledge certainly pleased many Conservative MPs. Some 81 of these out of a group of 306 rebelled against the government and demanded a referendum on the UK's EU membership in October 2011.[62] However, support for the idea was far from unanimous in the Parliamentary party, where there were still many "pro-European" MPs, or in Cameron's Cabinet, where his closest colleague, the Chancellor of the Exchequer, George Osborne, opposed it on the grounds that the British business community would be hostile to it and the government would not be able to negotiate a good deal with the other member states to put to Britons in a referendum.[63] Immediately prior to his 2013 Bloomberg speech, voter support for the UKIP was estimated to be 9 percent.[64] This was three times as high as the party's vote at the 2010 Parliamentary elections. While, despite its share of the vote in the 2015 Parliamentary elections virtually stagnating, the Conservative Party won a majority of the seats, Cameron's pledge did not prevent the UKIP from quadrupling its share of the vote in the 2015 Parliamentary elections to 12.6 percent. The UKIP leader, Nigel Farage, welcomed the Conservatives "coming to play on our pitch."[65]

In any case, however, although intra-party politics and party competition did push Cameron toward making the referendum pledge, they were, in his own words, "not the determining force" for his decision.[66] The UKIP was "still a small force" when he had begun to contemplate staging a referendum.[67] The main reason he made this choice was his conviction, as a self-proclaimed "pragmatic Eurosceptic"[68] that, mainly because of the Eurozone crisis, the EU was changing and integrating in ways that were incompatible with British interests or with the Conservative Party's and his conception of Europe. Therefore, for the

UK to remain a member, the terms of British EU membership had to be renegotiated and the new ones approved in a popular referendum.[69] His referendum pledge was not dictated by structural constraints. Rather it was an expression of agency – a choice Cameron made relatively autonomously, based on his own political orientation and beliefs. Economic constraints – the likelihood, in the almost unanimous view of economic research institutes and commentators, that a Brexit would inflict significant damage on the British economy – seem not to have impinged at all on Cameron's thinking. At least he makes no reference to them in his memoirs.

The third choice was a collective one, made by the UK and its EU negotiating partners, over the proposed new terms of the UK's membership. The deal that Cameron negotiated with the remainder of the EU failed to mollify many British Euroskeptics, whether in his own party, the mass media (which had grown much more Euroskeptic compared with the time in 1975 when the first UK referendum on EU membership had been held), or the mass public.[70] Cameron himself admits to having allowed expectations about "what could be achieved through a renegotiation to become too high" and failed to do more to "focus people's minds on what was really possible."[71] Conceivably, the heads of most other EU governments did not make more far-reaching concessions because they did not think that Britons would vote for Brexit anyway.[72] For his part, Cameron denies having "complacently assumed that 'remain' would win" and claims rather to have thought it "very possible" that the UK would vote to leave.[73] According to other accounts, however, he was very confident that "remain" would win the referendum, even by as much as 70 to 30 percent.[74] If he was indeed so certain of victory and told other EU leaders so, it is comprehensible that the outcome surprised – or shocked – many of them.

The most salient issue in the referendum campaign – and the one on which the deal secured by Cameron arguably fell furthest short of meeting public expectations in the UK – was immigration to the UK from other EU member states, especially those in Central and Eastern Europe that had joined the EU since 2004.[75] The main provision relating to immigration in the deal negotiated by Cameron created the possibility for the British government to limit the amount of state welfare benefits paid to employees from other EU member states – an instrument that was generally considered to be unlikely to curb immigration into the UK.[76] Most Central and Eastern European governments opposed these measures initially, but they saw the UK as an important ally in the EU and NATO and finally accepted them because they did not want to "go down in history" as having "kicked the British out of the EU."[77]

Cameron would have liked to impose quantitative restrictions on the inflow of EU immigrants. However, the legal and political constraints on implementing such restrictions were so high that he refrained from raising the demand in the negotiations.[78] The EU treaties provided for the free movement of workers between member states and forbade governments from discriminating against the citizens of other member states based on their nationality. To restrict immigration to the UK from other member states would thus have been illegal unless the treaties themselves were changed. However, there was, according to the then UK Permanent Representative to the EU, "zero preparedness" in key capitals, West and East, as well as in the [EU] institutions' to accept such a change.[79] Some leaders, including Merkel, were skeptical as to whether immigration was an issue or problem in the UK. As she told Cameron: "You have low unemployment, a booming economy, you're growing faster than most of Europe. There is no social crisis. And you are pulling in highly qualified labour, cheaply. Explain to me what the problem is."[80] In any case, no other governments wanted to agree to treaty changes, as in some countries these would have had to be ratified in public referenda and ran a strong risk of being rejected. Central and Eastern European governments were vehemently opposed to any quantitative controls on immigration between member states. So too were Merkel and the German government, which, concerned to avert any unraveling of the single market and not to create any precedent that could lead to the unwinding of the EU, strongly defended the four freedoms (of the movement of goods, service, capital, and persons) in the EU treaty.[81]

The fourth choice that increased the likelihood of a vote to leave the EU was that made by the Conservative Party politician and then Mayor of London, Boris Johnson, to support Brexit. Although he had long been a critic of the EU, Johnson hesitated for a long time before declaring his position. In 2013, he had said that there wasn't even a "bunch of crackpots" in London who wanted to leave the EU: "Do you think the elite of this country – the political leaders, high-level civil servants, newspaper editors, university presidents, big business people – have an interest in leaving the union? Absolutely not. We want to influence the rules of the common market. We have to stay in the EU, if only to stop it doing nonsense."[82] Johnson described his decision as having been "agonizingly difficult" and confessed that on this issue he had been "veering all over the place like a shopping trolley."[83] His indecision was allegedly so great that he had drafted three declarations for the news media, one opposing Brexit and the other two supporting it.[84] As Johnson was the most popular and highest-profile pro-Brexit campaigner, it is plausible that his choice, which a prominent "remain" campaigner described as "devastating," indeed had a decisive influence on the referendum result.[85]

The fifth choice that may have contributed to the referendum outcome was Cameron's decision during the campaign not to make any "blue-on-blue" attacks on the Conservative leaders of the Leave campaign, notably Johnson and the Cabinet member, Michael Gove. Cameron's closest ally, Osborne, pleaded with him to return their fire: "These are now your opponents. They're killing you … You've got to destroy their credibility."[86] Uncertain that this tactic would work and presumably in the interests of party unity, Cameron refused: "I wanted others to fire the weapons in our armoury that we couldn't" – or wouldn't.[87] The opposition Labour Party, however, did not do him this favor, to the extent that its (left-wing) leader, Jeremy Corbyn, a long-standing critic of the EU, sat on the fence in the campaign. Alternatively, the Prime Minister possibly believed that it was not necessary to attack his intra-party opponents, as he remained confident that the Remain camp would win the referendum, a mistaken optimism that might have been nourished by the wildly inaccurate analyses of his opinion pollsters, who assured him on the day of the referendum itself that opinion had shifted "decisively in his favour" and that he would win it with a 60 to 40 percent margin, "maybe better" (as quoted in Parker 2016; Cameron 2019: 677).[88]

Overall the Brexit crisis and its outcome were therefore not the result of the inexorable interplay of structural constraints and forces that had key EU decision-makers in a vice-like grip that left them powerless to make any major decisions differently. Compared with the choices made in the other three big crises, more of those made on the issue of Brexit, especially by the British Prime Minister Cameron, were relatively autonomous. Indeed, even after the referendum, notably in autumn 2019, when the Labour Party and the Liberal Democrats forewent an opportunity to overthrow the minority government of Prime Minister Boris Johnson and install a government that could have called a second referendum, some conceivable opportunities to avert Brexit were left unexploited. The most far-reaching manifestation of political disintegration that occurred in the EU after 2010 was the one that was the most contingent and could most easily have been avoided.

Coronavirus

Compared with the Brexit crisis, the scope for actors in the EU to exercise agency in managing the coronavirus was much more limited and the corridor defining the range of feasible political choices much narrower. In some respects, this crisis and the way it was managed by the

EU displayed parallels with the earlier Eurozone crisis. In others, however, the two crises – and the EU's response to them – diverged. Numerous elements of the context within which the coronavirus crisis unfolded enabled the EU to master this threat to its survival much more swiftly than it did the Eurozone crisis and on terms that promoted both closer political integration and greater cohesion and solidarity between the member states.

The coronavirus spread rapidly across the EU in spring 2020. It quickly became not only a public health, but also a socioeconomic and, for the EU, a political crisis. Within the following year, more than 23 million people, roughly one person in every twenty, caught the virus in the EU and the European Economic Area (comprising Norway, Iceland, and Liechtenstein) and well over half a million died from it.[89] Owing largely to the measures taken by governments to contain the virus, the EU economy contracted by more than 7 percent in 2020, making it by far the deepest recession in the EU's history. The rise in unemployment – from a rate of 6.6 percent in January 2020 to 7.3 percent a year later – was limited by a rapid, countercyclical expansion of government budget deficits as a proportion of GDP from only 0.6 to an estimated 8.4 percent that was facilitated by historically low interest rates.[90] Compared with the Eurozone crisis, the coronavirus crisis hit the EU economy faster, harder, and far more broadly and the pressures on member state governments and the ECB to take measures to counter it built up more quickly. The rhetoric of EU political leaders and notables reflected these facts. Chancellor Merkel echoed the views of many of her counterparts in labeling this the hitherto "gravest crisis" in the EU's history,[91] as did the former European Commission president Jacques Delors when he described the EU as being in "mortal danger."[92] Once again, as at the height of the Eurozone and refugee crises, there was an elite consensus that the EU's very survival was at stake – and that this scenario had to be averted. The ideational-normative pressures on EU leaders to intervene to keep the integration process on the rails were extraordinarily strong.

The economic, financial, and political pressures on the EU to steer against the rapidly deepening crisis were also extremely powerful. Although the crisis was felt everywhere, its – public-health, economic, and financial – impact on them diverged widely. The number of deaths per 100,000 citizens in the first year of the pandemic ranged from below 500 in Finland, Cyprus, and Denmark to more than three times this ratio in eight other member states and over 2000 in the Czech Republic. The worst hit member state at the outset was Italy, which, at the same time, belonged to the states with the highest levels of both state indebtedness and support for Euroskeptic populist movements. The parlous state of

Italian public finances made actors on international bond markets nervous about lending to the Italian government, leading quickly to a growing 'spread' in the interest rates paid on the loans raised by Rome and Berlin and threatening effectively to bankrupt the Italian government and destroy any scope it had to pursue a countercyclical fiscal policy against the crisis. This situation raised the specter of a rerun of the Eurozone crisis and a collapse of the Euro, given that, on this occasion, a much bigger economy, which would be far more costly to rescue, would be at the eye of the storm.

Not only market, but also political dynamics threatened to tear the EU apart. Even before this new crisis struck, Euroskeptic populist movements were already very strong in Italy, where they captured over 50 percent of the vote in the 2018 Parliamentary elections. The initial reflexes of most EU member states were predominantly protectionist. An Italian request for emergency medical supplies and equipment was met in Brussels by silence; a few governments even banned the export of such goods to other EU members. As Italy was left to its own devices to combat the crisis, public opinion rapidly turned more vehemently against the EU. Surveys showed that no more than about 35 percent of Italians thought favorably of the EU and 67 percent that it was disadvantageous to belong to it.[93] This trend provoked growing fears in other EU capitals that, in the absence of corrective action, the crisis could unleash an unstoppable movement toward an "Italexit." It was not just the future of the Euro and Italy's EU membership that looked to be on the line. Within a month of the outbreak of the crisis, twenty-one of the twenty-six member states of the Schengen Area imposed border controls, raising fears that, although such measures, provided they were temporary, were legal under EU law, passport-free travel in the area might be durably curtailed.

The EU's capacity to address the public-health dimensions of the crisis was strongly restricted by EU treaty provisions that limited it to playing no more than a complementary and coordinating role, except where, as in the – later controversial – area of vaccine procurement, member state governments judged this to be to their mutual advantage. In the issue-areas of monetary and fiscal policy, however, the scope as well as pressure for EU intervention was much greater. In the sphere of monetary policy, a week after its new president, Christine Lagarde, declared that it was not its job to limit the spread between Italian and German government bonds, the ECB changed tack and launched a new bond-buying program that immediately assuaged bond-market actors' fears about the viability of southern members' projected budget deficits. In respect of fiscal policy, the Commission suspended the application of the EU's state-aid and budget-deficit rules so that member states could expand financial support for companies and jobs that the economic recession would otherwise have destroyed. However, given the pre-existing divergences in the stock of government debt, this measure underlined the disparate capacities of member state governments to cushion their economies against the impact of the crisis. As the worst-hit states were already comparatively heavily indebted, they rejected the idea of borrowing much more heavily, above all if similar strings were attached to loans to those extended by the ESM during the Eurozone crisis. Rather they insisted this time on the creation of EU-wide financial instruments that would provide grants to member states according to their crisis-induced needs.

The demand for the creation of collective 'corona bonds' opened up a major distributional conflict within the EU. The cleavage ran broadly, as during the Eurozone crisis, between the northern and worse hit southern member states, notably Italy and Spain, but also France. During the Eurozone crisis, the northern member states, led by Germany, had successfully resisted these demands. In the coronavirus crisis, however, this conflict was settled differently, with the EU's adoption of a €750 bn so-called recovery fund, of which more than a half was to be made up of grants. Although this accord was to be a one-off measure, it was widely acclaimed to be an important step toward a "more federal, solidaristic and integrated" EU, a "taboo-breaker" and a "leap towards genuine integration" or a "landmark moment" in European integration.[94] This breakthrough was made possible by a German U-turn that transformed the balance of power in the EU on this issue.

This accord quelled, for the time being at least, any further speculation or worries that the coronavirus crisis might destroy the EU. Germany's change of stance can be traced to developments at three (international, EU, and domestic German) levels that transformed the context in which this crisis was managed compared with that which prevailed during the Eurozone crisis. These developments concerned (EU – especially German – leaders') perceptions of the changing international geopolitical environment, the resurgence of France as a major player in the EU, and changes in the domestic political context in Germany. Combined these changes brought about a renaissance of the Franco-German relationship whose role in mediating this conflict was decisive.

Internationally, since the middle of the decade the EU's external environment had become significantly more turbulent and uncertain. Russia's invasion and annexation of Crimea, covert invasion of southeastern Ukraine and military intervention, overt or covert, in Syria and Libya confirmed its growing propensity to deploy military force in conflicts on the EU's periphery. A similar trend also became increasingly manifest in Turkish foreign policy. The EU became increasingly nervous about the growing power of an increasingly authoritarian and self-confident China. The Brexit referendum and process symbolized the ominous growth of nationalist sentiment within the EU itself. Above all, the election of Donald Trump on a platform of "America First" as the US president in November 2016 not only raised a serious question mark over the extent of the United States' commitment to guarantee Western and Central Europe's security through the NATO (North Atlantic Treaty Organization), but also inflicted a major blow on internationally coordinated efforts to tackle such international challenges as climate change. The growth of military conflicts, the rise of authoritarian politics and the decline of international multilateralism were regarded with particular alarm by the German political elite, which, as the hope of "1989" dissipated, was increasingly persuaded of the need to shore up the EU as a bulwark against these menacing trends for Germany's security.[95] Berlin's views, one observer noted in 2020, were becoming "more French by the day ... Merkel has embraced Macron's sovereign Europe narrative."[96] In the worldview of Germany's political elite, the maintenance of a very close relationship with France arguably assumed greater importance than had been the case prior to the middle of the decade.

The second – and related - development that facilitated the accord over the EU recovery fund was the return of France as an agenda-setter and pacemaker in the EU with Macron's election as president in May 2017. Macron campaigned on a bold, unequivocally "pro-European" platform.[97] In contrast to his two predecessors, Nicholas Sarkozy and François Hollande, whose respective political camps were divided over European integration, Macron had the advantage of being backed by a cohesive pro-European domestic political constituency in the big French metropolitan areas.[98] From his election onward, he launched a series of initiatives to promote closer European integration and tried to mobilize support for them in Berlin. Of these projects, the most important involved creating a budget and finance minister for the Eurozone.[99] The new president's early efforts to reform the French welfare state and labor market, and to reduce the government budget deficit more radically than his predecessors, were motivated in part by his goal of raising the credibility of French demands for Eurozone reform.[100] Prior to the coronavirus crisis, he had made some limited, but not yet any decisive, progress in this regard. As the crisis deepened, he raised the pressure on Germany to acquiesce in a more radical project of fiscal integration. Along with eight other, mainly southern, member states, France pleaded for the creation of a "common European debt instrument" to provide financial aid to states to combat the virus.[101] Macron raised the pressure on the German government with public interventions in which, for example, he described the crisis as a "moment of truth" for the EU. Without greater solidarity from the richer member states, such as Germany and the Netherlands, the Euro and the EU could collapse: "Failure to support the EU members hit hardest by the pandemic will help populists to victory in Italy, Spain and perhaps France and elsewhere."[102]

The German government's initial reaction to the appeal of the French and Southern European governments was, as in the past, hostile. At the European Council meeting in March, Merkel told Italian Prime Minister Giuseppe Conte that corona bonds would never come, as the German Bundestag would never accept them.[103] With such demands Conte, she said, was creating expectations that would be frustrated. At the next Council meeting a month later, Merkel again insisted that, whereas the EU could offer member states loans, "grants do not belong in the category of what I can agree."[104] Gradually, however, German opposition to a large fund, comprising grants rather than loans, weakened. The chancellor reputedly saw now that Germany had to make a "grand gesture" to show that it had not abandoned the southern European member states worst hit by the pandemic, which otherwise could destroy the single market or even the EU itself.[105]

"After weeks" of discreet bilateral discussions between Paris and Berlin, Macron and Merkel thus suddenly launched a proposal to establish a €500 bn recovery fund comprising grants that would be financed by issuing common EU debt.[106] Even now, however, Merkel gave her support to this initiative only at the very last minute. The new Franco-German project formed the basis of a proposal to the Council by the Commission under its new president, the former German defense minister, Ursula von der Leyen. In lining up with France on this issue, Germany split from the other, mainly northern member states, led by the Netherlands, that had been its traditional allies in resisting large-scale financial transfers between EU member states. With Austria, Sweden, Denmark, and, at a very late stage, Finland, the Dutch government led the opposition to the Franco-German-initiated project. The so-called Frugal Four – if not Five – succeeded in gaining some concessions and reducing the volume of grants in favor of loans in the accord ultimately reached at the EU leaders' summit in July 2020, but the Commission's Franco-German-inspired proposal "remained largely intact."[107] The approval of the fund reflected the "remarkable revival of the recently dormant Franco-German alliance."[108] Macron described the accord as the "fruit of three years' work between France and Germany."[109] In the view of his finance minister, it owed "everything or almost everything to the resolve of France and Germany."[110]

Growing German anxiety about the shifting international geopolitical environment, France's increasingly energetic push for greater fiscal solidarity in the EU and the consequent galvanization of the Franco-German tandem were arguably necessary conditions of Germany's U-turn in the coronavirus crisis. But they may not have been sufficient. Berlin's change of course was also facilitated and expedited by several changes or events in the German domestic political context.

The first of these was the rapid growth of Merkel's popularity and political authority as a result of her government's comparatively successful management of the coronavirus crisis in Germany – the other side of the coin of which was a decline in support for the extreme right-wing AfD. This trend eased the pressure on Merkel to pursue a hard line on EU fiscal issues, as did the fact that, compared with the Eurozone crisis, German public opinion was significantly more favorable to fiscal transfers in the EU, supporting them at a ratio of five to three.[111]

The second was the transfer of control of the Finance Ministry from the CDUCSU to the SPD in the Grand Coalition government that was renewed after the 2017 federal elections. The German Social Democrats, the new finance minister Olaf Scholz and his team were significantly closer to the French stance on EU fiscal issues than the Christian Democrats and the previous finance minister, Wolfgang Schäuble. Already before the coronavirus crisis, Scholz had been cooperating closely with his French counterpart Bruno Le Maire on Eurozone reform issues.[112]

The third factor was the shifting, more accommodating attitude of German business to EU fiscal transfers. In a joint paper with its French and Italian counterparts, the peak association of German manufacturing industry, the BDI (*Bundesverband Deutscher Industrie* – The Federal Association of German Industry), called for more fiscal solidarity in the EU. This reflected worries in German industrial circles that loans might "not be enough." Germany could not afford to see its key European markets collapse. Fiscal transfers would be in their self-interest as "most of the money we give to other EU members will come back to us in the form of orders for our companies."[113]

The fourth factor that facilitated the German U-turn was ideational-normative in nature. Whereas, during the Eurozone crisis, the government's stance had been influenced by Ordoliberalism (see above), the allure of this school of economic thought had meanwhile faded. This trend was symbolized by the publication of a memorandum in March 2020 by seven eminent German economists, including economists close not only to the trade unions, but also to organized business, who pleaded for a creation of an EU bond fund worth €1000 bn.[114] Widely regarded formerly as nonnegotiable, the notion of large-scale fiscal transfers between member states came increasingly to be seen as indispensable to hold the EU together.

The fifth (coincidental) factor – related to the legal context – was the judgment of the German Federal Constitutional Court in early May 2020 that a government-bond-buying program that the ECB had launched during the Eurozone crisis was illegal. This ruling created a risk that the ECB's capacity to steer against the coronavirus crisis with monetary policy instruments might be restricted because the German Bundesbank might at some stage be banned from participating in ECB bond-buying initiatives, so heightening the pressure on EU governments, especially the German, to counter the crisis more vigorously with fiscal policy measures.[115]

The confluence of these trends and events significantly expanded the domestic political scope for Merkel and her coalition government to acquiesce in the demands of France and the southern member states for greater fiscal solidarity. Once the accord had been reached, the political crisis over the coronavirus pandemic in the EU rapidly subsided. A conflict over whether subsidies should be withheld from member governments, notably the Hungarian and Polish, that were deemed to be failing to uphold the rule of law, was settled by a compromise in which both camps of protagonists in this dispute traded concessions. Provided that the member states did not fall out seriously over the potentially controversial disbursal of the agreed grants once the recovery fund was up and running or over the distribution of vaccines, which they had agreed should be shared equally and at comparable speeds between them, there was a good prospect that the coronavirus crisis would end up forging a fiscal-politically more integrated EU.

The scope for EU decision-makers to exercise agency in managing the coronavirus crisis was significantly more limited than in the refugee and Brexit crises. The ideational-normative, economic-financial, EU-political, and domestic German legal constraints moulding the context in which they acted pushed them strongly toward crafting a major fiscal policy intervention along the lines that was finally adopted. The ideational-normative constraint consisted in the still-dominant "pro-European" consensus according to which it was imperative to avert the EU's possible disintegration. The economic-financial constraint required a major initiative to be undertaken to reassure international bond markets that the rest of the EU would come to the aid of the worst hit member states, above all Italy. The EU-political constraint dictated that decisive action be taken to head off a rapidly intensifying political backlash against the EU from becoming unstoppable in Italy and driving it out of the EU. The domestic German legal constraint – in the form of the jurisprudence of the Federal Constitutional Court – meant that the EU could not rely to the same extent as in the Eurozone crisis on unilateral action by the ECB to save the Euro.

If structural imperatives, mediated through the perceptions of EU political leaders, created powerful pressures in favor of the "grand gesture" that the EU adopted, the achievement of the accord over the recovery fund was nonetheless not a foregone conclusion, given the ferocity of the distributional conflict that the crisis unleashed and the stubborn opposition to it mounted by the four or five "frugal" northern member states. However, these small states could in the end be bought off by concessions that addressed some of their key concerns about the project without it being fundamentally diluted. The critical variable that paved the way for the accord was the German U-turn that was driven by German insecurity in the face of an increasingly turbulent international geopolitical environment that increased the importance to Berlin of a strong EU as well as close relations with France, by the (consequent perceived) need for it to accommodate France, whose president put the German government under intensifying pressure to acquiesce in a major step toward fiscal-political integration, and to the growing fear that, if such a project were not adopted, the EU was in dire danger of disintegrating. At the same time, the domestic political hurdles to launching and backing such a project in Germany were significantly lower than they had been in the Eurozone crisis. Correspondingly, the EU could respond to the economic dimensions of the coronavirus crisis faster and more radically than it did to the Eurozone crisis. The management of this crisis distinguished itself from the other three that the EU confronted between 2010 and 2020 by the stabilizing hegemonic leadership provided by the Franco-German tandem, which, under Macron's impulsion, experienced a striking and impactful renaissance.

Conclusion

Never in its 70-year history did the EU have to traverse so many severe crises so close together as during the decade from 2010 to 2020. It did not survive them unscathed. Above all, for the first time one of its member states seceded. Whilst it lost no more than one of twenty-eight, the UK was its second-largest economy, the second-largest member in terms of population, and, with France, the only member with nuclear weapons, a permanent seat on the UN Security Council and a significant capacity to deploy military force abroad. Brexit thus threatened to diminish the weight of the EU on the international stage. For its part, the refugee crisis destroyed any semblance of a common EU refugee policy, underlined how fast and easily the Schengen Area could disintegrate and saw several member states challenging and undermining the authority of several of the EU's organs: the European Commission, the Council, and the ECJ. These cases of political disintegration notwithstanding, the EU nonetheless proved to be relatively robust and resilient to crises. It emerged from the other – Eurozone and coronavirus – crises more closely integrated in respect of financial regulation and fiscal policy.

Two factors relating to EU political elites served to shore up the EU. The first is that they were linked by a pervasive and common atmosphere of crisis. Except arguably for Brexit, which was not widely anticipated, each crisis provoked widespread fears that it could destroy the EU or some important pillar of it, whether, for example, the Euro or the Schengen Area. At no point was there any danger of the EU's political elites underestimating the EU's fragility. This perception of the EU's fragility and vulnerability was best illustrated by Chancellor Merkel, for whom, judging by her public statements, each successive crisis (but for Brexit) seemed to pose a greater risk to the EU's survival than its predecessor. The second factor is that, albeit they did not all share the same conceptions of "Europe," EU political elites were united in their conviction that the EU should not be allowed to disintegrate. This reflected the continued dominance of domestic politics in most of the member states, particularly the biggest and most powerful ones, of "pro-European" political parties of the moderate left, center, and moderate right. This elite consensus arguably helped to limit the political polarization among member state governments as to how the various crises should be managed.

A pervasive atmosphere of crisis and an elite consensus in favor of European integration provided no guarantee, however, that the EU's political leaders would succeed in holding the EU together. There were fierce distributional conflicts between competing groups of member states over how to manage the Eurozone and coronavirus crises and irreconcilable, values-related conflicts between especially Germany and other, especially Central and Eastern European, member states over how to handle the refugee crisis. In the Eurozone and refugee crises, solidarity, a key ingredient in the preservation of political orders, was in very limited supply.[116] Conflicts had sometimes to be mediated under intense time pressures, whether these were imposed by international financial markets, flows of refugees facilitated by third-country governments or a dangerous and fast-spreading virus. Given the context in which EU negotiations took place and the nature of EU decision-making processes, which for the most part precluded unilateral or majoritarian choices, the agreements reached were typically improvisations that sufficed to avert worst-case collapse scenarios without necessarily providing definitive or durable crisis solutions.[117]

The two crises from which the EU emerged politically more closely integrated were, in key respects, managed differently. The conflict over the Eurozone was settled primarily by a unilateral intervention of the ECB, which, given its powers and independent status, did not have to negotiate and find a common denominator among divided member states. That over the coronavirus crisis was resolved by decisive Franco-German leadership of a kind that had not been provided in any of the three preceding crises, but that, in time-honored fashion, managed to mediate the conflict by forging a compromise that accommodated the interests of northern and southern as well as eastern member states. The other common trait of these two crises was that the principal actors in them had to heed relatively tight ideational-normative, economic-financial, and in part legal and domestic political constraints that defined a relatively narrow corridor within which solutions to the crisis had to be – and were in fact - sought.

Compared with these two crises, the refugee and Brexit crises were different, as in both of these the key actors possessed significantly more agency, that is, greater freedom of choice. Hence there was a clear alternative to the unilateral choice that was made by Chancellor Merkel and her government in September 2015 to keep Germany open for political refugees – a choice that profoundly destabilized the EU. Merkel, however, was forced to act in response to the exodus of refugees from Turkey at the time. One way or another, she and her government had to decide. In contrast to this and the other two crises, the origins of the Brexit crisis were not exogenous, but rather the result of a judgment made autonomously by the British Prime Minister Cameron, motivated primarily by his ambivalent attitude to European integration. The divergent pattern of EU crisis outcomes thus tells us that heroic leadership by autonomously acting "great men" or "great women" is not the best recipe for effective crisis management, defined here for the EU as the prevention of its (partial or complete) political disintegration. Paradoxically, structurally constrained decision-makers with a more restricted range of choice seem to come up more often with system-stabilizing policies, perhaps because the integrative processes by which their decisions have been reached provide these with greater legitimacy and therefore consent.

The preceding analysis must, however, carry a very important caveat. Structures are never so constraining as to reduce the scope for statecraft to zero. Actors and actor constellations always matter, if to varying extents. Independent of the crisis at hand, contexts can also evolve and change in ways that reduce or increase the likelihood of successful crisis management.

These points may be illustrated by reference to the coronavirus crisis. If Brexit had not occurred, would the UK have prevented an accord over the recovery fund – or would the other twenty-seven governments have bypassed it if necessary by launching the fund as an intergovernmental agreement outside the EU treaties?

Would the German government have been so amenable to the creation of the EU recovery fund if, during the preceding five years, the international geopolitical environment had not become so turbulent and menacing, making the preservation of the EU even more important to Germany than had previously been the case?

Would France have played the motor role it did if, in 2017, a political scandal had not destroyed the prospects of the more Euroskeptic traditional right-wing candidate François Fillon, leading to the election of the "pro-European" Macron as president?

Would the German government have finally warmed to the recovery fund project if the FDP (Free Democratic Party), which is very hostile to any notion of a fiscal "transfer union" between member states, had not withdrawn from postelection coalition negotiations with the CDU/CSU in 2017, leaving the way clear for the more "pro-European" Social Democrats to return to office with Chancellor Merkel?

If in Italy, the most strongly Euroskeptic mass party, the League led by Matteo Salvini, rather than provoking the collapse of the governing coalition in which it was a member, had still been in government in 2020 and above all if new elections had been held in 2019 and Salvini had become prime minister, how much more difficult might it have been for the EU to contain the political backlash in Italy against it?

Finally, if the Federal Constitution Court, entirely coincidentally at the height of the crisis, had not judged the government-bond-buying program launched by the ECB during the Eurozone crisis to be illegal, would the German government have made the U-turn it did less than two weeks later rather than relying, as it had done in 2012, on the ECB to "do whatever it takes" – or not – to try to save the Euro?

If some or any of these events had not happened, which is possible, it is conceivable that the outcome of the coronavirus crisis in the EU would have been different. This is to say that the EU's successful navigation of this crisis owed something, perhaps even a great deal, to contingency, to things that could have happened differently, and that, in the final analysis, neither this outcome nor that of the other crises was entirely preordained. By this logic, it also cannot be excluded that prospective future crises will have a more destructive impact on the EU than those that it traversed in the decade from 2010 to 2020.

Notes

1 Richard Ned Lebow, *The Rise and Fall of Political Orders* (Cambridge, MA: Cambridge University Press, 2018), pp. 7–8 and 20.
2 Ibid., p. 164.
3 Ibid., p. 164.
4 Douglas Webber, *European Disintegration? The Politics of Crisis in the European Union* (London: Red Globe Press, 2019), pp. 3–13.
5 Douglas Webber, "Trends in European Political (Dis)Integration. An Analysis Of Postfunctionalist and Other Explanations," *Journal of European Public Policy* 26, no. 8 (2019), pp. 1134–52.
6 John J. Mearsheimer, "Back to the Future: Instability in Europe after the Cold War," *International Security* 15, no. 4 (1990), pp. 5–56; Helen Milner, "International Political Economy: Beyond Hegemonic Stability," *Foreign Policy* no. 110 (Spring 1998), pp. 112–23; A.F.K. Organski, *World Politics* (New York: Alfred A. Knopf, 1959); Jack Snyder, "One World, Rival Theories," *Foreign Policy* no. 145 (November-December 2004), pp. 53–62; Stephen Walt, "International Relations: One World, Many Theories," *Foreign Policy* no. 110 (Spring 1998), pp. 29–46.
7 As quoted in Luuk Van Middelaar, *Alarums and Excursions: Improvising Politics on the European Stage* (Newcastle upon Tyne: Agenda, 2019), p. 91.
8 As quoted in Guy Chazan, "Angela Merkel: Germany's crisis manager is back," *Financial Times*, 27 March 2020.
9 Arend Lijphart, *Patterns of Democracy: Government Forms and Performance in Thirty-Six Countries* (New Haven and Yale: Yale University Press, 1999), pp. 42–7.
10 Fritz W. Scharpf, "The joint-decision trap: lessons from German federalism and European integration," *Public Administration* 66, no. 3 (1988), pp. 239–78 and "The Joint-Decision Trap Revisited," *Journal of Common Market Studies* 44, no. 4 (2006), pp. 845–64.
11 Ted Gurr, *Why Men Rebel* (Princeton: Princeton University Press, 1970), p. 234.
12 Douglas Webber, "Can the EU survive?" In Desmond Dinan, Neill Nugent and William E. Paterson (eds), *The European Union in Crisis* (London: Palgrave Macmillan, 2017), pp. 336–59.
13 Douglas Webber, "Agricultural Policy: The Hard Core," in Webber, ed., *The Franco-German Relationship in the European Union* (London: Routledge, 1999), pp. 111–129 and *European Disintegration?* Ulrich Krotz and Joachim Schild, *Shaping Europe: France, Germany, and Embedded Bilateralism from the*

Élysée Treaty to Twenty-First Century Politics (Oxford: Oxford University Press, 2013).
14. Maurice Couve de Murville, *Une politique étrangère 1958-1969* (Paris: Plon, 1971), p. 262 and Herman van Rompuy, interview, 28 September 2017 (https://resume.uni.lu/story/interview-herman-van-rompuy).
15. Charles Kindleberger, *The World in Depression, 1929-1939* (Berkeley, CA: University of California Press, 1973) and "Dominance and Leadership in the International Economy: Exploitation, Public Goods, and Free Rides," *International Studies Quarterly* 25, no. 2 (1981), p. 243 and Webber, *European Disintegration?* pp. 44–45.
16. The then French finance minister, Michel Sapin, as quoted in Yanis Varoufakis, *Adults in the Room: My Battle with Europe's Deep Establishment* (London: Bodley Head, 2017), p. 190.
17. William E. Paterson, "The Reluctant Hegemon? Germany Moves Centre Stage in the European Union," *JCMS Annual Review of the European Union in 2010* (Chichester: Wiley/Blackwell, 2011), pp. 57–75 and Simon Bulmer and Paterson, *Germany and the European Union: Europe's Reluctant Hegemon* (London: Red Globe Press, 2019), pp. 57–59.
18. Radoslaw Sikorski, "I fear Germany's power less than her inactivity," *Financial Times*, 28 November 2011.
19. Webber, *European Disintegration?* pp. 48–50.
20. Paul Lever, *Germany Rules: Europe and the German Way* (London and New York: Taurus, 2017), p. 166; Thomas Bagger, "The world according to Germany: Reassessing 1989," *The Washington Quarterly* 41, no. 4 (2019), pp. 53–63.
21. As quoted in "Angela Merkel warns EU: 'Brexit is a wake-up call'," *Financial Times*, 15 January 2020.
22. Webber, *European Disintegration?* pp. 106–34.
23. Andrew Moravcsik, "In defense of Europe." *Newsweek*, 7 June 2010, pp. 25–8.
24. Van Middelaar, *Alarums and Excursions*, p. 40 and 21–63; van Rompuy, interview; Webber, *European Disintegration?* p. 74.
25. Van Rompuy, interview.
26. Webber, *European Disintegration?* p. 95.
27. Varoufakis, *Adults in the Room*, p. 458.
28. "Alexis Tsipras: 'The worst is clearly behind us,'" interview, *The Guardian*, 24 July 2017.
29. Webber, *European Disintegration?* pp. 92 and 96.
30. "Tsipras warms to role as EU insider and populism critic," *Financial Times*, 29 June 2018.
31. Van Rompuy, interview.
32. As quoted in Marcus Walker, "Inside Merkel's Bet on the Euro's Future," *WSJ.com*, 23 April 2013.
33. Webber, *European Disintegration?* p. 81.
34. As quoted in "Wolfgang Schäuble: "Zur Überwindung der Krise gibt es keine einfache und schnelle Lösung,'" *Das Parlament: DebattenDokumentation*, no. 17 (22 April 2013), pp. 1–2.

35 German government official, as quoted in Webber, *European Disintegration?* p. 97.
36 Webber, *European Disintegration?* p. 91 and Viktoria Dendrinou and Eleni Varvitsioti, *The Last Bluff: How Greece came face-to-face with financial catastrophe & the secret plan for its euro exit* (Metamorfossi Attikis: Papadopolous, 2019), pp. 256–57.
37 Webber, *European Disintegration?* p. 72.
38 Simon Bulmer, "Germany and the Eurozone: Between Hegemony and Domestic Politics," *West European Politics* 37, no. 6 (2014), pp. 1244–63.
39 "Merkel keeps counsel as judges rule," *Financial Times*, 10 September 2012.
40 Bulmer and Paterson, *Germany and the European Union*, pp. 107 and 183.
41 German government official, as quoted in Webber, *European Disintegration?* p. 81.
42 German government official, as quoted in Webber, *European Disintegration?* p. 80; Adam Tooze, *Crashed: How a Decade of Financial Crisis Changed the World* (New York: Viking, 2018), p. 439 and Magnus Schoeller, *Leadership in the Eurozone: The Role of Germany and EU Institutions* (Cham, Switzerland: Palgrave Macmillan, 2019), pp. 180–82.
43 Draghi, as quoted in van Middelaar, *Alarums and Excursions*, pp. 57–58.
44 Schoeller, *Leadership in the Eurozone*, p. 180.
45 Peter Hall, "Varieties of Capitalism and the Eurozone Crisis," *West European Politics* 37, no. 6 (2014), pp. 1223–43 and Scharpf, "There is an alternative: The flexible European currency community," in Hansjörg Herr, Jan Priewe and Andrew Watt (eds), *Saving the Euro: Redesigning Euro Area Economic Governance*, (www.socialeurope.eu/wp-content/uploads/2017/06/EURO-web.pdf) (2017), pp. 155–74.
46 Schoeller, *Leadership in the Eurozone*, pp. 165–72.
47 Webber, *European Disintegration?* pp. 135, 137, 163, and 176.
48 As quoted in Robin Alexander, *Die Getriebenen* (Munich: Siedler, 2017), p. 58.
49 Ibid., p. 56.
50 Ibid., p. 61.
51 Webber, *European Disintegration?* pp. 155–7.
52 As quoted in Marcus Walker and Anton Troianovski, "Behind Angela Merkel's Open Door for Migrants," *Wall Street Journal*, 9 December 2015.
53 Webber, *European Disintegration?* pp. 157–58; Alexander, *Die Getriebenen*, pp. 23–24 and Thomas de Maizière, *Regieren: Innenansichten der Politik* (Freiburg: Herder, 2019), pp. 75–79.
54 As quoted in Henry Foy and Neil Buckley, "Barbed Rhetoric," *Financial Times*, 27 November 2015.
55 As quoted in "A last chance to rescue Europe's Schengen pact," *Financial Times*, 20 January 2016.
56 Erica Consterdine, "The huge political cost of Blair's decision to allow Eastern European migrants unfettered access to Britain," *The Conversation* (French edition), 24 November 2016 (https://theconversation.com/the-huge-political-cost-of-blairs-decision-to-allow-eastern-european-migrants-unfettered-access-to-britain-66077).

57 Ipsos MORI, *Issues Index: 2007 onwards* (www.ipsos.com/ipsos-mori/en-uk/issues-index-2007-onwards).
58 Webber, *European Disintegration?* pp. 188–90; David Cameron, *For the Record* (London: William Collins, 2019), p. 407.
59 Cameron, *For the Record*, p. 65.
60 David Laws, *Coalition: The Inside Story of the Conservative-Liberal Democrat Coalition Government* (London: Biteback, 2016), p. 241.
61 Ibid., p. 237.
62 Cameron, *For the Record*, pp. 330–32.
63 Ibid., p. 409.
64 Ipsos MORI (2013) *Ipsos MORI Political Monitor January 2013* (www.ipsos.com/ipsos-mori/en-uk/ipsos-mori-political-monitor-january-2013).
65 As quoted in Webber, *European Disintegration?* p.194.
66 Cameron, *For the Record*, p. 407.
67 Ibid., p. 407.
68 Ibid., p. 321.
69 Ibid., pp. 398–408.
70 Webber, *European Disintegration?* p. 199.
71 Cameron, *For the Record*, pp. 646–47.
72 Ibid., pp. 640–41.
73 Ibid., p. 400.
74 Webber, *European Disintegration?* p. 194.
75 See above and Webber, *European Disintegration?* p. 201.
76 Webber, *European Disintegration?* pp. 196–98.
77 *Eurocomment. February and March 2016: Migration Policy, the British Question and Economic Policy* (European Briefing Note 2016/1-3).
78 Webber, *European Disintegration?* p. 196 and Cameron, *For the Record*, pp. 632–37.
79 Ivan Rogers, "The real post-Brexit options," lecture delivered in the Policy Scotland Brexit series at the University of Glasgow, 23 May 2016 (https://pastebin.com/print/jMkxVUjs).
80 As quoted in Cameron, *For the Record*, p. 640.
81 Webber, *European Disintegration?* pp. 196–98.
82 As quoted in *M: Le Monde Magazine*,"'Il propose de saboter la monnaie unique': la première fois que *Le Monde* a parlé de Boris Johnson," 27 December 2019.
83 As quoted in Tim Shipman, *All Out War: The Full Story of How Brexit Sank Britain's Political Class* (London: Collins, 2016), p. 169.
84 Ibid., pp. 167ff.
85 Anna Soubry, as quoted ibid., p. 175.
86 Cameron, *For the Record*, p. 671.
87 Ibid., p. 671.
88 As quoted in George Parker, "The battle for Britain," *Financial Times*, 19 December 2016 and Cameron, *For the Record*, p. 677.
89 Statistics from European Centre for Disease Prevention and Control (ECDC) (www.ecdc.europa.eu/en/cases-2019-ncov-eueea).
90 European Commission, *European Economic Forecast Autumn 2020* (Brussels: DG For Economic and Financial Affairs, Institutional Paper 136, November 2020.

91 As quoted in Sylvie Kauffmann, "Merkel, l'Allemagne et le besoin d'Europe," *Le Monde*, 21–22 May 2020.
92 As quoted in "Coronavirus: les divisions de l'Union Européenne la placent face à un 'danger mortel'," *Le Monde*, 1 April 2020.
93 Marc Lazar, " Plus l'Italie fait nation face à l'épidémie, plus elle s'éloigne de l'Europe," *Le Monde*, 25 March 2020.
94 "Sommet de Bruxelles: le signal sans ambiguïté des Vingt-Sept sur leur volonté de préserver l'Union," *Le Monde*, 21 July 2020; Shahin Vallée, "With its recovery deal, is the EU finally starting to act as a unifying force? " *The Guardian*, 22 July 2020; "Recovery fund is a huge breakthrough for the EU," *Financial Times*, 21 July 2020.
95 Bagger, "The world according to Germany."
96 Joseph de Weck, "Pariscope: Germany is Becoming More French – and Paris Is Loving It," *Internationale Politik* 30 June 2020 (Pariscope: Germany Is Becoming More French—and Paris Is Loving It | Internationale Politik).
97 Emmanuel Macron, *Révolution* (Paris: XO Éditions, 2017).
98 Jérôme Fourquet, *Le nouveau clivage* (Paris: Cerf, 2018) and *L'archipel français: Naissance d'une nation multiple et divisée* (Paris: Seuil, 2019).
99 Macron, *Révolution*, pp. 226–29.
100 Macron, *Révolution*, pp. 228–29.
101 "Les trois semaines qui ont chamboulé l'orthodoxie économique européenne," *Le Monde*, 27 March 2020.
102 Macron, as quoted in "FT interview: Emmanuel Macron says it is time to think the unthinkable," *Financial Times*, 16 April 2020.
103 As quoted in "Coronavirus: les divisions de l'Union Européenne la placent face à un 'danger mortel'," *Le Monde*, 1 April 2020.
104 As quoted in "EU fails to settle rifts over size and shape of 'recovery fund,'" *Financial Times*, 24 April 2020.
105 "The chain of events that led to Germany's change over Europe's recovery fund," *Financial Times*, 22 May 2020.
106 "La France et l'Allemagne jettent les bases d'une relance européenne," *Le Monde*, 19 May 2020.
107 Stefan Lehne, "How the EU Managed Its Coronavirus Comeback," Carnegie Europe, 30 July 2020 (How the EU Managed Its Coronavirus Comeback – Carnegie Europe – Carnegie Endowment for International Peace).
108 John Palmer, "Is the EU finally moving towards an economic – and not just a monetary – union?," The Federal Trust, 21 July 2020 (Is the European Union finally moving to an economic – not just a monetary – Union? - The Federal Trust (fedtrust.co.uk).
109 As quoted in "Avec le plan de relance, Emmanuel Macron vante son action européenne, " *Le Monde*, 21 July 2020.
110 Bruno Le Maire, as quoted in "Au quatriéme jour d'un sommet difficile, les Européens trouvent un accord sur le plan de relance," *Le Monde*, 21 July 2020.
111 "Corona-Krise: Mehrheit der Deutschen findet EU-Krisenhilfen richtig,"*Der* Spiegel, 29 May 2020 (Corona-Krise: Mehrheit findet EU-Krisenhilfen richtig – DER SPIEGEL).

112 "Coronavirus crisis revives Franco-German relations," *Financial Times*, 13 April 2020.
113 As quoted in "German business body calls for European fiscal solidarity," *Financial Times*, 12 May 2020.
114 "Europäer sollen sich zusammen eine Billion Euro leihen," *Der Spiegel*, 21 March 2020 and Dorothea Bohnekamp and Holger Müller, "Les fissures de l'ordoliberalisme allemande," *Le Monde*, 12–14 April 2020.
115 "The chain of events that led to Germany's change over Europe's recovery fund," *Financial Times*, 22 May 2020.
116 Lebow, *Rise and Fall of Political Orders*, pp. 9 and 142.
117 Van Middelaar, *Alarums and Excursions*.

10 Conclusions

Richard Ned Lebow and Ludvig Norman

In the introduction we argued that leaders' estimates of robustness and fragility have important consequences for political orders. Depending on the circumstances, actor beliefs in robustness or fragility can prompt intervention or inaction, and either has the potential to strengthen or weaken orders. These effects we suggest are highly context-dependent. The problem is further complicated by the fact that some of the conditions and structures that appear to promote robustness can, under some circumstances be shown to have promoted fragility. These divergent outcomes can only be known in retrospect.

Actor estimates of robustness and fragility, their policy responses, and their possible consequences are historically and culturally contingent. Any account of them needs to be sensitive to how actors understand themselves and their social and political settings and the likely outcome of any intervention. In this conclusion, we draw on the preceding chapters to offer some tentative generalizations about the conditions associated with actor assessments and policy choices.

We posed a number of questions to our contributors. We asked them to identify how leaders assessed robustness and fragility – if they did; the range of responses they thought relevant to their situations, the reasons for their choices, and the consequences of their policies in cases where answers were evident. We also asked contributors to identify the particular, even idiosyncratic, contextual features of their cases that might affect assessments, responses, and outcomes. These include role models and the historical lessons they generated, leader estimates of their freedom of action and the timing and confluence of catalysts. We were particularly interested in anything that brought about dramatic and significant shifts in assessment or behavior.

Our cases include orders that were thought relatively robust by contemporary observers but turned out to be quite fragile, and those that were considered more fragile than they were. In some, leaders and other observers were sensitive to shifts toward robustness or fragility, and in others remarkably obtuse. It also includes contemporary orders, where there are differences of opinion about robustness and no definitive judgment is as yet possible. This variation prompts us to explore cultural and psychological explanations for willingness to recognize and address fragility or to remain obtuse to it and possibly engage in denial.

Our contributors address political order at the state, regional, and international levels. The state is a legal category that encompasses political units with wide variation, as our contributors have noted. They have certain features in common that affect fragility and robustness, but also differences that suggest the analytical utility of subcategories. As a political order, the Soviet Union was more of an empire than the United States and accordingly lacked many of the characteristics associated with nation-state. Their absence was a key reason for its demise. Some states build identity and loyalty on the basis of what the Germans formerly called *Blut und Boden* (descent and territory), and still others on a way of life or commitment to procedures and norms, as do France and the United States. Different foundations for national identity and different ways of building solidarity presumably have different implications for the robustness and fragility of political orders.

Regional organization is an even looser catchall category than the state. Douglas Webber suggests that the European Union (EU) does not fit easily within it. It was described by former European Commission president Jacques Delors as an "unidentified political object." For Webber, the EU constitutes something of a hybrid between a state and an international intergovernmental organization. He describes it as a consensual democracy. It differs from states in that it has no coercive means at its disposal. Its authority rests on implementing widely accepted norms. Unlike many states, integration has not generated a strong common identity; state or regional identifications come first for most people. In times of crisis, as in the last decade, the EU's decision-making capacity was facilitated and expedited by its hierarchy, which overrode and temporarily set aside the normally strong consensual EU decision-making norms.

Historically, France and Germany provided the EU with a form of stabilizing collective hegemonic leadership, in the sense envisaged by Charles Kindleberger.[1] From this perspective, the fate of the EU depended significantly more heavily on Germany's choices – specifically, how it exercised its broader scope for agency – than it did on those of other member states or of most of the EU's supranational organs.[2] Ludvig Norman's account instead emphasizes how the lack of broad politicization of European integration, proceeding instead through less visible legal and bureaucratic processes, explains its success. Indeed, with a few exceptions – most notably that of the UK – the political mainstream in most European countries were reluctant to make "Europe" a political issue. While questionable from a democratic perspective, this helped marginalize skeptics, keeping them at arm's length from the European political project.

Andrew Lawrence has authored our only chapter that bridges the three levels of political order. He starts with the assumption that climate change constitutes a serious crisis for all these orders. He asks why democratic and liberal national, regional, and international regimes have nevertheless failed to protect and empower populations in the face of this threat. He attributes their negligence to the triumph of instrumental reasoning over critical reflexivity, expressed in the institutional manifestations, and secondarily, to the practical consequences of colonialism, militarism, and economic approaches to the environment. Each of these causes represents different manifestations of the "imperial mode of living." It prompts – indeed, requires – elites to objectify nature in a manner that is blinkered and ultimately self-defeating. Elites, moreover, have unwarranted faith in their capability to control nature and convert uncertainty into risk. For Lawrence, these problems exist at every level of order, so there are no significant differences among states, regional, and international orders in addressing the climate crisis.

Most of our contributors address how assessments of fragility informed the outlooks of political actors, although they also have something to say about the consequences of these perceptions. Some chapters, most notably those of Brown and Petzschmann, explore the lessons that failures spawned. The collapse of the Weimar Republic and of communist regimes in Eastern Europe and the Soviet Union were unexpected by key actors and analysts, and when recognition dawned it was often only in the final stages of the process. In the case of Weimar, Paul Petzschmann tells us, denial continued after failure. Some intellectuals and administrators refused to regard the appointment of Hitler as chancellor as representing a collapse of the existing order because they anchored it in the civil administration; they expected it to endure and help preserve the dominant features of the Weimar order. Collapse is a social category with diverse meanings, which complicates our analytical task. It is, of course, an ex post facto determination, but as Weimar indicates, endings can also be contested.

Leader Assessments

Our contributors find important conceptual differences in understandings of robustness and fragility. Indicators of fragility are generally more obvious and thus more likely to draw attention and influence assessments. Political impasse, rising political and ethnic tensions,

Conclusions

demonstrations, and violence – some of the more common markers of fragility – are all readily observable and often widely commented on, either privately, or in the media in countries that allow free expression of opinion. A case in point is a recent report by Human Rights Watch suggests that more frequent and larger street demonstrations in Hungary, Turkey, China, Uganda, and Poland, and willingness of opposition parties to put aside their differences to collaborate against authoritarian regimes in Hungary and Turkey, indicate their growing fragility.[3] Theorized markers of robustness are less dramatic. They are more subtle, less newsworthy, less emotionally arousing and threatening, and may be more ambiguous in their implications. For these reasons, among others we expect leaders to be more sensitive to fragility.

Our privileging of fragility over robustness mirrors that of political leaders and analysts. Relatively little is written about robustness in comparison to fragility. In the latter half of the twentieth century, there was little discussion of robustness in the media. In the academic literature it had specialized foci. There was a spirited discussion of newly democratizing states and the difficulties and dangers of their transition.[4] It was followed by a more sustained discussion of "waves of democracy." Much of this literature was teleological as it was based on the belief that liberal capitalist democracy was the only rational response to the modern world.[5] A similar teleological outlook shaped studies of the European Union after the end of Cold War. European integration was the preordained future and the European project was expected to strike ever deeper roots and expand correspondingly in scope and authority.[6] We are not making judgments of robustness and fragility, but attempting to explain those of political actors. Our contributors emphasize the extent to which not only their assessments, but their openness to the possibility of fragility, are very much influenced by widely shared assumptions and expectations of their era.

To frame our discussion of leader assessments of fragility and their responses, we introduce a flowchart that connects such assessments to leaders' ability to implement effective responses. Each of the component questions included in the flowchart and their answers lead to additional questions and branching points, some of which we illustrate with examples from our chapters. Leader assessments, we argue, are closely connected with estimates of their own agency. The flowchart also highlights questions related to why leaders think some policy responses are appropriate and others to be avoided at all costs. For answers, we turn to role models, historical lessons, path dependencies, and beliefs and expectations common to the Zeitgeist. We conclude with some generalizations about contingency and agency and the different ways they affect perceptions of robustness and fragility at the state, regional, and international levels.

Leader assessments of robustness or fragility
   If regime or order is perceived as robust there is no need to act
   If perceived as fragile, leaders search for possible responses
   If they cannot find them, they may engage in suppression and/or denial
Leader assessments of their freedom to act
   If negative, they may resort to suppression and/or denial
   If positive, they consider their options.
Leader choice
   Policies that have worked in the past and are politically feasible
   If deemed successful, they may implement or be receptive to further measures.

     Figure 10.1 Feasibility Flowchart

Our flowchart is something of an ideal type. Max Weber had an evolving understanding of this concept but came to see it as an abstraction from reality that provided a useful template for studying real-world behavior.[7] It differs from the real world of politics in its assumption that leaders actually ask these questions and search for answers before they act – or do nothing. The flowchart also differs from rational choice models in that we make no assumption that leaders will behave rationally in the sense of having ordered preferences, search and evaluate information carefully, and, when required, make trade-offs between their goals. Leaders and entire elites may be prisoners of their ideologies, give too much weight to questionable historical lessons, apply good lessons to situations where they are inappropriate, or make inaccurate estimates in either direction of their freedom to act or misjudge the likely consequences of whatever policies they pursue. They may also shift their assessments of fragility in response to their estimates of the ability to respond.

Our flowchart suggests that leaders who believe their orders robust are likely to stay committed to the status quo and deny the need for major reforms. This situation will continue, as it did in the Soviet Union, until a new leader with different understandings and goals comes to power, or existing leaders question their estimates of fragility in response to new and unexpected developments. In some countries, most notably in Weimar Germany, elites were relatively insensitive to the fragility of their orders. At various times this was also apparent in Soviet Union, and to a lesser degree in Eastern Europe. Ariane Chebel d'Appolonia suggests that American elites were also overconfident, but in in the aftermath of the 6 January 2021 assault on the Capitol building, the pendulum appears to have swung in the opposite direction. Andrew Lawrence describes widespread denial regarding climate change and its consequences for the fragility of political orders. He attributes it to well-funded campaigns and deeply embedded cultural conceptions that exaggerate human ability to control nature. By contrast, Douglas Webber and Ludvig Norman document how beliefs in fragility informed the building of the European order from the outset.

Ned Lebow contends that exaggeration of vulnerability is the default in new orders as robustness is in long-standing ones. Different political and psychological mechanisms are at play. People everywhere tend to regard the status quo as stable and express surprise when dramatic changes occur. This phenomenon may have a cognitive explanation: The present is more vivid than any alternative future because it is experienced. To the extent that people are open to change, it is of the gradual kind for the same reason: It is easier to imagine minor changes than more sudden and far-reaching transformations. The latter require the mental construction of different worlds and credible pathways leading to them. This is a difficult task for most people. Beyond a good imagination it also requires a certain emotional security to escape from a world that is well-known into one that might be more threatening. If people can rise to this challenge, they are more likely to accept the possibility of significant change. Laboratory experiments – based on Tversky and Kahneman's classic work on the availability and simulation heuristics – find that people assimilate information to existing schemas. However, when primed by vivid, alternative scenarios they find it easier to imagine different worlds.[8]

Lebow notes that there is nevertheless ample evidence of people imagining catastrophes that involve dramatic political, economic, and social changes. Some of this pessimism is situation-specific. In new regimes, especially revolutionary ones, assessments of considerable fragility are pronounced, and may be warranted. Lenin and the Bolsheviks reasonably feared for the survival of their regime. It endured in part because they endorsed measures appropriate to the perceived threat.[9] As noted in our introductory chapter, Stalin greatly exaggerated the internal threats to the Soviet Union. Initially, this was a deliberate political strategy but later a manifestation of extreme paranoia.[10]

Exaggerated threat perception also occurs in what are generally regarded as robust orders. Conservatives in 1950s postwar America worried that rock 'n roll was corrupting the young and threatening the social and political order.[11] Since then every new generation have identified new threats to the young, whether in the form gangster rap, video games, or social media. The oil shock of 1973 convinced the Trilateral Commission, a group of American, European, and Japanese officials and policy intellectuals that thirty years of unprecedented growth was coming to an end due to stagflation: a combination of high unemployment and inflation. They feared – quite unreasonably – that the international order was on the verge of collapse.[12] It is, of course, too early to tell if the dire assessments now common in the United States after Donald Trump's denial of his defeat are equally exaggerated.

The rock 'n roll example suggests that threats to social values from people you can no longer control – teenagers in this instance – are likely to be regarded as severe. We may be witnessing a similar phenomenon on a world-wide basis today with regard to women, whose attainment of more equal rights has produced a strong and at times violent backlash from men.[13] Perhaps the best American example is the civil rights movement, where racists, among them, Federal Bureau of Investigation Director, J. Edgar Hoover, sought to brand Martin Luther King as a communist and his followers as dupes.[14] Anxieties voiced as fear for the social and political order may really reflect concern for the individual and collective status and authority of some of its members. When status and authority are connected with identity and self-esteem even minor changes can be perceived as very threatening. This argument resonates with recent studies on the factors that help explain support for far-right populist parties. Rather than narrowly defined material factors or disfunctions of political institutions, these studies point to importance of subjectively perceived social status, perceptions of general societal decline and the political mobilization of resentment for explaining such support.[15]

Douglas Webber recognizes that the European Union offers a parallel of sorts to revolutionary regimes. The European project is the most ambitious attempt at interstate cooperation ever attempted. Member states rose from six to twenty-eight and the powers of the European Commission, the European Parliament and the European Court of Justice increased at the expense of these states. Wide swathes of Europe are borderless and share a common currency, achievements that were almost unthinkable at the outset. There was good reason at the beginning to fear that such a novel project, and one, moreover, involving former enemies, would not succeed. Webber defines robustness in the first instance as the ability of a political order to weather crises successfully. In the last decade, the EU managed the Eurozone, refugee, Brexit, and Coronavirus crises. It proved more robust than expected by its leaders

Conclusions 277

and supporters, and recent opinion polls indicate that popular support for the EU is higher than it has been for a long time.[16] Really robust orders must also adapt and change in the course of coping with crises in a way that gains more popular support and makes them more likely to respond effectively to future challenges.

Webber argues that the pervasive concern for fragility has had positive consequences. In each of the crises he examined, it aroused widespread fears for the EU's survival EU or that of some of its important institutions like the Euro or the Schengen Area. There was accordingly great willingness to put other matters aside and cooperate to resolve the crisis. Also helpful was the fact that European actors did not share the same conceptions of "Europe." This was widely recognized and routinely finessed, which would be more difficult to do if the EU or its institutions began to disintegrate.

Turning to domestic political orders, the decline and collapse of the Weimar Republic offers a remarkable counter example of overconfidence. Paul Petzschmann finds that the pro-republican elite on the whole dismissed the gravity growing threats from authoritarian political movements at both ends of the political spectrum. Many officials opposed special intervention in the belief that the crisis would be mastered. Interestingly, this state of mind continued for some time after the republic's collapse. Petzschmann identifies two factors that encouraged elites to assume fundamental stability: the peculiarities of Germany's politics, and deep attachment to the ideology of statism. Elites saw continuity in German political development through the upheavals of the German revolution of 1919 and the Nazi seizure of power in 1933. Their belief in robustness encouraged administrative experimentation aimed at stabilizing Weimar democracy, but it also led administrators and politicians alike to underestimate the Nazi threat. The dedication to achieving stability "from above," and at any cost, helped to bring about the collapse of Weimar's constitutional edifice.

Petzschmann suggests that political stalemate at federal and state levels should have justified a more activist role for administrators. However, the dominant administrative ideology offered no guidance about how to create stable pro-republican majorities among Weimar's voters. More importantly, its conflation of political stability with administrative stability meant that administrative rule by decree was normalized. This, in turn, led administrators and scholars of public administration to seriously misjudge the severity of the Nazi seizure of power.

Archie Brown describes overconfidence in the former Soviet Union. He attributes it to the slowness of Soviet leaders – Gorbachev was not alone here – to acknowledge the power of nationalism. Nationalism had a ready-made base, Brown observes, because Stalin had organized the republics on a national basis, although did not allow them any real independence. The post-Stalin leadership successfully contained ethnonationalism with a combination of concessions to national languages and heritage but crackdowns against the slightest manifestation of nationalist deviation. The one glaring exception was Russian nationalism, which was tolerated but only when accompanied by proclamations of loyalty to the Soviet state. The union republics were generally administered by members of the nationality of that republic, but until the late 1980s, ultimate authority remained with the Central Committee in Moscow. Nationalism was omnipresent, but muted in expression, and only became an actively disintegrating force after Gorbachev had initiated fundamental reforms in the political system. Gorbachev remained insensitive to the power of nationalism until very late in the game.

We suspect that Gorbachev's naïveté was attributable to his ignorance of the effects of aroused publics. Alexander Yakovlev aside, neither Gorbachev nor any of his advisors had spent prolonged time in a democratic country. In May 1989, Gorbachev confided to Janice Gross Stein and Ned Lebow that he was under pressure to give more autonomy to the Baltic Republics. He and advisor Vadim Zagladin explained that they were in constant touch with the Baltic communist leaders who knew just how far they were allowed to go.[17] It seemed obvious to Stein and Lebow that once nationalist voices were raised and people came out on the streets these leaders would have to follow public opinion, and if not, would quickly be shunted aside. Familiar only with the workings of authoritarian regimes, the General Secretary and his advisors could delude themselves into believing that they could turn on and off political protests and demands as they would hot and cold water taps.

Petzschmann and Brown both write about orders we now know failed. Ariane Chebel d'Appollonia and Andrew Lawrence ask the same questions in existing orders at the national, and international levels. Chebel d'Appollonia emphasizes the cognitively constraining effects of the widespread and deeply entrenched belief in American exceptionalism. The "city on the hill" cannot fail, by definition. She documents how many prominent scholars have celebrated the American democratic experiment by focusing almost entirely on the positive side of their country's history and political culture. They recognize protest and dissent, but transform into a virtue because they depict it leading to positive changes.

Lawrence also maintains that there is considerable denial, facilitated by the complexity of the situation and powerful interests. It is motivated denial that is made necessary by commitments to libertarian individualism, generalized mistrust in government and science, a desire to maintain the status quo, loyalty to idealized national identities, and attachments to consumerist social norms.[18] An important contributing factor has been the growing adoption by both center-left and center-right political parties of austerity-driven fiscal policies. They encourage electoral abstention and votes for non-mainstream "populist" left-wing and right-wing parties. Alienation and the rise of the parties increases polarization and political destabilization and drives a growing sense of insecurity and precarity among large segments of the working class. These policies have arguably eroded a collective capacity for autonomous opposition and critique and make it political more difficult for leaders and governments to respond effectively to the climate threat.[19]

Judging from these cases leader assessments at every level of political order appear hit-and-miss. They are very much shaped by ideology, sensitivity to recent events, and the Zeitgeist. Cultural expectations and personality also appear important. Our cases indicate very little debate within elites about robustness or fragility as they do not have sharp differences in their assessments. In retrospect, it is apparent that faulty estimates were made in both directions: fragile regimes were considered robust, and robust ones fragile. Our next section addresses this diversity by turning to the second question in our flow chart, focusing on where assessments come from.

Role Models and Historical Lessons

Our cases suggest that critical importance of the frameworks policy-makers and analysts use to assess robustness and fragility. We have already noted ideology in this connection. In this section, we focus on historical role models and lessons.

The most influential twentieth-century role model for robustness and fragility is the Weimar Republic. It is an anti-role model in the sense that those who invoke it do so to prevent its repetition in another context. It has spawned numerous lessons, many of them of questionable accuracy or value.[20] They are by no means limited to Germany. In the United States, Paul Petzschmann notes, Weimar is the go-to political analogy. Commentators compared George H. W. Bush to Erich Ludendorff, Barrack Obama to Paul von Hindenburg, and Donald Trump to Adolf Hitler.[21] They invoked Ludendorff and Bush's invocation of the stab-in-the-back thesis to explain away military defeat, Donald Trump's political ambitions with those of Hitler, and the similarity between Mitch McConnell and Republican senators to parliamentarians who enabled Hitler to destroy democracy and consolidate his dictatorship. Historically, sophisticated Americans were repelled by the simplicity of these comparisons but this did not stop them from also mobilizing the lens of Weimar.[22] Their obvious attraction to journalists and the public may reflect deep distrust of democracy but also fears for its survival.

Petzschmann finds many of those who invoke the Weimar analogy are liberal to left in their politics. They believe that fascism remains a threat, that Weimar is the most relevant historical comparison, and that we should avail ourselves of its analytical and rhetorical power.[23] He goes further than Lebow in suggesting that historical analogies are like Rorschach's inkblots. We read meaning into them, and by doing so reveal our commitments and anxieties. Rorschach Tests have long been discredited in the field of psychiatry.[24] Petzschmann's observation strikes us as more defensible. He is not inferring complex psychological states or needs from the invocation of Weimar, only political concerns.

Ludvig Norman examines how the failure of the League of Nations became emblematic of stillborn international cooperation. Like Weimar, it spawned a number of policy lessons. The League and its failure continue to haunt the architects and officials of all other regional and international organizations. The EU lives very much in its penumbra and this is one reason, Douglas Webber infers, why EU officials consistently exaggerate the fragility of the European project.

Ludvig Norman describes how functionalism emerged as an implication of one of the principal "lessons" of the League's failure. It was a central inspiration for postwar European cooperation and motivated by a desire to prevent another round of violent interstate conflict. Functionalist ideas challenged state sovereignty as the fundamental organizational principle of international political order. David Mitrany, the great functionalist theorist, sought to decenter states and interstate relations in favor of organically generated forms of cooperation on well-defined problems of common concern. Mitrany saw states as on the whole standing in the way of functional cooperation.[25] He had a far-reaching agenda that sought to reduce identification and loyalty to the state by "the experience of fruitful international co-operation," which in turn would reduce support for war.[26]

Norman tells us that Mitrany was also influenced by Weimar. In Mitrany's view, public demands for welfare, nationally minded politicians, and special interests colluded to erode democracy and increase state control, or at least intervention, in all aspects of social and economic life. International connections and loyalties grew correspondingly weaker. The absence of any kind of international social policy and the failure to modernize liberal democratic theory and practice in the face of these changes paved the way for fascism. Mitrany joins other post-Weimar theorists in expressing deep skepticism about mass politics due to the ease with which uneducated publics can be aroused in support of destructive projects.[27] Mitrany was hardly alone in observing that "totalitarian movements use and abuse democratic freedoms in order to abolish them."[28] The Weimar Republic, and liberal democracy more generally, lacked the means for its own self-preservation.

Norman also analyzes the writings of constitutional lawyer and political scientist Karl Löwenstein, who emigrated to the United States when Hitler came to power. Löwenstein maintained that democracy needed to use defensive efforts to protect its core and should not refrain from decisive action due to what he called "democratic fundamentalism."[29] Constitutional scruples, he maintained, should not stand in the way of preserving fundamental rights and liberties.[30] His militant democracy, like Mitrany's functionalism, is rooted in the distrust of popular self-government because of the susceptibility of the demos to the spectacle of fascist politics. Löwenstein introduced an elitist logic at the heart of democracy, a parallel to Mitrany's desires to insulate technocrats from democratic intervention.[31] European unification was "too serious a business to be left to politicians."[32]

Functionalist and overtly protective notions of politics became influential in shaping the postwar European political order, the European Community, and later the European Union. However, functionalism, as developed by Mitrany, was used only selectively in shaping Europe's architecture. Nevertheless, the commitment to organize international cooperation in a way that removed core issues from oversight by elected politicians – equally central to functionalism and theories of militant democracy – is reflected in the core institutional structure of the EC and the EU.[33] The turn to administration as a substitution for democratic government rests on a questionable, if not downright fallacious diagnosis of the causes of Weimar's collapse. Weimar's emergency powers – now seen by many as the mechanism used to bypass and then destroy democracy – were regarded by Löwenstein and others as a good thing at the time. After Weimar's collapse, they were considered by many as a necessary protection against the evils of mass democracy.

Historical lessons – even bad ones – can become entrenched. Peter Breiner expands further on this theme. He documents how they become intellectual and rhetorical resources that people draw upon to analyze current events or persuade others to support their policy prescriptions. Weimar is front and center again in Anglo-American discourses because democracy is once again seen as threatened – and by the same kinds of right-wing, nationalist, authoritarian forces responsible for fascism between the Wars. Some of the more prominent scholarly analysts of the current situation pick up where Mitrany and Löwenstein left off. The "end of democracy" literature, spearheaded by Steven Levitzky and Daniel Ziblatt, David Runciman, and Yascha Mounk, once again foreground the alleged danger to democracy from authoritarian leaders, populism, or simple complacency. In his critique of these works, Breiner shows how they set up the problem to produce the response they desire. They identify democracy with liberal democracy, and liberal democracy with the minimalist Schumpeterian model of democracy. They imagine a degree of harmony and consensus in past party relations that never in reality existed, and blame the rise of antidemocratic authoritarianism on some equally questionable abandonment of liberal norms of liberal democracy, inadequate barriers to antidemocratic movements and politicians, and downright complacency. Some of these authors would follow earlier critics of Weimar democracy and turn to antidemocratic structures and procedures to save democracy.

Breiner insists that the end of democracy authors err as much as their Weimar predecessors in diagnosing the causes of fragility. They embrace the minimalist model of democracy, a political fiction that never achieves legitimacy. It fails to deliver political equality, uphold civil and political rights, and largely excludes entire demographics from recognition, status, and power. It therefore provides widespread resentment and a strong incentive and political space for right-wing authoritarian movements, leftist populist movements and parties, insurgent members of established political parties, and even social democratic parties willing to participate in political cartel arrangements at the expense of their traditional constituents. Minimalist democracy's solution is part of the problem.

Historical events and lessons help to explain leader, elite, and analyst estimates of robustness and fragility. We must nevertheless exercise care in this regard. We suspect that leaders and other political actors often invoke these events and lessons to justify policies they have decided on for other reasons. Even where they are determinative, we must ask why leaders and others are attracted to them. It may be a reflection of their more general political orientations and ideologies. They make certain events and lessons more attractive or convincing than others. This is especially true of Weimar where they are multiple lessons, some of them at odds with one another. What is interesting here is not only the invocation of Weimar but the particular use of the historical analogy. It could be to restrain the demos, enable it, support or oppose special powers, or to act with dispatch or restraint in face of authoritarian challenges to democracy. Historical lessons are, of course, only one source of framing, albeit an important one our cases indicate. As these lessons based on events like Weimar and the League of Nations are policy-focused, they provide a good entrée into the next question on our flowchart.

Leader Responses

Perceptions of robustness or fragility will prompt different responses. When leaders believe their order to be robust, they are unlikely to see any need to take extraordinary action to shore it up. They may continue to govern as they have in the past. Alternatively, they might exploit the perceived robustness of their order as providing them the political security to introduce major policy departures or innovations. The several reform acts in Victorian Britain were made possible by widespread belief in robustness among the political elite.[34] Perceptions of fragility, by contrast, are more likely to provoke insecurity, and with it, some kind of actions intended to shore up the order and stave off any possible collapse. Such fears may include various types of political and institutional reforms, sometimes accompanied by higher levels of repression. The other big difference is assessments of fragility, unlike those of robustness, are likely to arouse the emotions. Depending on the degree of fragility perceived, they can prompt anxiety, even fear.

Leaders who see internal existential threats to their order confront fundamental choices. They can attempt to strengthen their orders by coopting otherwise dissident groups, placating more general opposition through reforms, attempting to provide a new or additional basis for identification with and support for their order, or increase surveillance and repression. These are not either-or choices, and leaders can, and often have, relied on some combination of these strategies. There is the additional response of denial. Leaders can pretend to themselves that all is well, or that their order will somehow survive. Denial is not an effective policy response but it does reduce anxiety.

The most fundamental choice is between attempting to do something to strengthen the order or focusing more on reducing, suppressing, and silencing the opposition. Repression is the most common choice of authoritarian regimes; Hafez al-Assad, Vladimir Putin, and the Burmese generals offer contemporary examples. But democratic regimes frequently resort to repression, although not on the same scale. The United States did so during and after World War I, when it arrested those opposed to war or left-wing activists during the Red Scare.[35] It did so again in the McCarthy era.[36] In the aftermath of the terrorist attacks of September 11, 2001, far-reaching security measures were put in place.[37] In all these instances, repression was a response to greatly exaggerated fears of internal enemies. In the United States, the several Red Scares were encouraged and used by big business to go after labor unions and other forces of progressive change.[38] Similar dynamics can be observed in UK and France in the wake of terrorist attacks.[39]

Authoritarian regimes can also engage in meaningful reforms. One of the most dramatic examples is the Republic of South Africa under the presidency of F. W. De Klerk. He negotiated with Mandela to fully dismantle apartheid and establish a transition to universal suffrage. In 1993, he publicly apologized for apartheid's harmful effects. He oversaw the 1994 nonracial election in which Mandela led the African National Congress (ANC) to victory. Under Mandela and the ANC, formal white rule effectively came to an end.[40] Transitions to democracy in South Korea and Taiwan were less dramatic and more protracted, but shared in common with South Africa the belief by authoritarian leaders that change was necessary to sustain the political order. Both countries, like South Africa, engaged in massive repression against the political opposition, before ending it under new leaders and instituting freer speech and elections. All three regimes had found themselves unable to overcome their opposition by violence and subject to condemnation and, in the case of South Africa, sanctions by their major trading partners.[41]

Major reforms are difficult in regimes of all kinds, but especially in authoritarian ones. There are almost always members of the elite who worry that change will lead to more demands and weaken the order, as Leonid Brezhnev and his colleagues did. The likelihood of success, measured in terms of shoring up the present order, and creating a peaceful transition to a new one is not high. This may be one reason why such reform programs are only infrequently attempted. Another reason may be that the lives and livelihoods of political elites in authoritarian regimes are often intimately tied to the status quo, and that the end of such regimes are more likely to come with the threat of imprisonment, exile, and even death for former leaders. Lebow suggests that major reform programs, especially in authoritarian regimes, require the kinds of leaders whom Brian Rathbun characterizes as romantic. They believe in both the justness and necessity of their cause and convince themselves that their charisma and commitment will overcome any obstacles.[42] Examples include Anwar el-Sadat and Mikhail Gorbachev, the Young Turks, and Mustafa Kemal Atatürk.[43]

Archie Brown contends that Gorbachev convinced himself that *glasnost* and *perestroika* would succeed, just as he persuaded himself that he could end the Cold War and make the West his willing partner. He succeeded in overcoming Western suspicions and hostility by committing himself and his country to multiple acts of reassurance: withdrawal from Afghanistan, arms control, allowing Eastern Europe to choose its own political systems, and finally, the unification of Germany. The latter was the final step in ending the Cold War and a powerful symbol of East–West collaboration.[44]

Gorbachev was clever and very lucky – up to a point. He exploited a series of unexpected events early in his secretary general-ship – including the 1986 nuclear power plant disaster at Chernobyl and the 1987 surprise landing in Red Square of Matthias Rust's Cessna – to purge the military and civilian *nomenklatura* of hundreds of hardline officials who opposed his reforms.[45] Gorbachev deluded himself into believing that he could use reforms to generate pressure from below on recalcitrant bureaucrats and party officials. He also thought he could turn the tap of reform off when it threatened to carry the country in directions he did not wish to go.[46] Instead, he provoked a coup against him that failed but quickly led to the unraveling of the Soviet Union. One of the ironies of the Soviet system is that centralization gave the general secretary power to initiate the kind of sweeping changes that could not be made by a democratic leader. However, efforts to decentralize authority and increase political participation undermined the authority, not only of the leader but of the political system.[47]

Less fortunate was Egypt's Anwar el-Sadat. He was equally committed to transforming his country by ending its decades-long conflict with Israel and shifting Egypt's political and economic ties from the Soviet Union to the United States. He hoped this would bring peace, American aid and investments, and create the conditions for economic growth and political stability. Sadat's reforms were cut short by his assassination.[48] In the Soviet and Egyptian cases, Lebow argues, motivated bias played an important role in leader assessments. It encouraged overconfidence, which paid off in the ending of the Cold War, but was an impediment to reforming the political system.

Leaders in either authoritarian or democratic regimes not infrequently seek to mobilize nationalism in support of their regimes or orders, and all the more so when they appear fragile. Joseph Stalin famously sought a reset of this kind in the aftermath of the German invasion of the Soviet Union in June 1941, where resistance to the invaders was increasingly sold as defense of "Mother Russia" rather than of socialism.[49] Nationalism, and the spurring of nationalist sentiments by political leaders, has been and remains, one of the most powerful responses to perceived fragilities. Political orders of any kind that are able to convince people that they represent that nation are more likely to be regarded as legitimate. This is more difficult to do in countries where there are competing and conflicting nationalities, or where the nation is defined in terms of acceptance and loyalty to a set of governing principles as opposed to any kind of ethnic identity. It was also a problem in general for supranational communist regimes like the Soviet Union and Yugoslavia. Similar dynamics are in evidence in Europe's political order, the EU, where enthusiastic attempts among some elites to foster a common European identity, has generally found little resonance with broader publics. As Ludvig Norman demonstrates, political elites in the early stages of postwar European cooperation were less sanguine about the prospects of such a common identity, choosing instead to build the new institutions based on cooperation in concrete areas of industry.

National identity has been a source of strength in France and the United States but this unity has become frayed in recent years. Publics are more deeply divided, protests are greater and more extreme, and extremist candidates and office holders are more prominent. The invocation of a well-defined national identity in pluralistic societies comes with a sense of exclusion among minorities that do not fit the mold and may lead to heightened social and political tensions. In France, the principal cleavage is ethnic-religious, with many Muslims rejecting so-called secular French values, and the French government digging in its heels in defense of long-proclaimed policy of *laïcité* (secularism).[50] Éric Zemmour, who wants all Muslims expelled from France, became the darling of the French right. He campaigned unsuccessfully for the presidency of France, winning only 7 percent of the vote and being eliminated in the first round.[51] In the United States, the divide is cultural and political, with many Trump supporters, among them elected officials, in rebellion against the constitution and the rule of law. At the same time, underprivileged minorities, often mobilized along ethnic lines are challenging narratives of national pride that have worked to diminish the importance of their plight from the country's history.

Ariane Chebel d'Appollonia contends that the United States illustrates the Janus-faced nature of national myths and solidarity. Attachment to "the cluster of values and customs," loosely labeled as "the American creed," facilitates unity by providing incentives and benchmarks for individuals seeking to assimilate. Paradoxically, it also "stimulates nativist feelings and exclusionary practices." The constitution protects civil liberties, but the First Amendment perpetuates hate speech. The Second Amendment – as misinterpreted by Republican judges – legalizes guns of all kinds and allows a widespread culture of violence. The constitutional system of checks and balances at the federal level and between the central government and the states stabilizes the regime, but also encourages gridlock and polarization.

Archie Brown discusses another response to fragility: state control of discourses. It is the polar opposite of American freedom of speech. He attributes the survival of communist regimes for so long in part to their sophisticated system of institutional oversight, including censorship and strict management of the mass media. They used educational institutions and the media to propagate an ideology that purported to be scientific and to explain all political and social phenomena. Communism also developed and imposed a language of politics that determined how public political discourse was conducted and, in the case of long-lasting regimes, the categories in terms of which many people learned to think. Internalization of a communist discourse made it difficult to think outside of it or give credence to information that challenged it.[52]

Political orders sometimes face multiple threats, or are believed to do so by their leaders. In such situations they need to prioritize these threats and recognize the trade-offs that need to be made. But this is very difficult to do, cognitively and politically. Lebow offers the example of eighteenth-century Britain. In the 1760s and 1770s, the British government worried about the collapse of the East India Company and the survival of their domestic political system if they had to raise domestic taxes to pay for the maintenance of the empire in India and North America. Unwilling to tax the landed gentry, and already having placed a high tax burden on trades people and ordinary folk, they imposed consistently higher taxes instead on North American colonists. Vigorous opposition to the Sugar Act, Currency Act, Stamp Act, Townsend Acts, Tea Act, and Coercive Acts from Massachusetts to South Carolina prompted some amelioration. Colonial opposition did not compel the British government to rescind their taxation policies. Rather, they sought to impose their will on the colonies by means of a larger administration and armed forces paid for by local taxes. British policies provoked widespread anger and made local elites more sympathetic to radical calls for independence.[53] It is apparent that British leaders exaggerated their domestic threat and greatly minimized the overseas one.

In this situation, cognitive and political biases seem to have been mutually reinforcing. It was easier for British leaders to imagine disaster at home than abroad, making them more sensitive to the threat posed by the possible collapse of the British East India Company. That company and its investors also had more clout in parliament, in part because the colonies had no representation. British leaders did not appear to recognize and trade-off, and if they did, there was little doubt on which side they would come down. They exaggerated the domestic threat and minimized the colonial one – with very serious consequences. We suspect that this kind of problem is routine, and more evidence of the connection between leader assessments and policy choices, and between both and political outcomes.

Freedom to Act

By freedom to act, we mean the political freedom to initiate and implement the kinds of responses leaders think important or even necessary to stave off fragility. Leaders might understand the need for reforms but conclude – rightly or not – that their own freedom to act is limited. They might lack formal authority to act, see political forces arrayed against them, or believe they will pay too high a price politically. In these circumstances, delay is an obvious choice in the hope that they will gain more leverage in the future.

Leaders can misjudge their authority in either direction. They may fail to see, as Mikhail Gorbachev did, that their reforms would be sabotaged by other officials and the bureaucracy. In Egypt, Anwar el-Sadat's efforts at making peace with Israel as a precondition for far-reaching economic reforms led to his assassination. Underestimates are more difficult to document because they invariably result in the failure to initiative any kind of meaningful change. It only becomes possible to do so when we can make good intra-case comparisons. John Kennedy thought it impossible to get any significant civil rights bill through the Congress, but Lyndon Johnson proved him wrong. Of course, he may have benefitted from the changed political climate in the aftermath of his predecessor's assassination.

Over- and underestimates of freedom to act must be fairly common, especially in democracies where calculations can involve the decisions and interactions of multiple actors . Uncertainty provides an incentive for leaders to test the waters and to proceed or draw back depending on the kind of support or opposition they encounter. A recent example is President Joe Biden's failed attempts to gain congressional support for his infrastructure program, enhancement of voting rights, or changing the rules governing filibusters.

Many factors can influence leader assessments of their political authority. The success or failure with prior initiatives is no doubt important. So too are estimates by their associates or those on whom they would have to depend for support. Historical precedent counts as well. Brown and Lebow also point to the belief of some leaders – among them, Sadat and Gorbachev – that their skill and self-confidence would enable them to do what other leaders could not. No doubt, there are also leaders who err on the side of caution. Leonid Brezhnev may qualify, and some of the prominent Social Democrats of the Weimar era.

Role models are also important. They not only help shape beliefs about fragility, but help legitimate and delegitimize certain kinds of responses to fragility, and may influence leader assessments of their freedom of action. Our authors note the importance of revolutionary France, the collapse of Weimar Republic, and the failure of the Soviet Union as templates used by subsequent leaders to make all three kinds of assessment. They indicate that leaders in different countries can draw opposing lessons from the same event, and the same countries, the same leaders, can switch from one lesson to its opposite as conditions change. Lebow notes that Prussia and Britain drew different policy lessons from the French Revolution and then reversed their understandings. Prussia went from liberalization to repression, and Britain from repression to liberalization.

Chinese leaders and analysts came to see Gorbachev as a negative role model. They rightly understand Gorbachev's reforms as setting in motion a political process that led to the demise of communism in the Soviet Union and Eastern Europe and the breakup of the Soviet state. The Chinese elite has accordingly become extremely sensitive to the risks of democratic political change. They ordered the Tiananmen Square massacre while Gorbachev was at the height of his authority, and in retrospect, defend it as a proper and necessary response to organized opposition. Even Chinese who had once seen Gorbachev's perestroika as an inspiration and guide for China changed their views and reluctantly concluded that the CCP under Deng, not the CPSU under Gorbachev, had followed the correct path.[54]

Our authors suggest that the lessons leaders learn say at least as much about them and the situations they confront as they do about the countries or events on which these lessons are based. Lebow argues that liberalization was alien to Prussian political culture and a measure adopted only in extremis to retain and mobilize support among the population for the struggle with France. Repression was an exceptional strategy in Georgian Britain, where cooption and accommodation were the norm. It is not surprising that the pendulum swung in the other direction from Prussia once fear of domestic revolution subsided. As with France and its revolution, many possible lessons might have been learned from Gorbachev's reforms and the subsequent collapse of communism and the Soviet Union. The Chinese could have mimicked the British, who recognized that the collapse of the *ancien régime* in France was due to its failure to reform, but also that to succeed, reform had to be gradual and carefully managed. To understand why the Chinese elite learned the particular lessons they did we must look at the political culture and history of the Chinese communist party. Here, the lesson of the Cultural Revolution – that arousing the masses is certain to lead to chaos – predisposed Chinese leaders and intellectuals to understand the Soviet experience in a particular light.[55]

Role models may serve just as often as justifications for policies adopted for different reasons as they do as templates for formulating policy. Lebow offers the example of the 1989–90 debate in Germany over intervention as part of NATO in the former Yugoslavia. Arguments for and against turned on two different readings of German identity and of Nazi Germany as a negative role model. They led to two different policy lessons – no more war and no more Auschwitz – that were mobilized to support or oppose intervention. A third reading, that invoked 1914 and its lessons, made the case for caution on the grounds that the Balkans were a tinder keg.[56]

Douglas Webber examines the freedom from constraints, and actor understandings of the constraints they face, in the Eurozone, refugee, Brexit, and Coronavirus crises. Each crisis posed different kinds of challenges and its resolution involved different EU institutions and arrangements with member governments. These crises run the gamut in the degree of constraints acting on leaders, with arguably the least leeway in the Corona crisis. EU leaders and institutional officials were reasonably good at assessing their relative freedom of action; one of the reasons they surmounted these crises was their judgments about what kinds of initiatives were politically feasible.

The one exception was Brexit, where the constraints on the British side were greatly exaggerated by British leaders. Webber argues that British Prime Minister David Cameron had significant freedom of action. He did not have to propose a referendum but did so because he greatly exaggerated the threat posed to his position by his own anti-European backbenchers and by the soon to implode United Kingdom Independence Party. Even with a referendum, Cameron might have insisted on a 60 percent majority for Brexit to be implemented. Other British political actors misjudged their freedom of action. In autumn 2019, the Labour Party and the Liberal Democrats passed up an opportunity to overthrow the minority government of Prime Minister Boris Johnson and install a coalition government that could have called a second referendum. The most far-reaching manifestation of political disintegration that occurred in the EU after 2010 was accordingly the most contingent and the one that could most easily have been avoided.

In light of his assessments of these several crises Webber concludes that so-called structures are never so constraining as to remove any scope for political choice. Actors and actor constellations always matter, if to varying degrees. Situations can also evolve and change in ways that reduce or increase the likelihood of successful crisis management. In contrast to Cameron, Labour leaders, and Theresa May, clever leaders often find ways of manipulating key features of context to give themselves more latitude. Constraints can enable agency, according to Webber. Paul Petzschmann provides another example in his account of the ambitious reform proposals of Social Democratic politician Hans Staudinger and jurist Arnold Brecht. While Staudinger championed a version of Weimar Keynesianism through his proposal for a "communal economy," Brecht drafted far-reaching plans for reform that would have transformed Germany's disparate state administrations into an effective unitary state. Both men's belief in the system's robustness and assessment of the way it constrained political actors, created the space to conceive reforms they thought had a reasonable chance of success.

Lebow provides a more general discussion of leader assessments of their freedom to act. He suggests that leader goals are difficult to separate from their estimates of authority. Goals can expand and contract in response to what leaders consider feasible. This was apparent in the response of the US Supreme Court and successive American presidents to the civil rights movement. The famous 1954 Brown vs. the Board of Education Supreme Court decision that found segregated schooling inherently unequal was a milestone. The unanimity of the nine justices was made possible by leaving out of the decision any requirements for enforcement.[57] With more liberal justices, later court decisions were more interventionist.[58]

President Kennedy concluded, perhaps with reason that meaningful civil rights legislation would have to wait until his second term. In the aftermath of his assassination, President Johnson forged ahead with civil rights legislation, and brushed aside the objections of segregationists and their threats of filibuster.[59] His advisors told him the bill would fail and cost the president considerable political capital. To their surprise, Johnson achieved his goal: the first civil rights bill with "teeth" ever passed by the congress. He did so by exploiting Webber's structural opportunities. He manipulated Senate rules, exercised exquisite timing, and used a combination of carefully calibrated bribes and threats based on his intimate knowledge of what really mattered to friends and foes alike in the Congress. His maneuverings had the effect of increasing the constraints on his opponents and the pressures on those who were wavering in their support of the legislation.[60]

Constraints figured prominently in the calculations of Soviet leaders. Archie Brown writes that "Far from being unavoidable, fundamental reform was a nettle that would be grasped only by an unusually bold Soviet leader." Gorbachev was such a leader, but even he treaded cautiously at the outset. He introduced changes in a limited number of domains leaving others untouched. In the first five years of his leadership, the economy remained under the control of the technocratic Chairman of the Council of Ministers, Nikolay Ryzhkov. Some of Gorbachev's most dramatic initiatives required considerable support from other relevant officials, as did his withdrawal of Soviet troops from Afghanistan.[61] He also exploited structural opportunities and accidents (i.e., Matthias Rust landing his Cessna in Red Square, and Chernobyl) to retire numerous officials opposed to his radical reforms.[62]

Brown argues that Gorbachev coped well with stress. The General Secretary's seeming calm may have been due in part to his ability to convince himself that he would succeed in both his accommodation with the West and use of domestic reforms to generate pressure from below on recalcitrant bureaucrats and party officials. Lebow suggests that Gorbachev convinced himself in the face of considerable evidence to the contrary that the communist party could be transformed through glasnost and made a vehicle for positive reform; that he could shift his base of power from the communist party to democratic elements in the Soviet Union; that political change in Eastern Europe would bring "little Gorbachevs" to power who would be his natural allies; that the Cold War would end as a compromise between blocs, not with the disintegration of the Soviet Union; and that democratization would strengthen, not weaken, the Soviet Union. With respect to each goal Gorbachev was strongly motivated to exaggerate his ability to do what he thought necessary and appeared to deny for some time accumulating evidence to the contrary.[63]

Brown identifies Boris Yeltsin as the principal agent of the Soviet Union's disintegration. Yeltsin used his authority as Chairman the Congress of People's Deputies of the Russian Republic and then as its President, following his election in June 1991, to boost his own authority and Russian priorities at the expense of the Union. He steered through the Congress of Deputies a declaration of Russian sovereignty and then began by fiat to transfer rights and resources from the USSR to Russia in what became known as the "War of Laws."[64] In contrast to Gorbachev, Yeltsin had few, if any, illusions about what he was doing. His political judgments were accurate when it came to his ability to rally Muscovites against the coup, to increase his own authority by strengthening Russia. He judged correctly that the constraints that would have stood in the way in the past had all but evaporated due to the disillusion of vast numbers of people with the communist party and the Soviet state.

Once again, our cases show considerable variation, this time in leader assessments of their freedom to act and the kinds of constraints they faced. Some leaders facing constraints accepted them and limited their objectives. Others sought means of freeing themselves from these constraints, most often by attempting to increase or dramatize the constraints affecting their adversaries. Lyndon Johnson and Mikhail Gorbachev did this to introduce reforms considered unrealistic by observers. They both succeeded in the short term, but their reforms had dramatically different longer-term effects. Civil rights legislation and the Great Society strengthen the American republic whilst Glasnost, perestroika, and accommodation with the West undermined the Soviet Union.

Denial

Denial is a common mechanism to which people turn to reduce the anxiety that disconfirming or threatening information arouses. Leaders are well known to distort, ignore, or explain away such information, and take refuge in their illusions. They may also punish naysayers and those who warn them that their present or intended course of action is unlikely to succeed. Leaders and many high officials of the Austro-Hungarian and Russian empires in the decade before World War I engaged in extensive denial.[65] The same can be said of political elites in GDR in the period preceding the fall of the Iron Curtain.[66]

Our flowchart suggested a logical progression from assessments of fragility to the search for appropriate responses, and then to the political feasibility of enacting them. As noted, the flowchart is an ideal type and real-world actors do not always progress in this order. Their estimates of fragility and of advisable responses are frequently conditioned by their estimates of their freedom to act. If they lack the necessary authority, or if the threats they perceive are thought to be insurmountable, they have little political or psychological incentive to acknowledge the fragility of their order. Denial is most likely in these circumstances. It is a strategy that aims to reduce the anxiety aroused by threats that people believe they can do little to nothing to avert. Instead, they distance themselves from the problem or deny warnings and other threatening information. Leaders can rig the feedback networks of government to provide only positive information and the dismissal of threatening information as well as the people responsible for it.[67]

Another response to this situation is the "hot potato" strategy. Leaders acknowledge the problem but convince themselves that the status quo can continue long enough for the real crisis to come on their successor's watch. Margaret Thatcher treated the Falklands-Malvinas as a hot potato and tried to string along the Argentines with negotiations that led nowhere and were not intended to. The Argentines understood what was happening and forced the issue through preparations for invasion. The British missed or ignored the military buildup and associated even public warnings because they were in denial.[68] A costly domestic example of the hot potato strategy is the response of President James Buchanan to the secession of southern states. Weeks after Lincoln was elected as his successor, Southern states began seceding from the Union, precipitating the American Civil War. The lame duck Buchanan angered the North by not stopping succession and infuriated the South by not acceding to it. He supported the ill-fated Corwin Amendment in an effort to reconcile the country, but it was too little too late. He made an unsuccessful attempt to reinforce the defenders of Fort Sumter, but otherwise refrained from any military preparations. Many contemporaries blamed him for the war, and he was much reviled after his presidency.[69] As these examples indicate, both denial and hot potato can in different ways make matters worse.

Denial can exacerbate fragility, although its effects can take some time to become manifest. The leaders and most of the elites of the Austro-Hungarian and Russian empires in the nineteenth and early twentieth centuries refused to believe they were living on borrowed time. The novels of Joseph Roth and Robert Musil dramatize an Austro-Hungarian empire on the edge of collapse and the blindness of their leaders, officials, and many ordinary people to what is in store. But these novels were written in retrospect, after World War I and the Empire's disappearance. Leaders and top officials in all of these countries felt confident enough in the robustness of their orders to go to war in 1914. Franz Ferdinand was most unusual in his earlier prediction that a war between Austria and Russia would destroy both empires.[70]

These examples illustrate that under- and overestimates of stability have important consequences in terms of actor responses. Belief in robustness can sometimes be made self-fulfilling, but only in orders that are reasonably robust. If a majority of people believe their order to be robust, they are more likely to act in ways that make it appear this way to others. Their behavior in turn can enhance robustness. Inflated estimates of robustness are probably more likely to make leaders or political elites unreasonably confident and possible willing to risk behavior that makes their orders even more fragile. Far more likely in this circumstance is unwillingness to take such risks and sticking to the status quo. Biding time in fragile orders can postpone the inevitable. If lucky, the order might survive long enough to benefit from changing conditions over which leaders have little to no control. Many political orders have benefitted from world rises in the prices of raw commodities on which their societies are major producers.

Exaggerations of vulnerability can have equally divergent consequences. Ned Lebow recounts how in England in the decades after the Glorious Revolution fears of disorder were greatly exaggerated. They prompted repression but made the regime more pliant in other respects and keener to build support among wider constituencies. These fears became acute again after the French Revolution and led to a new series of repressive measures. They were never serious enough to stimulate the kind of popular backlash that might have raised the prospect of revolution.[71] The British were clever and lucky. The French Revolution's failure to find wide support among the masses in Britain – most rallied in support of king and country – convinced many parliamentarians to support Catholic Emancipation and the extension of the electoral franchise. These reforms proved central to Victorian stability and the country's evolution into a stable democracy.[72] In this instance, reforms bought leaders some breathing room, encouraging them to take further measures aimed at making their orders more robust. Alternatively, leaders may be content with what they have accomplished as they consider their orders less fragile. American efforts to address the civil rights issue in the late twentieth century offers examples of both responses.[73]

Outcomes

Our book focuses on the understandings political actors have of robustness and fragility and the responses they think appropriate. In this section, we engage the political world directly and explore some of the possible consequences of policy choices.

Interpretivists have long been aware of the interactions between our understandings of the world and the way in which it functions. Our conceptions can be made to some degree self-fulfilling, or alternatively, can prompt or accelerate unanticipated change. The links between beliefs and behavior are varied and complicated in their mechanisms and effects. One of the principal reasons for this is that outcomes are the aggregation of the behavior of multiple actors, whose interactions are difficult to predict.

With respect to fragility, leader initiatives can backfire, or be perceived to have failed, heightening perceptions of fragility. Failed initiatives and subsequent efforts at repression can set in motion an escalating spiral of new demands, failure to respond, more opposition and repression, and result in greater fragility. The Russian empire in the first decades of the twentieth century is the classic example. More recently, Syrian President Bashar al-Assad appears to have succeeded, with Russian assistance, in crushing the opposition to his rule, although largely destroying his country in the process.[74] As we write, Aleksandr G. Lukashenko, the dictator of Belarus, is beating up and arresting demonstrators.[75] In Myanmar, the ruling generals sought to gain some legitimacy by allowing carefully controlled elections and a civilian government. This "openness" proved too threatening to them, so they arrested the prime minister and others, provoking street protests, to which they responded by firing on the demonstrators.[76]

Similar developments can be found in post-Soviet Russia. In January 2021, police arrested more than 10,000 people at protests on consecutive weekends in January, according to independent monitor OVD-Info, including nearly 1,500 on the day opposition leader Alexei Navalny was sentenced to three-and-a-half years in prison. Nearly 1,300 demonstrators were sentenced to brief jail terms in Moscow and St Petersburg alone, while more than 90 faced more serious criminal charges. At least 140 protesters were beaten by police according to Apologia Protest, a public defenders' association that represents some of the demonstrators.[77] Our book goes to press several months after Russia's invasion of Ukraine, an initiative that clearly failed to achieve Putin's objective of a quick conquest of that country. It is too early to tell how the war will end and of its consequences for Putin's rule. Reports from Russia indicate the stalled and costly war has accelerated protests against the regime and efforts to suppress protestors and opponents.[78]

Ludvig Norman documents how the dominant "lesson" of Weimar – the political threat to democracy of mobilized masses – was central to the European project. From the very beginning, serious efforts were made to insulate regional institutions from democratic control and interference. Functionalism embraced and complemented this lesson by stressing the advantages of giving authority to experts. The understanding of democracy as fragile thus came to shape the institutional structure of European postwar cooperation. The consequences of these ideas and the cooperative arrangements that were put in place as a result were double-edged. Norman suggests that fear of democracy and the commitment to more technocratic forms of policymaking may account in part for the rather remarkable success and robustness of European cooperation over many decades. At the same time, they were responsible for the so-called democratic deficit that had made wide swathes of European opinion wary of the EU and stands in the way of meaningful democratization.

The same process was evident in some member states. Norman observes that Western European countries in general, and those of

Northern European in particular, greatly expanded their welfare and other state services in the postwar era. The functionalist approach to state functions encouraged bureaucrats, and some politicians, to view administration as largely technocratic in nature and to consider democratic governance a form of interference. In parallel, the second half of the twentieth century also saw the expansion of democracy in new social spheres.[79] The enduring tensions between pressures to democratize and to protect are in evidence today, in societies experiencing the increasingly palpable presence of far-right populist parties, as well as at the EU level.[80]

The Weimar lesson casts a long shadow. Fascism rose to power on the back of angry, mobilized people who rejected the political order. As we have seen, it prompted many observers to conclude that democracy had to be protected from the people. Among the most influential in this regard was Joseph Schumpeter, who sought to insulate the market and economic institutions from political interference.[81] His writings, those of Friedrich Hayek, and the network created and sustained by the Mt. Pelerin Society, were foundational to neoliberalism, which became the guiding economic philosophy within the EU.[82] The democratic deficit within the EU – and in constituent governments more generally, as Peter Breiner argues – was a major stimulant of alienation, the growth of antidemocratic, right-wing political movements.

Breiner, as noted, makes the strongest case for possible perverse effects associated with perceptions of democracy's fragility. He argues that minimalist accounts of democracy that espouse stylized understandings of populism encourage these theorists to offer proposals to shore up democratic regimes in ways that are likely produce responses diametrically opposed to what they intend. Their "solutions" encourage the political alienation and anti-system politics they are trying to overcome. He roots their approach in the Weimar lesson and the minimalist conceptions of democracy it spawned.

Ned Lebow tells a more positive story about unintended effects. It concerns Britain's transition from an aristocratic-authoritarian regime in the Georgian era to a more democratic one in Victorian times. Parliamentarians and others supporting Catholic Emancipation, doing away with rotten boroughs, extending the franchise, thought they were making concessions that would coopt opposition groups or future opponents, and by doing so preserve the existing order.[83] Instead, they set in motion a chain of events that undermined the old order in large part and set the stage for modern, mass politics and democracy. Support for the status quo was unwittingly the vehicle for its positive and peaceful transformation.[84]

Archie Brown offers another example of unintended consequences and this one at some remove from cause and effect. Stalin sought to make the Soviet Union "national in form, socialist in content." In doing so, he was oblivious to its longer-term consequences because he did not realize that basing administrative structures on national territories would institutionally reinforce national consciousness within the multinational Soviet state. The Stalin–Hitler Pact of 1939 allowed Stalin to annex the Baltic States and Western Ukraine. The latter was a hotbed of Ukrainian nationalism in 1989–90, and the former were the first units to declare their independence from the Soviet Union. Absent a national structure and these annexations, Brown reasons, the Soviet Union would have been more secure because nationalism would have been less pronounced.[85] Perhaps the most dramatic example of unintended consequences is theorized by Andrew Lawrence. He contends that the stability of the global political order, and the discourses and practices that underpin it, is undermining the robustness of our political and social orders in the fundamental sense of making the planet unlivable.

These multiple examples highlight the difficulty of assessing the longer-term consequences of any response to either perceived fragility or robustness. Even interventions that succeed in the short term have unknowable effects in the longer term. We cannot assume that seeming moves towards robustness or fragility will prove self-reinforcing. Some of the reasons that appear to make orders more robust in the present moment could make them less so in the future. Chebel d'Appollonia's chapter offers a nice illustration of this phenomenon in the United States. As we have repeatedly observed, short-term understandings of robustness and fragility and what interventions are likely to influence them are very difficult to come by, and for multiple reasons. Longer-term understandings are much more uncertain, if not altogether unpredictable.

Many physical and biological system tend toward equilibrium, which facilitates forecasts or even predictions. In politics, there is no evidence for this phenomenon, quite the reverse. Political orders of all kinds are constantly evolving, although leaders and analysts often mistakenly believe they return to or stay close to equilibrium.[86] In systems that tend to equilibrium fragility and robustness can be defined with reference events or processes that maintain equilibrium or bring about shifts to new equilibria. In politics, this is not possible. Robustness, as noted in the introduction, requires orders to evolve in ways that respond to changing material and ideational conditions and the demands they generate. This is the major reason why we can only make judgments with confidence about robustness and fragility after the fact. In the absence of

Conclusions 299

prior knowledge, there is no real way of knowing the longer-term consequences of our interventions.

Overcoming one set of constraints – those standing in the way of reforms, for example – can put a leader, an order, or a country, up against a second set of pressures and constraints, as Gorbachev discovered. Politicians are constantly evaluating their power and ability to influence others and doing what they can to gain more. In the process, they make judgments about their power and influence, that of competitors and of key gatekeepers. It is not surprising that they are better able to estimate what is politically possible than the likely consequences of their initiatives. Policy outcomes, as noted, are usually the product of much more elaborate and complicated aggregation. They require a different kind of analysis, knowledge, and skill set, not one we think most politicians possess. It may also be that political constellations within governments are more labile and manipulable than the institutions that must implement reforms and the public who must respond appropriately.

Archie Brown tells us that Gorbachev began by believing that the changes he espoused would improve the Soviet system through economic innovation, cultural relaxation, and a widening of the limits of what was politically possible. After three years in office he concluded that the system needed to be democratized and instituted competitive elections and a wide range of political freedoms.[87] Brown quotes Gorbachev's later recognition that since "the CPSU and state institutions were ineluctably interwoven a weakening of the party led to a weakening of the state." Lebow observes an even greater irony in the Soviet system. Centralization gave the general secretary power to initiate the kind of sweeping changes that could not be made by a democratic leader, but efforts to decentralize authority and increase political participation, undermined the authority, not only of the leader, but of the political system.[88] As Brown, observes, Gorbachev's public plea to Eastern Europeans to follow his example brought about significant shifts of power in the region, quickly putting an end to communist rule. Estonians, Latvians, Lithuanians, Georgians and Western Ukrainians – and other Soviet nationalities in their wake – grew bolder in their demands for national self-determination. Increasingly, they saw no reason why they should be deprived of the independent statehood now exercised by Poles, Czechs, and Hungarians. Demands for greater autonomy gave way to those for separate statehood.

As a general rule, it seems likely that leaders who can act with relative impunity have the most leeway to introduce really major changes in their political order. But these reforms also have a greater propensity to undermine the order. Elected officials in democratic orders face all kinds of constitutional and other political checks on their authority, as both Donald Trump and Joe Biden discovered in quite different ways. Leaders may occasionally succeed in strengthening their orders by far-reaching transformations, as Bismarck did during and after the unification of Germany. His carefully calibrated policy of repression, concessions and three victorious wars built a seemingly robust political order. Although it became apparent to many in retrospect, that the political order and Germany's position in Europe could only be maintained by somebody with Bismarck's extraordinary political skills and restraint.[89]

Brown notes a well-known mechanism that helps to explain popular mobilization, especially in situations characterized by high risks of violent repression. When people see that thousands of their fellow-citizens are defying a despotic regime, they will be much more willing to join the resistance. This was true of the Muscovites who took to the streets to halt the coup against Gorbachev in August 1991. In 2020, it was evident in the large-scale and sustained peaceful protests in Belarus against Alexander Lukashenko's rigged reelection and also in Myanmar against the general's coup de main. Mary Sarotte describes the return of East German vacationers to East Berlin as the catalyst for the series of events that led quickly to the unraveling of that country. Crowds swelled along the railway lines bringing back those who wanted to leave the country in fourteen so-called Freedom Trains, and then in town squares, effectively paralyzing the regime.[90]

Archie Brown suggests that these developments influenced political thinking elsewhere in the world. Gorbachev's transformation of Soviet foreign policy and the fall of Communism in Eastern Europe changed political calculations in South Africa. He cites Adrian Guelke on how Gorbachev's liberalizing change in Eastern Europe undermined the apartheid government's increasing reliance "on anti-communism to justify its policies internationally, particularly as any residual sympathy for racial oligarchy in the Western world faded."[91] The African National Congress in turn was encouraged to enter into dialogue with the apartheid regime to negotiate the transition to full democratic rights for the majority of the population.[92] The "Arab Spring" might be considered another parallel to the Soviet Union in the sense that it began with protests and internal changes in Tunisia but quickly affected other Middle Eastern countries in an amplifying ripple effect.[93]

Douglas Webber rather describes a process of consolidation through crisis. EU's largely successful responses to successive crises demonstrated its robustness and even deepened its integration in some areas. Brexit was the big exception as it led to a loss of an important member.

Conclusions   301

The refugee crisis did not lead to the breakup of the EU, but resulted in a reduction in the level of integration of refugee policy, in the scope of borderless travel in the Schengen zone, and in the authority of EU organs, notably the Commission and the ECJ. A decade of crises produced almost simultaneous and definitely divergent patterns of political integration and disintegration, he argues, that cannot be explained by either optimistic or pessimistic theories of integration.[94]

The two crises from which the EU emerged more closely integrated were handled differently in key respects. The Eurozone conflict was settled by unilateral intervention of the European Central Bank, which had sufficient authority to act without having to cobble together a consensus among member states. The deep distributional conflict over the COVID recovery fund was addressed by Franco-German leadership that, in time-honored fashion, forged a compromise agreeable to member states. The most important common feature of these two crises was that policy was made within tight and widely recognized normative, economic, legal, and domestic political constraints. There was no attempt to transcend or bypass them. Webber reasons that structurally constrained policymakers with restricted choices are more likely to come up with more order-stabilizing policies. This may be because of the consultative and integrative nature of the processes by which their decisions were reached provided greater legitimacy and therefore greater consent of those whose cooperation was essential to make their responses work.

For Webber, agency plays a prominent role in the EU, but laws, norms, established procedures, tradition, and political constraints dictate the kinds of choices that can be made. The pathways they encourage or allow keep actors on track. The exceptionalism of crisis is nevertheless important. It makes actors aware of the possibility of complete breakdown, compelling them to put aside lesser concerns. Actor choices, however constrained, can still have largely unforeseen consequences. Here there are striking parallels between the policies of Cameron and Gorbachev. Both miscalculated the way in which their initial actions would trigger processes that would work against their objectives.

Contingency and Timing

Contributions to our volume illustrate how outcomes in politics are often highly contingent. Archie Brown is very critical of the widespread determinism among Western analysts of the Soviet Union. Many of these commentators insist that the Soviet Union was in crisis in the mid-1980s; that reform was an unavoidable response to that crisis; and that any reforms were doomed to fail since Communism was unreformable. These propositions found few, if any, voices prior to Gorbachev, but were increasingly popular in the aftermath of perestroika and the Soviet collapse. Brown argues that the first two claims are wrong and the third an oversimplification. The end of Communist rule in Europe – not just in the Soviet Union – owed much to agency of particular leaders, especially a leader of the Communist Party of the Soviet Union unlike any of his predecessors. His choice was highly contingent and his reform program, as noted, was impacted by other, independent catalysts like Chernobyl.

Brown's conclusions are supported by George Breslauer and Ned Lebow, who use counterfactual experiments involving several possible Soviet and American leaders to explore diverse patterns of possible interaction, ranging from a different kind of settlement to intensification of the Cold War. They conclude that communism and the Soviet Union were likely doomed in the long term but might have endured for decades longer and their ultimate demise might have come about in different ways and as the result of different catalysts.[95] Counterfactual probing of East German politics offers more evidence for contingency. If General Secretary Erich Honecker had let vacationers and others leave the country through Hungary and Czechoslovakia he may well have delayed the mobilization of East Germans. Alternatively, if Honecker, or successor, Egon Krenz, had used force at the outset, it might have had the same effect. Whether East Germany could have survived in the longer term without the Soviet Union is doubtful. Douglas Webber employs counterfactuals in his chapter to consider the causes and contingency of the outcomes of his four EU crises. In only marginally different circumstances, he suggests, some of these crises would not have occurred or could have been resolved more or less effectively. Neither the crises nor their outcomes were preordained. He speculates that, Brexit aside, the EU may have been more lucky than robust in the last decade. We should not exclude the possibility that future crises, occurring amidst less fortuitous background conditions, will have a more destructive impact on the EU.

Timing is another important element of contingency. Seemingly marginal or out-of-the-blue events (e.g., Chernobyl, Matthias Rust's flight to Red Square) can create opportunities for change or establish self-reinforcing pathways from which it becomes increasingly difficult to diverge.[96] Situations that were once fluid become increasingly determined. The presence and timing of catalysts of all kinds is another cause of contingency.[97] They do not necessarily appear when conditions for change are ripe. Necessary catalysts often have causes quite independent from the events they are subsequently seen to have triggered, as was true of the assassinations that led to World War I.[98] Paul Petzschmann and Douglas Webber see the timing of catalysts or other events as critical to the outcomes of the Weimar Republic and several EU crises. In the absence of the Great Depression, the Weimar Republic might have survived, and much smaller changes would have forestalled a referendum on the EU in the UK or have led to a different outcome.

Conclusions

We have treated robustness as a positive good and fragility an evil – at least from the perspective of those in leadership positions. Here, we would like to suggest that the "sweet spot" for leaders should be somewhere between overconfidence in robustness and hypervigilance of fragility. The principal pushes for reform usually come from below but require the acquiescence of those in power. Some degree of tension and perceived threat is thus beneficial to the longer-term survival of political orders. It is likely to keep leaders on their toes, make them more alert and responsive to constituent demands, and even to extend the benefits of order to populations previously excluded and exploited. Taking robustness and survival for granted is likely to do the reverse. Some threat and tension, and the concern for fragility that it can arouse – while never welcome by status quo-oriented leaders and elites – can nevertheless prove to be in their interest and that of their orders. Threats and tension offer an incentive to address problems, inequalities, dissatisfaction, alienation, and opposition that might otherwise become more pronounced and threatening to existing orders.

There is a related conceptual point we want to make. In the introduction, we suggested how tempting it is to conceive of robustness and fragility as a binary. To some degree this is a useful framing because these political states are political opposites. It can nevertheless be misleading because they are closely related in the sense that the conditions seemingly responsible for one of them may also promote the other. Sometimes this happens sequentially, as Archie Brown suggests it did in the Soviet Union in the transition from Brezhnev and his short-lived successors to Gorbachev. Under these two leaders, centralized power and ideology had divergent consequences for fragility. In their treatment of Weimar and its lessons, Peter Breiner and Paul Petzschmann suggest a parallel. Federal and state bureaucracies helped to maintain order under Weimar but then became a tool for Hitler to consolidate his personal power.

Ariane Chebel d'Appolonia convincingly demonstrates how these divergent effects can occur simultaneously. The constitutional mechanisms that consolidated American democracy and its associated political cultures also helped to make them more fragile. The widespread belief in democratic values is counterbalanced by an intense political polarization of the meaning and scope of those values. External shocks – the 9/11 terrorist attacks – and internal ones – school shootings and the riots at the Capitol in January 2021 – energized efforts to secure national unity but also encouraged greater societal fragmentation and political division. Ludvig Norman argues in a similar vein that reliance on functionalist organization and technocratic politics is important in explaining the EU's robustness. At the same time, this form of institutionalization has created tensions and made the European political order vulnerable to criticisms for not living up to its stated democratic aspirations.

The seemingly opposing states of robustness and fragility are connected in another more indirect way. Seeming robustness and overconfidence are closely connected, as was evident in the Soviet Union, and the United States where seeming stability encouraged robustness, that in turn blinded leaders to conditions ultimately responsible for fragility. In the case of the Soviet Union, it also led directly to initiatives that destroyed the political order. Perceptions of fragility often prompt repression in lieu of any efforts to address serious problems, and they, at most, buy time for the political order while further depriving it of any legitimacy.

These findings support our prior point about there being a "sweet spot" in leader and elite perceptions. But the reality of political life rarely involves acceptance of nuance, uncertainty, or even moderation in claims and goals. Our chapters suggest that leader assessments are relatively stable, but by no means accurate, and when changes occur, they are more likely to be dramatic than gradual. Retrospective analysis indicates that leader and elite assessments bear only a passing relationship to any reality, but are critical in their understanding and responses to that reality. We have only scratched the surface in exploring this connection, but we hope, have convinced readers of its importance.

Notes

1 Charles Kindleberger, *The World in Depression, 1929-1939* (Berkeley, CA: University of California Press, 1973), "Dominance and Leadership in the International Economy: Exploitation, Public Goods, and Free Rides," *International Studies Quarterly* 25 no. 2 (1981), and "Dominance and Leadership in the International Economy," p. 243 Douglas Webber, *European Disintegration? The Politics of Crisis in the European Union* (London: Red Globe Press, 2019) pp. 44–45.
2 Webber, *European Disintegration?* pp. 106–34.

3 Human Rights Watch, *World Report 2022*, www.hrw.org/sites/default/files/media_2022/01/World%20Report%202022%20web%20pdf_0.pdf (accessed 13 January 2022).
4 Much of this research was sponsored by the Social Science Research Council or the American Council of Learned Societies and focused on the link between democracy and economic development. Prominent figures include Talcott Parsons, Walt W. Rostow, Gabriel Almond, Lucien Pye, Joseph Lapalombara. Michael Desch, *The Cult of the Irrelevant: The Waning Influence of Social Science on National Security* (Princeton, NJ: Princeton University Press, 2019); David C. Engerman, "Social Science in the Cold War," *ISIS* 101 no. 2 (2010), pp. 393–400.
5 Juan Linz, *The Breakdown of Democratic Regime: Crises, Breakdown, and Requilibration: An Introduction* (Baltimore, MD: Johns Hopkins University Press, 1978); Juan J. Linz and Alfred Stepan, *Problems of Democratic Transition and Consolidation: Southern Europe, South America, and Post-Communist Europe* (Baltimore, MD: Johns Hopkins University Press, 1996); Samuel P. Huntington, *The Third Wave: Democratization in The Late Twentieth Century* (Norman, OK: University of Oklahoma Press, 1993); Scott Mainwaring and Fernando Bizzarro, "The Fates of Third-Wave Democracies," *Journal of Democracy* 30 no. 1 (2019), pp. 99–113; Luke Martell, "The Third Wave in Globalization Theory," *International Studies Review* 9 no. 2 (2007), pp. 173–96; Larry Diamond, *Developing Democracy: Toward Consolidation* (Baltimore: Johns Hopkins University Press, 1999); Michael McFaul, "The Fourth Wave of Democracy and Dictatorship: Noncooperative Transitions in the Postcommunist World," *World Politics* 54 no. 2 (2002), pp. 212–44; Philip N. Howard and Muzammil M. Hussein, *Democracy's Fourth Wave? Digital Media and the Arab Spring* (Oxford: Oxford University Press, 2013). On democratic transitions and war, Edward D. Mansfield and Jack Snyder, "Democratization and the Danger of War," *International Security* 20 no. 1, (1995), pp. 5–38.
6 Hagen Schulz-Forberg and Bo Stråth, *The Political History of European Integration* (Oxon: Routledge, 2010).
7 Patrick T. Jackson, "The Production of Facts: Ideal-Typification and the Preservation of Politics," and Richard Ned Lebow, "Weber's Search for Knowledge," in Richard Ned Lebow, ed., *Max Weber and International Relations* (Cambridge, MA: Cambridge University Press, 2017), pp. 79–96 and 40–78.
8 Amos Tversky and Daniel Kahneman, "Extensional versus Intuitive Reason: The Conjunction Fallacy as Probability Judgment," *Psychological Review* 90 no. 2 (1983), pp. 292–315; Derek Koehler, "Explanation Imagination and Confidence in Judgment," *Psychological Bulletin* 110 no. 3 (1991), 499–519; Philip E. Tetlock and Richard Ned Lebow, "Poking Counterfactual Holes in Covering Laws: Cognitive Styles and Historical Reasoning," *American Political Science Review* 95 no. 4 (2001), pp. 829–43.
9 Kotkin, *Stalin: Paradoxes of Power, 1878-1928*, ch. 8; George Breslauer, *The Rise and the Demise of World Communism* (Oxford: Oxford University Press, 2021), ch. 7.

10 Stephen Kotkin, *Stalin: Waiting for Hitler: 1929-1941* (London: Penguin, 2017), chs. 7-8; Breslauer, *Rise and the Demise of World Communism*, ch. 10.
11 Harrison Salisbury, *The All Shook Up Generation* (New York: Harper & Row, 1958), p. 136; Simon Frith, *Sound Effects: Youth, Leisure, and the Politics of Rock and Roll* (New York: Pantheon, 1981); Glenn C. Altschuler, *All Shook Up: How Rock 'n' Roll Changed America* (New York: Oxford University Press. 2003), ch. 4.
12 Michael Crozier, Samuel Huntington and Joji Watanuki, *Crisis of Democracy: Report on the Governability of Democracies to the Trilateral Commission* (New York: New York University Press, 1975), p. 2.
13 Susan Faludi, *Backlash: The Undeclared War against American Women* (New York: Doubleday, 1991); Alisha Haridasani Gupta, "Across the Globe, a 'Serious Backlash Against Women's Rights'," *New York Times*, 4 December 2019, www.nytimes.com/2019/12/04/us/domestic-violence-international.html; Jelena Cupać and Irem Ebetürk, "The Personal is Global Political: The Antifeminist Backlash in the United Nations," *British Journal of Politics and International Relations* 22 no. 4 (2020), pp. 702–14; Katherine van Wormer, "Anti-Feminist Backlash and Violence against Women Worldwide," *Work & Society* 6 no. 2 (2008), pp. 324–37.
14 Stanford University, Martin Luther King, Jr. Research and Education Institute, "Federal Bureau of Investigation (FBI)," no date, https://kinginstitute.stanford.edu/encyclopedia/federal-bureau-investigation-fbi; Sarah Pruitt, "Why the FBI Saw Martin Luther King, Jr. as a Communist Threat," *History*, www.history.com/news/martin-luther-king-jr-fbi-j-edgar-hoover-communism; John Meroney, "What Really Happened Between J. Edgar Hoover and MLK Jr.," *Atlantic*, 11 November 2011, www.theatlantic.com/entertainment/archive/2011/11/what-really-happened-between-j-edgar-hoover-and-mlk-jr/248319/ (all accessed 2 December 2021).
15 Bart Bonikowsi, "Ethno-Nationalist Populism and the Mobilization of Collective Resentment," *British Journal of Sociology* 68 no. S1 (2017), pp. 181–213; Mark Elchardus and Bram Spruyt, "Populism, Persistent Republicanism and Declinism: An Empirical Analysis of Populism as Thin Ideology," *Government and Opposition* 51 no. 1 (2016), pp. 111–33; Noam Gidron and Peter, A. Hall, "The Politics of Social Status: Economic and Cultural Roots of the Populist Right," *British Journal of Sociology* 68 no. S1 (2017), pp. 57–84.
16 Catherine De Vries, *Euroscepticism and the Future of European Integration* (Oxford: Oxford University Press, 2018).
17 Richard Ned Lebow, Interview with Mikhail Gorbachev, Moscow, May 1989.
18 Gabrielle Wong-Parodi and Irina Feygina, "Understanding and Countering the Motivated Roots of Climate Change Denial," *Current Opinion in Environmental Sustainability* 42 (2020), pp. 60–64.
19 Evelyne Hübscher, Thomas Sattler, and Markus Wagner, M. *Does Austerity Cause Political Polarization and Fragmentation?* SSRN Electronic Journal, November 2020.
20 Richard Ned Lebow and Ludvig Norman, eds., *The Long Shadow of Weimar*, forthcoming.

Conclusions 307

21 Scott Horton, "The Weimar President," *Harper's*, 23 August 2007, http://harpers.org/archive/2007/08/hbc-90000996; Christopher R. Browning, "The Suffocation of Democracy," *New York Review of Books*, 25 October 2018.
22 Daniel Bessner and Udi Greenberg, "The Weimar Analogy," *Jacobin Magazine*, 17 December 2016, www.jacobinmag.com/2016/12/trump-hitler-germany-fascism-weimar-democracy/;
23 Sarah Churchwell, "American Fascism: It Has Happened Here," *The New York Review*, 22 June 2020, www.nybooks.com/daily/2020/06/22/american-fascism-it-has-happened-here/ (both accessed 27 April 2021).
24 Scott O. Lilienfeld, James M. Wood and Howard N. Garb, "What's Wrong With This Picture?" *Scientific American*, May 2001, https://scholarworks.utep.edu/cgi/viewcontent.cgi?article=1008&context=james_wood (accessed 1 December 2021).
25 Per Hammarlund, *Liberal Internationalism and the Decline of the State: The Thought of Richard Cobden, David Mitrany, and Kenichi Ohmae*. (Basingstoke: Palgrave Macmillan, 2005).
26 Paul Taylor, Introduction to David Mitrany, *The Functional Theory of Politics*. (London: London School of Economics, 1975), p x.
27 Leonie Holthaus, *Pluralist Democracy in International Relations: L.T. Hobhouse, G.D.H. Cole and David Mitrany* (London: Palgrave Macmillan, 2018), p. 192.
28 Hanna Arendt, *The Origins of Totalitarianism* (New York: Harvest Books,1951), p. 312.
29 Karl Löwenstein, "Militant Democracy and Fundamental Rights II," *American Political Science Review* 31 no. 4 (1937b) pp. 638–58.
30 Löwenstein, "Militant Democracy and Fundamental Rights I."
31 Anthoula Malkopoulou and Ludvig Norman, "Three Models of Democratic Self-Defence: Militant Democracy and its Alternatives," *Political Studies* 66 no. 2 (2018), pp. 442–58.
32 Karl Löwenstein, "The Union of Western Europe: illusion and reality: an appraisal of the methods," *Columbia Law Review* 52 no. 1 (1952), p. 55–99.
33 Martin Holland, "Jean Monnet and the Federal Functionalist Approach to the European Union," in Philomena Murray and Paul Rich, eds. *Visions of European Unity* (Boulder, CO: Westview Press, 1996), pp. 93–108; Cornelia Navari, "Functionalism Versus Federalism: Alternative Visions of European Unity," in Philomena Murray and Paul Rich, eds. *Visions of European Unity* (Boulder, CO: Westview Press, 1996), pp. 63-92.
34 J. C. D. Clark, *English Society 1688-1832: Ideology, Social Structure and Political Practice During the Ancien Regime* (Cambridge, MA: Cambridge University Press, 1985); Richard Price, *British Society, 1660-1880: Dynamism, Containment and Change* (Cambridge, MA: Cambridge University Press, 1999); Hilton Boyd, *A Mad, Bad, and Dangerous People? England, 1783-1846* (Oxford: Oxford University Press, 2008).
35 Joy Hakim, *War, Peace, and All That Jazz* (New York: Oxford University Press, 1995); Murray B. Levin, *Political Hysteria in America: The Democratic Capacity for Repression* (New York: Basic Books, 1972); Robert K. Murray, *Red Scare: A Study in National Hysteria, 1919–1920* (Minneapolis, MN: University of Minnesota Press, 1995).

36 Levin, *Political Hysteria in America*; Ellen Schrecker, *Many Are the Crimes: McCarthyism in America* (Boston, MA: Little, Brown, 1998).
37 Clem Brooks and Jeff Manza, *Whose Rights: Counter-Terrorism and the Dark Side of American Public Opinion* (New York: Russel Sage, 2013); Ludvig Norman "Theorizing the Social Foundations of Exceptional Security Politics: Rights, Emotions and Community," *Cooperation and Conflict* 53 no. 1 (2018), pp. 84–100.
38 Levin, *Political Hysteria in America*, is particularly good on this aspect of the Red Scares.
39 Todd H. Hall and Andrew A. G. Ross, "Affective Politics after 9/11," *International Organization* 69 no. 4(2015), pp. 847–79; Ludvig Norman, "Theorizing the Social Foundations of Exceptional Security Politics: Rights, Emotions and Community," *Cooperation and Conflict* 53 no. 4 (2018), pp. 84–100.
40 Steven Friedman and Doreen Atkinson, *The Small Miracle: South Africa's Negotiated Settlement* (Johannesburg: Ravan, 1994); Alasdair Sparks, *Tomorrow Is Another Country: The Inside Story of South Africa's Road to Change* (Chicago, IL: University of Chicago Press 1996), and *Beyond the Miracle: Inside the New South Africa* (Chicago, IL: University of Chicago Press 2006).
41 Chao, Linda, and Ramon Myers, *The First Chinese Democracy: Political Life in the Republic of China on Taiwan* (Baltimore, MD: Johns Hopkins University Press, 1998); J. Bruce Jacobs, *Democratizing Taiwan* (Leiden, The Netherlands: Brill, 2012); Larry Diamond and Byung-Kook Kim, *Consolidating Democracy in South Korea* (Boulder, CO: Lynne Rienner, 2000); John Kie-chiang Oh, *Korean Politics: The Quest for Democratization and Economic Development* (Ithaca, NY: Cornell University Press, 1999).
42 Rathbun, Realists, *Romantics and Rationality in International Relations*.
43 On the Young Turks, M. Şükrü Hanioğlu, *Preparation for a Revolution: The Young Turks, 1902–1908* (Oxford: Oxford University Press, 2001).
44 Archie Brown, "Gorbachev and the End of the Cold War" in Richard K. Herrmann and Richard Ned Lebow, eds., *Ending the Cold War: Interpretations, Causation and the Study of International Relations* (New York: Palgrave-Macmillan, 2003), pp. 31–57, and *The Rise and Fall of Communism* (New York: Vintage, 2010); Richard K. Hermann and Richard Ned Lebow, "Learning from the End of the Cold War," in Herrmann and Lebow, *Ending the Cold War*, pp. 219–38.
45 Archie Brown, *The Gorbachev Factor* (Oxford: Oxford University Press, 1997), ch. 6.
46 Interview with Mikhail Gorbachev, Moscow, 21 May 1989.
47 Brown, "Gorbachev and the End of the Cold War"; Hermann and Lebow, "Learning from the End of the Cold War"; Serhii Polkhy, *The Last Empire: The Final Days of the Soviet Union* (New York: Basic Books, 2014), pp. 29–30, 395–97.
48 Robert L. Tignor, *Anwar al-Sadat: Transforming the Middle East* (London: Oxford University Press, 2016), pp. 122–75; Thomas W. Lippmann, *Hero of the Crossing: How Anwar Sadat and the 1973 War Changed the World* (Lincoln, NE: University of Nebraska Press, 2016), chs. 2, 5.

Conclusions 309

49 Geoffrey Hosking and Robert Service, *Russian Nationalism, Past and Present* (London: Palgrave-Macmillan, 1998), p. 88.
50 See Etienne Balibar, "Dissonances within *Laïcité*," *Constellations* 11 no. 3 (2004), pp. 354–67; Myriam Hunter-Henin, "Why the French Don't Like the *Burqa*: *Laïcité*, National Identity and Religious Freedom," *The International and Comparative Law Quarterly* 61 no. 2 (2012), pp. 613–39.
51 Norimitsu Onishi, "From TV to the French Presidency? A Right-Wing Star Is Inspired by Trump," *New York Times*, 17 September 2021, www.nytimes.com/2021/09/17/world/europe/zemmour-france-presidency-trump.html; *Figaro*, "Éric Zemmour «n'a pas le droit de venir ici» : l'étonnante sentence d'un journaliste de France," 10 October 2021, www.lefigaro.fr/politique/eric-zemmour-n-a-pas-le-droit-de-venir-ici-l-etonnante-sentence-d-un-journaliste-de-france-info-20211009 (both accessed 13 October 2021); "Les résultats de l'élection présidentielle 2022," *Le Monde*, 25 April 2022, www.lemonde.fr/resultats-presidentielle-2022/ (accessed 4 July 2022).
52 Archie Brown, *The Rise and Fall of Communism* (Bodley Head, London, 2009), pp. 574–86.
53 Anthony. G. Hopkins, *American Empire: A Global History* (Princeton, NJ: Princeton University Press, 2018), pp. 107–08, 114.
54 John W Garver, *China's Quest: The History of the Foreign Relations of the People's Republic of China* (Oxford: Oxford University Press, 2018), p. 527.
55 Yang Jisheng, *The World Turned Upside Down: A History of the Chinese Cultural Revolution*, trans. Stacy Mosher and Guo Jian (New York: Farrar, Strauss, and Giroux, 2021); Pankaj Mishra, "What Are the Cultural Revolution's Lessons for Our Current Moment?" *New Yorker*, 25 January 2021, www.newyorker.com/magazine/2021/02/01/what-are-the-cultural-revolutions-lessons-for-our-current-moment (accessed 1 March 2021).
56 Alice Cooper, "When Just Causes Conflict with Acceptable Means: The German Peace Movement and Military Intervention in Bosnia," *German Politics and Society* 15 no. 3 (1997), pp. 99–118.
57 James T. Patterson, *Brown v. Board of Education: A Civil Rights Milestone and Its Troubled Legacy* (New York: Oxford University Press, 2002), pp. 46–69.
58 Ibid., pp. 118–69.
59 Robert A. Caro, *The Passage of Power*, vol. IV: *The Years of Lyndon Johnson* (New York: Random House, 2012), vol. IV, pp. 489–91.
60 Ibid., 488–91, 498, 585.
61 Richard K. Herrmann, "Regional Conflicts ad Turning Points: The Soviet and American Withdrawal from Afghanistan, Angola, and Nicaragua," and Matthew A. Evangelista, "Turning Points in Arms Control," in Richard K. Herrmann and Richard Ned Lebow, eds., *Ending the Cold War: Interpretations, Causation, and the Study of International Relations* (New York: Palgrave-Macmillan, 2004), pp. 59–82, 83–106.
62 Archie Brown, *The Gorbachev Factor* (Oxford: Oxford University Press, 1996), ch. 6.
63 Richard Ned Lebow and Janice Gross Stein, "Understanding the End of the Cold War as a Non-Linear Confluence," in Herrmann and Lebow, eds., *Ending the Cold War*, pp. 219–38.

64 Jeffrey Kahn, *Federalization, Democratization, and the Rule of Law in Russia* (Oxford University Press, Oxford, 2002), p. 94.
65 Stephen Kotkin, *Stalin: Paradoxes of Power, 1878-1928* (London: Penguin, 2015), ch. 4; John W. Mason, *The Dissolution of the Austro-Hungarian Empire 1867-1918*, 2nd ed. (London: Routledge, 1996); Pieter M. Judson, *The Habsburg Empire: A New History* (Cambridge, MA: Harvard University Press, 2018), ch. 7.
66 Mary Elise Sarotte, *The Collapse: The Accidental Opening of the Berlin Wall.* (New York: Basic Books, 2014).
67 Janis and Mann, *Decision Making*, pp. 57–58, 74, 107–33. See Lebow's chapter for an overview.
68 Richard Ned Lebow, "Miscalculation in the South Atlantic: The Origins of the Falklands War," in Robert Jervis, Richard Ned Lebow, and Janice Gross Stein, *Psychology and Deterrence* (Baltimore, MD: The Johns Hopkins University Press, 1985), pp. 89–124.
69 Michael J Birkner, ed., *James Buchanan and the Political Crisis of the 1850s* (Selinsgrove, PA: Susquehanna University Press, 1996); John W. Quist, and Michael J., Birkner, eds., *James Buchanan and the Coming of the Civil War* (Gainesville, FL: University Press of Florida, 2013).
70 Holger Afflerbach, "Topos of Improbable War Before 1914," in Holger Afflerbach and David Stevenson, eds., *An Improbable War: The Outbreak of World War I and European Political Culture Before 1914* (New York: Berghahn Books, 2007), pp. 161–82; Richard Ned Lebow, *Forbidden Fruit: Counterfactuals and International Relations* (Princeton, NJ: Princeton University Press, 2010), ch. 3.
71 Robert Tombs, *France, 1814-1914* (London: Routledge, 2014), pp. 329–53.
72 Lebow, Rise and *Fall of Political Orders*, ch. 7.
73 Julian Bond, *Eyes on the Prize: America's Civil Rights Years, 1954-1965* (New York: Penguin, 2013); Sara Bullard and Julian Bond, *Free At Last: A History of the Civil Rights Movement and Those Who Died in the Struggle* (New York: Oxford University Press, 1994).
74 Sam Dagher, *Assad or We Burn the Country: How One Family's Lust for Power Destroyed Syria* (Boston, MA: Little, Brown, 2019); Christopher Phillips, *The Battle for Syria: International Rivalry in the New Middle East*, rev. ed. (New Haven, CT: Yale University Press, 2020).
75 Ivan Nechepurenko, "'You Cannot Say No': The Reign of Terror That Sustains Belarus's Leader," *New York Times*, 14 November 2020, www.nytimes.com/2020/11/14/world/europe/belarus-lukashenko-protests-crackdown.html, and Belarus Jails 2 Journalists for Covering Protests," *New York Times*, 18 February 2021, www.nytimes.com/2021/02/18/world/europe/belarus-protests-lukashenko.html; Philip Roth, "Nicole Krauss: on stealing from life as a livelihood," *Financial Times Magazine*, 28 February 2021, www.ft.com/magazine (all accessed 28 February 20121).
76 Richard C. Paddock, "Military Crackdown in Myanmar Escalates With Killing of Protesters," *New York Times*, 1 March 2021, www.nytimes.com/2021/02/28/world/asia/myanmar-protests.html?action=click&module=Well&pgtype=Homepage&section=World%20News; Michael Safi, "Myanmar

Conclusions 311

police fire stun grenades at rally, critically injuring three protesters," *Guardian*, 2 March 2021, www.theguardian.com/global-development/2021/mar/02/myanmar-police-fire-stun-grenades-at-protesters-ahead-of-regional-talks (both accessed 2 March 2021).

77 Max Seddon, "Russian crackdown brings pro-Navalny protests to halt," *Financial Times*, 13 February 2021, www.ft.com/content/e8889644-051c-41f6-a991-6a32091e5c54 (accessed 13 February 2021).
78 Anton Troianovski, "In Putin's Russia, the Arrests Are Spreading Quickly and Widely," *New York Times*, 4 July 2022, www.nytimes.com/2022/07/04/world/europe/russia-putin-arrests.html (accessed 4 July 2022).
79 Birte Siim *Gender and Citizenship: Politics and Agency in France, Britain and Denmark*. (Cambridge, MA: Cambridge University Press, 2000).
80 Ludvig Norman (2021) "To Democratize or to Protect: How the Response to Anti-System Parties Reshapes Europe's Transnational Party System," *Journal of Common Market Studies* (published as EarlyView) https://doi.org/10.1111/jcms.13128.
81 Wolfgang Streeck, *Buying Time: The Delayed Crisis of Democratic Capitalism*, 2nd ed. (London: Verso, 2017); Paul Pierson, *Dismantling the Welfare State? Reagan, Thatcher, and the Politics of Retrenchment* (Cambridge, MA: Cambridge University Press, 1994); Angus Burgin, *The Great Persuasion: Reinventing Free Markets since the Depression* (Cambridge, MA: Harvard University Press, 2012).
82 Ibid.
83 Lebow, *Rise and Fall of Political Orders*, ch. 7.
84 J. C. D. Clark, *English Society 1688-1832: Ideology, Social Structure and Political Practice During the Ancien Regime* (Cambridge, MA: Cambridge University Press, 1985); Richard Price, *British Society, 1660-1880: Dynamism, Containment and Change* (Cambridge, MA: Cambridge University Press, 1999); Hilton Boyd, *A Mad, Bad, and Dangerous People? England, 1783-1846* (Oxford: Oxford University Press, 2008), p. 30; Lebow, *Rise and Fall of Political Orders*, ch. 7.
85 Archie Brown, *The Human Factor: Gorbachev, Reagan, and Thatcher and the End of the Cold War* (Oxford: Oxford University Press, 2020), p. 376; Serhii Plokhy, *Last Empire: The Final Days of the Soviet Union* (New York: Basic Books, 2015), pp. 400–01.
86 Lebow, *Rise and Fall of Political Orders*, ch. 3.
87 Brown, *The Rise and Fall of Communism*, pp. 101–14 and 503–21.
88 Brown, "Gorbachev and the End of the Cold War"; Hermann and Lebow, "Learning from the End of the Cold War"; Serhii Polkhy, *The Last Empire: The Final Days of the Soviet Union* (New York: Basic Books, 2014), pp. 29–30, 395–97.
89 Otto Pflanze, *Bismarck and the Development of Germany*, 3 vols. (Princeton, NJ: Princeton University Press, 1963-90).
90 Sarotte, *Collapse*, ch. 4.
91 Adrian Guelke, "The Impact of the End of the Cold War on the South African Transition," *Journal of Contemporary African Studies* 14 no.1 (1996), pp. 87–100.

92 Archie Brown, "Transnational Influences in the Transition from Communism," *Post-Soviet Affairs* 16 no. 2 (2000), pp. 177–200.
93 David W. Lesch and Mark L. Haas, eds., *The Arab Spring: Change and Resistance in the Middle East* (Boulder, CO: Westview, 2012); Mark L. Haas and David W. Lesch, *The Arab Spring: The Hope and Reality of the Uprisings*, 2nd ed., (London: Routledge, 2016).
94 Douglas Webber, "Trends in European Political (Dis)Integration. An Analysis of Postfunctionalist and other Explanations," *Journal of European Public Policy* 26 no. 8 (2019), pp. 1134–52.
95 George Breslauer and Richard Ned Lebow, "Leadership and the End of the Cold War: A Counterfactual Thought Experiment," in Herrmann and Lebow, *Ending the Cold War*, pp. 161–88.
96 Brian W. Arthur, "Competing Technologies, Increasing Returns, and Lock-in by Historical Events," *Economic Journal* 99 no. 1 (1989), pp. 116–31; Paul David "Clio and the Economics of QWERTY," *American Economic Review* 75 no. 2 (1985), pp. 332–37.
97 Paul Pierson, *Politics in Time: History, Institutions and Social Analysis* (Princeton, NJ: Princeton University Press, 2004); Ludvig Norman, *The Mechanisms of Institutional Conflict in the European Union* (Oxford: Routledge, 2016).
98 For a debate about the independence and importance of catalysts in political change, see, Richard Ned Lebow, "Contingency, Catalysts and International System Change," *Political Science Quarterly* 115 no. 4 (2000–2001), pp. 591–616; William R. Thompson, "A Streetcar Named Sarajevo: Catalysts, Multiple Causation Chains, and Rivalry Structures," *International Studies Quarterly* 47 no. 3 (2003), pp. 453–74; Richard Ned Lebow, "A Data Set Named Desire: A Reply to William P. Thompson," *International Studies Quarterly* 47 no. 3 (2003), pp. 475–58.

Index

Adichie, Chimamanda Ngozi, 141
administration, 162
Adorno, Theodor, 133, 135
African National Congress, 158, 284, 300
agency, 13, 16, 18–19, 26, 30, 37, 39,
    46–47, 132, 145, 161, 164, 166–67,
    169, 229–32, 235–36, 246–47, 250,
    252, 259, 262, 271, 273, 288, 291,
    301–2
Albania, 145, 147
alienation, 279
Andropov, Yuri, 152, 167
anti-Americanism, 144
anxiety, 37, 258, 283, 293
apartheid, 158, 284, 300
Arab Spring, 28, 34, 300
Armenians, 159
Association of South Asian Nations
    (ASEAN), 195
Atatürk, Kamal, 41, 284
Aung San Suu Kwi, 143
austerity, 119, 234, 238, 241, 279
Austria, 2, 28, 31, 33, 35, 42, 190, 244,
    257, 294
Austria-Hungary, 31, 33, 35, 42
authoritarianism, 43, 47, 58, 61, 73–75,
    141, 143, 146, 169, 209, 282
authority, 30, 32, 40–41, 43, 55, 63, 72,
    79–80, 100, 105, 121, 147, 153–54,
    162, 165, 190, 216, 219, 223, 230,
    244, 258, 261, 271, 273, 276, 278,
    285, 288–89, 291–93, 296, 299–301

backsliding, 3, 56, 59, 212
Baltic states, 16, 158, 274, 298
Batista, Fulgencio, 145
Bean, Charles, 128
Benton, Ted, 133
Berlin Wall, 28, 43, 157
biases, 12, 25, 203, 287
biosphere, 116–17, 121, 132
Black Lives Matter, 210, 221

Bloomberg, Michael, 249
Blyth, Mark, 78
bolstering, 37
Braun, Otto, 95, 109
Brecht, Arnold, 93, 95–96, 100, 102–3,
    109, 291
Brexit, 18, 191, 195, 230, 234, 236,
    247–48, 250–52, 256, 259, 261–63,
    276, 290, 300, 302
Brezhnev, Leonid, 6, 28, 40, 45, 146, 150,
    152, 154, 167, 284, 289, 303
Bricker Amendment, 207
Brüning, Heinrich, 96, 99–101, 106
Burke, Edmund, 184
Bush, George H. W., 210, 279

Cameron, David, 247–48, 290
Canovan, Margaret, 74
Carr, E.H., 184
cartel, 14, 62, 65, 78–79, 84, 282
caste, 66–67, 77, 80, 98
Castro, Fidel, 145
catalyst, 7, 10, 29, 275, 300
Catholic Emancipation, 34, 45, 295, 297
censorship, 42, 146, 160, 169, 287
Cerf, Bennett, 208
checks and balances, 204, 206, 212–13,
    216, 286
Chernenko, Konstantin, 152
Chernobyl, 41, 285, 292, 302
Chiang Kai-shek, 144
China, 7–8, 27, 32, 40, 46–47, 144–45,
    150, 247, 256, 273, 289
Christian Democratic Party (Germany),
    234, 241
Churchill, Winston, 39
civil rights, 220
civil service, 97, 100, 104, 110–11
cleavages, 61, 233
Clegg, Nick, 249
climate crisis, 15, 115–18, 124–26, 130,
    272

313

Clinton, Bill, 210
cognitive psychology, 31
Cold War, 3, 27, 41, 44, 46, 118, 160, 163, 165, 167, 169, 187–88, 208, 211, 233, 236, 273, 284–85, 292, 302
colonialism, 115, 272
Comecon, 152, 167
communism, 143, 145, 147–48, 150, 158, 166, 169, 211, 287, 300, 302
Communist Party (Soviet Union), 147, 160
Concert of Powers, 233
Congress of Vienna, 233
constraints, 18, 30, 46, 94, 108, 168, 230–32, 234, 237–38, 241, 243, 246, 248, 250–52, 259, 262, 290–93, 299, 301
Conte, Giuseppe, 257
context, 1, 9, 12, 17, 19, 26, 29, 32, 44, 46–47, 94, 96, 100, 103, 111, 117, 131, 135, 153, 176–77, 181, 192, 194, 202, 204, 207, 213, 223, 233, 237, 246, 253, 255, 258–59, 261, 270, 279, 291
Corbyn, Jeremy, 252
corona bonds, 255, 257
Council of Europe, 176, 184, 186
counterrevolution, 27
Court of Justice of the European Union, 194
COVID-19, 196
Croats, 163
Crouch, Colin, 76
Cuba, 144
cultural determinism, 169
Cyprus, 238, 240, 253
Czech Republic, 165, 246, 253
Czechoslovakia, 28, 144–45, 147, 157, 164–65, 302

Dahl, Robert, 76, 143, 213
Dahms, Harry, 130
De Klerk, F. W., 284
decommodification, 125
defensive avoidance, 37, 39, 42
Delors, Jacques, 233, 253, 271
demagogue, 61
democracy, 3–6, 8, 10–11, 13–15, 17, 34, 47, 54–58, 60–69, 71–72, 77, 80–82, 84, 92–94, 96–97, 100, 103, 105, 108–9, 111, 128, 141–43, 148, 150–51, 154, 157, 161, 166, 168–69, 176–77, 179–83, 185–89, 191, 193–94, 196, 202–19, 221–24, 233–34, 271–73, 277, 279–82, 284, 295–97, 304

democratic deficit, 187, 297
Democratic Party (United States), 208, 245, 263
democratic theory, 180, 280
democratization, 3, 16, 57, 117, 143, 150, 154–58, 161, 166, 169, 177, 187, 195–96, 292, 296
Deng Xiaoping, 150
denial, 18, 28, 40–41, 43, 115, 118, 122, 128, 204, 224, 271–72, 274–76, 278, 283, 293–94
Denmark, 191, 253, 257
depoliticization, 189
Descartes, René, 15, 115
deterrence, 45
dissent, 7, 43, 45, 161, 190, 278
Draghi, Mario, 242–43
Durnovo, Pyotr, 43

East India Company, 287
economic determinism, 169
economic policy, 72, 102, 149, 189
Eilstrup-Sangiovanni, Mette, 29
electoral college, 142
Elliott, David, 144
emergency powers, 106, 281
England, 11, 34, 44, 128, 295
equality, 13–14, 54–55, 61, 63–64, 68–69, 71, 76–77, 80–81, 83–85, 117, 121, 134, 180, 191, 202, 206, 210, 218, 282
Estonia, 16, 151, 162
Euro, 177, 189–90, 237, 239–40, 242–44, 248–50, 254, 257, 260–61, 263, 277
European Central Bank, 230, 301
European Coal and Steel Community, 185
European Commission, 229, 244, 246, 253, 261, 271, 276
European Community (EC), 176, 185, 187, 281
European Council, 230, 233, 237, 242, 247, 257
European Court of Justice, 229, 276
European Parliament, 188, 192–93, 229, 276
European Union, 2, 8, 17–18, 94, 176–77, 185, 191, 229, 239, 271, 273, 276, 281
Euroscepticism, 191
Eurozone, 18, 230, 232, 234, 236–44, 246–49, 253–56, 258–61, 263, 276, 290, 301

fake news, 4, 215
Falun Gong, 7
Farage, Nigel, 249

Index

fascism, 180–82, 185, 280–81
Faymann, Werner, 245
Federalist Papers, 206, 216
Ferdinand, Franz, 31, 33, 43, 294
Fillon, François, 263
financial crisis, 189, 191, 194, 219
Finland, 253, 257
fiscal policy, 238, 247, 254, 259, 261
foreign policy, 13, 15, 143, 149, 155, 158, 166–67, 169, 207, 217, 256, 300
fragility, 1–3, 5–15, 17–19, 25–28, 30, 35–36, 39, 43, 46–47, 54, 68, 83, 92, 94, 105, 110, 115–16, 120, 127–28, 130, 132, 134–35, 143–44, 147, 155, 157, 164, 166, 169, 176–77, 179–83, 186, 189, 191, 194, 196, 202–5, 209, 212–13, 222, 224, 231, 261, 270–75, 277, 279–80, 282, 287–89, 293–95, 297–98, 303–4
France, 3, 27, 31–32, 40, 42–43, 65, 83, 176, 204, 233, 235, 240, 255–60, 263, 271, 284, 286, 289
Free Masons, 42
Fried, Amy, 212
Friedman, Thomas, 3
Fukuyama, Francis, 211
functionalism, 94, 105, 176, 180, 182, 185, 194, 280–81

Gagarin, Yuri, 161
gatekeepers, 60
Georgians, 5, 159
German Democratic Republic (DDR), 28
Germany, Nazi, 6, 32, 93–94, 103, 105, 107, 109, 146–47, 151, 160, 163, 222, 277, 290
Germany, Weimar, 6, 14, 29, 31, 92–111, 180–81, 222, 272, 274, 277, 279–82, 289, 291, 296–97, 303
Gilens, Martin, 212
Global warming. *See* climate crisis
Goebbels, Joseph, 181
Goldman, Marshall, 149
Goldwater, Barry, 212
Gorbachev, Mikhail, 6, 16, 28–30, 32, 40–41, 44–45, 148–53, 155, 157–59, 161–62, 164, 166–67, 169, 274, 277–78, 284–85, 288–89, 292–93, 299–301, 303
Gove, Michael, 252
Great Depression, 4, 29, 97, 119, 204, 217, 219–20, 303
Greece, 65, 154, 238–41, 245–46
Guelke, Adrian, 158, 300

Habermas, Jürgen, 75
Harris, Douglas B., 212
Hartz, Louis, 209
Harvey, David, 126
Hasen, Richard, 218
Hegel, G. W. F., 15, 115, 122
hegemonic stability theory, 231
Helsinki, 161
Hilferding, Rudolf, 98
Hill, Fiona, 142
Hindenburg, Paul von, 279
historical lessons, 1, 12–13, 18, 25–26, 29, 45–47, 270, 273–74
Hitler, Adolf, 6, 31, 45, 107, 272, 279, 281, 298, 303
Hofstadter thesis, 57, 71–72
Hollande, François, 256
Hume, David, 27, 142
Hungary, 2, 6, 28, 33, 43, 60, 145, 148, 150, 156, 191, 212, 244, 246, 273, 302
Huntington, Samuel, 210
hypervigilance, 39, 303

Iceland, 253
ideology, 8, 15, 17, 32, 62, 71, 93, 103, 110, 115, 119, 121, 144, 147, 163, 165, 182, 202, 214, 272–73, 277, 279, 287, 303
inclusion, 14, 58–59, 64, 68, 75–81, 84, 134, 187, 215
influence, 1, 10, 13–14, 16, 18, 26, 29, 31, 47, 58, 61, 64, 66, 68, 70, 72, 76, 78, 80–81, 84, 105, 109, 124, 144–45, 156–58, 161, 165, 187–89, 191–94, 211–12, 216, 221, 236, 241, 251, 272–73, 288, 298–99
integration, 126, 176, 187, 194, 229–38, 241, 243–44, 247, 253, 255–56, 260–62, 271, 273, 300
intelligentsia, 8, 167
International Labour Organization, 185
international society, 229
Ireland, 11, 31, 44, 238
Iron Curtain, 293
Italy, 3, 65, 190, 242, 246, 253–55, 257, 259, 263

Jackson, Andrew, 216, 219
Janis, Irving L., 13, 26, 37, 39, 41
Jews, 159
Jim Crow, 220
John Paul II, 155
Johnson, Boris, 251–52, 290
Johnson, Lyndon B., 288, 293
Joseph II (Austria), 42

Kádár, János, 150
Kagan, Robert, 219
Kaplan, Robert, 211
Karl, Emperor of Austria, 2, 35
Kennedy, John F., 30, 206–7, 288, 291
Keynes, John Maynard, 125, 128
Keynesianism, 93, 97, 99, 119, 291
KGB, 7, 146, 149, 160
Khrushchev, Nikita S., 6, 45, 150–52, 167
Kindleberger, Charles, 271
Kipling, Rudyard, 208
Krenz, Egon, 28, 43, 302
Kryuchkov, Vladimir, 7
Kuper, Simon, 132
Kyoto Protocol, 127

Labour Party (UK), 252, 290
Laclau, Ernesto, 74
Laos, 144
Latvia, 16, 151, 162
Le Maire, Bruno, 258
League of Nations, 8, 178–79, 185, 280, 282
Lebow, Richard Ned, 1–19, 25, 204, 222, 270
legitimacy, 54–85
Lenin, Vladimir I., 27, 36, 146, 153, 275
lesser evil perspective, 205
Levitzky, Steven, 13, 282
liberal regimes, 15, 54, 68, 74, 115
liberalism, 54–55, 62, 64–67, 71, 74, 83
liberalization, 15, 149, 157, 161, 166, 170, 289
Libya, 2, 255
Lieberman, Robert C., 219
Liechtenstein, 253
Lincoln, Abraham, 218
Lindbergh, Charles, 207
Lindblom, Charles, 75
Linz, Juan, 143, 160, 168
Lipset, Seymour Martin, 208, 214
Lisbon Treaty, 188, 234
Lithuania, 16, 151, 159, 162
Locke, John, 223
Löwenstein, Karl, 6, 17, 177, 181, 281
Lukashenko, Alexander, 143, 300

Maastricht Treaty, 188, 238, 241
Mair, Peter, 73
Malthus, Thomas, 133
Malthusian, 132
manifest destiny, 208
Mann, Geoff, 134
Mann, Leon, 37
Maoism, 150

Martin, Terry, 160
Marx, Karl, 15, 106, 115, 122
Marxism-Leninism, 155, 165
Matlock, Jack, 151
meritocracy, 68
Merkel, Angela, 232, 237
Mettler, Suzanne, 219
Michnik, Adam, 159
Mikoyan, Anastas, 159
militarism, 95, 115, 127, 133, 272
military-industrial complex, 149, 160, 162, 165
Miller, Perry, 208
Milošević, Slobodan, 164
Mitchell, Timothy, 123
Mitrany, David, 177–78, 280
monetarism, 119
Monnet, Jean, 185, 229
Morgenthau, Hans, 184
Mounk, Yascha, 13, 56, 62, 282
Müller, Jan-Werner, 54
Musil, Robert, 33, 294
Myanmar, 143, 296, 300
Myrdal, Gunnar, 214

Napoleon Bonaparte, 31
National Socialism, 93, 109
nationalism, 42, 45, 67, 131, 158, 162, 164–65, 206, 209, 277, 285, 298
neoclassical economics, 115
Netherlands, 191, 257
New Deal, 61, 93, 204, 214, 216, 220
New School of Social Research, 93
New Zealand, 11
Ng, Karen, 122
Nicholas II (Russia), 43
Nixon, Richard, 217, 219
non-interference, 195
North America, 3, 33, 165, 287
North Atlantic Treaty Organization (NATO), 256
North Korea, 29, 44, 144
Norway, 253
Nove, Alec, 160
nuclear war, 118, 128

Obama, Barrack, 206, 214, 217, 240, 279
oligarchy, 65, 149, 154, 158, 300
Orbán, Viktor, 244
ordoliberalism, 241, 258
Organization for Standardization, 124
Orwell, George, 150
Osborne, George, 249
Ottoman Empire, 2

Index

Page, Benjamin, 212
Pakistan, 44
Palazhchenko, Pavel, 155
path dependency, 19
pathways, 12, 25–26, 31, 35, 44, 168, 275, 301–2
perceptions, 3, 15, 17–18, 26, 29, 35–36, 44, 46–47, 92, 115, 118, 142, 164, 176, 184, 189, 193, 195–96, 203, 232, 255, 260, 272–74, 276, 295, 297, 304
plebiscitary leadership, 107
pluralism, 76, 106, 152, 158, 214
Poland, 6, 144–45, 147–48, 155–56, 191, 212, 246, 273
populism, 13, 54–57, 62, 65–67, 71–74, 77, 82–85, 177, 192, 211, 216, 282, 297
Portugal, 3, 154, 238
power, 4, 6–7, 14, 16, 27, 30–31, 34–36, 39, 41–42, 56–57, 59–60, 64, 68–71, 75, 77–82, 84, 93, 103, 105, 107, 109–10, 117, 119, 121, 126, 129, 131, 133–34, 142–47, 149–50, 152–55, 157, 160, 162–63, 165, 167–69, 177, 183–84, 191, 203–5, 207, 213, 216, 218–19, 223, 231–33, 235–36, 241, 244, 255, 274, 277, 280–82, 285, 289, 292, 297, 299, 303
power transition theory, 231
Prague Spring, 144, 148, 157
preemption, 4
protest, 28, 81, 83–85, 143, 146, 148, 242, 275, 278
Prussia, 14, 31, 42, 94–98, 100–3, 109, 111, 289
Przeworski, Adam, 56
Putin, Vladimir, 169, 283

racism, 72, 204, 214, 219
Ramsey, Frank, 125
Rancière, Jacques, 84
Rathbun, Brian, 13, 26, 37, 39, 284
Reagan, Ronald, 39, 143, 166, 203
realism, 82, 120, 231
Realpolitik, 8
recession, 111, 189, 253, 255
referendum, 234–35, 239, 248–50, 252, 256, 290, 303
reflexivity, 115, 124, 272
reform, 14, 28–30, 40–43, 45, 47, 72, 83, 92–93, 97–98, 100–2, 106, 110–11, 119, 143, 148–50, 152–53, 166–69, 220, 256, 258, 283–85, 289, 291–92, 301, 303
refugees, 131, 232, 244, 246–47, 261–62

representation, 14, 65, 68, 101, 106, 131, 134, 177–78, 183, 185, 187, 193, 195, 218, 287
repression, 7–8, 16, 28, 31, 34, 42–45, 98, 152, 157, 166–67, 283, 289, 295, 300, 304
resistance, 83, 142, 163, 220, 240, 242, 285, 300
revolution, 5, 27, 31, 34–35, 42–43, 144–45, 148, 160, 165, 180, 206, 277, 289, 295
ripple effect, 28, 300
risk, 5, 11, 29, 37, 39, 58, 95, 100, 108–9, 118, 120, 125, 157, 190, 195, 218, 233–34, 238, 241, 247, 249, 251, 259, 261, 272, 294
robustness, 10, 141, 273, 298
role models, 1, 13, 18, 26, 30, 32, 36, 44, 46–47, 270, 273, 279, 289
Roosevelt, Franklin D., 96, 208, 216
Roth, Joseph, 33, 294
Republican party (United States), 163
Rukh, 158
rule of law, 191, 209, 223, 259, 286
Runciman, David, 13, 56, 219, 282
Russia, 16, 33, 35, 42–43, 146–47, 158, 162, 166, 168–69, 217, 241, 255, 285, 292, 294, 296
Rust, Matthias, 285
Ryzhkov, Nikolay, 149, 292

Sabin, Paul, 213
Sadat, Anwar el-, 40–41, 284–85, 288
Saddam Hussein, 2
Salvini, Matteo, 263
Sarkozy, Nicholas, 256
Schäuble, Wolfgang, 258
Schengen, 230, 244–48, 254, 261, 277, 301
Scholz, Olaf, 258
Schuman Plan, 185
Schumpeter, Joseph, 68, 297
Scotland, 44
segregation, 60–61, 75
Serbs, 163
Slanský, Rudolf, 145
social democracy, 13, 83
social policy, 180, 280
socialism, 27, 32, 99, 155, 181, 185, 209, 211, 285
Solow, Robert, 123
Solzhenitsyn, Alexander, 150
South Africa, 284, 300
sovereignty, 14, 63, 68–69, 72, 74, 77, 80–82, 84, 121, 162, 164, 178, 184, 190, 207, 210, 280, 292

Soviet Union, 2–3, 6, 8, 10, 15–16, 27–29, 32, 34, 40–41, 44–45, 143, 145–48, 150–55, 157, 159–61, 163–67, 169, 271–72, 274–75, 277, 284–85, 289, 292–93, 298, 300–4
Spain, 3, 34, 65, 145, 154, 238, 242, 255, 257
Stalin, Josef, 6, 27, 45, 145, 151–52, 159–60, 163, 167, 275, 278, 285, 298
statism, 93–94, 96, 103, 105, 109–11, 277
Staudinger, Hans, 93, 95, 97–100, 109, 291
Stepan, Alfred, 143, 160, 168
Stolypin, Pyotr, 43
Sweden, 191, 257
Syria, 255

Thomas, Clarence, 216
Tiananmen Square massacre, 7, 289
timing, 29–30, 44, 97, 100, 102, 152, 243, 270, 291, 302
Tito, Josip Broz, 163
Tocqueville, Alexis de, 42, 208
tolerance, 15, 60–61, 68, 77, 82–83, 150, 161–62, 165, 220
Tooze, Adam, 73
totalitarianism, 180
tradition, 8, 104–5, 122, 141, 168, 177, 209, 215, 301
Treaty of Westphalia, 233
triangle trade, 121
Trilateral Commission, 32, 276
Trotsky, Leon, 36
Trump, Donald, 4, 29, 59–60, 141, 207, 210, 213, 256, 276, 279, 300
trust, 11, 56, 141, 209, 211–12, 221, 223
Tsipras, Alexis, 239
Tuđman, Franjo, 164

Turgot, Anne Robert Jacques, 40
Turkey, 246–47, 262, 273
Tusk, Donald, 247

Ukrainians, 2, 159, 161, 167, 299
uncertainty, 8–9, 46, 115, 125, 128, 232, 238, 245, 272, 304
United Kingdom, 11, 92, 191, 248, 290
United States, 60, 66, 93, 105, 129, 131, 142–44, 168, 202–4, 206–9, 212–14, 218, 222–23, 271
Ustinov, Dimitri, 167

Vietnam, 144–45, 204, 219, 221
vigilance, 39, 142, 165
von der Leyen, Ursula, 257

Wainwright, Joel, 134
War on Terror, 127, 129
Warsaw Pact, 145, 148, 152, 155–58, 167, 169
Watergate, 205, 210, 213, 217, 219–20
Weber, Max, 80, 103–4, 177, 274
Wilhelm II, (of Germany), 35
Wilson, Woodrow, 207–8
Winthrop, John, 205
World War I, 29, 32–35, 45, 208, 233, 283, 293–94, 303
World War II, 32, 45, 64, 233, 241

Xi Jinping, 7

Yeltsin, Boris, 16, 151, 154, 161, 292
Yugoslavia, 3, 32, 145, 147, 163, 165, 286, 290

Ziblatt, Daniel, 13, 56, 59, 212, 282

Printed in the USA
CPSIA information can be obtained
at www.ICGtesting.com
LVHW021916190124
769091LV00003B/129